Praise for *Resisting Borders and*

"This volume . . . holds a mirror up to the everyday violence of borders that rarely capture widespread public attention, much less outrage. The essays and case studies that follow draw our attention to the policies and technologies that governments and companies are deploying quietly and viciously, tearing into people's lives, ripping families apart, and hunting down the most vulnerable, one computer bit at a time."
—Ruha Benjamin, author of *Race After Technology: Abolitionist Tools for the New Jim Code*, from the foreword

"The essays in *Resisting Borders and Technologies of Violence* are all excellent, but collectively they add up to more than their parts: a keyhole look into the future, where new repressive technologies will be met by new forms of creative resistance. Mizue Aizeki, Matt Mahmoudi, and Coline Schupfer have put together a vital collection of essays that help us imagine escaping what they have in store for us."
—Greg Grandin, author of *The End of the Myth: From the Frontier to the Border Wall in the Mind of America*

"In a world awash with violent borders, this book serves as a beacon of hope guiding us toward a more just future."
—Reece Jones, author of *Nobody Is Protected: How the Border Patrol Became the Most Dangerous Police Force in the United States*

"A valuable resource for those trying to dismantle technologized regimes of state terror around the world and create something life-giving in their place."
—Ben Tarnoff, author of *Internet for the People: The Fight for Our Digital Future*

"*Resisting Borders and Technologies of Violence* is an essential book for the difficult times we find ourselves in. This collection provides vital insight and nuance about the political, social, and technological dynamics of borders and technologies of coercion. Far more than just lines on a map, as this book illuminates, modern borders are more fluid and complex than ever. But perhaps most important, we can organize against them. Through compelling case studies and meticulous research, the book is an essential

resource for building movements that can fight back against technological authoritarianism in various forms."
—Lizzie O'Shea, author of *Future Histories: What Ada Lovelace, Tom Paine, and the Paris Commune Can Teach Us about Digital Technology*

"This brilliantly curated collection brings a much-needed understanding of how technology, geopolitics, and imperial domination by the United States and Europe are fragmenting the world through borders reinforced by surveillance drones, myriad tracking devices, and massive databases that use our own biometrics to undermine our freedom. But far more than a chronicle of oppression, *Resisting Borders* offers analysis and case studies of resistance fighters outsmarting the 'smart' borders to inspire us to continue the fight to save the planet and our humanity."
—James Kilgore, author of *Understanding E-Carceration: Electronic Monitoring, the Surveillance State, and the Future of Mass Incarceration*

RESISTING BORDERS AND TECHNOLOGIES OF VIOLENCE

Edited by Mizue Aizeki, Matt Mahmoudi, and Coline Schupfer

Haymarket Books
Chicago, Illinois

Published in 2023 by
Haymarket Books
P.O. Box 180165
Chicago, IL 60618
773-583-7884
www.haymarketbooks.org
info@haymarketbooks.org

ISBN: 978-1-64259-911-4

Distributed to the trade in the US through Consortium Book Sales and Distribution (www.cbsd.com) and internationally through Ingram Publisher Services
International (www.ingramcontent.com).

This book was published with the generous support of Lannan Foundation, Wal-
lace Action Fund, and the Marguerite Casey Foundation.

Special discounts are available for bulk purchases by organizations and institutions.
Please email info@haymarketbooks.org for more information.

Cover and book design by Jamie Kerry.
Cover art by Anuj Shrestha.

Printed in Canada by union labor.

Library of Congress Cataloging-in-Publication data is available.

10 9 8 7 6 5 4 3 2 1

Contents

Part 3: Digital IDs: The Body as a Border

Part 4: Bordering Everyday Cities

Part 5: Looking Forward

Borders & Bits: From Obvious to Insidious Violence

Ruha Benjamin

"Horrible." "Shocking." "Heartbreaking." So were some of the reactions to photographs and videos showing US Border Patrol corralling Haitian migrants attempting to cross the Rio Grande into the United States in September 2021. The agents straddled horses, wielding whips and shouting expletives in scenes that seemed to evoke a prior era of racial slavery. Social media erupted with charges of racism at the routine dehumanization of Black, Latinx, and Indigenous migrants, a stark contrast to the border crossers coming into the country from Canada, or those entering the country by plane, including the recent arrival of Ukrainian refugees.

"One group is being met with food, cheers, places to live, etc.—which is what welcoming looks like. And the other group is being met with cowboys with leather straps or ropes and detention by force," said Nana Gyamfi, the daughter of Ghanaian immigrants and executive director of Black Alliance for Just Immigration (BAJI).[1]

On Instagram, I scrolled past vintage drawings of slave catchers in the 1800s juxtaposed with this recent footage of US Border Patrol agents hovering over the drenched bodies of families carrying their belongings in trash bags.[2] Scrolling further, I saw a friend's post of a video of Joe Biden in a 1994 PBS interview with Charlie Rose, saying, "If Haiti just quietly sunk into the Caribbean or rose 300 feet into the air, it wouldn't matter a whole lot in terms of our interests."[3] Another friend posted the words of poet Warsan Shire, "You have to understand, no one puts their children in a boat unless the water is safer than the land," floating above the image of a girl clinging to her father as he waded through the water.

The Biden administration knows the land is unsafe for those in Haiti. It acknowledged the dire conditions in the country earlier in the year when the administration announced that Haitians already living in the United States were eligible for Temporary Protected Status. But *new* arrivals seeking asylum need not apply.[4] Instead, the administration proceeded to expel migrants crossing from Mexico, many of whom had been residing in South America since the 2010 earthquake in Haiti, deporting them to a country experiencing political violence and ongoing humanitarian disasters.

"The US government showed a total disregard for the right to seek asylum when it sent agents on horseback with reins flailing to control and deter this largely Black migrant population," said Alison Parker, US managing director at Human Rights Watch. "This violent treatment of Haitians at the border is just the latest example of racially discriminatory, abusive, and illegal US border policies that are returning people to harm and humanitarian disaster."[5] But it is not simply border agents on horseback that make the scene violent—it's *borders*, period.

The political construction of borders perpetuates global inequalities and routinizes state-sanctioned murder. It does so both by limiting people's mobility and by punishing those who actively challenge the border regime. As political geographer Reece Jones writes, "By refusing to abide by a wall, map, property line, border, identity document, or legal regime, mobile people upset the state's schemes of exclusion, control, and violence. They do this simply by moving."[6] And in upsetting the state, mobile people become targets for repression.

The violence visited upon people of Haitian descent in the US-Mexico borderlands in September 2021 is only one manifestation of such repression. This high-profile spectacle of border violence against Haitian migrants captured widespread attention, perhaps because it falls on the most obvious end of a carceral continuum that seeks to contain racialized populations in the name of public safety and public health.[7] But what of the more insidious end of the spectrum—the end that appears nonviolent, but effectively does most, if not all, the same work as the overtly violent?

Here's an example: the Dominican Republic now employs a digital ID system that provides people with proof that they are Dominican citizens. As discussed in many of the essays and case studies that follow, states laud such technologies as a more effective way to ensure citizens get access to public goods and services. Encouraged by the World Bank and the United Nations, many countries have taken similar steps as that of the Dominican Republic in the name of fighting structural forms of exclusion and marginalization. However, this techno-fix, it turns out, has an ugly underside. The Dominican state has effectively weaponized the ID system to discriminate against people of Haitian descent living within the country. It has done so by blocking the Haitian-descended population from accessing and renewing their IDs.[8] Such practices build upon a history of horrific racialized and nationalized violence by the Dominican state against people of Haitian descent, coupled with long-standing exploitation of that population for reasons of economic (and political) gain.[9]

This demonstrates a point made by special rapporteur E. Tendayi Achiume in a November 2020 report prepared for the United Nations General Assembly. Achiume notes that many of the emerging digital technologies employed in immigration and border policing have "historical antecedents in colonial technologies of racialized governance." This speaks to how "not only is technology not neutral, but its design and use typically reinforce dominant social, political and economic trends." Indeed, the report finds that national governments employ these technologies in ways that "advance the xenophobic and racially discriminatory ideologies which have proliferated in part due to widespread perceptions of refugees and migrants as *per se* threats to national security."[10]

It is also a manifestation of what I call "the New Jim Code": the employment of technologies that reflect and reproduce existing inequities but that are promoted and perceived as more objective or progressive than the discriminatory systems of a previous era. A 2015 audit of California's gang database reveals a very different reality.[11] The audit found that Black and Latinx individuals constituted 87 percent of those listed. Moreover, many of the names turned out to be babies under the age of one, some of whom were supposedly "self-described gang members." So far, no one has explained how this could have happened, except by saying that some combination of zip codes and racially coded names constitutes a risk.

Such outcomes raise serious questions about what it means to deploy supposedly neutral technologies in a context that embodies an unjust set of social relations. Innocence and criminality are not objective states of being that an algorithm can detect, but are *created* through the interaction between technology and a deeply racialized history, in which a certain type of person is coded as a criminal. Once someone is added to the database, whether they know they are listed *or not*, they undergo even more surveillance and lose a number of rights.[12] Inclusion in this context is more akin to possession, as in the conceit in Frantz Fanon's plea that the "tool never possess the man," where possession alerts us to the way that freedom is constrained. The goal is thus not simply to tweak the technology to make it "less biased." Designing surveillance technologies to be less biased simply enables them to better carry out the racially discriminatory violence mandated by an already racist, white supremacist, xenophobic state. The goal must instead be to address the socio-political and economic conditions that give rise to injustice and surveillance in the first place.

The task of this volume, then, is to connect obvious forms of harm and discrimination with more insidious technologies—immigrant databases, digital IDs, and electronic tracking systems, to name a few. For all the talk of "smart" borders, which use the latest in facial recognition, aerial drones, and data fusion centers, borders are just becoming more sophisticated sites of racialized surveillance, displacement, and death. Here we must understand "smartness" as the ability to more "efficiently" categorize and distinguish desirables from undesirables, rich from poor, expat from migrant and refugee, and capital from labor.

In this sense, these advancements scale colonial efforts of times past to enclose and condemn communities to a life of performing free labor and generating value or capital. Today, these technologies are used to determine everything from who gets to access safe harbor in a new country, welfare services, and shelter, to who is booked for or released from prison, and who is targeted and persecuted for exercising their right to protest. The eugenicist underpinnings of both artificial and organic intelligence and its primary directive—to categorize and rank humans—are predictable, but not inevitable.[13]

This volume, like the flood of images depicting Haitian migrants determined to find refuge, holds a mirror up to the everyday violence of borders that rarely capture widespread public attention, much less outrage. The essays and case studies that follow draw our attention to the policies and technologies that governments and companies are deploying quietly and viciously, tearing into people's lives, ripping families apart, and hunting down the most vulnerable, one computer bit at a time.

The power of these technologies rests on a false assertion of neutrality. They count on us believing that they are more objective, even more "humanitarian," than a scowling border agent wielding a whip. But there are many types of violence—some spectacular and swift, others quiet and methodical.

One example is the executive order that President Joe Biden signed on January 20, 2021, his first day in office. The presidential directive ordered a pause on the construction of Trump's southern border wall. On the same day, the White House sent a bill to Congress, the US Citizenship Act of 2021, calling for the deployment of "smart technology" to "manage and secure the southern border."

The United States and the European Union employ a wide array of technologies to surveil and patrol land and sea, and to determine, by way of algorithms, who can and cannot cross their borders.[14] A digital fortress has been layered upon imperial projects already built on a substratum of white supremacy and global apartheid. Concrete brutality has been exchanged for covert brutality. Moreover, the deployment of smart borders against migrants *out there* offers up new tools for patrolling racialized individuals via smart cities *in here*—those social borders within the nation-state that carve up our neighborhoods, schools, and institutions, structuring access to resources and letting us know where we belong and do not belong.

The power of the New Jim Code is that it allows racist habits and logics to enter through the back door of tech design, whereby the humans who create the algorithms are hidden from view. We need abolitionist tools that counter tech-mediated policing in the United States just as we need tools that push back against oppressive borders globally.[15]

If the coronavirus pandemic has taught us anything, it is that borders are a futile and outmoded tool for keeping us safe, that humanity is inextricably connected, both biologically and spiritually, and that any way forward must safeguard the well-being of everyone (not just those with the right passports). This involves employing creative tools to subvert the racist status quo—not only critiquing the world as it is but reimagining it for what it could be. This text invites us to question and organize against high-tech border imperialism globally—particularly in a time of unparalleled inequality across the world and myriad challenges on both the ecological and epidemiological fronts—even as we imagine a world without borders.

Resisting Technologies of Violence and Control

Mizue Aizeki, Matt Mahmoudi, and Coline Schupfer

International boundaries fortified by high-tech surveillance infrastructures developed by military contractors and Silicon Valley and Israeli tech corporations. Massive databases where police and immigration agents can do searches on hundreds of millions of people's biometric and biographic information gathered by refugee agencies, police, customs agents, and data brokers. "Smart" streetlights, intended to save energy, that end up serving as surveillance cameras for local police and immigration agents. National digital ID systems that enable governments to track, sort, exclude. The border- and surveillance-industrial complex—post-9/11, growing into one of the dominant forces organizing governments, markets, and societies—has exponentially expanded the power and reach of bordering regimes that extend far beyond physical international boundaries. In other words, through the deployment of information and surveillance technologies, the *border* has moved far beyond typical geographic bounds of enclosure—traversing not only state boundaries, seas and oceans, but also reaching deeply into other countries. Through the confluence of information technology systems, biometric collection databases, domestic policing regimes, and more, "smart borders" cut deep into the interior of the nation-state—into our cities and our societies, intersecting our bodies and our communities.

This book should not be necessary. Nonetheless, it is necessary, because wealthy nation-states around the world are increasingly denying one of the most basic freedoms—mobility—to the vast majority of the world's population. As for the borders themselves: By 1989, there were six physical border walls across the world. By 2020, this number had risen to sixty-three. This is just one manifestation of a global system of border and migrant policing, which affords hypermobility to a minority of the world's population at the expense of the rest. This reinforces global apartheid—a neoliberal world in which racialized systems of labor control and resource extraction are undergirded by unjust hierarchies of class, race, and nationality.

This book emerged from conversations attempting to stitch together local struggles to draw a clearer pathway toward abolishing border policing regimes and the global apartheid that they engender. We, the editors of this anthology, met in January 2019 through conversations about fighting different manifestations of the tech-fueled migrant control regime in different countries, on different continents. It became clear that we were confronting many of the same actors and logics—whether we were struggling against criminalizing immigration raids in the United States, digital IDs in New York City, experimentation with technologies of control in refugee camps in Jordan and Greece, or surveillance in the United Kingdom. Another common thread included activists being intercepted by repressive surveillance technologies deployed to curb dissent, by targeting them through spyware and facial recognition, cementing fears that the exercise of their basic rights somehow warrant persecution. We recognized that our separate fights are intimately interconnected, that we needed to share information and analysis, and that we must break down silos in order to dismantle and abolish borders and confront and resist global apartheid.

As such, this book pulls together threads that are core to our work to combat the increasing deployment of technologies to track and discipline mobility in service of capital and social and political control. An idea for a common medium emerged—in part a guide, a collection of campaigns, a shared analysis and vernacular—one that identifies common threads that we can weave together into fabric strong enough to hold together the resistance against the violent infrastructure of inequality created and reinforced by global bordering. The choices made in this book, too, are grounded in this original vision. For one, the book focuses on comparative trends in Europe and North America—regions of origin not only for our advocacy and organizing, but also the dominant forces in the historical and current production of the ideologies and violent technologies deployed in bordering and empire-building. The book also includes essays on other countries, including Israel—a key producer and worldwide exporter of hostile technologies—and India, as laboratories and global standard bearers for biometric ID systems. It is not, however, an exhaustive overview of the totality of states and actors involved in perpetuating this violent infrastructure. It is worth noting that we could not do justice to the importance of both China and Russia as important rivals to US imperial power: we did not include examinations, for example, of the Chinese surveillance regime and Russia's ongoing invasion of Ukraine and the connected risks of global cyber warfare. These important developments fall beyond the scope of this book. The book does, however, include case studies that connect and ground the essays' analyses in the textured, local realities of people around the world facing up to global apartheid. These are stories of resistance, of revolt, of grassroots struggles and the power of organizing.

As this volume shows, the violent infrastructure is not new but is instead steeped in history. We see how the contemporary techno-authoritarian moment fits into and follows a historical continuum of combating Western colonialism, imperialism, militarism, racial capitalism, and neoliberalism. It also shows how the violence of this system can only be resolved through strategies that lead to the abolition of all forms of the apparatus and ideologies of migrant control—whether they are the hard power of walls and boots on the ground or the soft power of radio towers and risk assessment algorithms.

The Growing Centrality of Migrant Control

Wars and internal conflicts, economic destabilization due to neoliberal policies and practices, climate catastrophes, public health pandemics, and the desire to reunite with loved ones are just some of the factors that compel people to migrate outside their homelands. Despite full awareness of these crises and driving forces, nation-states prioritize securitization over human rights—investing in wall building, migrant policing, and technological barriers to mobility at an unprecedented scale. Despite the visible harms—migrant deaths and injuries, family separation, highly exploitable labor conditions, impoverishment due to land dispossession, to name a few—border and migrant control regimes that criminalize and further marginalize racialized, Indigenous, and dispossessed people flourish, as do the surveillance and IT industries that fuel those regimes.

Wealthy countries carry much of the responsibility in creating the conditions driving mass migration in the first place, which has resulted in unprecedented numbers of people displaced today. These conditions have been economic, political, and especially ecological, with climate catastrophes in the next few years predicted to generate millions more climate migrants, predominantly from Latin America, sub-Saharan Africa, and Southeast Asia. The states of these very same regions, however, also invest heavily in internal and external migrant tracking and surveillance mechanisms encoded with Western carceral methods of exclusion and control. This includes a proliferation of "smart" biometrics and algorithms. Far from being "neutral" technologies, these tools hard-code suspicion, detention, deportation, and intolerance, into physical and abstract categories derived from assumed characteristics such as one's race, gender, sexuality, class, and country of origin.

As countries of destination—rich, high carbon–emitting nations—work to stave off migration flows from their shores, they justify regimes of exclusion by constructing threats—the "terrorist," the "criminal," the "unauthorized migrant"—and innovating the bureaucracy to make it easier to repel, detain, and deport. The political status quo that legitimates the state violence of border policing is contingent on the cultivation of a public fantasy that presents those in precarious positions as threatening and undeserving—a fantasy that reinforces a racialized hierarchy of worthiness that lies at the core of what Cedric Robinson called "racial capitalism." As Ruth Wilson Gilmore explains in her interview in this volume, "capitalism requires inequality and racism helps to enshrine that inequality." Under racial capitalism, the state and the market work together to ensure mobility of global capital and to maximize its ability to extract labor and resources—this is entirely dependent on capital's ability to contain and exploit racialized bodies and labor. The management of these racialized threats serves as the rationale for governments to invest billions in sophisticated surveillance. The techno-security-industrial complex thrives on keeping the fantasy of this threat alive—thereby further enabling the hostile politics of xenophobic political factions. In this way, capital is kept in circulation between governments and tech companies. Meanwhile, those upon whose subjugation capital depends—migrants, undocumented workers, peasants, indigenous groups, and other people on the political-economic, social, and nation-state "margins"—are in a constant state of physical and bureaucratic immobility or precarity. These are the modern-day dynamics of racial capitalism: while the companies that provide the tools through which governments can further assert their power of subjugation thrive, the majority of the global population loses.

From its inception, the project of building the post-9/11 "homeland security" apparatus was crafted by governments in partnership with corporate capital—and the technology and military industries were central to this. The tech sector itself has a long-standing engagement with enclosure, mass incarceration, and violence. As early as 1933, US-based IBM was courting Nazi Germany, eventually providing more than two thousand units of their Hollerith "punch card and card sorting" machines (the early twentieth-century equivalent of sophisticated data management infrastructure), which were used to operate every major concentration camp in Europe. IBM was also one of many information communication technology providers to equip the apartheid regime of South Africa with more advanced computational infrastructure.

Today, tech corporations, notably the biometrics and data industry, play a critical role in border policing regimes providing states with cutting-edge means to rapidly identify, categorize, and contain "unruly" or "undesirable" bodies. This infrastructure of control has grown markedly since the late twentieth century. As technological interventions under the auspices of "economic development" and migration control have converted the Global South and transient spaces such as borderlands and routes of refuge into neocolonial laboratories for new and largely experimental technologies. These spaces become laboratories and the people that traverse them become test subjects and end targets for the widespread collection of biometrics, databases that facilitate information sharing between policing agencies across countries, digital ID systems that track movements, "smart border" systems, cloud services, predictive analytics, facial recognition algorithms, and more. This effort has significantly escalated globally since 9/11, one of its manifestations being the introduction of the very same technologies into cities worldwide.

These systems govern regimes of control in carceral spaces as diverse as the increasingly digitized bureaucracy involved in accessing welfare, right through to facial recognition–enabled smartwatches that promise more "humane" forms of incarceration. Through case management software, server infrastructure, biometric identification systems, and other so-called artificial intelligence tools, Silicon Valley giants like Microsoft, Amazon, Palantir, and start-ups alike are helping state authorities rapidly define, target, and scale their desired threats for incarceration, detention, deportation, separation, displacement, and experimentation. Cities in particular are unavoidably laden with these digitally reinforced borders; "smart city" initiatives that purport to connect people with services are converging with tracking and policing surveillance to control the everyday lives of everyday people. As part of this strategy, massive amounts of data are collected and analyzed from public transactions and interactions, meanwhile increasing the corporate stake in everyday forms of technology-augmented bordering.

Through a mosaic of preventative policies (offshore processing and technological forms of interception such as drone surveillance), post-facto policies (offshore detention and criminalization), and more critically, the large-scale displacement of asylum applications, assessments, and processing to third countries via financial and other development aid incentives (e.g., the United Kingdom's 2022 plans to process incoming asylum seekers from around the world in Rwanda, or the US investment in the militarization of the southern Mexican border), states move their borders far beyond their actual physical borders. In doing so, they engage in the wholesale export of the violent ideology of border imperialism and its associated technologies. The European Union has arrangements with at least thirty-five countries outside the EU to process asylum and immigration claims far beyond its borders, the majority of which are known for harboring high-risk human rights environments. Similarly, in the United States, asylum seekers crossing the sea in search of safety have since the 1990s been interdicted at the Guantanamo Bay military base for refugee status determination, without any access to legal representation.

Dismantling Border Imperialism and Racial Capitalism

Borders have become impermeable for those violated by them. These walls, sustained by the logics of racial capitalism, organize the production (and deployment) of machines that, in essence, are not only destructive of human lives and communities, but also of our political imaginations. To fight them, organizers must contend with both racial capitalism as a structure and the immediately visible violence inflicted by the technology industry. A singular focus on the latter inhibits our ability to take on what is fast becoming an all-encompassing techno-racial system of global apartheid.

Our job, then, through reading, learning, and acting together, must be to politically and radically imagine a world void of the border- and surveillance-industrial complex; void of racial capitalism. We impart cracks in these structures, in part, by chipping away at violent technologies and their political economy wherever we find them. We must interrogate and understand exactly how the structures we wish to undo are upheld, obscured, and reinforced by these violent technologies that promise greater efficiency, convenience, and security. Tech companies have always been involved in propping up borders and racialized forms of enclosure, yet technology production and border enforcement have long been treated as distinct processes. To fight either, we have to understand them as fundamentally intertwined, and how they are driven by the incentives of racial capitalism.

The goal of this book is to strengthen our collective analysis of the technologies of violence and control that reinforce global apartheid, and to help us build, nurture, and accumulate our power of organizing and resistance—locally and transnationally—against these technologies. We start in the first section with a look at the logics that permit containment and border violence, with a focus on critical histories of homeland security state building as the driving pillars of the contemporary moment. Next, in the second section, we turn to the fictitious construction of racialized "threats," which create the conditions for technology-augmented domination. Following that, we focus on digital and biometric identification systems that are deployed globally in an effort to essentialize hierarchies into machine-readable identities, creating borders out of bodies. The fourth section then spotlights how everyday interactions in cities are increasingly governed by technologies that border and police us—from access to housing, education, and health care to connectivity, work, and social services. Finally, we end the volume by calling for abolition at multiple intersections—the national security paradigm, imperial borders, the prison- and military-industrial complexes. In this (albeit not exhaustive) mosaic that illustrates the ways in which technology-augmented violence against mobile bodies are exercised and resisted, we hope to show that our separate fights are not separate. They are all converging in this present moment. So, let's weave, let's resist, and let's chip away and crack open the structures upholding racial capitalism and global apartheid.

Part 1

IDEOLOGIES OF EXCLUSION

1

The Border Is Surveillance: Abolish the Border

Harsha Walia

To be a modern state presupposes the existence of a secured border. Even in the middle of a global pandemic, nation-states were drawing and delineating new borders on the world map. Overriding Indigenous Inuit jurisdiction, Canada and Denmark divided Hans Island in the Arctic, while Qatar and Saudi Arabia drew new lines through the southern shore of the Khor al Udeid region. Yet, as I argue in *Border and Rule: Global Migration, Capitalism, and the Rise of Racist Nationalism*, borders are not fixed or static lines marking territory, and most maps do not conceptualize the shifting cartography of borders. In fact, the border is less about a politics of movement per se and is better understood as a key method of imperial state formation, hierarchical social ordering, labor control, and xenophobic nationalism.

Borders are an ordering regime, both assembling and assembled through racial-capitalist accumulation and colonial relations that create migrants yet criminalize migration. Borders function to maintain asymmetric relations of wealth accrued from colonial impoverishment and racial capitalism, ensuring mobility for some and mass immobility and containment for most—essentially, a divided working class and system of global apartheid determining who can live where and under what conditions. Classifications such as "migrant" or "refugee" don't represent unified social groups so much as they symbolize state-regulated relations of governance and difference made through selective inclusions and mass expulsions. The production and social organization of difference is, in fact, at the heart of border-craft. The violence *at* borders upholds the imperial, racial, social violence *within* and *across* borders.

"He burned his fingertips so he could apply for asylum like a new person." Across the European Union, refugees like Awet routinely burn and mutilate their fingertips to avoid detection in EURODAC, the world's first multi-national biometric system.[1] The biometric system centers on a mass fingerprint database used to enforce the EU's Dublin Regulation, mandating that refugees must seek asylum in their first European country of arrival. Once a refugee's fingerprints (and often facial image scans) are taken, they are entered into EURODAC.[2] This data then becomes searchable by all police forces and immigration authorities across the EU, who use it to carry out deportations and removals in accordance with the Dublin Regulation. By the end of 2019, the EU had stored almost 6 million peoples' fingerprint sets in EURODAC.[3] The EU spends billions of dollars to maintain Fortress Europe[4] through an intricate system of "smart border" databases, virtual surveillance, military-grade drones, sensor systems, sound canons, AI detectors, thermal cameras, and Orwellian surveillance centers.

The border has become a dystopic testing ground everywhere, constituting a $500 billion border security and virtual walling industry. In the United States, unmanned aerial vehicles were first tested on the U.S.-Mexico border before they were used in imperialist drone attacks on Yemen and Pakistan. Private contractors like Amazon, Palantir, Anduril, Elbit Systems, and European Dynamics are being granted billions of dollars by governments to build virtual walls with their promises of infallible high-tech drone surveillance and infrared technology.

Often advocated for by neoliberal advocates, techno-solutionism in migration management has two common justifications—that electronic surveillance is a purportedly better alternative to immigration detention, and that the so-called objectivity of automated algorithmic-driven processes will eliminate human decision-making biases in immigration processes.

On the former rationale, President Biden claims that a buildup of a virtual border wall is a "softer" version to Trump's physical wall. Biden has also grown the e-carceration Intensive Supervision Appearance Program, erroneously touted as an alternative to detention, to $475 million.[5] In the UK, facial recognition smartwatches and GPS tags collecting intrusive data are being introduced as the latest form of monitoring technology to drastically expand the surveillance net over foreign nationals in the country.[6] Amid all the techno-hype and dizzying jargon of "smart borders," "predictive analytics," and "artificial intelligence" is the simple fact that the primary purpose of these technologies is to further entrench—not mitigate—border imperialist violence.

These technologies have been particularly critical in outsourcing border violence; border controls no longer exist solely at the site of the border itself but extend far beyond nation-state's territorial limits. The management of global migration through technological enforcement across the skies, waters, and remote lands has globalized the violence of borders. The EU coordinates surveillance, interdiction, pushback, and detention strategies deep in the Sahel region of Africa and the Middle East. Similarly, the US maintains an imperial stronghold across Latin America by funding a series of security and surveillance initiatives to deter, prevent, intercept, and criminalize migration from Mexico and Central America through the Mérida Initiative and the Central American Regional Security Initiative.

Part of the challenge in recognizing these widespread anti-migrant initiatives and surveillance technologies as modes of carceral violence is that, as J. Khadijah Abdurahman puts it, "these new geographies of policing, regulation, and management are largely invisible."[7] Israeli-made drones in the Mediterranean, facial recognition technology at and beyond US land and maritime border crossings, automated surveillance cameras in refugee camps across Europe, AI in immigration decision-making processes in Canada, intrusive biometric systems piloted in Australia, and the global buildup of data infrastructure all serve to constrict, contain, and criminalize migrant/refugee mobility. In its #NoTechforICE campaign, Mijente and ally organizations compellingly argue, "The digital border is part of the same militarization logic, the same deportation logic, the same surveillance logic, and the same carceral logic that undergirds the entire immigration enforcement system."[8] Common xenophobic media depictions of migrants/refugees as "swarms" and "floods," and the accompanying rhetoric of "migrant crisis," have become a pretext to shore up immigration enforcement and technological surveillance, when, in fact, mass migration is a displacement crisis created by enduring legacies of capitalism, wars, and climate change.

On the claim of novel migration management technologies being "neutral and objective," it is important to remember that oppression and repression are constitutive, and not a random consequence, of technological-driven surveillance. Technological surveillance and data criminalization are rooted in long-standing patterns of racial categorization and control. For example, it is well documented that facial recognition technologies misrecognize images labeled "Black women" twenty times more frequently than images labeled "white men."[9] Yet, in both the domestic policing and border-crossing contexts, the use of these technologies is increasing. The United Nations Special Rapporteur on Contemporary Forms of Racism, Racial Discrimination, Xenophobia and Related Intolerance has warned that the rise in digital bordering is "uniquely experimental, dangerous, and discriminatory in the border and immigration enforcement context" and "being deployed to advance the xenophobic and racially discriminatory ideologies that have become so prevalent."[10] Mapping who is most vulnerable to displacement and then subjected to the violence of data criminalization reveals the fault lines between rich and poor, and between whiteness and Black, Indigenous, and racialized "others."

In 2021, for instance, it came to light that the United Nations refugee agency had improperly shared data collected from Rohingya refugees in Bangladesh.[11] Refugees were told the data was necessary to issue them smart cards to access essential services and refugee aid. The data was shared with the Bangladesh government, which submitted the names and biometric data of over 830,000 refugees to authorities in Myanmar to verify people for possible forced deportation back to the very violence and genocide they had initially fled.

Simone Browne's extensive work, including *Dark Matters: On the Surveillance of Blackness*, urgently highlights how contemporary surveillance technologies did not emerge in a vacuum, and are continuities of—in fact, founded upon—the policing and criminalization of Black life.[12] From the US-Canada border to British outposts in Asia, early surveillance technologies such as birth certificates and passports were key pillars of population management and movement regulation within racial capitalism and colonial empire. A 2022 report, *From Data Criminalization to Prison Abolition*, examines the interlocked machineries of data criminalization and migrant surveillance, describing how today's sprawling surveillance machinery of immigrant criminalization draws "from centuries of racialized capitalism and social control, anti-blackness, settler-colonial expansionism, and US imperialism."[13]

In her essay "Home," Toni Morrison writes, "The contemporary world's work has become policing, halting, forming policy regarding, and trying to administer the movement of people."[14] We are witness to the horrific impacts of this categorization and control of people. While borders are hierarchically organized and permeable for expats, a handpicked immigrant diaspora, and the rich investor class, they form a fortress against the millions in the "deportspora," who are shut out, immobilized, and expelled.[15] Suffocation in cargo trucks, dehydration in blistering heat, unmarked graves in deserts, lethal pushbacks of migrant caravans, and wet cemeteries are the deathscape of those killed by borders every day, especially in the US and EU. Bordering regimes produce and police the "good versus bad" or "real versus bogus" migrant/refugee, as well as produce and police the colonial, racial, gendered, sexualized, ableist, and classist orderings among all of us. The border, the prison, the sweatshop floor, the refugee camp, the reservation, and the gentrified gated community are all part of the same bordering, carceral system operating through dispossession, capture, containment, and immobility.

The fight to abolish border surveillance is thus better understood as a fight to abolish the border itself. The freedom to stay and the freedom to move, which is to say a world without borders, is reparations and redistribution long due.

2

Multiplying State Violence in the Name of Homeland Security

Mizue Aizeki

Well, the story of how that happened—it was unbelievable. . . . I was sleeping; Jennifer was sleeping. The kids were each in their own rooms. We hear knocking, and Jennifer gets up and . . . asks who's at the door. They say police—they don't say immigration, they don't say ICE. So, we opened the door. I still live in a bad neighborhood, so the police, you know, are always knocking just to find out information if anything bad is happening. We didn't really think anything of it, and she opened the door, and they rushed my wife, put her to the side and just barged into my apartment.

I got up from my bed because I heard the ruckus. . . . They started asking me questions of who I am, asked me where's my ID. They told me do not move. My kids got up at that time because my wife is going hysterical. [My kids] start crying. One ICE agent goes into my daughter's room, [one] goes into my son's room—[and they] tell them to stay where they're at, to not move. . . . They're going through my stuff—finding my ID—they grab my ID. They don't answer any questions, you know. They handcuffed me, and they take me away.

I mean . . . it was horrible. . . . My wife is asking, "What is this about?" And they didn't answer anything. It's after they handcuff me and detain me is when they said—oh, oh we're, um, agents of the immigration, and we're taking you. . . . That was the only information that he told me. They threw me in a van and took me to 26 Federal Plaza. They left Jennifer here with the kids—crying—like not knowing what was happening, just like that.¹

first met Jose in 2015. Owing to a twenty-year old felony conviction, he was facing mandatory deportation to Panama, a country he had not stepped foot in since he came to New York as a legal permanent resident when he was a baby. Jose has no family in Panama, and he does not speak Spanish, the national language. After US Immigration and Customs Enforcement (ICE) agents stormed his Bronx apartment at 5:30 a.m. and arrested him, Jose, desperate to stay in the only home he has ever known, reached out to multiple organizations. After being turned away from them all because his case offered no clear legal avenues due to his criminal record, he reached out to the organization where I then worked, the Immigrant Defense Project.

When we first met, Jose was exasperated by the prospect of being forcibly removed to an unknown country and losing the stability he had built. He asked, why hadn't anything he had done in the fifteen years after prison—raising a family, for example, working as a public employee—counted for anything? While the government refused to see him as anything other than a threat, Jose insisted, "God knows my heart is good." Jose, like millions of immigrants with prior criminal convictions, have become part of a pool of individuals that ICE can target for deportation at any time, depending on the politics of the moment. For people like Jose, there are almost no legal avenues to fight a deportation order because of laws passed in 1996 that exclude many immigrants from protections under the law.

Since 2007, much of my work has focused on challenging the normalization of the policing, punishment, and exclusion of people who have been deemed to be "perpetual threats"[2] —in particular those who have criminal convictions or have crossed borders without legal authorization. A key part of this work has been ending the increased collaboration between local and federal police that emerged as part of the "War on Terror" that followed the attacks of September 11, 2001. This work increasingly includes combating a dramatic expansion of a surveillance-industrial complex deployed in service of internal and global migrant policing.

This period of organizing has been defined by the ascendancy of the US Department of Homeland Security (DHS), founded in 2002 under the broad mission to protect "national security." Each presidential administration that has overseen the now twenty-year-old DHS—from George W. Bush to Obama to Trump to now Biden—shifted the bull's-eye, however slightly, on how to define "security," and consequently, who is deemed a "threat," yet both parties continue to share consensus that more control, punishment, and policing to protect against named threats are legitimate and necessary.

Now, twenty years after the founding of DHS, we have to take stock of the sheer magnitude and global reach of the border walls, police, databases, surveillance, and prisons. These are all-powerful manifestations of the perspective articulated by the 9/11 Commission in 2003: "The American homeland is the planet."[3] Below, I briefly explore the rise of DHS and how it has built consensus around its agenda. I show how the merger of the ongoing US "wars" on crime, drugs, and terror has been central to the success of DHS's migrant control regime and has fed into the development of DHS's massive surveillance apparatus—at the border, in the interior, and globally.

The migration and border control budget of DHS has more than tripled since the department's founding, enabling it to oversee the most massive apparatus of immigrant exclusion, incarceration, and expulsion in US history.[4] Authorities justify these "national security" policies and practices by invoking threats. But who constitutes a target for state repression is not necessarily a given—these "threats" are constructed and shift over time based on political utility. Jose became a target of ICE's mass deportation regime at a time when DHS was deliberately elevating the threat of people with criminal convictions as one of the central concerns of, and justifications for, the homeland security state. Today, exiling immigrants with criminal convictions is widely accepted as one of the legitimate policing functions of the US federal government. Yet, it is this very construction of threats that is at the heart of the state violence fueled by the "War on Terror." We must confront this violent process of othering that has disrupted, and frequently destroyed, countless lives in the name of "homeland security." The fight to end carceral state violence requires that we redefine safety and dismantle DHS and the homeland security state.

Producing the Threat

Representations of "dangerous outsiders" or "the enemy within"—and the need for violent measures to protect against such "threats"—play an integral role in capitalist nation-building. Since the colonial settlement of the

United States, US immigration law has served as a key mechanism to shape the nation by creating and enforcing categories of belonging—including who is allowed to be mobile, who is allowed to stay, and who has access to socioeconomic and political rights. While many herald the United States as a "nation of immigrants," this necessarily violent nation-building process has always required dispossession and economic exploitation, facilitated by marginalizing groups deemed unassimilable and undesirable—Native Americans, formerly enslaved persons and their descendants, people from China, people of Japanese descent, Mexicans, and Haitians—among others.[5] The project of nation-building has also excluded people on the basis of social standing or bodily attributes (the poor and those with mental or physical disabilities, for example), and because of political ideology (in the case of radical labor organizers and leftists during the Red Scare, for instance).[6]

The US government did not eliminate race as a bar to immigration and citizenship until 1952.[7] Yet racialized, politicized, and class-based exclusion persists—in the post–civil rights era it has just been more veiled. As the government is no longer authorized to exclude based on racial categories, racialized proxies have become the named targets—"criminal aliens," "illegal border crossers," "terrorists." This is one manifestation of how the ongoing project of defining the "nation" under racial capitalism requires the constant articulation of who belongs and is granted full rights and who does not. As Craig Gilmore and Ruth Wilson Gilmore explain, "The state's management of racial categories is analogous to the management of highways or ports or telecommunication; racist ideological and material practices are infrastructure that needs to be updated, upgraded, and modernized periodically."[8]

For much of US history, large-scale migrant policing was episodic. It was not until the 1970s and 1980s that border and migration control began to be widely embraced as a "necessary" function of state control to address an ongoing "crisis."[9] In these decades, enhanced immigration control and border policing dovetailed with the punitive neoliberal policies in response to a racialized moral panic around drugs, crime, and low-income people,[10] which together contributed to increasingly naming immigrants as a threat to social services, national security, and white homogeneity.[11] Since then, "controlling the border" has become a central political focus of both the Democrat and Republican parties—a focus defined more by consensus than difference. What is understood by the ruling powers, but rarely articulated, is how borders are a tool of social control that can be weaponized as economic or political conditions dictate—this includes, for example, the use of border policing to create a precarious and highly exploitable labor pool both within and outside the United States.[12] Relatedly, border policing and associated manufacturing of threats facilitates US geopolitical practices outside its boundaries—including a "War on Drugs" that has enabled neoliberal land dispossession and privatization in Latin America[13] or a "War on Terror" that masked US imperial objectives to secure control over energy reserves and social movements in the Middle East.[14]

Central to the foundation of the current migrant control regime are a series of laws that Congress passed in the 1980s and 1990s. These legal tools were firmly based in the dominant "law and order" penal framework,[15] and embraced "sealing" the border from unauthorized migration, mass detention, and the deportation of immigrants with criminal convictions.[16] This included initiating what is now called the Criminal Alien Program, which has led to deep collaboration between jails and prisons and immigration agents.[17] Two laws passed in 1996 dramatically accelerated the punitive trend and significantly grew the ability of the government to exclude, detain, and deport people at a mass scale.[18] These laws increased border policing, enhanced penalties for unauthorized entry, and established a framework for police collaboration with immigration officials. They made it much harder for immigrants to obtain legal status and much easier for the government to deport even longtime permanent residents by vastly expanding the criminal offenses that trigger deportation and by severely limiting due process.[19] Passed ceremoniously a year after two US citizens, Timothy McVeigh and Terry Nichols, bombed a federal building in Oklahoma City and killed scores of people, the 1996 laws included provisions that markedly increased the government's ability to target those suspected of terrorism—in particular non-citizens.[20] Yet even with the passage of these harsh laws, it became clear that the only way for the government to "rid the country of criminal aliens" would be through "an enormous increase in resources or a significant realignment of inter-governmental responsibilities."[21] These developments laid the foundation for a post-9/11 migrant securitization regime that relies on progressively broader categories of criminalization through which to enact broad-sweeping state violence.

Homeland Securitization: Building DHS

Founded in 2002 under George W. Bush's post-9/11 War on Terror, the US Department of Homeland Security represents the institutionalization of what is effectively a perpetual state of emergency. In other words, DHS constitutes an institutional response to what are framed as never-ending threats in the form of unauthorized immigration, crime, and terrorism. Consolidating multiple agencies under the mission of "homeland security," DHS became "the most militarized federal entity after the Pentagon."[22] By realigning intergovernmental responsibilities under one institutional umbrella, the United States turbocharged its power to control—and to create—those deemed as threats and enemies. It also activated broad corporate interest in advancing its global securitization agenda.[23]

Central to DHS's goal to "secure the nation"[24] is maximizing the state's ability to *know* and *see* all residents.[25] Through its pursuit to be all-seeing, DHS has cast an expansive web that reaches inside and beyond the boundaries of the United States.[26] There are several broad groups that have been central targets of DHS's all-seeing eye: Arabs and Muslims, undocumented workers, people who crossed the border without authorization, and immigrants who are arrested by police. To achieve the hypervisibility of those deemed to be a "threat," DHS has enlisted a vast complex of military and technology corporations, as well as research institutions, to design, produce, and operate surveillance hardware and data-driven policing tools—fueling a growing border and surveillance-industrial complex.[27]

An early initiative of the War on Terror focused the all-seeing eye on Arabs and Muslims through the implementation of "alien registration," a tactic used historically to catalog and track perceived threats.[28] Under the program, men from twenty-four Arab and majority-Muslim countries (plus North Korea) had to report to immigration offices, where they were interrogated and required to submit biometric and biographic information. More than two hundred thousand men underwent this "special registration." While none were charged with terrorism, many were subjected to surveillance and detention, and close to fourteen thousand were put into deportation proceedings.[29]

Another early national security initiative to increase the visibility of "undesirables" involved federal investment in an infrastructure for interior immigration policing, giving rise to a new agency within DHS: US

Immigration and Customs Enforcement. In its first strategic plan—"Operation Endgame"—the agency explained its mission: "Simply stated, [ICE's] ultimate goal is to develop the capacity to remove all removable aliens."[30] The agency made clear that its success required more resources and information technology infrastructure to "identify, locate, apprehend, process and remove aliens who are unlawfully present in the United States."[31] And it got those resources. This included massive resources for data gathering and other surveillance systems. And in 2003, ICE created the National Fugitive Operations Program (NFOP)—teams deployed to conduct arrests of immigrants at homes, workplaces, and on the street. Initially the core of the ICE policing apparatus, NFOP was its fastest growing program—its budget grew over 24-fold (from $9 million to over $218 million) in its first five years.[32] And justifications for expanded funding continued.

The commitment to ICE and border policing has been consistent across the two main US political parties. Since the founding of DHS, the primary difference between parties has been mostly tactical or rhetorical. For example, in the early stages of DHS under G. W. Bush, the main named "threat" were Muslims and undocumented workers, as well as what ICE calls "fugitive aliens"[33]—people with outstanding orders of deportations. Under the Obama administration, as described below, the policing agency's main stated focus became immigrants with criminal convictions. Yet, under all administrations that have overseen DHS, it is clear that public safety is not the genuine objective, but rather a political agenda that is served through mass exclusion and deportation achieved by targeting the broad range of people without citizenship whose rights are not protected under the law.

The substantial buildup of DHS infrastructure and staffing reflects the degree to which the homeland security state has been institutionalized. Between 2003 and 2021, the US spent over $333 billion on immigration policing in the interior and at the border.[34] DHS has the second largest information technology budget in the federal government (second to the much larger Department of Defense). DHS staffing expenditures, including for Border Patrol agents and ICE police, are its most substantial costs.[35] Notably, the unions representing ICE and Customs and Border Protection (CBP) officers have become formidable promoters of anti-immigrant policies,[36] exemplifying how, similar to the prison-industrial complex, DHS policies and practices have strengthened "interest groups with incentives to 'reinforce the stability' of punitive policies."[37] The power of the nation's immigration police force was on display under Trump. ICE and CBP police displayed great enthusiasm under his presidency, as one of his early acts upon taking office was to "take the shackles off" agents, authorizing deportation without restrictions.[38]

The use of the criminal legal system has been critical for DHS to identify and arrest, as well as demonize, immigrants. ICE's first strategic plan named coordination with jails and prisons as a critical part of achieving its mission—and this coordination has grown dramatically, particularly through the use of technology.[39] Under Obama, DHS accelerated the police-to-deportation pipeline through the implementation of "Secure Communities"—a fingerprint sharing program where information collected by police at booking is automatically shared with DHS, making every police precinct a feeder into the deportation system. This data sharing—combined with the vilification of people with criminal convictions—became a key tool in the historically unprecedented rates of deportation during Obama's presidency.[40] His administration deported over 3 million people in eight years, more than the total deportations from 1892 to 2001.[41]

One way the Obama administration methodically elevated ICE as necessary to protect against "threats" was through highly publicized raids targeting immigrants with criminal convictions—people like Jose. In one such sweep in 2012 under ICE's Operation Cross Check—occurring periodically since 2011 to focus on immigrants with convictions—ICE arrested 3,100 people over six days. To conduct such operations, ICE draws agents from field offices across the country, from other DHS agencies, and from federal, state, and local law enforcement partners.[42] ICE's director at that time, John Morton, justified these actions by suggesting that the arrestees were permanent threats to public well-being. "When ICE arrests and removes [deports] a particular offender, the rate of recidivism for that particular offender drops to zero," he said. "Public safety is significantly improved by deporting those involved in crime."[43]

In a 2014 speech encapsulating the immigration agenda of his administration, Obama, drawing from liberal law-and-order ideologies, invoked the "rule of law," and stated "felons, not families," are the targets for deportation.[44] The president reinforced the notion that laws are just and people who violate them must be punished. By evoking a dichotomy of "good" versus "bad" immigrants, he legitimated and normalized the widescale exile of people with convictions as "public safety threats." This framing and the associated efforts to hunt down immigrant "felons" had a profound impact on the immigration policing paradigm and on the immigration movement overall. By centering carceral state logics including equating public safety with policing and punishment, the administration solidified the legitimacy of the deportation regime, thereby strengthening it for the administrations that followed.[45]

DHS and Its Force Multipliers

Today, close to twenty years after its founding, ICE, and DHS more broadly, have made tremendous progress toward achieving its "Endgame"—an unprecedented ability to identify, categorize, and track people and the capacity to "remove all removable aliens." Under DHS, the United States has deported more than 6 million people—more than double the number of the previous 110 years—and in the process, has defined and normalized the US "solution" to migration control. DHS has not reached this point on its own.[46] Military contractors and technology corporations—cashing in on lucrative data and surveillance markets—have played a "mission critical" role by developing sophisticated tools that support and enhance DHS's work.[47] Various domestic and international agencies have also played a key role in helping DHS extend its reach. These "force multipliers" have helped bring about a transnational collaboration of agencies that make up the securitized immigration policing regime, further entrenching US state power on the domestic and global fronts.[48]

DHS force multipliers enabling an "everywhere border," operating at different geographical scales, and involving police, civilians, foreign governments, technology corporations, and more. Key examples include:

- **The Internal Border:** DHS has made *interior* immigration policing[49] a regular feature of the border control regime.[50] ICE has increased its power by amassing multiple DHS agencies—such as Enforcement and Removal Operations, Homeland Security Investigations, and Customs and Border Protection—as a "surge force" to conduct large-scale raids.[51] The Trump administration deployed DHS agents at

Black Lives Matter demonstrations,[52] and CBP used drones to surveil Indigenous organizers defending against pipelines.[53]

- **Local, State and Federal Police:** DHS actively recruits police to act as immigration agents under the 287(g) program,[54] making local and state police a "massive force multiplier" for deportation.[55] Local and state police also communicate information to ICE in myriad ways, including via a tip line or automatic sharing of biometrics at arrest.[56] ICE also sends notifications to police when releasing certain immigrants from detention, ostensibly to assist in narrowing "the pool of potential suspects" in criminal investigations.[57] Moreover, the power of DHS is fueled by "mega spy centers,"[58] where DHS intelligence is combined with information gathered by other policing agencies in "fusion centers."[59]

- **ICE Intelligence Centers, Commercial Data Brokers, and Big Data Analytics:** ICE's Targeting Operations Division oversees three intelligence centers with distinct but coordinated functions.[60] Through contracts with corporations such as Thomson Reuters, LexisNexis, Palantir, Clearview AI, and Deloitte Consulting, the three centers form a Big Data surveillance dragnet that provides the technical infrastructure for the police-to-deportation pipeline. They also provide generalized surveillance of social media and personal data, which contributes to the generation of target lists for ICE raids.[61]

- **DHS's Global Police Force:** Externalization of the US border policing regime has been a central objective of DHS.[62] As of 2022, ICE had eighty-six offices located in foreign countries, which, among other activities, collect information from those nations' law enforcement agencies to track and identify potential migrants.[63] The United States, moreover, has over a hundred agreements with countries to aid its efforts to police migration.[64] Mexico and Central America, a region with a long history of US intervention, are key sites for such efforts. For example, border security agreements signed in 2019 deploy ICE and CBP agents to Central America to "advise and mentor host nation police, border security, and immigration and customs counterparts."[65] In addition, DHS has been building a digital infrastructure of interoperable databases that seamlessly communicate with each other across borders.[66] This includes information gathered from domestic police, as well as agreements with countries to share biometric and biographic information, and criminal history.[67]

- **The External Border:** Mexico's Southern Border and the War on Drugs: In 2007, the US shifted its drug war focus from Colombia to Mexico, Central America, and the Caribbean.[68] The infrastructure of this "war" has converged with DHS objectives to externalize the US border policing regime. Under the Mérida Initiative (2007), a bilateral US-Mexico drug war security initiative under which the US has spent $3.5 billion, and Programa Frontera Sur (2014), Mexico has built up a formidable detention and deportation apparatus. Mexico, which DHS has cultivated as a key partner in its southern border policing regime, has developed one of the world's largest immigration detention systems, detaining more than 150,000 per year to prevent migration to the United States.[69] Between 2002 and 2017, Mexico deported more people from Honduras, El Salvador, and Guatemala (1.9 million) than did the United States (1.1 million).[70] Through the Central American Regional Security Initiative, the US government has granted funds of upward of $1 billion since 2008 for countries to remedy "border security deficiencies."[71]

- **Massive Biometric Collection and Interoperable Databases:** DHS is currently developing one of the world's largest biometric databases, the Homeland Advanced Recognition Technology System (HART). Hosted on the cloud by Amazon Web Services, HART will enable DHS and other users to link the biographic information of more than 260 million people to biometrics like fingerprints, iris scans, and facial recognition images, as well as DNA and more.[72] HART will allow DHS to expand "database interoperability" (info sharing) between police, foreign governments, other US agencies, and more. This includes the Department of Defense, which collected biometrics from civilians in Iraq and Afghanistan.[73] DHS also has a biometrics-sharing agreement with the United Nations High Commissioner for Refugees to share data on refugees, including fingerprints, iris scans, and facial images.[74]

- **"Smart Borders"**: The US government increasingly speaks of "smart borders," which includes a growing list of what CBP calls "technology force multipliers."[75] These include Integrated Fixed Towers,[76] drones, ground sensors, mobile tracking systems, biometric collection systems, robot dogs, and much more.[77] DHS recruits R&D partners at universities and has ensured that the United States is the single largest market for border security corporations.[78]

- **Winning Hearts and Minds:** ICE and CBP engage in a variety of public relations activities aimed at building support for their activities. This normalization of border and immigration policing—a manifestation of what sociologist Nandita Sharma has referred to as the "territorialization of people's consciousness"[79]—includes sponsorship of "Border Patrol Explorer" posts for teens and Christmas visits by a Border Patrol "Santa" to border communities near Mexico.[80] In 2020, ICE announced that it would host a "Citizen Academy" in Chicago to train civilians in deportation tactics, including "defensive tactics, firearms familiarization, and targeted arrests."[81] The Border Patrol has held similar academies across the country since the late 1990s.[82] In addition, efforts to modernize migrant control through the deployment of surveillance and data-driven technologies is often promoted as a "humane" or "smart" approach to migrant policing—effectively masking the violent enterprise that these technologies advance.[83]

This partial list of DHS's policing capacity illustrates the jaw-dropping power it has amassed in only two decades of existence. This securitization regime taps deeper and deeper into, and consequently fortifies, the power of the carceral state[84] as well as the power of US imperialism, of which militarism is just one component.[85] US expenditures on policing migrants currently exceeds total spending by some of the world's largest militaries.[86] Military contractors, Silicon Valley tech corporations, policing agencies at multiple geographic scales, foreign governments and other federal agencies together create a formidable homeland security apparatus that is continually expanding its ability to track, analyze, identify, arrest, and control.[87] Abolishing this apparatus—which requires challenging the legitimacy of DHS and the logics that fuel it—must be central to any fight aiming to bring about a just world for all.

Conclusion

When I first started working on immigration issues in the early 1990s, there were only a few miles of border fencing along the US-Mexico boundary. DHS and ICE did not exist, nor did much of the technology that fuels it today. And although bordering and the creation of the "other" has long been a powerful means of social control, we have seen it become even more so since the founding of DHS. The agency is a well-resourced hydra—a multiheaded mythological monster that grows two heads when one is cut off—continually sprouting justifications for its existence.

The United States is not alone in building such a technology-fueled apparatus of control and exclusion. As tragically manifested by, among other phenomena, the deaths of illegalized people on the move across the world, the "violent borders" of the United States illuminate what is increasingly a problem of global proportions, one brought about by a whole host of countries, corporations, and other actors.[88]

For this reason, there is no shortage of stories of individuals harmed by borders of violence—whether by those of the European Union, the United States, or other entity. I share Jose's story not to illustrate that a "bad" immigrant can in fact become a "good" one, nor to reinforce an argument that he should be spared from the brutality of deportation because he is an exceptional and virtuous person. Our fight is not to push people up or down a hierarchy of worth. And no one should have to prove themselves exceptional to escape a category that legitimates systemic oppression—like the "criminal alien" category in Jose's case. Jose narrowly avoided deportation—not because the immigration system offered him an avenue to remain, but because he had the rare opportunity to eliminate the criminal conviction that made him subject to mandatory deportation. He shares his story in the hopes that it can create the possibility for others to also be able to remain wherever they call home. His story shows that securitization governance requires that the state must deem certain categories of people as a "threat" and perpetually "violent" to mask and justify state violence: dispossession, containment, exlusion and more.

If we value the lives of all humans, there is no ethical reason for the forcible removal of millions of residents of the United States (or any other country for that matter)—a deeply destructive practice that exiles people, often permanently, to countries where they may lack a social network, and where employers and government agencies often stigmatize and discriminate against them.[89] If we value life, there is also no defensible argument to legitimate the barriers to mobility that are put in place by the historical drivers of dispossession, inequality, and destabilization.

That such actions are "normal" practices of nation-states manifests the dangers of an international order predicated on national sovereignty rather than on human rights. As Achille Mbembe states, "The ultimate expression of sovereignty resides . . . in the power and the capacity to dictate who may live and who must die."[90] We need to directly confront such power as it manifests in border and migrant control regimes. What must die is the apparatus that embodies such power. An understanding of the many ways in which DHS functions as a tool of state violence and of the ways it fuels corporate power will enable us to build pathways to dismantle it and to build a world where the ability to move, to stay, to live, and to thrive is available to all.

3

Empire's Walls, Global Apartheid's Infrastructure

Joseph Nevins and Todd Miller

In January 2020, U.S. Customs and Border Protection (CBP) agents in Guatemala participated in the arrest, detention, and deportation of Hondurans who were heading northward to the United States to request asylum. According to *The Guardian*, US agents aided Guatemalan police as they "swept up hundreds of migrants, returning them to the Honduran border and in effect dashing their plans to travel together in a 'caravan' to the United States."[1]

It turns out that the actions of the CBP agents contravened an agreement between the US Department of Homeland Security, within which CBP is an agency, and the US State Department. As a US Senate Foreign Relations Committee report asserted, "DHS personnel stationed in Guatemala conducted a reckless operation that breached restrictions on their funding." The funding had come from the State Department's Bureau of International Narcotics and Law Enforcement Affairs. Among the purposes of the funding was the provision of training to civilian police and border authorities in Guatemala—for "mentoring, advising and capacity-building purposes *only*," according to the agreement.[2]

Much of the post-incident reporting focused on DHS's misapplication of the funds.[3] But what is of far greater significance than the misuse of funds is the very presence of US border agents in Guatemala in the first place. It manifests not only a reality of growing border policing, particularly along the boundaries between relatively wealthy and poor parts of the world, but also the proliferation and externalization, or pushing outward, of those boundaries by powerful countries such as the United States, or by supranational entities in the case of the European Union. As the opening story reflects, it is an undertaking that increasingly involves the enrollment of the governments of countries from where illegalized or unwanted migrants come or whose territories they pass through. These multinational regimes of exclusion are part and parcel of what is effectively an empire of borders.

This imperial regime of border policing is tied to the hypermobility across global space enjoyed by a minority of the world's population. This speaks to how movements of people, as Tim Cresswell writes, are "products and producers of power (and thus their attendant inequities)."[4] In a world of deep inequality, these inequities are tied to hierarchies such as class, gender, race, and nationality, as well as the places with which they are associated. In other words, the ability to traverse the earth and national boundaries—in terms of the ease or difficulty and legal sanction with which one does so—is apartheid-like. Similar to the impact that apartheid in South Africa had, it limits where people can go, work, and live—and under what conditions—based on their geographic origins and ancestry (real or imagined). In this case, however, the apartheid is global in scope. In both cases, there is an inherent double standard: a significant body of rights for some, much fewer for others—a disparity, like that associated with racialized inequities, that comes about by accident of birth.

This results in a world of highly restricted mobility—especially that involving travel between relatively poor and rich countries—for the majority of the world's denizens. This constrained mobility compels them, if and when they do migrate, to do so by unauthorized and highly risky means— by traversing international waters in insufficiently seaworthy boats, for example, or by walking great distances across arduous terrain in an effort to circumvent obstacles intended to stymie their movement.[5]

The border apparatuses that police such movement have many tools. They range from physical walls and armed guards to the sophisticated monitoring and surveillance technologies that characterize what are euphemistically referred to as "smart borders." While most of the world's countries are involved in this global border system in various ways, it is not a partnership of equals, but one dominated and disproportionately shaped by a handful of the world's wealthiest and most powerful countries. And it is the United States that is the central player.

The roots of the global border system are embedded in imperialism, nation-state-building, and associated processes of violence. That said, this empire of borders has greatly expanded over the last thirty years or so. In what follows, we provide a brief overview of this period, with a focus on the United States. We explore the unfolding and impacts of this regime of hardening borders in the post–Cold War era, while highlighting the growing role of technology in the apparatus of exclusion.

From the Cold War to Free Trade and Unfree Borders

Referring to the fall of the Berlin Wall thirty years earlier, Michael Hirsch asserted in 2019, in relation to national borders, "It meant the vanquishing of all walls, a giddy flinging-open of all doors."[6] And certainly in terms of the flow of capital and goods, there is considerable truth to Hirsch's statement. Consider, for example, the North America Free Trade Agreement (NAFTA), implemented in 1994. NAFTA liberalized cross-border investment and trade between Canada, Mexico, and the United States. In the case of migration, however, NAFTA, while enhancing the cross-border travel of professionals, did nothing to free up movement of workers between the three countries.[7] This is indicative of how what Hirsch characterizes as "a giddy flinging-open of all doors" was actually quite different—not least along the US-Mexico border, the policing of which increased dramatically in the years following NAFTA's implementation.[8] More broadly, the post–Cold War era has proven to be one of marked growth in border policing apparatuses across the world, with particularly dire consequences for low-income people trying to move from poor and unstable parts of the planet to wealthy and secure areas. According to one report, at the time of the fall of the Berlin Wall in 1989, there were six physical border walls across the world, for example, while as of 2020, there were at least sixty-three.[9] Not surprisingly, barriers arose along the boundaries of relatively prosperous countries. Leading the way in post–Cold War wall building was the United States.

It is unclear when the US government first began constructing barriers along the boundary with Mexico.[10] Through most of the twentieth century, however, border barriers were few and far between, generally located near urbanized areas and often in a state of disrepair, and also easily breachable.[11]

A key year in the transformation of the nature and extent of US border barriers was 1990; that year federal authorities constructed the first literal wall (rather than a chain link fence, for example) along part of the US-Mexico boundary. A few years later, under the Clinton administration, the boundary-policing apparatus exploded with the emergence of geographically focused "operations" and a spike in enforcement-related resources.[12] It was a time when concerns about crime, national security, growing unauthorized border crossings, and economic insecurity converged. Political actors in Washington and elsewhere manipulated these concerns so that they translated into a focus on an "out-of-control" US-Mexico divide and unauthorized immigrants. In this context, barricades became a basic tool in a much larger and fast-growing border policing toolbox.

The explosive growth in the US-Mexico border policing apparatus that began in the early 1990s occurred around the time when NAFTA, which came into force on January 1, 1994, was unfolding. While the simultaneous "hardening" and "opening" of the US-Mexico boundary may seem contradictory, they manifest the complementary coupling of what Matthew Sparke calls "securitized nationalism" and "free market transnationalism."[13] In other words, the goal of US authorities is to create a filter along the country's boundaries. This filter is one that aims to catch the unauthorized and illicit and allow passage to the officially desired and welcome across the US boundaries with Canada and Mexico, two of the United States' three biggest trading partners (along with China). The US government, explains Peter Andreas, seeks "to have it both ways: Create borders that perform as better security barriers and as efficient economic bridges at the same time."[14]

The attacks of 9/11 had the effect of intensifying the focus on the US-Mexico border as a security barrier, leading to a host of efforts in the White House and Congress to enhance the boundary-policing apparatus. Prior to 2005, there were in place 78 miles of "pedestrian fencing" and 57 miles of low-lying vehicle barriers along the US southern border with Mexico. By the time Donald Trump entered the White House in 2017, there were 354 miles of walls and fences, and 300 miles of vehicle barriers.[15] When Trump left office in January 2021, there were 80 additional miles of walls along the border. Most of the wall building undertaken during his administration involved replacing what it perceived as inferior barriers or ones that were dilapidated with newly designed ones.[16]

That said, physical barriers are simply one technology among many used to control entry into the United States—and this has always been the case. In 1919, five years before the founding of the US Border Patrol, the US War Department established a short-lived US Army Border Air Patrol, an armed aerial surveillance and reconnaissance unit, for example. Manned surveillance towers were present in the 1940s.[17] In the early 1970s, US authorities deployed in-ground motion detectors—technology adapted from the horrific US war in Vietnam.[18] And the use of technologies like night-vision equipment goes back to at least the 1990s.

Today, many leading Democratic and Republican politicians champion "smart borders"—the expansive use of surveillance and monitoring technologies including cameras, drones, biometrics, motion sensors, and more. Many do so for reasons of effectiveness, while some go so far as to claim that they offer a humane alternative to physical barriers. However, the championing of high-tech enforcement over physical barriers obscures the fact that both have long been central to the border and immigration policing regime.[19] Also central to the regime are personnel, the numbers of which have increased dramatically. In the case of US Border Patrol agents, for example, there were about 4,200 in 1994; in 2022, there were around 20,000.

Still, there are unique aspects of contemporary "smart borders." One is the sophistication of the technologies they embody, the scope of the personal data they are able to collect, and the integration of various data collection systems with one another. Second is their centrality to what are framed as complementary efforts to stymie unauthorized movement and to facilitate the smooth flow of authorized border crossings.

Borders of Inequality, Empire, and Apartheid

Economic inequalities between countries have declined somewhat in recent decades. However, across the world—in other words, if we analyze the world's population as a whole—they have grown markedly during this time, manifesting rising inequalities *within* most countries. Indeed, according to a 2022 report, present-day global inequalities are similar to those of the early twentieth century, a time when Western imperialism was at its peak. In 2021, the top 10 percent of the world's population received 52 percent of global income; the bottom 50 percent garnered only 8.5 percent. Wealth inequities are even more pronounced, with the top 10 percent having 76 percent of the world's wealth, and the bottom 50 percent having a measly 2 percent.[20]

As William Robinson states, "extreme inequality requires extreme violence and repression."[21] This helps explain why the number of walls along international boundaries has exploded in recent decades.[22] The biggest predictor of who constructs physical walls and where they do so, for instance, is the wealth gap between the nation-state constructing the barrier and the place and population defined as a threat. It is those on the upper end of the wealth gap who are the wall builders.[23] The United States' barricades along the country's southern border with Mexico is an obvious example. Others include Spain's formidable barriers along the boundaries of its North African enclaves of Ceuta and Melilla with Morocco, Botswana's electrified fence on its border with Zimbabwe, and the Dominican Republic's wall along its land border with Haiti.[24]

These infrastructural developments are both enhancements of national sovereignty and part of an emerging global border system. This system involves governments of relatively wealthy and powerful countries sorting, classifying, and repelling or incarcerating people from poor and disadvantaged parts of the world—directly and indirectly. Indirect means entail the enrollment of other countries, largely from the Global South, as extensions of the border policing of the North, the presence of US CBP agents in Guatemala being just one example. Mexico, for instance, now effectively serves as an extension of the US policing apparatus and the associated regime of exclusion, stymieing the ability of many people on the move to even reach US territory and to request asylum (something they are entitled to do under both international and US law).[25] The United States also helped to establish, train, and fund border policing agencies in a wide array of countries ranging from the Dominican Republic and Honduras to Kenya and Kosovo. In the case of the Dominican Republic, for example, its border policing agency, CESFRONT, was established in 2007, the same year that what was described as a group of "US experts" raised concerns in an official report about what they saw as an insufficiently policed border between the Dominican Republic and Haiti. About one month later, the country's president issued a decree creating CESFRONT.[26]

Another manifestation of the increasingly geographically extensive nature of the US border regime is that there are now at least eighty-six ICE offices worldwide.[27] Additionally, since 2003, the CBP has had attaché offices abroad; the first ones were established that year in Belgium, Canada, and Mexico. As of May 2022, there were CBP attaché offices in at least twenty-four countries.[28] And the US Border Patrol has offices in four Canadian cities, and two in Mexico. Together, these developments extend US borders outwards, whether by scrutinizing US-bound people and shipments before they board or are loaded onto planes or ships, by using the War on Terror as a justification to protect private companies' "supply chains," or by supporting border policing agencies abroad.[29]

In this regard, empire is not simply concerned with territorial expansion. Instead, it involves the harmonization of relationships between dominant groups in different countries to bring about and maintain a profoundly hierarchical system that allows a global elite, as well as activities, goods, and services with which they are associated, to cross national boundaries with ease, while stymieing the movement of a poor, global majority. In terms of North America, Thomas Shannon, US assistant secretary of state of Western Hemisphere Affairs, succinctly described what this meant during a 2007 summit between the United States, Mexico, and Canada. The three countries, he said, had to understand "North America as a shared economic space," one that "we need to protect," not only on the border but "more broadly throughout North America," through improved "security cooperation."[30]

What this entailed effectively, according to Shannon, was that the three countries were "armoring NAFTA." This was, to put it in a more global context, the armoring of capitalism, a phenomenon that provides stability for investors by surveilling, policing, and repressing challenges—particularly by social movements—to their activities. And through expansive federal expenditures in the rapidly growing "homeland security" market, with global revenues now in the hundreds of millions of dollars each year, it helps to enrich particular sectors of corporate capital.[31] One way it does so is by producing different levels of exploitation and thus a hierarchy of people, making some non-citizens essential to national well-being when it is advantageous and effectively disposable when it is not.

Take, for instance, what unfolded in the United States in the early months of the coronavirus pandemic. In March 2020, the US State Department announced that it would suspend the processing of immigration visas; this would have had the effect of ending the flow of seasonal agricultural workers (most of whom would come from Mexico) to the United States. Quickly, however, the State Department, under pressure from agribusiness interests, changed the decision, announcing that the H-2A program (which provides time-delimited visas and work permits to farmworkers from abroad) would continue as "a national security priority."[32] Around the same time, the Department of Homeland Security officially defined farm laborers—the majority of whom are undocumented—as "essential workers." The day before the DHS declaration, ICE announced that it was adjusting its policing operations to focus on "public safety risks and individuals subject to mandatory detention based on criminal grounds," and that it would not police those who fall outside these categories. In response to the change, one farmworker explained to the *New York Times*: "Those of us without papers live in fear that immigration will pick us up. . . . Now we are feeling more relaxed." In this case, however, the ability to feel relaxed was only temporary. As ICE made clear in its announcement, the new policy would only last until the pandemic passed.[33] Similarly, while Israel has long arrested and deported "illegal" Palestinians from its territory, the Israeli state opens and closes its border to Palestinian workers when it deems it politically and economically advantageous.[34] In 2020, for example, the Israeli state intentionally created breaches in what it refers to as its security barrier with the occupied West Bank to allow and encourage (officially unauthorized) Palestinian laborers to enter the country. And during the pandemic, Israel compelled approximately thirty thousand Palestinian workers to remain within the country for weeks because of the need for their labor in the construction and agricultural sectors, preventing them from returning to their homes in the Palestinian territories.[35]

Such "flexible" borders help maintain and exacerbate inequalities that are central to the contemporary global order and its inequities of race, class, and nationality. They manifest a world in which the few—the relatively rich and disproportionately white—are generally free to travel and live wherever they would like or have the means to access the resources they "need." Meanwhile the relatively poor—who are largely people of color—are forced to subsist in places plagued by dangerous levels of insecurity or where there are not enough resources to provide sufficient livelihood. Border regimes that reflect, produce, and maintain such inequality are the embodiment of global apartheid.[36]

In order to overcome the resulting deprivation and insecurity, many feel compelled to leave their home countries and risk their lives in the quest to circumvent the ever-stronger boundary controls put into place by the countries of privilege that they attempt to enter. And if they succeed in reaching the territories to which they are denied, these officially unwelcome individuals must endure all the indignities and hazards associated with being marked as "illegal." Even if they are allowed to enter a particular territory—say, in the case of individuals on temporary work visas—their rights are typically greatly limited, which serves as a form of discipline and heightens their exploitability by capital.

Whether the borders that individuals on the move encounter are "smart" or conventional—or a combination of both (which is typically the case)—is irrelevant from the standpoint of human well-being. In addition to contributing to the deaths of thousands of people across the planet each year, as illegalized people are compelled to take ever more dangerous routes to circumvent the obstacles put in their way, all border policing tools have a common goal. That goal is to control human beings, to limit the rights of those deemed as foreign, and to deny entry and residence to those deemed undesirable or undeserving. In a world of stark inequities, it is a goal that is both a product and producer of unequal—and unjust—life and death circumstances. It thus speaks to the need for a radical shift in how we think about migration—as a fundamental right.[37] This entails a transformation of territorial boundaries, the need for which is only heightened in a time of intensifying climate change, so that they are no longer borders of death.[38]

Contesting what activist, writer, and educator Harsha Walia calls "border imperialism" requires efforts on multiple fronts.[39] Moreover, just as the fight to overturn apartheid in South Africa required struggles by those most harmed by that system of racial segregation, any collective endeavor to end global apartheid necessitates struggles by those most harmed by the empire of borders.[40] It also requires alliances with, and great efforts by, many of those who are the intended beneficiaries of the borders that uphold and reproduce the system of global apartheid.[41] And, again, just as efforts to end apartheid in South Africa proved to be, the fight against global apartheid will prove to be hard, but winnable—if we help make it so.

4

Fortress Europe's Proliferating Borders

Miriam Ticktin[1]

On August 20, 2021, less than one week after the Taliban overthrew the Western-backed government in Afghanistan, Greece announced that it had completed a 25-mile-long wall along its border with Turkey, explaining that the barricade's purpose was to prevent Afghan refugees from entering Greek territory.[2] Less than three months later, violent clashes unfolded along the razor-wire fence dividing Poland and Belarus as thousands of refugees from countries like Syria and Iraq on the Belarusian side of the border fought Polish police, who were trying to prevent them from moving westward.[3] That same month, twenty-seven individuals—mostly Kurds fleeing Iran and Iraq—drowned as they tried to cross the English Channel from France to the United Kingdom in an inflatable dinghy.[4]

These borders are not simply expressions of nation-states, but those of a supranational entity, the European Union. The wall building, the violent clashes, and the deaths all took place along the EU's perimeter, a perimeter that is located both around the formal territory of the Union and increasingly elsewhere. This manifests how Europe is increasingly a border zone, or "borderscape," where control is performed in settings well beyond its official territorial boundaries.[5] In other words, the European border regime is both mobile and manifold. It is more than a coincidence that the countries that were historically the world's major colonial powers are at the center of this regime. Similarly, it is not a coincidence that the vast majority of the peoples on the move, targeted by the regime, come from countries and territories that European powers colonized, ravaged, and plundered—and continue to dominate and exploit to this day, often greatly contributing to the very migration they want to block.[6] The EU's move to immediately open its borders to Ukrainian refugees following the Russian invasion of Ukraine that began in February 2022, while keeping them closed to others, has rendered explicit the racialized nature of this regime. In this sense, the border regime manifests enduring, as well as changing, forms of the European empire and its violence and injustice.

Four key developments characterize this ever-growing European border regime: a hardening of Europe's official territorial borders; a pushing outward, or externalization, of the EU's boundaries; an associated proliferation of the EU's policing and immigrant control infrastructure in the waters and lands both within and beyond Europe; and a marked increase in the deaths, among other forms of hardship and injury, of illegalized people on the move toward and within Europe. I examine each of these manifestations below, after providing a brief background to the making of the EU's contemporary border regime.

Hardening Territorial Boundaries: Walls, Walls, Walls

The EU's origins lie in the creation of an economic association among six European countries in 1957. Over the decades, the resulting European Community (EC) grew in size and scope, a key development being the 1985 Schengen Agreement, which established freedom of movement within the EC's borders. In 1993, the EU, promising even greater levels of European cooperation, replaced the EC. Today, there are twenty-seven member states in the European Union. While almost all these countries are members of what is called the Schengen Area—the area of control-free movement at their shared borders—the EU does not directly map onto the Schengen Area. The Schengen Area comprises twenty-six countries, some of which are not part of the EU, such as Norway and Iceland, while some members of the EU have opted out of Schengen, such as Ireland, which wants to control its own borders. The slippage (and confusion) between these two political formations has ultimately enabled greater policing and exclusion.

More specifically, the development of the Schengen Area has enabled a selective hardening of Europe's external borders, even as these border zones change and shift. Coupled with Schengen's liberalization of movement between member states (seen as an opening of borders), this was a requirement to achieve greater control over external boundaries (a corresponding closing of borders)—a key development in the making of what many have come to call Fortress Europe.[7] This requirement has been most impactful on countries on the periphery of Europe, typically countries that have experienced the greatest number of individuals seeking to cross their borders in the quest to find refuge within Europe. More than a dozen countries—including Italy, Greece, Portugal, and Spain—were not allowed to join the Schengen Area until they demonstrated that their border controls were sufficiently strong. To help them achieve such strength, the EU has provided extensive funding—among other resources.[8]

Perhaps the most visible expression of this growing regime of border and migrant control is the more than 600 miles of walls—in total, more than six times the length of the Berlin Wall—many of which are reinforced by sophisticated detection and surveillance technologies. While walls are not part of any formal or official EU mandate, and are often disparaged in the name of what some present as more "humane"[9] surveillance systems, they are increasingly part of the EU's border policing regime.[10] A prime example is the barriers around Ceuta and Melilla.[11] The enclaves have the most militarized borders within the European Union, with four layers of fencing (one on the Moroccan side, three on Spain's), some sections of which are thirty-three feet tall; and with barriers that are complemented by a variety of technologies aimed at stymieing the movement of people through, under, or over them. Since the first fences were built in the 1990s, dozens of individuals have died from being shot or beaten, and from injuries sustained while trying to cross the barriers. For instance, in June 2022, over twenty died and seventy-six were injured trying to cross into Melilla, some falling to their deaths while others were the result of violent clashes with the Moroccan security forces.[12] Many have drowned trying to swim around the walls to enter the two enclaves by sea from neighboring Morocco.[13]

Naval patrols in the Mediterranean and virtual or "smart" walls complement physical barriers along Europe's perimeter. So, too, do the personnel of the assorted national border policing apparatuses of Schengen Area member states as well as an EU agency called Frontex, or the European Border and Coast Guard Agency. Founded in 2004, Frontex coordinates in various ways with national border police agencies and coast guards. Its formation and growth reflect the broader militarization of security regimes that emerged in the aftermath of the 9/11 attacks in the United States, the 2004 train bombings in Madrid, and the 2005 underground bombings in London. Together, these events, exploited by political actors within Europe, helped exacerbate xenophobia and conflate "otherness" with "terrorism." They also helped justify the very creation and development of Frontex. The EU agency brings together existing national systems—from defense and disease control to maritime safety—of all EU member and Schengen Area countries to create what it calls "the system of systems." The public systems are increasingly partnering with private enterprises—from global technology companies to military contractors.[14]

Externalization of Borders: Pushing Europe into Africa

As Europe is working to shore up its formal territorial perimeters, a second face of its border regime is also under construction. It involves the proliferation and expansion of what many have referred to as Europe's "external borders," pushing its border regime ever deeper into Africa and elsewhere. Frontex, for example, has engaged in "pushback" operations at sea—a potentially illegal practice—stopping migrant vessels from entering EU waters and from landing on the shores of places like Greece, Italy, or Malta, putting those on board at great, and often deadly, risk.[15] Indeed, a central goal of Frontex is to achieve total surveillance of Europe's increasingly thick borderlands. These include not only the Mediterranean and the border areas of North Africa, but "anywhere" from which migration could originate, justifying an ever-widening terrain of policing and surveillance. By pressuring African states—ranging from Niger to Sudan—to participate in the EU migrant policing apparatus and inducing them to do so via trade deals, arms transfers, and aid programs, the European Union has effectively pushed its borders into sub-Saharan Africa. It has also strengthened some of the region's most authoritarian states.[16]

The EU's surveillance systems include unmanned aerial vehicles along Libya's desert borders, optronic and radar technologies that scan the Mediterranean from the air, and surveillance towers that use visual and electromagnetic identification techniques to scan the Strait of Gibraltar and the Moroccan coast. There are also many surveillance-enabling technologies specific to the sea. These include optical and thermal cameras, radars, vessel tracking tools, distress signal mechanisms—which indicate geo-referenced coordinates—wind and current data collection devices, and image-producing satellites, which help track where a boat is, might be, or where it was recently.[17] They play a significant role in the interception of migrants en route and their detention in a series of camps in North Africa—in Algeria, Libya, and Morocco—paid for by the EU. Human Rights Watch and other organizations have revealed that imprisoned migrants face regular and sustained violence by local police or militia groups in these countries, to which the EU's border and immigration apparatus has been effectively outsourced.[18] Libyan authorities and what is referred to as Libya's Coast Guard (an entity with links to militia groups), for example, have intercepted tens of thousands of migrants at sea—often in international waters—in the last few years, and forcibly brought them back to Libya, holding them in what are often squalid and physically violent conditions.[19] Moreover, Libya is a country where national law allows for the indefinite detention and punishment with forced labor of unauthorized foreigners. EU equipment, funding, and training have made much of this possible.[20]

Incarceration: The Prisons Within

Closer to the formal territorial borders of Europe, illegalized and unwelcome people on the move are encountering ever greater levels of direct and structural forms of violence, which constitutes a third face of the border regime.

This third aspect is perhaps most visible in the proliferation of camps, or spaces of externalization and legal exception, even when on European territory. Those who manage to circumvent such obstacles and cross the sea, or who take new and treacherous land routes, often get stopped at the edges of Europe and put into overflowing frontier camps. For instance, Moria refugee camp on the Greek island of Lesbos (or Lesvos) held up to twenty thousand migrants in 2020, in a space designed for three thousand. This produced conflict with the otherwise welcoming local population and amplified the already huge risk of COVID-19 after the pandemic began.[21] A fire destroyed the camp in September 2020, leaving thousands unhoused. When the migrants then demonstrated and demanded the right to leave the island and go to the EU's mainland, Greek police responded with tear gas.[22] As of September 2021, they were still occupying what was supposed to be a temporary tent camp on Mavrovouni beach, near the island's capital, Mytilene.[23]

Deeper into Europe's "interior," one also finds camp-like establishments, except that they are called detention or retention or holding centers. Both formal and informal, the camps are located in private hotels, city buildings, airports, on the outskirts close to borders. They are sometimes even located within cities, as is the case in Paris.[24] These carceral facilities are composed of a mixture of formal and informal housing—ranging from shipping containers to tents.

Just as camps and immigration prisons are proliferating in the "interior," so, too, are smart border technologies.[25] Those coming from outside the EU are made to face AI lie detectors,[26] DNA collection, and other invasive and experimental technologies,[27] which defer responsibility for judgment and classification of people to technologies that have been shown to be untrustworthy. The AI lie detectors, for instance, are part of a largely untested automated system, and the facial recognition algorithms on which this system relies have been shown to have high error rates, particularly with women and people of color.[28] Racialized minorities are surveilled in places like train stations with these same technologies, legitimating racism and racial profiling.[29] In this sense, wherever they are found, migrants—and the racialized minorities with whom they are conflated, revealing Europe to be a fundamentally racist project—serve as experimental subjects for these technologies.[30]

Death: Mass Graves on Land and in the Sea

While there are many forms of violence that illegalized people encounter within Europe or as they try to reach Europe, death is the ultimate expression—the fourth and final face of the EU's "violent borders."[31] In the case of the Mediterranean, which is effectively Europe's most geopolitically significant border zone, it has the distinction of becoming the site of the greatest number of lethal border crossings in the world; indeed, it has become a mass grave. Between 2014 and 2020, according to the Missing Migrants Project of the International Organization for Migration (IOM), more than twenty thousand individuals lost their lives while trying to cross the Mediterranean, circumvent the border policing apparatus of the European Union, and reach Europe's shores. Smart borders have furthered migrant deaths at sea by forcing migrant vessels to take different routes, requiring the use of smugglers, and by coordinating maritime responses to stop ships with migrants from docking in any EU port, leaving many to simply drift and die. While migrants are always fighting back, working in solidarity with others to find new strategies to cross and to live decent lives, the human costs are enormous.[32]

On land, hundreds more have died within Europe, according to the IOM, and countless others have perished within Africa. Authorities in countries like Libya and Morocco sometimes deport migrants into the desert, leaving them to die. Moreover, a combination of vehicles getting lost or breaking down in the desert areas of North and sub-Saharan Africa, with attacks by bandits, has led to many fatalities. As Ambassador Raul Mateus Paula, head of the EU delegation in Niger, admitted: "We know that many people are dying in the Mediterranean. But many are dying in the desert as well, and we have not many statistics."[33]

European Apartheid

The EU justifies much of its border work through the framework of humanitarianism. Frontex officials, for example, often position themselves as the rescuers of imperiled people at sea or as the protectors of individuals threatened by the practices of ruthless smugglers.[34] However, it is clear that the EU's multilayered border control apparatus is first and foremost about maintaining a hierarchy of humanity, one in which "citizens" (even while this citizenry is itself stratified) and a small number of other (authorized, and generally already privileged) individuals are granted high levels of rights and resources, while the rest—with rare exceptions, the cumulative effect of which is to bolster border rule—are subject to exclusion and violent borders.[35] It is thus hardly surprising that border technologies, of both conventional and "smart" varieties, have been primarily used not to rescue but to prevent migrant vessels from arriving on the shores of Europe, or to tag and track migrants wherever they go, producing what Étienne Balibar predicted and named in 2001: "European apartheid."[36]

5

Frontex and Fortress Europe's Technological Experiments

Petra Molnar

The borders of the European Union (EU) are the setting in which thousands of people have been violently set adrift, unable to penetrate Fortress Europe without succumbing to the depths of the sea or freezing to death along land borders. Europe's regional border force, Frontex, is a leading player in the perpetuation of increasingly deadly border regimes underpinned by systemic and historical racism, facilitated by technology.

From the Poland/Belarus frontier to Greece to the English Channel, borders continue to be the setting of various migration management experiments supported and actively encouraged by the EU, codified in its 2020 New Pact on Migration and Asylum, or "New Migration Pact,"[1] and reconfirmed at various recent press conferences with EU officials.[2] The New Migration Pact is a set of policy documents that set out Europe's new approach to migration, asylum, and border management and integration, and consolidate the EU's internal and external migration policies. These EU policies are replete with explicit messaging regarding the "management" of migration,[3] a Europeanized deportation process, the protection of the border, and the strengthening of the work of Frontex, or the European Border and Coast Guard Agency. The Pact also explicitly opened the door to increasingly more draconian tools of surveillance.[4] The EU has increasingly explored how to strengthen this migration management machine and expand the power of its border force through various technological experiments.

Frontex, a pan-European agency, plays a leading role in setting the agenda for policymaking, bolstering a growing international border industrial complex and a web of actors profiting from the use of border technologies that target communities crossing borders and violently ensnare people seeking protection.[5]

Frontex and Border Technologies

Frontex has been one of the leading actors in the development and deployment of high-risk technologies for migration control across the EU, having made technological innovation a cornerstone of its strategy and operations. Over the last number of years, the agency has positioned itself as the vanguard of technological development, piloting and deploying various interventions for border surveillance and migration management. For example, in March 2021 Frontex commissioned a report from the RAND Corporation on various uses of artificial intelligence (AI) in border operations.[6] In November 2021, Frontex committed to flying surveillance airplanes over the English Channel, after the death of twenty-seven people at sea attempting to reach the shores of the United Kingdom. And as of autumn 2022, the agency has issued various procurement notices for even more border technologies,[7] including taking its surveillance into the stratosphere.[8] It is a major player in the political economy of a lucrative multibillion-dollar border industrial complex that is feeding the global development and deployment of these violent technologies.[9] Frontex spent €434 million between 2014 and 2020 on military-grade surveillance and IT infrastructure.[10]

However, Frontex also does not operate alone. The agency is integrated in a broader ecosystem of high-risk border technologies, bolstered by a framework of data sharing and surveillance activities at the heart of EU's border and migration management. These projects include EUROSUR, an information-exchange framework shared between EU member states.[11] There are also many other interoperable databases used for border control, such as EURODAC, first introduced in 2003, which maintains an EU-wide database of biometrics including iris scanning and fingerprints.[12] These databases blur the lines between data collected for border management, law enforcement, and national security, and directly infringe on people's right to privacy, nondiscrimination, and freedom of movement.[13] In addition, over the last few years, more draconian surveillance and border technology has been rolled out around the frontiers of Europe in a push to militarize migration management.[14] Some of these experiments include high-tech prison-like refugee camps in Greece;[15] Long Range Acoustic Devices (LRADs) or sound cannons;[16] and aerostat surveillance cameras at the Evros land border between Turkey and Greece,[17] as well as along the Balkan route in countries like Croatia and Albania; and AI-powered lie detectors at borders.[18] Some of these projects have been even challenged in court for their discriminatory and life-threatening impacts. Yet this increasingly lucrative ecosystem creates the perfect high-risk laboratory of experimentation with migration control technologies, playing out at Europe's edges.[19]

Technological Frontiers of Fortress Europe

Frontier countries like Greece, or "Europe's Shield," often act as testing grounds for new technologies and surveillance mechanisms.[20] "Shield," or "aspida" in Greek, was a term Ursula von der Leyen, the European Commission's president, used to thank Greek authorities for deterring refugees, after announcing an additional $795 million in EU support to step up border infrastructure and management. The term was quoted widely as accurately naming the EU's handling of migration in the Mediterranean and the Aegean, and the EU's active role in creating and fueling a deadly migration deterrence regime.

Greece has been hosting the majority of refugees in Europe since 2015, and has come under fire for the decrepit conditions on its island camps in the Aegean Sea. Tragedy struck again in September 2020, when Moria, Europe's largest refugee camp, burned to the ground on the island of Lesbos, rendering thousands of people without shelter. I have visited Lesbos and the other Aegean islands in the aftermath of this fire numerous times to document the building of new high-tech refugee camps and map out how this context fits into broader narratives of technological experimentation in Fortress Europe. The five new Multi-Purpose Reception and Identification Centers (MPRICs) on Lesbos, Samos, Chios, Leros, and Kos all include "camera surveillance with motion analysis algorithms monitoring the behavior and movement of center residents."[21] These camps are funded by the EU to detain people—and those inside describe them as a prison.[22]

This surveillance of people on the move follows a long-standing historical tradition of containing and surveilling racialized groups and communities made historically vulnerable. The recent war in Ukraine has clearly shown how Europe's migration policies are highly discriminatory against non-white refugees. In March 2022, during a monitoring trip to Ukraine, I saw refugees being welcomed with open arms at the Polish-Ukrainian border, while mere kilometers away people from Africa, South Asia, and the Middle East continued to freeze in the forest,[23] aided by a replica of the Greek border surveillance system.[24]

Discrimination is also baked into the technology itself. Much of these border technologies are automated and rely on vast amounts of data and algorithmic decision-making. Yet, algorithms that feed these technologies are vulnerable to the same decision-making concerns that plague human decision-makers: transparency, accountability, discrimination, bias, and error. The opaque nature of immigration and refugee decision-making creates an environment ripe for algorithmic discrimination. To identify these risks is not mere speculation. Biases at the border have far-reaching results if they are embedded in the emerging technologies being used experimentally in migration. For example, Greece was also one of the pilot countries for the now widely derided iBorderCTRL project,[25] an AI-powered lie detector to be deployed at airports. The project claimed that passengers' faces would be monitored for signs of lying, and if the system became more "skeptical" after proceeding through a series of increasingly complicated questions, the person would be flagged as a "risk" and identified for further investigation.

But how can these so-called lie detectors deal with cross-cultural communication differences, or even the impact of trauma on memory? Decisions in these systems—from determining whether a refugee's life story is "truthful" to whether a prospective immigrant's marriage is "genuine"—are highly discretionary, and often hinge on an assessment of a person's credibility. Facial- and emotion-recognition technologies are also very racially biased.[26] Border technologies are underpinned by an increasingly violent regime of border enforcement, bolstered by the rise of far-right anti-migration sentiments and fears about "uncontrollable masses" of the unwanted overrunning Fortress Europe.[27]

This increasingly normalized technological violence culminates in the most egregious manifestation—assistance for Frontex and other national actors like the Greek Coast Guard with pushbacks, or the practice of returning people seeking asylum to Turkey, Libya, or other unsafe countries. These practices are in direct contravention of international law and the fundamental right of being able to claim asylum. These pushbacks, which are facilitated by surveillance technologies, have led to thousands of deaths around Europe.[28]

Why Is This Violence Allowed to Continue?

Frontex has been allowed to operate with relative impunity for years, covering up pushbacks and other human rights abuses.[29] The entity operates in an ever-growing tapestry of the increasingly powerful and global border industrial complex[30] that legitimizes violent technological experiments[31] at the expense of human rights and dignity, strengthening the violent borders around Fortress Europe.[32] As the EU explicitly moves toward shutting its borders to people seeking protection, the technological experiments at the heart of EU's migration policies also do not occur in a vacuum. Powerful actors—including the private sector[33]—increasingly set the stage regarding what technology should be developed and deployed, while communities experiencing the sharp edges of this innovation are consistently left out of the discussion.

These uses of technology create far-reaching risks to fundamental human rights, including the right to not be discriminated against, the right to privacy, and freedom of movement; and procedural justice rights such as the right to an impartial decision-maker and meaningful access to mechanisms of redress.[34] The complexity of human migration is not easily reducible to an algorithm. Yet the EU—and states globally—are willing to experiment with these new, unregulated border technologies precisely because migration is a discretionary space of opaque decision-making. The EU continues to make its priorities clear: containment, surveillance, and techno-solutionism at the expense of human rights and dignity. These priorities are also in direct opposition to how the EU positions itself as a leader in data protection and privacy, through its fairly robust General Data Protection Regulation (GDPR) and the proposed Act to Regulate Artificial Intelligence (the "AI Act"). Both of these regulatory frameworks extend protections to citizens while leaving people on the move out of the regulatory regime.[35]

However, various grassroots and community-led campaigns such as Abolish Frontex have made headway in highlighting that reform of agencies like Frontex is not enough, calling for abolition of the agency,[36] while parliamentary hearings have begun to question the absence of adequate checks and balances on Frontex's operations.[37] When it comes to border technologies, civil society and academics are also currently calling for amendment to the EU's AI Act to introduce redlines around the use of predictive analytics for the purposes of pushbacks or border interdictions by actors like Frontex.[38]

Nonetheless, as an agency with half a billion euros ($545 million) of annual funding, Frontex continues to weather serious and mounting allegations of harm against people seeking asylum in Europe. The ranks of Frontex continue to swell, while thousands of people on the move are stranded, detained, and in the worst instances pushed back out of European territory by the gatekeepers of Fortress Europe. The technological experiments at the heart of Frontex and EU border control are just one part of a violent global migration machine that people searching for safer shores now have to navigate as they seek refuge in an increasingly destabilized world.

6

Abolish Migration Deterrence

Jenna M. Loyd

I n the international migration context, "deterrence" refers to state policies and practices that aim to prevent people on the move from reaching their destination. These practices have become increasingly well known in connection with highly visible exercises of state power such as Frontex patrols in the Mediterranean, Australia's use of the island of Nauru for detaining asylum seekers, and the US policy of "prevention through deterrence" that diverts people from moving through cities to cross the US-Mexico boundary to remote and difficult desert terrains. In all of these cases, governments rely on a punitive theory that increasing the "costs" of migration will cause people on the move to weigh their risks and choose their options accordingly. Critics of migration deterrence contend that these policies do not stop people from trying to move in the interests of safety, livelihood, or family. Rather, deterrence policies have only made these journeys more dangerous and deadly for people on the move.

Migration deterrence—with roots in punishment and military theories—has been implemented around the world to become a fundamental part of what activists and critical migration scholars call a system of global apartheid.[1] So how did punishment theory get integrated into migration policy?

Seen from today's vantage point, with the displacement of people globally at a historic high, the political terrain for migrant and refugee rights in the late 1970s seems hopeful. President Carter had signaled his interest in human rights, which was rapidly becoming a central part of social movements.[2] The US was in the midst of what remains its largest moment of refugee resettlement, namely of people displaced from conflicts and US-led wars in Southeast Asia. Consequently, the Refugee Act of 1980 created the United States' first asylum and refugee law.[3] Concurrently, when it seemed that asylum and refuge might be put on a solid human rights footing, the US also implemented deterrence policies of mandatory detention and interception at sea to prevent the US from becoming a country of first asylum. This fateful connection between refugee legislation and migration deterrence was rooted in geopolitics and has only deepened since that time.

The event that prompted deterrence policy was the arrival of 125,000 Cuban and 25,000 Haitian asylum seekers by boat to Florida.[4] Each group had been treated in terms of Cold War geopolitical calculations: because Castro was a foe, people fleeing Cuba were welcomed as freedom-fighters, while those who left the shores of US-allied Haiti were treated as economic migrants. In the 1990s, the US continued these deterrence policies with interception of Haitian boats and confinement of Haitian refugees at its Guantánamo Bay naval base. Cold War foreign policy continued to inform treatments of asylum seekers from Central America. Ronald Reagan invoked already racialized hysteria over migrants from Mexico to warn of "a tidal wave" of "feet people" fleeing civil wars in Central America. The US backing of these wars either went unmentioned by US officials or was justified in Cold War terms.[5] Rhetorics of crime, lawlessness (often related to the drug trade), and a not-so-distant Communist threat fueled restrictionist politics in California, Arizona, and Texas, which soon collided with national tough-on-crime efforts.[6] In 1994, President Clinton passed legislation that expanded reliance on migration detention and instituted the Border Patrol policy of prevention through deterrence. Almost immediately, residents living in the US-Mexico borderlands began to see shifts in migration patterns, and a largely new phenomenon of injuries and deaths among migrants attempting to traverse strenuous, sometimes mountainous, desert terrains.[7] The numbers of migrants who have lost their lives to state policies is a matter of dispute, but researchers contend the figure is in the thousands.[8]

When Ronald Reagan signed the executive order authorizing interdiction at sea in 1981, refugee scholar Guy Goodwin-Gill called it "the model, perhaps, for all that has followed."[9] Alison Mountz traces how deterrence became more global in the late 1990s, when Europe, Canada, and Australia also began instituting practices of "externalization," which refers to a variety of policies and practices that aim to keep people from a particular territory.[10]

These policies have continued to evolve into a suite of practices, including (1) the movement of border enforcement locations "offshore" from immediate boundaries; (2) the movement of processing (such as visa checks) and detention sites to countries of transit; and (3) the use of island detention sites and refugee camps to confine people from reaching their destinations.

The result is what international law scholars Thomas Gammeltoft-Hansen and James Hathaway call a "world of cooperative deterrence," another way of saying "global apartheid."[11] Today, most internationally displaced people continue to reside in the Global South, and less than 2 percent of refugees are ever resettled. Wealthier nations employ deterrence measures *and* modest refugee resettlement to forestall the collapse of the global refugee regime system because they fear its failure would result in even greater migration to the Global North. Countries in the Global North have been teaming up with each other and with countries in the Global South (often former colonies or neo-colonies) to carry out deterrence measures that now span transnational transit routes linking wealthier nations and places of major conflict or other significant displacement. These arrangements can include financial incentives, the provision of training and equipment for border patrols, and joint migration operations.[12] Seen in this light, deterrence is the iron fist in the velvet glove of refugee resettlement.

How does deterrence work, in theory? When criminologists and philosophers discuss the origins of deterrence as a theory, they typically begin with the eighteenth- to early nineteenth-century thinkers Cesare Beccaria and Jeremy Bentham. In the Italian and British contexts in which they respectively wrote, Beccaria and Bentham were interested in reforming the existing systems of punishment, which they regarded as cruel, arbitrary, and ineffective in preventing crime. Together, they advanced the premise that punishments would dissuade unwanted acts if they were certain, swift, and severe enough.[13] In the US context, interest in this utilitarian model surged in the late 1960s in the groundswell of neoliberal political theorizing (such as economist Gary Becker's rational choice theory) and increasing bipartisan embrace of law-and-order politics. The idea that lengthened prison terms, mandatory minimums, and harsh penalties would prevent crime became common sense among lawmakers, "despite four decades of accumulating evidence to the contrary" that harsher punishments deter violent, property, or drug offenses more effectively than lesser ones (they don't); imprisonment deters one from committing another offense (it often increases that possibility); and capital punishment prevents homicide better than any other punishments (it does not).[14]

It was within this historical and ideological context that deterrence made its way explicitly into US migration policy. Despite the origins of deterrence in punishment theory, its place in migration policy has been examined mainly by international law and migration scholars on legal, theoretical, and ethical grounds, which I examine in turn.[15] National security commentators and legal scholars alike draw attention to the questionable legality of deterrence, particularly for nations that have signed on to the 1951 Convention Relating to the Status of Refugees and the 1967 Protocol.[16] For them, deterrence practices may undermine foreign policy objectives and create legal blurs between national and international obligations.[17] For Gammeltoft-Hansen and Tan, the emergent deterrence regime is inherently unstable. Its effectiveness and legality are increasingly in question, but most importantly the proliferation of deterrence practices "creates a systemic risk to the entire refugee protection regime," an undesirable outcome for countries of the Global North.[18] This optimistic view of the efficacy of international law, however, is tempered by remembering the Cold War and decolonization-era roots of international refugee policy, which the West largely shaped.[19] From this perspective, the emergence of containment and virtual collapse of resettlement are fully in line with migration policies that have become increasingly restrictive toward members of former colonies or neo-colonies.

The basic tenets of deterrence theory have been widely questioned by migration scholars (echoing critiques by criminologists and military strategists).[20] In order for deterrence to "work" on its own theoretical terms, at least three assumptions must be addressed: (1) that people on the move know about the legal and policing landscape; (2) that perception of potential "costs" of an action informs their decisions; and, given these concerns, (3) that rational choice accurately depicts human-decisionmaking. The assumption that people's knowledge of the law will change their migration decisions is the basis of public policies and information campaigns intended to signal that migration is unlawful or otherwise unsafe and unwanted. Yet legal scholar Emily Ryo finds that there is little evidence that people on the move are aware of these legal conditions; rather, many "assume that the law cannot be so unjust as to confine them in jail or jail-like facilities upon apprehension."[21] Further, for many people who take great risks to migrate, staying put is not an option due to severe conditions of violence or obligations to family and community members. As Cecilia Menjívar writes, "Compared to the [other] expected risks—such as rape or death—detention is actually less serious and thus less likely to function as a significant deterrent."[22] Finally, the idea that human behavior can be explained through rational cost-benefit calculations has been widely criticized (including by national security strategists) for failing to account for emotions, the context of decision-making, and collective decision-making processes. The question is not reason vs. unreason. Rather, as Ryo, Menjívar, other migration scholars, and migrants themselves have repeatedly observed, military conflict, sustained police violence and impunity, and other forms of systemic violence create conditions in which people have no better option but to take great risks. When anthropologist Wendy Vogt asked a young Honduran man about whether he feared returning home, as he traveled through Mexico to reach family in the United States, he replied, "Yes: my country, it takes your smile away."[23]

Finally, I turn to ethical critiques of deterrence. The fatal and otherwise harmful effects of deterrence draw into question the legitimacy of this form of state violence. For Cox and Goodman, "government strategies that would maximize deterrence are off limits when they run afoul of ethical redlines," such as imposing emotional anguish on families.[24] In theory, deterrence was supposed to result in a more just criminal justice system that reduces crime, but instead has resulted in lengthier, harsher punishments. Some criminologists think it still could work, in a drastically narrowed scope. But prison abolitionists (and radical criminologists) have questioned whether punishment and policing can ever be separated from racialized, class, and gendered forms of social control.[25] From this perspective, the terror, bodily endangerment, and violation that are built into deterrence make it inherently violent and utterly indefensible.[26]

The horrors of deterrence made evident during the Trump administration's Zero Tolerance family separation practices put deterrence on the political landscape as an ethical redline. According to journalist Caitlin Dickerson, Marine Corps General John Kelly had rejected family separation during the Obama administration on moral and practical grounds, particularly given the difficult conditions people were fleeing in Central America.[27] We know that such express acknowledgment of deterrence's ethical violations and practical inefficacy did not hold sway in the Trump administration. I view this as a small but tangible opening toward ending deterrence. Building a world in which all people—not just militaries, tourists, and the wealthy—are able to move freely must necessarily abolish the deterrence practices that sustain global apartheid. The abolition and "no borders" frameworks offer world-changing theory and practice.[28] Given that borders have proliferated into mobile and transnational operations, "no borders" politics questions the legitimacy of migration policies and citizenship as a basis of allocating power and resources. Abolition and no borders are about dismantling these institutions and transforming the social, political, and economic conditions that enable these violent institutions to persist, often in the name of safety, security, and well-being. For leading abolitionist Ruth Wilson Gilmore, "abolition requires that we change one thing: everything."[29]

As these new worlds are being created amid the wreckage of deterrence, Naomi Paik offers radical sanctuary as a practice of welcome integrating a "defensive logic of protecting people from imminent harm" and efforts to "create equitable conditions in which everyone has what they need."[30] Abolishing deterrence should also involve forms of reparative justice. Joe Nevins argues, "Migration involving the movement of people from exploited and relatively impoverished parts of the world to countries of relative wealth and privilege, is, or at least should be, a right born of debt—an imperial debt. The right to migration, in other words, is a form of reparations."[31] Reparations would also include the right for people who have been deported to reunify with families and communities.[32]

For wealthy nations to continue to reject migratory reparations, Suketu Mehta writes, they also "would have to stop propping up dictators, stop starting savage and unnecessary wars, restrain their multinational corporations from ripping off mineral wealth of poor countries and make sure that global trade is more equitable."[33] Mehta's contention also forms the basis of no borders as a politics. As Harsha Walia writes, "A meaningful no borders politics requires an end to forced displacement caused by the brutalities of conquest, the voraciousness of capital, and the wreckages of climate change."[34] Deterrence cannot be made ethical. It must be abolished as part of changing the everything of colonialism and racial capitalism.

7

Cruel Fictions in the Black Mediterranean

Ida Danewid, The Black Mediterranean Collective

> *A border, like race, is a cruel fiction*
> *Maintained by constant policing, violence*
> *Always threatening a new map. It takes*
> *Time, lots of people's time, to organize*
> *The world this way. & violence. It takes more*
> *Violence. Violence no one can confuse for*
> *Anything but violence. So much violence*
> *Changes relationships, births a people*
> *They can reason with. These people are not*
> *Us. They underestimate the violence.*
> *It's been awhile. We are who we are*
> *To them, even when we don't know who we*
> *Are to each other & culture is a*
> *Record of us figuring that out.*

—Wendy Trevino, "Brazilian Is Not a Race" from *Cruel Fiction*

That borders are cruel fictions is something that Isa Muazu knew all too well. In 2011, he sought asylum in the United Kingdom after fleeing Nigeria and the violence of Boko Haram. Two years later his application was rejected and he was taken to Harmondsworth removal center near Heathrow airport. In protest, he went on hunger strike: "I am not afraid," he explained, but "they—the authorities—have not treated me as a human being and that is wrong."[1] Refusing any food and drink, Isa's physical and mental health rapidly deteriorated. Doctors soon declared him medically unfit for detention, but the UK Home Office refused to release him: instead, it issued an "end of life plan." After three months without food, Isa was finally deported. Strapped to a stretcher, he was brought onboard a private jet and flown to Nigeria. It is unclear what happened to him after this and whether he survived.

There are many horrifying aspects of Isa's story, but the most disturbing is perhaps that there is so little that is unusual about it. In the last decade, EU countries have annually deported more than one hundred thousand migrants; over the same period, more than twenty thousand migrants drowned in the Mediterranean.[2] The majority of those that are turned away, detained, deported, and left to drown are—just like Isa—Black migrants who travel from sub-Saharan countries that until recently were under European colonial rule. In spite of this, Europe generally regards migrants as "uninvited guests," "charitable subjects," and "strangers" to whom it owes nothing; that "they are here because you were there" is often and conveniently forgotten.[3]

In recent years, scholars and organizers have challenged this narrative by drawing on the concept of the "Black Mediterranean."[4] Inspired by Paul Gilroy's seminal text *The Black Atlantic*, the Black Mediterranean invites us to place the current migrant "crisis" within a much longer history of European empire, transatlantic slavery, and colonial conquest.[5] As the Black Mediterranean Collective explains, "What is unfolding in the Mediterranean today is, in part, constitutive of an unparalleled crisis—not a crisis of humanitarianism or of territorial sovereignty, but of Eurocentrism."[6] For some, such as Christina Sharpe, the Black Mediterranean is a continuation of "the semiotics of the slave ship";[7] for others, it is part of a long history of racialized exploitation, expropriation, and extraction in the Mediterranean Basin, including the recent military interventions in the Middle East and North Africa as well as decades of structural adjustment programs, resource extraction, and land grabbing. For all these writers, the migrant "crisis" is ultimately not an exception or a break with European normality but rather, as Cristina Lombardi-Diop explains, a "repetition of the subjection of Black life through the same old means: borderless apparatus of surveillance, containment, captivity, forced displacement, forced labor, the slave markets, and dehumanization."[8]

The European border regime today consists of a vast carceral network that stretches across and beyond Europe's actual borders. This includes Frontex, or the European Border and Coast Guard Agency, tasked with policing the Mediterranean; the border fences in the Spanish North African enclaves in Ceuta and Melilla; an extensive visa and biometric regime that prevents migrants from reaching the physical borders of Europe by any means other than those that put them at risk; a number of "hotspots" in Greece and Italy, where migrants are fingerprinted and registered; offshore containment centers in neighboring countries, including Libya, Morocco, Sudan, and Niger; countless detention estates across the European continent; and different forms of community policing and surveillance programs designed to extend borders into public life *within* Europe. As an analytic, the Black Mediterranean reminds us that these bordering practices build on techniques and technologies that derive from histories of empire, enslavement, and (settler) colonialism.[9] From the Middle Passage to the plantation economies, to indentured labor, the "pass laws" in South Africa, and the "White Australia" policy, migration control and border surveillance emerged as part of a global racial-colonial project seeking to control the movement of the enslaved, colonized, and racial poor. In Radhika Mongia's formulation, modern immigration restrictions thus have a "crucial colonial genealogy."[10] Frontex, like Moria camp on Lesbos and Yarl's Wood detention center in the UK, is merely its latest manifestation.

In retrieving this racial-colonial history of borders, the Black Mediterranean ultimately challenges hegemonic ways of thinking about migrant justice. While (liberal) appeals to human rights, citizenship, and more open borders might go some way toward alleviating migrant suffering, they are incapable of uprooting the violent structures that render migrants disposable, precarious, and super-exploitable. European borders were, and continue to be, designed to control and keep out the Global South's racial poor. Rather than an unfortunate humanitarian crisis—to which an ethic of empathy, rescue, and hospitality is the solution—the Black Mediterranean exposes Europe's migrant crisis as a distinctively racial and colonial crisis.[11] As S. A. Smythe explains, "These deaths, unlike the rising of the sea, are the result of racial calculus, not 'nature.'"[12]

In place of such humanitarian and state-centric approaches, the Black Mediterranean rearticulates the struggle for migrant justice as part of a wider struggle against global capitalism, state violence, and the many afterlives of empire: in short, as a struggle for abolition rather than hospitality.[13] Inspired by the Black radical tradition and, in particular, by W. E. B.

Du Bois's notion of "abolition democracy," this is a liberatory politics that seeks to abolish all institutions complicit in upholding racialized oppression, including police, prisons, and borders.[14] In the words of No Border Kitchen Lesvos, "We demand and fight for the end of this system built on and sustained by cages, prisons and violence."[15] This, then, is at once a rejection—of immigration controls, detention centers, mass deportations, and other forms of state violence that seek to police mobility—as well as an affirmation of other ways of being and belonging.[16] With Saidiya Hartman, we can think of this as a dream, not of nationhood, but of autonomy: as "an elsewhere . . . where the stateless might, at last, thrive."[17]

In the end, borders, like race, *are* cruel fictions. If we listen to the counternarrative that is the Black Mediterranean, then we too might come to understand that those fictions can, and indeed must, be abolished.

8

CASE STUDY: How We Fight Against (Tech-Facilitated) Persecution of Uyghurs in China and Abroad

World Uyghur Congress

WHO WE ARE

The World Uyghur Congress (WUC) strives to promote democracy, human rights, and freedom for the Uyghur people through peaceful, nonviolent, and democratic means in order to determine their political future.

KEY CONCEPTS

What is China's Integrated Joint Operations Platform (IJOP)?

The IJOP is a data program that collects and stores personal data. As a policing program that culls from aggregated data to single out Uyghurs for detention, the IJOP has served as the central system through which Chinese authorities have built profiles of Uyghur persons. Data is collected from the East Turkistan's surveillance networks and through government officials' input. The IJOP receives information from "convenience" police stations and security checkpoints—featuring closed-circuit surveillance cameras (also known as CCTV) equipped with facial recognition software.

Why does the WUC refrain from referring to the Uyghur Region as "Xinjiang"?

The name "Xinjiang" invokes the colonial occupation of the territory. The WUC therefore uses "East Turkistan," but, as this might be confusing or political, we also use "Uyghur Region," with reference to the name the People's Republic of China uses (Xinjiang Uyghur Autonomous Region) after first mention. Therefore, for clarity, throughout this case study we refer to the East Turkistan geographical and historical region as the Uyghur Region.

BACKGROUND

Ever since the establishment of the People's Republic of China in 1949—the same year East Turkistan was occupied by the People's Liberation Army and subsequently made part of the Chinese state—successive Chinese regimes have used tactics of social control. In the late 1980s, against the backdrop of the collapse of the Soviet Union, pro-democracy protests in China, and later, with the advent of the internet and the growing digitalization of society, these social control tactics were increasingly enforced through emerging technologies.[1]

One group disproportionately affected by these developments are the Uyghurs—an ethnic Turkic people who are culturally, religiously, and linguistically distinct from China's majority Han Chinese population. In recent years, the persecution of Uyghurs through discriminatory and exclusionary policies has been heightened further through data-driven mass surveillance to control and monitor the Uyghur population inside and outside East Turkistan,[2] including in service of facilitating their mass arbitrary detention in internment camps.

The construction of the mass internment camp system coincided with the introduction of AI-assisted computer systems, which were brought together into the IJOP—a data program that collects information on members of the Uyghur community, on the basis of which it flags "suspicious" or "untrustworthy" persons to the police.[3] Authorities have also collected biometrics of all residents in the Uyghur Region between the ages of twelve and sixty-five.[4] Further surveillance measures include QR codes on the doors of Uyghur homes through which police can immediately access information about Uyghur residents, and the assignment of Han "relatives" to live with Uyghur families to monitor them.[5]

Even as the Uyghur Region has been transformed into a police state, Uyghurs who have fled overseas remain targets of Chinese attempts to surveil and control them. Through the spreading of malware, the hacking of electronic devices, and cyberattacks, the Chinese government is trying to surveil the Uyghur diaspora and prevent activists from speaking out about human rights abuses at home. It is not uncommon for Uyghurs abroad to receive phone calls from Chinese state agents demanding information or threatening their safety or that of their family members in the Uyghur Region if they refuse to end their activism.

NAVIGATING DIGITAL RISKS

In its advocacy and in its pleas for support from national governments and international institutions, the WUC has continuously highlighted the role of the IJOP and other repressive technologies in the persecution of Uyghurs. It has frequently drawn attention to the complicity of Chinese tech companies, such as Huawei, Dahua, and Hikvision, in the mass surveillance of Uyghurs and the risk their products pose to democratic values and social and political freedoms worldwide.

In carrying out this work, the WUC faces frequent cyberattacks and attempts to hack the organization's devices and online systems. This is why, in recent years, the WUC has taken its digital security increasingly serious, participating in digital security trainings and carrying out regular audits of its devices and networks. However, its resources as a nongovernmental organization are often inadequate to fully prevent state-sponsored digital attacks from an economic powerhouse like China.

Another of the organization's main priorities has been to educate the Uyghur diaspora about China's transnational repression. For young Uyghur activists, active mostly on social media and other online platforms, the risks are particularly high. Through frequent trainings and workshops on digital security, the WUC has sought to build the capacity within the Uyghur diaspora to recognize online threats and for Uyghurs to protect themselves against surveillance attempts.

LOOKING FORWARD

Though this evidence only shows a fraction of the workings of the police state that the Uyghur Region has become, it provides insights into how the Chinese government has used data-driven surveillance to profile, monitor, and detain Uyghur people en masse. Indeed, what is increasingly being recognized as a genocide could not have been orchestrated without high-tech surveillance.

This also highlights the need for a broader understanding and increased support of the digital security of persecuted diaspora communities. Governments of the countries in which these communities reside need to be more active in protecting activists and others at risk. At the same time, civil society, including representative organizations, can also play an important role by launching capacity-building initiatives to ensure communities are aware of the risks and able to better protect themselves. Educating the Uyghur youth has been an important step in this direction. Since they constitute the future leadership of the Uyghur movement, it is imperative for young activists to be aware of how repressive technologies and surveillance programs shape as well as threaten their own activism.

9

CASE STUDY: Why We Took the UK to Court for Its Discriminatory Visa Streaming Algorithm

Chai Patel & Foxglove

WHO WE ARE

Foxglove is a UK-based tech-justice nonprofit organization. The Joint Council for the Welfare of Immigrants (JCWI) is a UK-based migrants' rights charity. In 2020, Foxglove and JCWI teamed up to bring a judicial review challenge to the use of a discriminatory visa streaming algorithm that the UK Home Office was using. This case was the first-ever successful challenge to a public sector algorithm.

KEY CONCEPTS

What is the "hostile environment"?

The "hostile environment" describes a set of policies introduced in the UK in 2012 by the then home secretary, Theresa May. "Hostile environment" encompasses all those policies that are aimed at deterrence and make it difficult for immigrants to live a dignified life in the UK.

What is the Windrush scandal?

The Windrush scandal broke in April 2018. The UK had targeted hundreds of British residents of Caribbean heritage who had arrived in the UK between 1948 and 1973 ("the Windrush generation"). The UK deprived these individuals of their legal rights, subjecting them to hostile immigration policing and deportation.

What are streaming algorithms?

Streaming algorithms process large data streams and compute a very small "summary" output (a snapshot of the data). In these models, the algorithm has very short processing time per item and often only has access to limited memory.

THE PROBLEM

Foxglove and JCWI discovered that the Home Office had been using a secretive visa streaming algorithm since 2015.[1] The algorithm was a "streaming tool" that we believe was being used to process every visa application to the UK. The Home Office was incredibly secretive about this algorithm and refused to disclose much information about how it works. In the course of our legal case, we learned that the algorithm scanned applications and directed them either into a fast lane (green), a slow lane (yellow), or they were flagged (red). We were seriously concerned that people's right to come to the UK to work, study, or see loved ones was being affected by a shadowy and unaccountable government algorithm.

We were concerned that this algorithm could be yet another example of the "hostile environment" policy toward immigrants that brought us "Go Home" vans[2] and led to the Windrush scandal. In the course of the case, we learned that the Home Office had a secret list of undesirable nationalities. If you were a visa applicant belong to one of those nationalities, the Home Office would automatically put you into the "red" queue and treat your application differently. Caseworkers looking at a red-flagged application were given more time to process applications, and their supervisors would double-check their work if a visa was granted. There were clear incentives and nudges that led to a greater likelihood of red-flagged applications being refused.

In addition, the data on which the nationality risk register was based was deeply flawed. The system scanned for past incidences of non-compliance with visas, or refusals from each country, but did not correct for the fact that immigration enforcement and raids already specifically target certain countries because their nationals are easier to remove. Even worse, new decisions made under the algorithm were fed directly back into the data, reinforcing any existing prejudices, and creating a feedback loop where once a country was assigned a higher risk, the risk would likely continue to increase as more of its nationals were refused.

Nor did the system vet the data for racial bias. Reference was made to "intelligence," but often this comprises anonymous tips made by members of the public. For obvious reasons, there is a grave risk of racial bias in such tip-offs, and the independent chief inspector of borders and immigration has raised concerns about their accuracy. But no data is collected on ethnic or racial bias within the immigration enforcement system or intelligence, which means that the data sets used would inevitably reproduce both institutional biases and the racism that exists in society.

Using the UK Equality Act and data protection law, we took the government to court. We asked the court to declare the visa streaming algorithm unlawful, and to order the end of its use in processing visas. Before the case could be heard in court, the Home Office caved in, writing to us in August 2020 that it would scrap the algorithm and redesign the system, with a promise to think about how nationality should be used in these systems, or whether it should be used at all.

LOOKING FORWARD

Despite the success of our legal case, the Home Office doesn't seem to be shying away from the use of algorithms and nationality discrimination to make consequential decisions about our lives. It has now introduced a new streaming algorithm, and once more nationality forms part of the risk assessment, though within a more complex system than the one in place before. JCWI and Foxglove are closely inspecting this new system and will consider further action, although we are waiting for the Home Office to provide crucial documents about the way the system works. The use of these systems may be growing further, as just recently it was reported that the Home Office has been using a similar algorithm to detect sham marriages.

The fight continues.

Part 2

CONJURING THE PERFECT THREAT: TECHNO-SECURITIZATION AND DOMESTIC POLICING

10

Building the #NoTechforICE Campaign: An Interview with Jacinta Gonzalez

Mizue Aizeki

Jacinta Gonzalez is the Policy Director of Mijente and has organized the immigrants' rights movement for over fifteen years, focusing on the criminalization of migration, deportation defense, and ICE's use of tech and data. She leads Mijente's #NoTechforICE campaign.

Mizue Aizeki: How did you start organizing around issues of migrant justice, and when did you get concerned about tech and ICE?

Jacinta Gonzalez: I started organizing in New Orleans post–Hurricane Katrina. I was in college and went to participate with an organization centered in the Ninth Ward where students came to help do demo and construction work for folks that were trying to come back home. When I got to New Orleans, they told me about an organization that was just starting to organize both Black workers and immigrant workers that were helping in the reconstruction. They really needed people that were bilingual, so I was like, "Okay, I'll plug in." There, I started organizing day laborers. When I first started organizing, I was following the instructions of labor organizers who had been doing the work for a very long time and would explain the basics of how to do wage theft cases. That was a huge problem that folks were confronting.

But it became really clear pretty early on that we couldn't do any of that work without addressing issues of policing. The reason why it was hard for day laborers to find work was because at that time, the National Guard was still supporting the police in New Orleans, and you literally couldn't even look for work without having the police come after you. And ICE would also be doing raids on the corner. That was actually one of my first experiences doing work in New Orleans—ICE raids on the corners.

Aizeki: You couldn't address workers' rights without also addressing policing and immigration?

Gonzalez: Yeah, we couldn't talk about labor and worker rights without talking about policing and immigration. One of the first things we did—I'm glad it didn't pass—was trying to pass an ordinance to criminalize wage theft. The way that it was happening was that folks would not get paid and they would call the police. But the police would come and actually arrest them for whatever the boss had said.

Through that process, folks came to talk about the right to remain in New Orleans—not to be treated as disposable workers, but actually have the right to be able to build and remain in the community as they were starting to have their families come. That led us to where we started to realize that the local sheriff for the Orleans Parish Prison was working with ICE and submitting to ICE hold requests. This was a really funny time because a lot of people across the country were talking about Secure Communities,[1] but we started to see that ICE was trying to build up an infrastructure to be able to share information with the police. In New Orleans, they didn't have Secure Communities, but they had detainers anyway.

We started a multiyear campaign to push back against the sheriff and we actually won. We were able to get the first detainer policy in the South, and one of the most comprehensive in the country. It not only had the sheriff not submit to detainers, but actually required ICE agents to get judicial warrants to enter into the jail.

Aizeki: What was the impact on ICE tactics on the ground?

Gonzalez: After that happened, ICE had to figure out how to retaliate and they started to do raids in communities. The way that they would do these raids is they would go into neighborhoods and would literally go to supermarkets and Bible study groups. They would go into people's apartments as they were doing Bible study, and make them come out of the house, take the Bibles out of their hands, and take their fingerprints with these mobile biometric devices. And that's when I started to think, what is going on with this technology? There was already this conversation around how ICE was sharing information with local police departments and around detainers, Secure Communities, and 287(g) agreements. But the fact that they had these mobile biometric devices just put alarm bells in my head.

Aizeki: ICE was taking surveillance technology to people's everyday spaces.

Gonzalez: Once we started to do some research, we realized that these were ID machines, and that a lot of them had actually been created for war zones. This was the strategy that the military used in the war in the Middle East to try to create files on people because they didn't actually have a lot of information on folks. They were going around and trying to use the technology in this same way. That just started to really get me thinking about what was happening, what kind of industry was being built up. As time went on, we started to understand more and more. People were calling us asking these questions like, "How did ICE get my address if I've never had any problems with the cops?" or, "How did they know that this person was my cousin or that this was the car I was driving?"

Aizeki: Did it make you wonder who were the companies providing this military-grade technology to ICE?

Gonzalez: Between New Orleans and joining Mijente, I went back to Mexico to work with an organization called Poder that does corporate accountability work. I was organizing in rural Mexico, doing corporate accountability—human rights lawsuits against both the company and government agencies for an environmental disaster related to mining. That's where I had really gotten exposed to some of these ideas of corporate capture and accountability—like, what are the interests, and how do you actually hold not only government agencies accountable for their actions, but also corporations?

With both of those experiences, and talking to you and to Paromita [Shah, executive director of Just Futures Law], we started understanding that this is the direction that things are going. That's what got us to think doing #NoTechforICE[2] and doing the *Who's Behind ICE?* report.[3] And that was at the same time that child separation was happening at the border, and a lot of workers within tech companies were starting to push back. It just felt like the right moment to both think about how to expose these things and about how to create a multi-sector movement against what these tech companies are doing in our society.

Aizeki: Can you talk a bit more about the multi-sector organizing?

Gonzalez: I remember reading the stories about what was happening within Google around Project Maven and seeing that it was tech workers within Google that were exposing this and fighting back. They had found out about things because there was a huge movement around killer drones, and how they are being used for war.

A lot of tech workers were trying to cancel their contracts with ICE and CBP (Customs and Border Protection) under Trump. I thought about what it would require to actually have a movement of folks that are pushing back against that. But not just workers, because tech workers are just really hard to organize for a lot of reasons. For us it was like, how do we actually create space for a lot of people to be pushing back in their own kind of way? That also included—given our traditions and beliefs around organizing at Mijente and a lot of the groups we were working with—how do we create space where stakeholders from all vantage points can participate, and you can actually create different points of leverage?

So that included tech workers and future tech workers. Student organizing became really clear and really crucial. The thing that's hard about organizing around tech is tech is the invisible hand. People might not see the technology behind this, but they see the ICE agent, they see the government policy. There was also a need to be able to create education materials and different experiences for people to understand how surveillance was impacting them and what the consequences were. And then, obviously, these are private companies within capitalism. So there also just had to be a space for investor organizing given their impact and their influence on the corporations.

For us, it was important to have popular education around the subject and to be able to expose these companies in the media as a way of gaining power, to organize current workers, and then future tech workers or students on different campuses—especially knowing the role that academia has played in validating a lot of these horrible technologies—and have engagement with investors, and then also local policies, given that that's a place where local communities can try to build some pressure.

Aizeki: What were the specific companies you targeted and what was their role in the deportation machine?

Gonzalez: For us, it's helpful to think about them in different categories. One category is data brokers, as ICE has not only relied on getting information from local police departments or local jails but started to expand its reliance on getting private information from companies. Data brokers like Thomson Reuters, or RELX, are companies that are frequently thought of as legal research companies, or publishers, but are actually creating entire systems of a data economy that is exposing people's most private information to policing authorities.

There are many ways that information can flow, from paying your utilities or the cable bill, and that's how your address can get into a database that then can be accessed by ICE. Data brokers can be selling information like your address, or also aggregate information that they can scrape from the internet the way Clearview AI does for facial recognition technology.

Then there's companies that provide data analytics for ICE. Data at this point is worth more than oil at the global scale. But just having more information doesn't mean that it can be used or can be accessible. And that's why data analytics companies can be so crucial. There's one company, Palantir, who actually custom-built the software for ICE to be able to have the data analytics to create files on people that they use in their enforcement operations. They're also founded by Peter Thiel, who was also really crucial in getting Donald Trump elected.

It's incredibly alarming that not only are they custom-making software for ICE, but also for the IRS, and for the Census, and for Health and Human Services. So we see that they're also contributing to the building of a business model where a lot of these companies are profiting tremendously from our tax dollars, even though they're unaccountable and incredibly harmful.

Then there's the companies that are providing cloud services to ICE. One of the things that we realized during our research was that Amazon Web Services is the primary cloud service provider for ICE and for a lot of the companies that make programs for them, like Palantir. That was also really important to expose during a time where Amazon was trying to create their second headquarters in New York City.[4]

It was really exciting to kind of see that information used as part of a broader movement, and a movement against Amazon. Being able to say not only are they anti-worker, not only are they going to be bad for housing, not only will they be bad for all of these other reasons, but they're also building up this infrastructure for ICE. To have that be a successful campaign was really inspiring and shows the power that grassroots groups can have in holding these companies accountable.

The fourth category is biometrics. What we're starting to see is that there's a growing industry of needing to track people and identify people through different biometrics, whether that be iris scans, palm prints, DNA, your voice. This is a huge industry that is growing globally. ICE is really pushing for biometrics to be used more and more in ways that can be really terrifying.

Aizeki: Can you give an example of a campaign in which these different allies and tactics came together?

Gonzalez: With Palantir, we had to do a lot of research to be able to describe and expose all of the ways that Palantir does work for ICE, and why that means that they should cut that contract. It's been exciting to see students at UC Berkeley, SLAP—Students for the Liberation of All People—taking on this campaign and protesting the company on their campus when it tries to do recruitment events, and also going directly to their former headquarters in Palo Alto—to do banner drops, to flier workers and tell them about the contracts and engage workers in that way. We know this led to conversations internally within the company around some of these contracts.

Alex Karp himself, the CEO, has said that workers have left Palantir because of these contracts. When Palantir moved their headquarters to Colorado, there were already immigrant rights groups that were ready to protest the company and to take action because they had learned about the national campaign, which is really exciting.

Also, there's been different levels of investor advocacy, including human rights groups putting out investor warnings against the company.[5] This has led to different conversations around what's happened with those funds. That's just one example of where that happened. When the company decided to go public, we had a group of street theater artists put on a play outside of Palantir's offices, describing not only their connections with ICE, but a lot of military contractors as well. The video from that action was used for mass education around who the company is and how they work. There's been several places like that where we've been able to bring different elements together in one campaign.

Aizeki: How does this work fit into the broader US migrant justice landscape? What has changed over the course of the #NoTechforICE campaign?

Gonzalez: We know at the end of the day, it's the policies that have to change—it's not about what technology they use or don't use, it's whether or not we actually have a police force dedicated to enforcing immigration law, which is what ICE is. We know that is at its core the problem. The problem isn't what kind of technology they use, but actually the fact that they exist.

At the same time, organizers have the impossible job of having to tear down infrastructure that's been built over centuries to police Black and brown bodies, as well as the struggle of understanding these companies and the forces that we are fighting. There is the challenge of anticipating what the next chapter is going to be. I think that's where the #NoTechforICE campaign comes in—not only being able to hold that the problem is the existence of ICE to begin with, but also understanding that they're the tip of the spear in terms of where policing is going in the future. Because we know that they are deeply invested in these structures and their ability to cause harm. They're always trying to reinvent themselves. We're trying to mark out that this is where the future is going, and so I think that's a contribution we've made.

It's something that we can see in this current moment, with the new Biden administration, where there has been movement to address harmful frameworks or rhetoric—that we can't be talking about the need for more enforcement or more deportations in exchange for a path to citizenship. But we still see an emphasis on trying to use technology and surveillance as a way of ensuring safety and being vigilant. One of the contributions that we can make right now is trying to interrupt that conversation and show how that they can be equally harmful and continue the path of state control and state violence against different communities.

11

Big Tech, Borders, and Biosecurity: Securitization in Britain after COVID-19

Nisha Kapoor

Shortly after Boris Johnson informed the nation that the British government's strategy for dealing with the COVID-19 pandemic would center on herd immunity, in March 2020, Downing Street held a summit (informally referred to as the "Digital Dunkirk"), attended by around thirty different companies from across the technology and science sectors, asking them what they would be able to offer the British government in its war against coronavirus.[1] Among those in attendance were Google's London-based DeepMind artificial intelligence research unit, Palantir, Amazon, Microsoft, Apple, and the UK-based artificial intelligence start-up Faculty, as well as Uber and Deliveroo. Palantir, headed by US libertarian Peter Thiel and Alex Karp, pledged to commit its engineering staff to assist with the government effort. Amazon offered its video conferencing tools alongside cloud computing services to the health service for free. Dominic Cummings, then chief advisor to the prime minister, put the volunteers in touch with the management of NHSX—the National Health Service's digital transformation arm—and soon after, work commenced. Big Tech began excavating NHS data to build a "COVID-19 datastore." Palantir, which had been eagerly attempting to vie its way into the NHS for two years, was awarded its first contract with it, volunteering forty-five of its UK-based engineers for the sum of just over one US dollar. In exchange, it was granted access to the Personal Demographics Service, a database compiled by NHS

Digital, which is one of the most complete collections of personal information on people in England and Wales.[2]

The infiltration of private Big Tech corporations, particularly Palantir, into Britain's public (but progressively privatized) health care system for managing the pandemic provoked much alarm, protest, and dissent because it indicated an extension of security technologies and practices customarily associated with external border policing into the NHS. The health care system has for some time now been deeply imbricated in Britain's deportation and counterterrorism regime through "hostile environment" policies and the Prevent counterterrorism policy. Given the growing emphasis on biosecurity as the new frontier of securitization, whereby managing disease and "diseased bodies" is becoming pivotal to state security work, it seems worthwhile to reflect on the securitization of health care as a key portal through which the security state is expanding and evolving, with direct effects on migrant control regimes of the UK. The War on Terror resourced an expansion of securitization both ideologically and materially, erecting a regime that has played out most acutely at state borders and has depended on systems of immigration control for administering law and order. COVID-19 has exposed the growing salience of public health care as a conduit for maintaining and developing these phenomena, since emerging forms of biosecurity draw on the expertise developed in the counterterrorism context by mimicking the governing techniques, reproducing the institutional structures, and borrowing the personnel of the counterterrorism industry. In turn the health care system is repurposed as an internal border checkpoint, fortifying migrant control systems as a result.

The realities of health securitization can be considered as operating on two fronts: first, we see the NHS being incorporated into the institutional apparatus of the security state, and second, we observe biosecurity logics being superimposed onto established policing and immigration control regimes and practices. Here the symbiosis between the surveillance regimes, cultures, and technologies used for the War on Terror and for border policing and migrant control are starkly evident.

Securitizing Health Care

Arguably, one of the most effective elements of the War on Terror's surveillance strategy was the harnessing of community organizations, social and welfare professionals, and service providers for the purpose of intelligence gathering.[3] We tend to focus on the advance of digital surveillance technologies, the amassing of Big Data, and the scrutinization and manipulation of our online activities when tracing the tools used under the auspices of "security" in the War on Terror. Yet, the acceptance and incorporation of ubiquitous digital surveillance technologies has to some extent followed an earlier cultural shift that extended security logics into the day-to-day practices of health care and social workers, teachers, doctors, and youth workers. With the adoption of the Prevent Strategy, launched in Britain in 2006 (and subsequently exported to several countries across the world including the US), which imposed an obligation on social, welfare, and education arms of the state to gather intelligence on students and patients within their care deemed as suspects, as well as report any suspicious activity to law enforcement agencies, we had the institutionalization of a surveillance culture beyond the policing and security arms of the state that utilized and infiltrated personal and professional relationships built on trust.[4] Within the context of Britain's health service, Prevent normalized the idea that health workers, nurses, and general practitioners, who had usually received little if any education in anti-racist praxis, ought to be trained in how to spot signs of radicalization and report their patients to state prevention programs should they observe any such signs in those under their care.[5] The impetus for better "joined-up" coordination across law enforcement agencies, health, and social services and the recognition that health care surveillance could be beneficially used for "national security" was thus nurtured as part of the ramp-up of securitization that came with the War on Terror.

This short step from "national health" to "national security" emerged again with the introduction of the UK's "hostile environment" policy, a set of laws and regulations introduced in 2015 that aimed to make life for immigrants—undocumented as well as those with unsettled and precarious legal status—as difficult as possible. Policies included raising charges for non-UK citizens to access essential health care, extending the border by mandating that health care and welfare services, schools and universities, landlords, and the Driving and Vehicle License Authority carry out passport checks before offering their services, and promoting fear in immigrant and minority neighborhoods by circulating Home Office–sponsored marketing vans advising those communities to "Go Home" if they were in the UK without legal authorization.[6] Securitization's expansion thus infiltrated the norms, codes, ethics, and practices of health care, merging the roles of caretaker and counterterrorism official, doctor and border guard.

The use of digital technologies has been key to enabling, accelerating, and effecting this cultural shift. Hostile environment policies, which came into place around the same time US Immigration and Customs Enforcement (ICE) commissioned Palantir's investigative case management system in the US, sanctioned data sharing between the Home Office and the NHS as well as other state institutions, with aspiring plans for the creation of a networked database that links discrete data sets (a project for which Experian, the credit rating and surveillance company, was originally commissioned).[7] Even in its initial iteration, mere access to the Personal Demographics Service was integral to Home Office immigration enforcement and deportation raids. A Freedom of Information disclosure by Statewatch UK showed that in the first eleven months of 2016, the Home Office made 8,127 information requests from NHS Digital; 5,854 of these led to people being traced.[8] Though this arrangement between the Home Office and the NHS was suspended in 2018 following a legal challenge, subsequent contracts with Palantir and other private companies open up the easy possibility of its return with greater speed, efficiency, and likely even less transparency.

The War on Terror, Big Tech, and Securitization

It is perhaps with the awarding of NHS contracts to Palantir that the technologies of violence connecting "national security" and "biosecurity," with all the implications for immigrant communities and people of color, was made most stark. Among those tech start-up firms nurtured by US military and intelligence agencies as part of their objective for seeking "Total Information Awareness," Palantir has gained a particularly notorious reputation.[9] Backed by the CIA's venture capitalist arm, In-Q-Tel, during their formative years as tech leaders,[10] Palantir's cofounders Peter Thiel and Alex Karp have marketed the company by selling its established reputation for work on security and defense, branded as "the intelligence services firm of choice," and "the War on Terror's secret weapon" for the surveillance technologies it built for the US military.[11] For tech corporations, state surveillance contracts offer deep learning opportunities—to access Big Data sets, to experiment with new technologies, and to gain seed funding to pilot these ideas. As was noted in a presentation to the US National Security Commission on Artificial Intelligence, surveillance remains "one of the first and best customers" of AI start-ups, and an entire generation of "AI unicorns [the term used to denote start-up companies worth over $1 billion] is collecting the bulk of their early revenue from government security contracts."[12] Such gains by Palantir have been made not only in the US; its software has been used with enthusiasm by the UK government's intelligence and security organization GCHQ (Government Communications Headquarters) since 2008.[13] And alongside such security contracts that are not required to be publicly declared, Palantir has secured numerous contracts from the Ministry of Defense, including one for $38 million in 2018, taking the total value of UK government deals won by the company at that point to at least $53 million.[14] According to reports, it has been awarded more than $62 million in public contracts by the UK government and NHS since the start of 2020, including a subsequent COVID contract with the NHS worth £23 million (roughly $26 million).[15]

The appeal of Palantir's surveillance technologies is that they are able to synthesize multiple strands of structured and unstructured data, personal and abstract data, and combine manifold analytical tools. These are technologies that have enabled US Special Operations forces and their allies to identify targets and carry out military operations in Afghanistan and Iraq. It is the same technology, known as Palantir's "Gotham" software, that has been used by US Homeland Security and ICE for identifying, apprehending, and detaining undocumented and documented migrants, highlighting the explicit continuities between surveillance technologies used for border control and those for counterterrorism and military and civilian policing.[16] The genius of Palantir's technology in terms of its military and immigration control objectives is that it has allowed for the synthesizing of multiple state and commercial databases that otherwise operate discretely, enabling information sharing between different state institutions and allowing for real-time live updates that are networked across different interfaces. Drawing on this more comprehensive knowledge set, Palantir's Investigative Case

Management System is able to draw on the biometric data of someone apprehended by military or border personnel, locate them, and ascertain their status and other intelligence, which can then be used by law enforcement and welfare agencies. It is exactly this capability that enabled Palantir to present itself as an attractive solution to the management challenges of the pandemic where concerns for public health were reduced to issues of biodata management, "track and trace," and frictionless administration. Observers anticipate that alongside the many lucrative business opportunities that come with the NHS data set and privatization of the health service, Palantir's trade in connecting discrete data sets for border and counterterrorism security may well now extend to more seamlessly connecting the Home Office with health data, augmenting the "hostile environment."

It is worth noting that such developments have been met with ongoing resistance. In September 2021, following legal action taken by openDemocracy and the tech-justice group Foxglove to prevent the government from extending Palantir's NHS contract beyond the COVID-19 pandemic without public review, the Department of Health and Social Care terminated a data contract with Palantir for adult social care, though the extent of Palantir's continued role with NHS data management remains unclear.

From National Security to Biosecurity

The hardening of securitization is not limited to a realignment and repurposing of the National Health Service; it is also felt in the investment in "biosecurity," now also a named priority for government security, intelligence, and military agencies. With the onslaught of policing and state powers passed through law and justified in the wake of the COVID-19 pandemic, Boris Johnson's government, on par with trends elsewhere, pursued a criminal justice response to a public health crisis. It was a militarized response that discursively invoked a plethora of World War II references and metaphors, and structurally involved the establishment of a Joint Biosecurity Centre, itself modeled on the Joint Terrorism Analysis Centre and set up by the former director-general at the Office for Security and Counter-Terrorism, Tom Hurd. Here regimes of biosecurity, where coronavirus threat levels are decided in tandem with terror threat levels, reproduce racialized suspicion, violence, and systems of exclusion. And since national biosecurity thrusts an acute focus on border management and control, for immigrant communities this means being subject to overlapping forms of "dataveillance," where biometric and antigen metrics concur to classify and produce people whose life histories, struggles, and determinations are reduced to distorted pathologies. That is, border surveillance practices operate to classify migrants and produce immigrant subjects through a series of biometric data recordings, distorting and often erasing the complex lived histories and politics that frame migrant life as well as adding another "threat" dimension against which migrants must be secured. In Britain, among the most concerning of the plethora of additional powers is the authority to detain "potentially infected people."[17] Potentiality appears as another nod to policing premised on the tentative and the hypothetical, the adjacent and the latent, now all too familiar. It is another reiteration of the pre-emptive policing institutionalized under community and counterterrorism policing where its racialized framing means there is little distinction between suspect and convict, and where conviction scarcely reflects culpability. Policing regimes being sanctioned under COVID-19 thus layer biosecurity onto border security to fortify all too familiar law-and-order regimes.

12

Targeting Muslim Communities in NYC: Interview with Fahd Ahmed

Mizue Aizeki and Coline Schupfer

Fahd Ahmed is a grassroots organizer and activist. Since 2000, he has been involved with Desis Rising Up & Moving (DRUM), supporting families targeted for deportation, surveillance, and policing. He is currently DRUM's executive director.

Mizue Aizeki: Can you tell us more about your organization and your work?

Fahd Ahmed: DRUM organizes working-class, South Asian, and Indo-Caribbean people across New York City for immigrant rights, worker rights, racial justice, educational justice, gender justice, and global justice—which links to issues of migration globally, and issues of war and militarism. We see all those things as interconnected.

Pre-9/11, the surveillance of Muslim communities existed already, mostly in the form of targeting of Arab or Muslim prominent activists, especially those focused on Palestine. But it was really in the aftermath of 9/11 that it ramped up exponentially—there were massive sweeps in our communities, especially in New York and New Jersey. At least 1,200 men were picked off the street, from their homes, from their workplaces. We received phone calls from children saying, "A bunch of police came to our house last night, they took my father, and we don't know where they took him."

Most of the people picked up in the sweeps ended up in county jails in New Jersey, Passaic County Jail, Hudson County Jail, and Middlesex. Among these 1,200 people, law enforcement found zero connections to terrorism, which was the premise under which they were picked up, but in those first six months post-9/11, they effectively had a green light to do anything.

It was on Martin Luther King Day in 2002 that we really kicked things off. We had a press conference in Union Square, where a woman, Uzma Naheed, spoke about her husband and her brother, who were taken from their home and held incommunicado in one of the detention centers. After the Union Square rally, we organized caravans to Passaic County Jail and Hudson County Jail, and held rallies outside those jails. This was coordinated with the detainees on the inside, who kicked off a hunger strike that day.

Eventually, this caught the attention of the media, as did the conditions under which people were held in detention. Questions started being raised, like, "Why are you holding these people in these conditions when you're not finding any ties to terrorism?" There were calls for greater scrutiny. The government started getting bad criticism and pushback, and it also started to become an issue within Congress.

In that moment, we started to see a pivot, with law enforcement reaching out to community leaders and saying, "We want to work with you to find 'the right people,'" to try to figure out the best way they could move their agendas forward. Because we had people in DRUM that had been trained by people that went through the history of the Black Panther Party and the Young Lords and knew how surveillance and counterintelligence worked in the sixties and seventies, we were able to warn community leaders, "Don't do this, this will just lead to bad things."

Aizeki: But communities still ended up being recruited to work with the police?

Ahmed: The level of fear was very high, so most of the community leaders gave in and agreed to collaborate, hoping that this would ease some of the pressure. What happened then is that the community leaders opened their doors to law enforcement, who would then come into mosques and community centers. Police even got a forum and would essentially get to speak and say, "We want to work with you, we want to support people, and we want to make sure that your rights are protected."

Of course, people were living in a state of fear. A bunch of people would bring their immigration files to the forum, to show that they are undocumented, express their fears of being picked up and deported, and ask if they could get help with documentation. Others would raise that they were being prosecuted for a thing that should not be happening and asked for help to dispose of the case. People were desperate, afraid. And all this was happening because when you provide law enforcement with a platform to speak, you are providing them legitimacy within the community. Why else would the community leader invite them into community spaces? You were essentially unofficially saying, "We trust these people."

We identified those people in those forums who sought help with their cases and documentation, and told them, "Don't do this." But those people were desperate. A week or two later, however, some of those same people would call on us. They would tell us, "I met with that FBI guy and they asked me information about my Imam, or they asked me questions about what happens at the mosque, or questions about people in their community, or they're asking me to collect license plate numbers outside of the mosque"—those sorts of things.

This became the beginning of the surveillance state *inside* our communities. It largely started with people being recruited to be informants, because at that point, there weren't many officers from our communities. Those forums also become opportunities to recruit people to become officers, though that generally took a bit longer, another year or two. This is how the surveillance apparatus started to build into our communities.

Aizeki: We think often about technology-fueled surveillance—but how much of it was human, and possible due to the precarities people faced?

Ahmed: We think of the surveillance apparatus at three levels. The lowest level is very general surveillance and includes information like the name of the mosque, religious and political orientation, about the leadership, and about the ethnic makeup of its members, that level of information. The second level is the most insidious and involves informants and undercover officers. These folks are just watching, collecting information and reporting back. Level 2.5 is when these folks are poking and prodding people and saying things like, "Oh, you see what's happening in Iraq, how does that make you feel?" That sort of stuff.

The things that happened over the Obama years was hard surveillance— level 3—the mosque raids, the use of informants and undercovers to entrap people in manufactured cases. In between levels 2 and 3, was the growth of the Countering Violent Extremism program, which really borrows from the UK's Prevent program. And it really creeps in social services and other places where they try and get into—in effect latching the surveillance apparatus into the public life infrastructure. Again, while a lot of it is human-based, we're sure that there's some technology being used as well. One place that we know of is the DHS grants to install security cameras in mosque synagogues, but DHS retains access to that technology and the footage.

Coline Schupfer: You spoke about poking and prodding—what specific tools are being used, whether in the form of phone hacking or other tracking devices?

Ahmed: What we learned, when the Associated Press leaked documents of the NYPD surveillance program in 2011, is that most of this was human surveillance. But in some of the mosques and community centers, technology was used in primarily two places. Firstly, in the form of data collection, to track and store information on a database. Secondly, there was the actual use of digital surveillance in some of the mosques, but I think for that level, they did have to get some level of approval. All this other lower level of stuff, however—they were able to do that without having to show anything. I would imagine, in third-tier cases, some greater tools of technology would have been triggered. The third tier is when those informants and undercover officers are actually successfully able to instigate people.

There wasn't any extremism or terrorism within the communities. But law enforcement was spending all these resources surveilling, so they had to prove and justify why they were doing this. Therefore, undercovers and informants would then start to instigate people. They would start talking about what's happening in Iraq, in Afghanistan, and once it feels like there's sufficient emotional agitation, they would say, "We should do something about this!" And as soon as you agree to do something, then it becomes a conspiracy. That's when people get mad, then they arrest people, and then they prosecute them. We started seeing those cases as early as 2004. There may have been some earlier cases, but by 2004, we were able to read the pattern and say which cases have really been instigated and manufactured by the undercovers and the informants.

There are these three levels, which is about general surveillance, but there are also the more prominent cases of surveillance of Muslim communities.

Then there is the specific targeting of activists and of community leaders. I think that's where you see technology used a bit more aggressively, the hacking of phones, the tapping of phones, the examination of people's social media, and the use of that information in prosecution.

Aizeki: Was there any enduring restructuring of policing practices? The NYPD now has a huge counterterrorism unit—how has this shaped policing?

Ahmed: Yes, so I'll take us one step back, to the dynamics of surveillance policing and law enforcement budgets. Initially, they could just say, "We have to do this surveillance, and we need money for it." But then, if they're not producing results, then they have to produce results. This is where the third tier kicks in, where the instigation starts. And those instigated cases are the primary ones that they can then use to justify their budget needs, or a budget increase. If you look at the press releases, every time they bust one of these manufactured cases, they say, "This is why we need to be vigilant." Just like that, it becomes this self-perpetuating cycle: they use cases to expand their budget; an expanded budget means expanded operations; and to justify those operations, they need to produce more things. But what happens is, as those budgets keep expanding, you're gaining more and more technology, and more tools.

And the use of those is not limited to counterterrorism. Those tools spread across police departments and are used in all sorts of ways—almost like a Hydra that just grows more and more heads, and then it's able to consume more and more.

Aizeki: Initially there were massive roundups of people targeted without evidence, and then they built this entire infrastructure to construct suspects. Is there a cautionary lesson about how we can challenge this moving forward?

Ahmed: I think one is that we need to be vigilant, and we need to push back against any expansion of the law enforcement apparatus, and against the expansion of the surveillance state. This requires being able to look at specific instances of people being set up, but it also requires looking at it more systematically: "What is their interest in creating cases like this?" There are multiple cases like this, because they're trying to grow this Hydra, this beast, this machine. We need to be vigilant of any expansion of state power. There is the use of informants, undercover officers, and mosque raids. Then there's what is called "community outreach efforts," which are effectively efforts for extracting information.

Aizeki: We see similar counterinsurgency tactics with Prevent in the UK. One of the things they did in the UK was propaganda about Western liberalism, arguments about how women have more freedoms in the West, those kinds of things. Did you see that in New York?

Ahmed: My sense is that most of the indoctrination was within law enforcement internally. The NYPD and the FBI had, for example, their own versions of reports around extremism and countering-radicalization and would use frameworks of, "Here's how these people think, here's how they are able to take advantage of our society, our freedoms, etcetera." Essentially liberalism. I think law enforcement uses a comparatively lighter touch. But then, as you see with the right wing, the non-state right wing, they are a lot more explicit, and use all that to justify restrictions on freedoms, to justify the surveillance apparatus.

Schupfer: You spoke about tech encroachment on every part of life, from everyday policing and into public life, including housing and education, and how this impacts the relationship between the state and the people, as well as intercommunal relations. Can you share how we can reverse the logic of community surveillance?

Ahmed: Yes, I think I would just go back to the lesson of orientation, and that we can't always act on it, but to give no inch, no ground, to law enforcement. Don't give them anything that they can use to expand on. They will always come up with the sharpest justifications to legitimize infringing on rights. There's the use of drones, there's the use of gang databases, there's surveillance and there's a lot of suspicious activity reporting—a lot of low-level things. But those seemingly low-level things keep building the apparatus bigger. The growth in some ways is not linear; there's something organic to it in how it picks up momentum. So, the growth ends up being exponential. And that's what we must confront. We may not have the capacity to confront all of it, but we need to have an orientation that all of it is wrong and is going to be used against us. The challenge then becomes, what about the actual risks? What about crime? What about gangs? What about terrorism?

In recent years, there were seeds of this in the work that we were doing before. But I think with the increasing prominence and insights from abolitionist approaches, it has made it easier to talk about the concerns that you are raising. As in, we could simply invest in people. We could be investing in communities and meet a lot of their needs. What you're trying to criminalize is poverty and people on the basis of their race or religion or beliefs. On the other hand, yes, there are some antisocial activities that exist. But rather than trying to use a hammer, or law enforcement, you could invest in those people, in those communities, and you could probably resolve 80 or 90 percent of those things. If you had youth centers and programming that engaged people, how much would that take care of things like gang involvement or potential extremism? I think that provided some framing that allowed us to be able to talk about these things in a better way, not just what we're against. So, on the issue of expanding the surveillance state, it's not just that we're against it, but about why we don't just invest in all of these other things instead. Using this logic, we don't need surveillance.

13

Global Palestine: Exporting Israel's Regime of Population Control

Jeff Halper

I srael has been labeled the world's "Homeland Security/Surveillance Capital," a reputation that arises out of the special conditions under which Israel develops its systems of population control.[1] The Occupied Palestinian Territory (OPT—the West Bank, East Jerusalem, and Gaza) has increasingly been referred to as a laboratory in which the Israeli military, security services, police, and even private companies can perfect weaponry, technologies of surveillance and repression, and techniques of population control over a captured population, with no oversight whatsoever.[2] Each Israeli security firm has a niche of its own, but all stress that their operatives and services come from "years of experience" in the Israeli Defense Forces (IDF).

Israel, moreover, may just as well be known as the world's capital of military and security technologies, the construction of population control systems, and the tactics—ranging from military through policing—that sustain daily control.[3] Beyond all this, it deserves yet another title: the world's capital of *hasbara*—public relations—a sophisticated strategy of "disappearing" its settler-colonial project and the ravages of occupation, enabling it to successfully peddle itself as the "only democracy in the Middle East" and a "Jewish" democracy despite its continued—and visible—displacement and violent repression of the indigenous Palestinian population.[4]

This stems from the multi-layer "security" tasks Israel faces. At base, Israel faces problems of migratory labor and border control vis-à-vis the Palestinians that are similar to but also different from those of other countries, since the "unwanted" population of laborers and potentially immigrants, Palestinian Arabs, comes from within.[5] How, then, to maintain the "Jewish character" of an Israel that since 1967 has expanded all the way to the Jordan River and which contains a Palestinian majority; how to control the movement of Palestinians, especially within pre-1967 Israel "proper," whether it be Palestinian citizens of Israel who are carefully segregated or Palestinians of the OPT; and how to conceal Israel's repressive practices in order to continue garnering international support? How, in short, to normalize the Zionist settler-colonial project now extending over the entirety of historic Palestine?

The last task is key to the global significance of Israel's regime of population control. Realizing that other countries face issues of migration and of internal unrest as their working class (and increasingly, their middle class) struggle with the depredation wrought by neoliberalism (which they also frame in terms of "security"), Israel has strategically parlayed what might have been a political problem—colonialism, occupation, and the construction of a regime of repression against Palestinians—into a positive model of population control and internal security that speaks to the needs of its friends and (potentially malleable) foes alike.[6] Its export of technologies of repression, tactics of daily control, and key pieces of its regime of population control play a key role in assuring Israel's international standing and in repulsing attempts to pressure it into making concessions to the Palestinians. In essence, by carving out such a niche, instrumental both for control of external threats and for suppressing internal dissent, Israel makes itself useful to a broad range of countries. That, in turn, affords it a "pass" for its treatment of the Palestinians.

And Israel has endeavored to globalize that niche. Key to its *hasbara* and foreign relations is its contention that as the world's most besieged state, it has succeeded in finding effective solutions to virtually every kind of security threat any other country might face. Israel's message is: "You shouldn't be condemning us for our treatment of the Palestinians, you should be imitating us. You have a problem with domestic terrorism coming from particular neighborhoods or regions of your country? You need to protect your society against foreign migrants? Just look at what we have done. Israel has created a vibrant democracy with a flourishing economy and a high degree of personal security for its (Jewish) citizens in a situation where *half* the population under our control are terrorists. If we can succeed in that, imagine what we can contribute to your country's security!"[7]

Israeli security firms, part and parcel of Israel's military establishment and marketed as such by SIBAT, the marketing arm of the Ministry of Defense, offer a wide range of "solutions" for border and police forces long preoccupied with the challenge of surveilling and controlling populations and their movements and activities, and doing so under adverse, highly populated, or concealed conditions. The deployment of UAVs (unmanned aerial vehicles) for surveillance, and perimeter defense and access controls; dense networks of video cameras equipped with image identification capabilities; sensors and threat detection systems for cargoes; "biometric borders" in airports and via smart-card IDs, credit cards, and passports—all these enhance the operations of border and police forces. But beyond weaponry, high-tech security technologies, or tactics of "counterinsurgency," Israel is ultimately offering something much more comprehensive: a systemic solution to problems of population control embodied in a security state. A version of a police state, the Israeli model is driven by the logic of securitization. Its attraction is its seeming ability to effectively address society's deep sense of insecurity (which has often been intentionally instilled into the population as a means of control), yet in a technical manner that appears to leave democracy intact.[8] Thus, by concealing the security state's repressive policies and actions behind a democratic facade, as Israel does vis-à-vis the Palestinian population both inside Israel and in the OPT, democratic processes and compliance with international law can be subordinated to security concerns yet remain palatable to the public.

Let's begin our examination of how Israel has used its "conflict" with the Palestinians to construct and export its security regime by briefly looking at the system itself, what I call its "Matrix of Control."

The Matrix of Control

After more than half a century of an occupation that has become a permanent and normalized "fact on the ground," it is clear that left to its own devices, Israel will not allow a truly independent and viable Palestinian state to emerge in the OPT. Since at least the days of Menachem Begin in the late 1970s, Israel's position has been consistent: the best the Palestinians will get is "state-minus, autonomy plus," a phrase coined by prime minister Benjamin Netanyahu.[9] The Palestinians may "receive" a demilitarized mini-state with limited sovereignty in enclaves of the West Bank and Gaza, but even so Israel will remain firmly in control, a "solution" resembling the Bantustans of apartheid South Africa more than Palestinian independence.

Enter the "Matrix of Control," a maze of laws, military orders, planning procedures, limitations on movement, Kafkaesque bureaucracy, settlements, and infrastructure, accompanied by prolonged and ongoing low-intensity warfare, that effectively conceals the fact of occupation—a form of political and military control Israel denies even having—behind a facade of "proper administration" and "defense against terrorism." Through three interlocking levels—military control and strikes, creating "facts on the ground," and using bureaucracy, planning, and laws as tools of occupation and control—the Matrix enables the maintenance of the image of a liberal Western democracy, lowering the occupation's military profile to a point where repression disappears from public view.[10]

Together with these political, economic, military, and physical measures, a far less visible form of what Harsha Walia calls "discursive control" also plays a key role in Israel's ability to retain its regime of population control indefinitely.[11] While many democracies expend great energies justifying migrant control and attempting to place it within some fundamentally inclusive set of regulations, as a settler-colonial project, Zionism eliminated that need from the start. Aiming to establish a "Jewish" ethnocracy,[12] it displaced the indigenous Palestinian population first and foremost from its national narrative: the Land of Israel was a "land without a people" (in the sense that in the Zionists' view "the Arabs" did not constitute a national collective with rights of self-determination) and the Jews were "returning home" to "reclaim" their exclusive national heritage. "The Arabs" were excluded discursively in Zionism, so that the ongoing process of displacement of Palestinians from the land, together with their controlled entry into the Israeli labor market, goes virtually without challenge.[13]

Territorial diffusion or expanding the "border" to include all the territory where migrants live and come from, a second element of Walia's border control regime, constitutes another key strategy of Israeli population control. Where "military necessity" is found to be an inadequate justification, Israel simply denies the applicability of the Fourth Geneva Convention, claiming that there can be no occupation since no sovereign state ruled the West Bank, East Jerusalem, and Gaza before 1967. Whatever the strategy, the diffusion of the border zone throughout the West Bank created a zone of military enforcement enabling Israel to control the Palestinian population in a proactive way, long before migrant laborers approached the actual border crossings.

Finally, as a precursor to the Matrix of Control in the OPT, Israel constructed a matrix within the framework of the military government it imposed on Palestinian citizens of Israel from 1948 to 1966, elements of which continue to determine their life opportunities today. Having driven 85 percent of the Palestinians out of what became Israel and then preventing them from ever returning (an exclusion later extended to the inhabitants of the OPT,[14] the third element of Walia's regime of control), Israel employed a series of laws and regulations to seize control of Arab land and reclassify it as Israeli "state land," and then prohibited "non-Jews" from "owning, leasing, or working on the 97 percent of state-held land" reserved for exclusive Jewish use.[15] Emergency regulations inherited from the British; the imposition of a military government over its Palestinian population; laws such as the Absentees' Property Law of 1950, the Land Acquisition Law of 1953, the Law of Return (1950), and the Nationality Law (1952)—all of these effectively denationalized Palestinian citizens of Israel (now referred to as "Israeli Arabs") and prevented the return of the refugees or their claims to lost properties.

The OPT as a Laboratory of Population Control

The very longevity of the Matrix of Control speaks not only to the ongoing security threat represented by a restive, incarcerated Palestinian population, for which there exists no political horizon whatsoever, but to what Israel considers a permanent existential threat: the "demographic bomb," awaiting to explode. As the West Bank becomes ever more incorporated into a "Greater" Israel, the Jews will find themselves a distinct minority unable to control millions of Arabs despite imposing an apartheid regime (as was the case in South Africa). No less threatening, the presence of an assertive Palestinian national majority makes it increasingly difficult to defend the existence of Israel—especially a "Greater" Israel—as a Jewish state.

The limited mobility of workers into Israel, and the immobility of Palestinians inhabiting the different areas of the OPT as well as the segregation of

Palestinian citizens of Israel must be enforced through surveillance, military technologies of repression, and physical constraints, all backed by security regulations or laws such as the Citizenship and Entry into Israel Law. Israeli securitization, then, spans and integrates conventional warfare, counterinsurgency tactics, and weaponry used in "asymmetrical" conflicts and policing as a form of routinized population control. "Israeli capital, with considerable support from the US and Israeli governments," comments Stephen Graham, "has taken its skills, expertise and products beyond the more obvious markets surrounding urban warfare, and expertly projected them towards the much broader and ever-extensible arena of global securitization, securocratic war, 'homeland security' and counterterrorism."[16] Indeed, the linkage of border security, homeland security, and counterterrorism is key to Israeli marketing, helping authorities "sell" their policies and technologies to the public by criminalizing migrants and other "unwanted" populations.[17]

In its *Homeland Defense Sales Directory*, SIBAT lists forty categories of homeland security applications offered by Israeli companies.[18] And its marketing strategy highlights Israel's "unique" advantage of having the technologies of control it exports derive not from military laboratories and testing grounds, but from the *real* controlled-conflict laboratory of the Occupied Territory.[19]

This marketing strategy applies in particular to Israel's vaunted border security technologies that can easily be adapted to centralized civilian hubs of hyper-surveillance such as the NICE Systems' "Safe Cities" program, through which commercial technologies of social sorting and monitoring are sold to municipalities and airports throughout the world.[20] The ability of Israeli firms to "borrow" electro-optical, laser, and infrared applications from military reconnaissance and avionics applications, together with such military-based technologies as data mining and intelligence gathering, certainly does confer on them distinct marketing advantages.[21]

Some 416 Israeli companies specialize in homeland security, constituting 21 percent of the high-tech sector, most having to do with surveillance.[22] The precise revenues of Israel's civilian homeland security/surveillance industry cannot be separated from those of its military industry, both because of the dual civilian-military use of many products and the engagement of many Israeli firms—Elbit Systems being a graphic example—in Israel's defense industry as well as in commercial marketing.[23] Twenty-one Israeli homeland security companies, including Elbit, are traded on the NASDAQ.[24]

Propagating the Israeli Model
of Securitization, Exporting the Security State

In many cases, Israeli security technology sells itself, and a direct transfer
of security and weapons systems is transacted with the client country or
agency. The Safe Cities program, for example, is sold by Israeli companies
to police forces throughout the world.[25] A "Safe City" refers to an intersection between different elements of communication, command and control,
sensors, biometrics, IT connectivity, cyber security, and more. Israeli-made
systems and devices of video surveillance and civil security air surveillance
maintain public safety and security during routine times and emergency
situations. In order for a city to qualify for a "Safe City," program, however,
it must integrate all its security-relevant information on a cross-cutting IT
platform. Thus public safety information coming in from video surveillance,
sensors, biometrics, and access control is combined with other information
providing a clear situational picture citywide via communications and command and control networks—all displayed on digital maps and GIS for
quick and effective emergency response.[26]

How this all comes together, and how technology transfers occur, is
well illustrated in the case of what has been called provocatively the "Palestine-Mexico border."[27] Here the US government awarded Elbit a contract
to surveil its border with Mexico using its Hermes 450 drones,[28] while the
Mexican government contracted with the Israeli firm Aeronautics Defense
Systems to supply its Orbiter UAV and Skystar 300 aerostat systems for surveillance on Mexico's side of the border.[29] Magna BSP, which provides surveillance systems surrounding Gaza and on the new barrier being built along
the Egypt-Israel border, has partnered with US firms to enter the lucrative
"border security" market, while NICE Systems provides CCTV for notorious
anti-immigrant Sheriff Joe Arpaio's Maricopa County Jail system in Arizona.[30] As far back as 2003, in the wake of the 9/11 attacks, the US Department
of Homeland Security established a special Office of International Affairs to
institutionalize the relationship between Israeli and American security officials. "Since 9/11," the American-Israeli lobby group AIPAC reports on its
website, "the United States and Israel have intensified their homeland security cooperation. Israel shares priceless information about terrorist organizations with the United States and is one of five countries participating in the
U.S. Counterterrorism Technical Support Working Group."[31]

The high degree of internal-external overlap between Israel "proper" within the 1949 armistice lines and the occupied West Bank has given rise in Israel to a ubiquitous concept known as *bitachon*, "security," which combines "homeland security" and "homeland defense." This has given rise to an Israeli model of securitization that eliminates the "wall," long considered essential for Western democracies, between internal and external, civilian and military. In its view, Israel exports far more than discrete commodities of weapons, security systems, and technologies of repression; it peddles to the democracies of the Global North—an integrated model of an entire security state, one resembling the supremacy of state security common to the Global South, in which democracies continue to espouse democratic values and retain their democratic institutions, yet *de facto* subordinate democracy to security through militarizing its police and citing transcendent "security" concerns as the Patriot Act demonstrates.

One of the ways in which Israel propagates its doctrine of securitization is by exporting military combat training programs in forms custom-made for domestic law enforcement.[32] That doctrine and the institutional changes it requires consist of several elements:

First, close ties between field operations, technologies of population control, and tactics. "What grew out of a direct military need with a high-tech edge," says the Israel Export and International Cooperation Institute, "has developed into a core element of the Israeli economy and placed Israel at the forefront of the global security and HLS [homeland security] industry. . . . With the military providing a fertile breeding ground for future generations of engineers and entrepreneurs, many non-defense-related, high-quality technologies and solutions have been developed."[33] It is this which sets apart the "Israel model" from the others and makes it marketable.

Second, Israeli military, security agencies, and police all act under a permanent state of emergency, based on the 1945 British Defence (Emergency) Regulations. This allows the security forces to ignore or compromise due process and other safeguards against violations of human rights such as ethnic profiling—what in most countries would be considered excessive use of force or the use of administrative detention without charge or trial.

Third, Israeli counterterror and security operations focus on preventing attacks or any manifestation of a security threat, meaning interdiction and the weakening of the infrastructures of resistance, crime, or terrorism.[34]

The ability to develop these systems in the OPT laboratory with the Israeli military gives Israeli companies like NICE, Verint, Check Point, Narus, Amdocs, Black Cube, Celebrite, NSO Group, Candiru, WiSpear, and dozens of others that grew out of the IDF a distinct edge on the market, the acceptability of their products limited only by the laws of their clients' countries.[35] At the same time, protections against arbitrary arrest or imprisonment are lacking in Israel. All this involves "interactive intelligence" and ethnic profiling, both illegal in most democracies but not in the security state promoted by Israel.

Israeli exports of technologies and tactics of repression are only part of its contribution to global population control. Aware that the systems and the practices they require contradict the structures, laws, and values of Western democracies, Israel has had to invent a state framework in which they find acceptability. That it has done in its advocacy for the security state, which has three main components:

(1) The securitization of all parts of its national polity. The state must be equipped to fight wars abroad while also keeping a close watch on the potentially subversive activities of its citizens at home, especially if there is a perceived demographic threat.

(2) Employing security as a rallying point to unite different organs of the state, often invoking race- or threat-baiting incitement.

(3) Employing security as a neutral, threat-based, rational response that in reality conceals the powerful economic, political, military, and social interests motivating it.

As we witness the rise of the security state in Europe and North America—joining the security states in most of the rest of the world—and become ever more aware of its threat to human rights, including people's right to the fundamentals of a decent life where they live and the right to mobility if they decide to move, the export of Israel's occupation represents nothing less than the global Israelization of borders and the global Palestinianization of migrants and the poor.

14

Chicago's Gang Database Targeting People of Color: Interview with Xanat Sobrevilla and Alyx Goodwin

Mizue Aizeki and Coline Schupfer

Xanat Sobrevilla leads campaign and coalition work for OCAD (Organized Communities Against Deportations). Along with supporting anti-deportation campaigns, Sobrevilla ensures that OCAD plays a meaningful role in the Erase the Gang Database Coalition and pushes back on the ways surveillance is used to target immigrants for deportation.

Alyx Goodwin is currently a deputy campaign director at Action Center on Race and the Economy, organizes with BYP100 (Black Youth Project 100) Chicago, and is a cofounder of and contributor to LEFT OUT Magazine. Her writing, organizing, and activism are broadly centered on building Black power and self-determination, on sustaining its momentum and dealing with its challenges.

Mizue Aizeki: Please tell us a bit about your organizations, and how you came together in the "Erase the Database" campaign against Chicago's gang database?

Sobrevilla: I'm Xanat, an organizer with OCAD (Organized Communities Against Deportations). We're a group of undocumented, unapologetic, and unafraid organizers building a resistance movement against deportations and the criminalization of immigrants and people of color in Chicago and its surrounding areas.

In 2009, we had a friend in proceedings and realized we had the power to intervene. We decided to formalize this relationship as undocumented folks. In 2013, we began to focus on deportation defense. And, noticing the

trends and the ways in which US Immigration and Customs Enforcement runs itself and its excuses for conducting raids and removals, we started seeing a lot of people get criminalized—not starting from ICE, but from local policing.

Back in 2016, we were looking at how people were being targeted in Chicago. We were told that because they were in a gang database, they would be denied bond, or they would be removed, because being a gang member is an automatic, no-relief situation.

Then, in 2017, there was a very violent raid in the South Side of Chicago. We tried to figure out what initiated this, and what we found was that ICE was using the Chicago gang database to legitimize breaking into people's homes without permission. They used the database as an excuse for breaking a person's arm, and for locking them up for eleven months. In this instance, we were lucky because one of the persons concerned was able to file a lawsuit against the city of Chicago, its police officers, ICE, and McHenry County Jail.[1] Through this lawsuit and investigation, we were able to find out more about Chicago's gang database, and about CLEAR [Citizen and Law Enforcement Analysis and Reporting].

By then, OCAD was already working with BYP100 at a very conscientious level, trying to figure out how we can fight together and how to challenge local policing in ways that show up at the federal level. Alyx, correct me if I'm wrong, but I believe this was around 2016 when we did an action together, when a bunch of cops, even from other countries, came to be trained.

Alyx Goodwin: Yeah, that's correct, and that was a great overview of the campaign. So, I'm Alyx, an organizer with BYP100. I've been a part of the organization since 2016, which has been around since, I want to say, 2013 or 2014. BYP100 is a national, member-based organization of Black 18- to 35-year-old activists and organizers, dedicated to creating justice and freedom for all Black people. We operate through a Black queer feminist lens, and are an abolitionist organization that firmly believes that none of us are free until we're all free. And I say that as a description of the organization because it's what drives our politics and the campaigns that we are a part of. As Xanat mentioned, we have been working with OCAD for that exact reason.

In terms of BYP100, we understand that as Black people, we are safe nowhere. There is no sanctuary for us. In particular, Chicago is not a sanctuary city for Black people. It's not a sanctuary for Latinx people. None of us are free until we're all free. We are fighting in solidarity, for the sanctuary of safe spaces, against police violence, against the evils of racial capitalism. And, knowing that the issue of sanctuary cities also impacts Black immigrants on the issue of police violence, and that the gang database impacts Black Chicagoans, campaigning against it was a no-brainer. Those are just some added points as to why BYP100 is involved.

Coline Schupfer: Thanks for sharing what drives you and how you came together in such an incredible display of solidarity. Can we backtrack a bit and zoom into the gang database—what it looks like, how it affects people's lives, and any consequences it carries?

Sobrevilla: The database is hard to understand, because the city gives us different versions and explanations of what it looks like. What we know is that the gang database is a list where people are designated as gang members and monitored as a direct consequence. Sometimes folks are arbitrarily designated as belonging to a particular gang, but sometimes folks are not and are simply listed as "gang member." One of the overwhelming things was learning that there are many different databases. We're told that there is no one computer or database where they keep all the information, but we know they use Citizen and Law Enforcement Analysis and Reporting (CLEAR), an automated predictive policing system. It is accessed by over five hundred agencies, with ICE and Chicago Public Schools being among the top ten users of the database. Through a Freedom of Information Act (FOIA) request, we also learned that churches have access to it. We also know that the database is racist.[2] Black and Latinx people make up almost 95 percent of the database. I believe it's 70 percent Black and 23 percent, Latinx.

There are many ways to get into this database. We learned that people were being placed into the database through schools—either by teachers or school resource officers. There's been young people—some as young as nine and we've also seen younger—who are placed on this gang database. They're impacted from a really young age and when they grow older, they will face issues getting housing, work, licenses, as well as risk deportation. Once on the database, you can't get out of it. When one of the people detained as a direct consequence of the database sued the city, the city conceded that he was wrongfully placed on the database twice, but they could not get him off the list, and that all they could do is write a letter to admit that they were mistaken.

Goodwin: The gang database has taught us a lot about the larger scope of what we're up against. This gang database has sharing agreements with around five hundred other agencies. It illuminates the length that the police and the state are willing to go, that corporations are willing to go, to keep the status quo in place. It's like we are all being surveilled in some form or fashion. And the purpose of that is social control, through violent policing and mass incarceration. These things have created this ugly cycle of poverty and divestment, of lack of resources, and lack of love in our communities. This has really been illuminating for me as to what the larger system is exactly.

Aizeki: What reasons did they give about why they couldn't get him out of the database, despite the mistake? They could only write a letter? How is this related to your campaign to get Cook County to stop the database?

Sobrevilla: Exactly. We were told that there is no mechanism for removing a name from the list and that all they could do is write a letter to the city saying, "We were mistaken," and now the different agencies that can access the database can see the letter and find out the information isn't correct. I guess they can look for the letter when they plug in a name.

We learned that Cook County was about to transfer their database to another unknown agency. We tried to intervene publicly with a campaign pushing for its erasure instead of a transfer of hands. At that point, their share was too much to hold, so they wanted to get rid of their database, for legal or cost reasons. Instead of transferring, we pushed for it to be destroyed. And it happened. The County's gang database was eventually eliminated.

Goodwin: Yes, and after the campaign made enough noise, the Office of Inspector General initiated an investigation of Chicago's gang database and through their investigation discovered that everything that we were claiming and saying was accurate. This was really important—the city's independent auditor finding that the Chicago Police Department was using a database that was not only inaccurate, but also racist. Therefore, the City's and the CPD's conclusion was to get rid of this particular gang database. However, there's plans to implement a new one, we just don't know much about the timeline.

Aizeki: So the campaign made enough noise to get the Office of the Inspector General's attention. Please elaborate a bit more and on any tactics that you used. Also, you filed another lawsuit?

Sobrevilla: Yes, in 2017, we filed a lawsuit. By then, we had learned about the database, and how we could get a letter at a minimum. We therefore decided to publicly challenge the city. At first, it was just OCAD and BYP100. Then we started inviting other folks who wanted to join. We filed a lawsuit ourselves. Through that lawsuit, from 2018 until 2020, we learned that the city is preparing to create a new database, one that they hope cannot be challenged in the courts, but one that would be equally harmful and useless, as the BYP100 also determined.

Eventually, we withdrew as organizational plaintiffs, and the individual plaintiffs went on to reach a settlement. We withdrew—knowing that the courts were not going to get us the transformation and the abolition that we were seeking—rather than institute reforms that were just as dangerous. Through that settlement, the four plaintiffs got some financial compensation at least. Thereafter, we closed that chapter. The process did allow us to learn more about the database and gave us a public platform, but we know that our goals are beyond reform.

Goodwin: Yes, and the research that went into it was also really important. There's a report called *Tracked and Targeted* on the Erase the Database website.[3] Once that report was public, there were a couple of actions that we did. One action included shutting down traffic in front of City Hall.

Sobrevilla: We have also been constructing an ordinance that we hope to introduce in the spring of 2022, to not only get rid of the database, but also prevent other databases from coming in, and to find ways of getting reparations for people adversely impacted. There's over 160,000 people that we know are in it, and thousands are added year after year. Regardless of whether they're gang affiliated or not, they're being harmed by the state. More recently, we also joined the fight with GoodKids MadCity, who have been developing a "peace book" to provide communities with the resources to be able to say, "What are the actual solutions in our neighborhoods?" "What will actually address the violence that we're seeking to address?"[4] The peace book could be a resource that all the people would have, in terms of the actual things that can reduce violence. And it's been constructed by young Black people. There's also the idea of a peace commission: being able to have a group of people from the community with an actual understanding of what the causes of what we're seeing in our neighborhoods are, and then being able to say, "This is how we use the money." "This gets prioritized in the budget." By nature, policing is not a solution.

We've also been doing teach-ins in the community, where the impacts of the gang database are very much felt. If you're being impacted by it, you might not know because you're not notified either. So, oftentimes, when we're doing block parties, training, or teach-ins, we're talking with people that have a sense that they might be on that database.

Right now, the only way that you can find out if you're in it is through a FOIA request. On our website, we also created text that people can use to find out if they are on the database. It doesn't always work, but sometimes this is how people are able to find out. So, when we do block parties, teach-ins, or training sessions, we have a space for people to do that. Sometimes we also offer to do it for people with a different email. This is because one time, we saw a young person being visited at their home by cops after they requested their information. It's also just about getting the word out and, if you feel you're being affected, this provides knowledge and tools, and us as a support system to challenge it.

Schupfer: Can you reflect on any lessons learned? Also, you mentioned earlier that you're undocumented-led. When it comes to insecure legal status, there's a lot of personal risk, especially when engaging in this kind of work. Could you share how you all manage risk, and what you do to protect your safety?

Sobrevilla: The hope is that, since we created a network where people can challenge it if they want, we are able to support them through our campaign. For OCAD, this campaign has also been very important in helping us unpack the many ways in which we are criminalized, as Black and brown people; treated based on labels in the courts; and disposed of.

We learned really early on that being organized and having a network is really powerful. In the Obama era, how they [undocumented folks] were being perceived and how the police detained people mattered. Public campaigns were essential in order to push back, and oftentimes that was what kept us safe. I would say in the Trump era, we learned that that's not always necessarily the case. In June 2020, we did lose an organizer to deportation,[5] but managed to get him back a year later.[6] It's about having each other's backs as people. Even though being public can be a risk, it can also be an asset and a way to protect ourselves. We're in this because we believe it's unacceptable to keep living under this stress, and so the only option is to organize and to fight, and even though it's risky, it's also the only way we can protect ourselves.

As for lessons learned, we must remind ourselves that there are different ways and better ways to address what we need. We've been deprived of so many resources for so long. And the only solution that we keep being told is: "We need more policing." In Chicago, our violence prevention workers that go out and de-escalate conflict often are folks that are in the database themselves. And their work has resulted in less violence in neighborhoods. But oftentimes that's not what gets in the news, because of the capitalistic interest of keeping a policing force. We already know that incarceration isn't working. It's been in practice since the eighties. We only see more and more suffering because of it. But we keep being told that it must exist. And I think it's pushing for alternatives, pushing for the resources that we've been needing for the longest time, because that is what is actually going to solve the issues we see. Even if you think about COVID-19 and wanting more surveillance because of it—to track people through their phones, for example—this is a knee-jerk reaction to surveillance and policing as a solution, yet there are so many other options, better options that are actually solutions.

Goodwin: We have all been socialized to believe that police surveillance is public safety, and there are a lot of challenges to be tackled in moving people's imaginations, to continue this work. We could have given up when the city decided to just create a new gang database. But we recognize that this struggle is rooted in the love for our people. We literally cannot give up, because folk's lives are at stake.

15

Building Community Power in Unequal Cities:
Interview with Hamid Khan

Mizue Aizeki

Hamid Khan is an organizer with the Stop LAPD Spying Coalition, a grass-roots group that builds community power toward abolishing the police state.

Aizeki: Can you tell me about your work and how Stop LAPD Spying came to be?

Khan: Stop LAPD Spying Coalition is basically a continuation of the work that I've been involved in, over the last thirty to thirty-five years, organizing in various capacities in Los Angeles. Going back into the late eighties, early nineties, this included founding a grassroots organization primarily focusing on the immigrant communities from South Asia. I'm originally an immigrant myself from Pakistan. I was born and grew up in Pakistan.

For about twenty years, I was very involved with the immigrants' rights movement. I organized against the police state and witnessed a lot of oppression—deportations, how people were being excluded, how people were being targeted. Surveillance and other information-gathering tools were already present at the time, whether through tracing and people-tracking, through bank or visa information—surveillance and the presence of the police state has always been there.

It got really heightened in the early nineties. When we look back at the 1994 Crime Bill and the 1996 Illegal Immigration Reform and Immigrant Responsibility Act, for example, the police state was central to those legislations. From an immigrant rights' perspective, the 1986 Immigration Reform and Control Act was one of the first laws in which enforcement was a central idea. 9/11 then added fuel to what we were already seeing—a massive expansion of the national security police state. We also saw an increased use of technology and particularly information-processing technology, including emerging developments around machine learning and artificial intelligence.

Concurrently, the infrastructure to support this massive expansion was reconfiguring itself too. The post-9/11 Commission Report played a key role in where we are today, with the main thesis being that the events happened because information was not being shared between agencies.[1] That report led to Congress passing a critical law in 2004, the Intelligence Reform and Terrorism Prevention Act, which introduced several things, including the establishment of the Office of the Director of National Intelligence, which brought together major agencies and all the intelligence agencies under one umbrella. It mandated the executive branch to create a massive information-sharing environment, the key pieces of which are known as "fusion centers," which are the central warehouses of information gathering, storing, and sharing—in other words, the infrastructure that makes it all go around.

Aizeki: How did this change policing in the US?

Khan: One of the key practices was the tactic that was imported from England, that started thirty to thirty-five years ago at the Kent Constabulary, referred to as "Intelligence-Led Policing." The central themes of this are behavioral surveillance and data mining—how behavior could become an indicator of somebody's activity or lead to activity that could be "potentially" criminal in nature. At that time, there was not enough technology available, but, connecting the dots, it laid the foundation of something similar to what we now call social media monitoring and social network analysis.

As this information-sharing environment was being developed, additional layers were added to legitimate speculative policing. That's what led to the creation of the "suspicious activity reporting program," which initially came out of the Director of National Intelligence. The idea was that local law enforcement agencies needed to be enlisted in the suspicious activity reporting program, operating as the eyes and ears for national security. Then, in March 2008, the LAPD was the first law enforcement agency—and Bill Bratton was then chief—that incorporated the suspicious activity reporting program into their daily policing. Bratton was one of the first instigators and main players who brought this type of intelligence-like behavioral surveillance and data mining into policing on this side of the Atlantic, and who positioned it so it became the primary vehicle in the late nineties and post-9/11. After that, with the advent of machine learning / predictive analytics types of technology, it went into overdrive.

Aizeki: How did Bratton and company decide what constituted potentially crime-related data? How did they calculate "suspicious activity"?

Khan: There was no precedent for how suspicious activity was defined, so it was defined by the director of national intelligence as "observed behavior, reasonably indicative of preoperational planning, of criminal and/or terrorist activity." When you break that down, you find that it's just behavior being observed; it indicates there is no reasonable suspicion, there's no probable cause, or any other standards. "Reasonably indicative of preoperational planning" essentially means somebody's thinking of doing something. They then set up these activities, supposedly, that would be constitutionally protected, but can be considered suspicious in nature. Some of these activities included taking photographs in public, using video cameras, walking into infrastructures, and asking for their hours of operation. Others included normal routine type activities—drawing diagrams in public, taking notes, and so on.

Aizeki: So, the LAPD effectively criminalized everyday life?

Khan: It was very evident to me, as I was involved in organizing around the national security police state, that counterterrorism tactics were being incorporated into domestic policing, including predictive policing. This is where Bill Bratton becomes critical, since he was a big supporter of predictive policing as it was developed on the battlefields of Iraq and Afghanistan through a 2005 academic grant by the DOD [Department of Defense] with the claims of predicting insurgent activity. By 2009, realizing the profit potential, these academics formed their own company called PredPol. LAPD was one of the first law enforcement agencies to experiment with it, and it was clear who was going to be on the receiving end—Black, Indigenous, migrants, and poor communities. This is what really led to folks coming together, because this surveillance, spying, and infiltration infrastructure was expanding and becoming deeply entrenched. Incorporating advanced technology, it also provided opportunities to bring in pseudoscience, like algorithms that they claimed were free of racial bias.[2] The writing was very much on the wall. This led to the creation of the Stop LAPD Spying Coalition, with people coming together in late 2010, early 2011.

Aizeki: You've explained to me previously how human surveillance is still the most pervasive. How can we understand the interaction between human and tech surveillance?

Khan: Human-based surveillance has always been there and remains a primary vehicle for gathering information. But the processing of information is also being done. For example, crime is everywhere in the city, and predictive policing and PredPol algorithms process information and provide potential hotspots covering five hundred square feet.[3] Ultimately, however, it's the analysts who decide which hotspots to deploy law enforcement to. Human-based intelligence is therefore still in the driver's seat. It's the analysts, again, who are in these fusion centers when the suspicious activity reports go in; who make an assessment whether there's any nexus to crime or criminal or terrorist activity, and who should be further investigated by the Joint Terrorism Task Force or the other federal task forces.

The Suspicious Activity Reporting program in LA, which is called "iWATCH: See Something, Say Something," is in effect the same as community informants calling on people about suspicious activity. We also need to look at the culture of deputization, how volunteers that are being deputized into law enforcement activities are celebrated and become honorary cops in that sense. That whole snitch culture is very much there.

This culture of deputization, this culture of volunteer cops, and of neighborhood watch—they are very much a part and parcel of the white supremacist DNA, very much driven by sunset towns, Jim Crow, and various ways of segregation. That's where one of our main guiding values at the coalition comes from, that this is not a moment in time, but a continuation of history. And in that continuation of history, there's always the creation of the "other" that justifies enforcement, to maintain and preserve white supremacy by demonizing the other and then justifying legislation and structures and institutions to criminalize the other.

Aizeki: Can you talk about the significance of the apparatus built up around 9/11, DHS, and the permanent War on Terror and counterinsurgency?

Khan: The creation of DHS was a tremendous opportunity for the powers to bring together what was happening, the war abroad and the war at home. There's this whole language around community policing, but it's really about counterinsurgency—practices that have been ongoing pretty much since the colonization of the Philippines. These locations became laboratories to test and deploy these practices. Especially after Vietnam, we saw this partnership between law enforcement and the US military. They—the war in Iraq and in Afghanistan and the domestic vilification of Indigenous communities, of peoples of African descent, and of migrant populations—are part and parcel of that same DNA, because of how these populations were perceived as threats to the white supremacist system.

In relation to counterinsurgency, what we have seen over the last forty or fifty years is this rise in sanitizing the overt violence of the police. It is about building relationships and trust in the communities through an iron-fist-velvet-glove-type approach. The idea is to identify certain people as leaders, prominent folks in their community, and to build relationships with them. It is about, then, capitalizing on those people's desire for proximity to power, and for them to feel safe around law enforcement. And if you pump enough money on them, you can basically hold them hostage.

Another layer of community policing is to start building relationships with the local population, including children, and presenting yourself as a benign force that is only there to build a partnership. Yet, at the same time, it is to keep an eye on the community, to make sure that that population remains under control. The classic example of community policing, at least in LA, is the way in which it is implemented in public housing projects. Because people are dependent on housing, there's already a certain level of coercion, and law enforcement then comes in and makes sure they are monitored. It creates almost like an equivalent of a panopticon effect, a 360-lens on the community, through community informants, through providing resources that should be going to people in the first place anyways. Making people resource-dependent means they are also dependent on building relationships with law enforcement.

Aizeki: You mentioned the continuum of history. I'm curious about your experience organizing under the first three presidents that have overseen DHS. Under Bush, the slogan very much was, "We got to get the terrorists." Then, under Obama, it was, "We got to get the 'criminal aliens.'" And then Trump compounded the vilification of all the "dangerous others" who had been presented as a threat to security over the previous administrations. What strategies have you used against the continual construction of "threats" in your organizing against the national security state?

Khan: So that's exactly our second guiding value that we've built our work around: that there's always an "other."

The creation of the other has always been central. It just keeps on expanding because the system requires it. There are multiple "faces" that have been created that provide a justification for laws to be created. So, for example, why hold Indigenous and Native Americans in reservations? Because of the "savage native," and that face of this savage native has been paraded and Hollywood-ized over time. It's a process of demonization.

Or the face of Black people, which has been criminalized in perpetuity—whether through narratives of protecting the white woman, or that paint them as inherently criminal by virtue of their DNA. This assumption of criminality is central to maintaining and preserving systems of public labor, slave labor, incarceration. Then there is the face of the illegal Latino—it immediately sidelines any conversation around the occupation and colonization of Mexico, or of the states of California, Arizona, New Mexico, and Texas. That whole illegal-ness creates stigma. And then there's the disloyal and manipulative Asian, the classic argument that persons of Japanese ancestry contain enemy race blood, hence are inherently disloyal. Earlier on, this whole narrative provided fuel to the Chinese Exclusion Act.

More recently, all of this has become more pronounced around the face of the Muslim terrorist, or South Asian, or Arab. It has its own historical significance—almost as if the Crusades never ended. The conflict between the Crescent and the Cross has always continued. It has its own sort of significance in popular imagination and the culture of the public. Other faces include that of the deviant trans, or the conniving femme body.

But for us, it was critical to highlight that it is not just a moment in time, but a continuation of history. We developed these tools for organizing. On our website we developed this whole timeline of surveillance, of the LAPD and national security. We had twelve pages and blew up each page into posters. Then we got these panels that we used as visuals for organizing. We placed them on the streets and had people walk through that historic time-line, which brought up many "aha" moments. These tools for organizing help people understand who is on the receiving end of all of this, historically. It also reminds us there are many of us "others" and that we have a lot of power; and that we need to come together and fight.

So that became one of the primary vehicles of street organizing, and organizing was a primary way of building power on the ground, rather than looking for legislative or judicial fixes. There's no privacy if you're Black, Asian, or an immigrant body.

So, the typical response usually is, "Let's find a case, let's file a lawsuit." We flipped the script, saying it's not just about privacy invasion, but it is about the use of surveillance as a primary tool to police race and poverty and "suspect bodies" through the white gaze. Ultimately, it's about control of land. It's about who controls the land and who needs to be banished, and who has the privilege to loot the land.

Aizeki: You talked about two of your guiding values, and I wonder if you could elaborate more on the others?

Khan: Yes, there are four elements, and the third is "de-sensationalization." De-sensationalizing the language, the rhetoric of national security, this rhet-oric of the "Russians are coming, the communists are here, the anarchists are here, the terrorists are here, the hordes of immigrants are here," about how our whole culture is "being poisoned by trans people."

This then becomes the justification for protecting this serene, untainted shining city on the hill, and it extends into the rest of the United States. The question becomes, how do you preserve whiteness? How do you preserve the system that upholds whiteness? For us, it was crucial to de-sensational-ize all this, to flip the script on the language of national security and that poverty is an issue of national security.

Coming back to Skid Row, this is why the issue of surveillance has al-ways been so critical. How are you seen through the white gaze? For us, this is what all this comes down to. And there's the question of how technol-ogy ultimately works in service of banishment, gentrification, and devel-opment. Through public records, we have mapped out how communities like Skid Row are placed into these hotspots for two different six-month periods. What it shows is a quarantining effect of Skid Row, almost like a digital wall; a digital boundary that is created to protect the new downtown, the development that's going on in the art district, and in the warehouse district. They are quarantined because they are seen as undesirables, and this is where the sensationalization comes in—the language around risk assessments and all that.

Finally, the fourth element is that our fight is rooted in human rights, rather than just looking at the importance of constitutional rights and civil liberties. Here, again, we are falling into this trap of citizenship. Non-citizens are dehumanized, and the same goes for those seen to be implicated with gangs and those incarcerated. You become a statistic; it's like you're leaving your humanity at the door and are no longer seen as a human being. When we talk about human rights, it's not rooted in the very white, Western conception of human rights—but by the simple fact that as part of the natural universe, you are a human being with rights, with autonomy. It's not driven by mandates or paragraphs, it's not codified, but as simple as, "I claim my humanity as part of the natural universe." So, with that, fuck your borders, fuck your police, and fuck your infrastructure. Those are my closing comments.

16

CASE STUDY: Why We Are Suing Clearview AI in California State Court

Paromita Shah & Just Futures Law

WHO WE ARE

Just Futures Law is a women-of-color-led legal organization defined by our partnerships with grassroots groups, and is working to end criminalization, deportation, and surveillance. We believe that the law can be a transformative tool in support of organizing and political movements. One of our priorities is tech surveillance because it is supercharging mass incarceration and mass deportation systems.

KEY CONCEPTS

How big is Clearview AI's database?

As of April 2023, it purports to have over 30 billion photos, which is much bigger than the FBI's database, and includes images "scraped" without consent from websites like Facebook, Twitter, and Venmo. Clearview AI's founder claims that US law enforcement has accessed it over a million times since 2017.[1]

What is scraping?

The process of using automated computer software to gather and copy data from websites into a database for retrieval and analysis.

What is biometric information?

A person's distinct and immutable physical characteristics, such as the position, size, and shape of the eyes, nose, cheekbones, and jaw, that can be used to later identify that person, for example, from a scraped image.

THE ISSUE

Clearview AI has built the most dangerous facial recognition database in the country, and allows law enforcement and government to identify, locate, and track people—where they go, who they're with, and what they say—at the touch of a button on a mobile device. The backbone of this powerful technology relies on a vast database of photo images and biometric information illicitly collected by scraping websites and social media.

Clearview AI sells access to its database for commercial gain. The database allows users, including law enforcement, to not only identify people in public spaces, but also to learn those people's professional roles, religious affiliations, familial connections and friendships, romantic partnerships, personal activities, political views, patterns of travel, and even home addresses, *all without receiving consent, obtaining a warrant, or providing probable cause to conduct a search.* This mass surveillance technology raises profound human and civil rights concerns. Black and brown people, including immigrants, are more likely to be surveilled, to have rights violated, and to be subjected to harmful policing. Concerns remain that facial recognition technologies perpetuate racial, gender, and age biases: Asians and African Americans are one hundred times more likely to be misidentified than white men. Moreover, surveillance technologies, such as Clearview AI, could be used to stifle the rights of—or retaliate against—protesters, activists, or organizers.

Immigration agencies in the United States have been using this dangerous technology. In June 2019, DHS began a paid pilot program with Clearview without a formal contract, with both Customs and Border Patrol, and Immigration and Customs Enforcement (ICE) Enforcement and Removal Operations initiating searches. On August 12, 2020, Clearview entered into a purchase order contract in which ICE agreed to pay $224,000 for "Clearview licenses."[2] In September 2021, ICE renewed the contract. Clearview

AI was also used by police departments during the racial justice uprisings, heightening concerns over civil rights abuses.

ABOUT THE LAWSUIT

In April 2021, plaintiffs filed a lawsuit in superior court in Alameda County, California, against Clearview AI and four California law enforcement agencies suspected of using Clearview.[3] The plaintiffs are two community-based organizations, Mijente Support Committee and NorCal Resist, and four individual activists. The individuals filing the lawsuit are all activists who have participated in various political movements critical of the police and ICE. They have supported Black Lives Matter, criticized ICE and the police on online platforms, and organized fundraisers for immigrants confined in detention facilities. The organizational plaintiffs have engaged in similar work. All of these activities open them up to retaliation by ICE and the police. Chilling the right to protest is a threat to democracy, and Clearview AI's powerful facial recognition tech runs counter to fundamental democratic values. Sejal Zota from Just Futures Law and BraunHagey & Borden LLP represent the plaintiffs.

The lawsuit aims to prevent Clearview AI from illegally acquiring, storing, and selling the plaintiffs' likenesses and the likenesses of millions of Californians in Clearview's quest to create a cyber-surveillance state. It is crucial to forefront concerns that runaway tech like Clearview AI can be used to surveil and retaliate against activists, particularly BIPOC (Black, Indigenous, and people of color) and immigrant activists, and to interject the idea that surveillance tech must be evaluated through a racial justice lens.

LOOKING FORWARD

Clearview AI has been criticized, repeatedly fined, or banned around the world for its disturbing practices. In January 2021, Canada banned Clearview AI altogether, ordering the company to cease operation in the country and delete all Canadians' data.[4] Australia's national privacy regulator ordered the company to destroy images and facial images of anyone living in Australia.[5] The European Data Protection Board, a European Union body, also recently said that Clearview's practices violate European privacy laws.[6] In 2022, privacy watchdogs in the United Kingdom, France, Italy and Greece fined Clearview AI nearly 70 million euros over its controversial facial recognition software.[7] Sweden fined its own police agency $300,000 dollars for using Clearview AI.[8] However, in October 2023, Clearview AI successfully appealed the UK's privacy watchdog's fines.[9]

Policymakers at all levels must intervene to end the abusive use of surveillance technology and shut down its devastating connection to detention, deportation, and criminalization. Our key recommendations include the following:

- States, municipalities, and federal agencies like ICE should terminate their contracts with Clearview AI.

- Federal, local, and state governments should follow the lead of communities, like those in Alameda County in California, who are organizing for the ban of the use of facial recognition.

- Federal, local, and state governments should reduce funding for surveillance programs by 50 percent.

17

CASE STUDY: Why We Need Local Campaigns to End Immigration Detention

Silky Shah, Detention Watch Network

WHO WE ARE

Detention Watch Network (DWN) is a national coalition that aims to remove one of the key drivers of mass deportations while also addressing the broader role of incarceration and criminalization in US society. In 2012, DWN updated its vision to include ending detention. We see the abolition of immigration detention as part and parcel of struggles against racism, xenophobia, discriminatory policing, mass incarceration, and border militarization.

THE PROBLEM

The United States' immigration detention system began to take its current shape in the early 1980s. During the early years of the War on Drugs, the mandatory detention of certain immigrants became part of a legal framework to facilitate mass deportation. Since then, the system has grown exponentially, reaching its height in 2019 under Trump, with a capacity to detain fifty-five thousand immigrants at any given time. The deportation machine went into high gear. Immigration and Customs Enforcement (ICE) officers were given more latitude to target immigrants residing in the US, as well as individuals arriving at the border. Detention numbers skyrocketed, and people were detained for much longer periods of time. ICE used this as an opportunity to expand the system, and overspent its budget only to be regularly bailed out by Congress, which increased detention capacity annually.

In the spring of 2018, then attorney general Jeff Sessions rolled out a "zero tolerance" policy that separated parents from their children if they attempted to enter the US without authorization. Owing to the rising detention numbers, the administration began using Federal Bureau of Prisons (BOP) facilities for ICE detention. Immigrants were incarcerated at five BOP prisons in Arizona, California, Oregon, Texas, and Washington. At the same time ICE issued requests for proposals for a massive expansion of family detention at military bases, including up to 15,500 additional beds.

COMMUNITIES NOT CAGES CAMPAIGN

In response to the proposed expansion by Trump, DWN launched the "Communities Not Cages" campaign in October 2018 to halt detention expansion, shut down existing detention centers, and stop the proliferation of ICE detention into other agencies such as the Department of Justice and Department of Defense. The campaign initially focused on stopping the use of the five BOP prisons and supporting coordination between organizers and lawyers to ensure releases. By November 2018, BOP ended the practice of detaining immigrants in ICE custody, but ICE was still expanding immigration detention across the country.

Much of the detention system operates through intergovernmental service agreements (IGSAs) between ICE and local counties and cities, contracts that are often quickly secured without public engagement. Local counties find these contracts quite lucrative, allowing them to supplement dwindling budgets in rural communities. All but five of the two-hundred-plus ICE detention centers are subcontracted out to local governments or private prisons. During the Obama era, many communities fought back against ICE collaboration with police by ending agreements at the city, county, and state level. This strategy proved to be successful especially in more friendly political environments. Since then, the passage of state and local sanctuary policies to end collaboration with police have limited ICE's ability to use local law enforcement as a direct pipeline for deportation.

More recently, to combat detention expansion and end contracts at existing detention centers, advocates and organizers have employed two strategies: (1) target local county commissioners and city councils to prevent the creation of contracts or renewal of existing ones; and (2) pass legislation at the state level to end the use of IGSAs or private prisons and phase out existing detention in the state. Over the course of the three years since the Communities Not Cages campaign launched, groups in at least twenty-seven states developed local strategies and learned about effective tactics utilized in other parts of the country. When Biden took office, DWN launched First Ten, a supplement to the Communities Not Cages campaign, calling on the administration to end detention and begin shutting down ten jails that exemplify the system's problems.

LOOKING FORWARD

There were a few impediments to the Communities Not Cages strategy, one being that many counties, dependent on federal income, did not want to end ICE contracts because they had no substitute for the lost revenue. In response, DWN has advocated a just transition away from detention economies including recommendations for federal financial support to counties closing detention centers. Additionally, within the national movement, some advocates were concerned that shutting down detention centers would lead to transfers far away, limiting access to family and counsel. While ICE's reasoning for transfers is often arbitrary and impossible to predict, DWN has worked with members to develop a plan for when closure of a detention center is imminent. Often this involves bringing organizers, lawyers, and advocates together to demand releases and not transfers through a combination of legal support for immigrants currently at the detention center, actions outside the jail, and pressure on ICE headquarters and field offices.

Another concern is that many advocates and members of Congress have offered "alternatives to detention" as an option to argue against physical detention. However, ICE's alternatives program, which mostly consists of electronic monitoring and phone tracking apps, often inflicts physical and psychological harm on those enrolled. Rather than reduce detention, alternatives have instead expanded the number of people under government control; many immigrants who would have otherwise been released without tracking are now put on an alternative. Existing as a tool for compliance and limiting one's range of movement, alternatives only serve to reinforce the immigration enforcement system rather than dismantle it.

Despite these challenges, the Communities Not Cages campaign has been remarkably successful at ending ICE detention contracts, halting expansion, and shifting the national discourse toward detention abolition. By late 2023, seven states passed legislation curbing detention expansion or phasing out existing facilities, and several other states plan to reintroduce legislation in upcoming sessions. In some of these instances, legislation has successfully halted expansion. For example, in Dwight, Illinois, where Immigration Centers of America tried to build a thousand-bed detention center, a bill to ban private detention in Illinois stopped the contract from moving forward. Additionally, the impact of the COVID-19 pandemic cannot be overlooked. In early 2021, detention numbers were at a twenty-year low and some counties that were hesitant to end contracts were more open to doing so after losing revenue due to empty beds. The campaign finally gained traction at the national level when in May 2021 and March 2022 the Department of Homeland Security announced the end of ICE detention at three county jails: Bristol in Massachusetts, Irwin in Georgia, and Etowah in Alabama. The latter two had been included in the First Ten list. This was the first time an administration had publicly canceled ICE contracts because of the facilities' abysmal conditions. More than fifteen county jails have stopped being used for ICE detention due to the efforts of Communities Not Cages local campaign partners. These wins have had an impact on the system overall. In Biden's 2023 budget request he called for a reduction in the capacity of immigration detention by nine thousand beds or 26 percent from the previous year's budget. Biden's budget request signals that we've finally moved the needle in the opposite direction when it comes to immigration detention.

18

CASE STUDY: Stop Urban Shield: How We Fought DHS's Militarized Police Trainings

Lara Kiswani, Stop Urban Shield Coalition

WHO WE ARE

This campaign was organized by the Stop Urban Shield Coalition, which included the Arab Resource & Organizing Center (AROC), BAYAN USA, Critical Resistance Oakland, Xicana Moratorium Coalition, American Friends Service Committee, Public Health Justice Collective, War Resisters League, and many others.[1]

KEY CONCEPTS

Urban Areas Security Initiative

This DHS program provides funding to police in "high-threat, high-density urban areas" as part of their counterterrorism initiatives. The police can use this funding to buy equipment, conduct trainings, and for increasing "security" at public venues. In 2021, DHS had $615 million in funds available for this program.

CONTEXT

The Stop Urban Shield Coalition was formed in 2013, following several years of mobilizations, to put an end to Urban Shield—one of the largest weapons expos and militarized policing trainings in the world. Taking place annually in the San Francisco Bay Area on or near the weekend of

124

9/11, this training and expo was created by Alameda County sheriff Gregory Ahern in 2007 and was held in Alameda County until 2019. Urban Shield imposed a militarized framework on how municipalities understood and deployed responses to human-made and natural "disasters" and emergencies. Emergency responders and law enforcement agencies came from across the country and world—including from the apartheid state of Israel and other human rights–violating regimes—to train under a highly militarized framework. Urban Shield was an expression of police militarization and the militarization of "public safety" in the post-9/11 period.

While policing has always had a militarized aspect to it, 9/11 marked a particular broadening of policing and an intensification of the relations between law enforcement, surveillance, imprisonment, and war-making on a global scale.

THE PROBLEM

Urban Shield represented everything our movements have fought against for a long time. It featured collaboration with ICE and hosted the far-right Oath Keepers militia organization as well as exchanges and training with Israel. The training aspect of Urban Shield mobilized deadly stereotypes in its depictions of Muslims, leftists, and other "criminals" through its wargame and disaster-response scenarios. During its weapons and trade expo, it glorified the most violent and militarized aspects of policing including blatantly racist imagery—the most popular shirt sold at the expo read "Black Rifles Matter." All of this was on taxpayers' dime. Urban Shield exploited real tragedies and natural disasters, and real public health needs. Post-9/11 militarism, along with an onslaught of neoliberal abandonment and divestment, has created real instability and vulnerability among communities in terms of structural violence, community-level violence, and potential impacts of natural and social disasters. Urban Shield, in true military-industrial logic, exploited this organized abandonment and vulnerability to increase the political, economic, and social hegemony of the militarism of local law enforcement, in effect doubling down on many of the root causes of instability. All the while, it abandoned more sustainable, more community-centered response programs and strategies while consolidating huge amounts of resources and significant political power in the hands of Sheriff Ahern and his right-wing agenda.

As we know, policing has been involved in the violence management and sometimes outright warfare against Black, brown, and poor communities since day one. What we've been seeing in the post-9/11 world, and which can be seen in a shockingly clear way in the police response to the 2014 Ferguson uprising, is that police militarization has rapidly intensified and become normalized since 2001. The process of militarization has given police forces increased resources to continue to militarize, and is an extension of the necessity of the neoliberal state to use increasingly sophisticated forms of violence to manage increasing austerity, instability, and inequality.

Through this hyper-militarized international training and expo, war was taught as a normal and necessary way of addressing "crisis"—both real and manufactured. This imperialist logic, of course, is not new. For US militarism, the enemy combatant would be the Black, Indigenous, Arab, Muslim, and racialized and demonized "others." Urban Shield utilized the same logic with the same combatants, only locally. But the problem was not only the militarized nature of the trainings—it was the use of policing itself.

As we know, George Floyd (and many others) were killed by police not outfitted with military hardware or part of those operations. They were killed by "regular beat cops," likely deployed under community policing strategies. The Urban Shield program illustrated these intersections—militarization, policing, and warfare—and the intense impact it had on all our communities.

STRATEGY AND SOLUTION

The Stop Urban Shield Coalition engaged in grassroots organizing, legislative pressure, strategic media and communications, direct actions, and popular education. The work of the coalition over many years dragged Urban Shield from the shadows and made it a highly controversial and visible hot-button issue for political candidates and social justice organizations in the Bay Area. In 2014, the coalition successfully compelled the City of Oakland to no longer host the Urban Shield weapons exposition and training event, garnering national attention to the racism and violence of the program. In 2016, the coalition organized a massive statewide mobilization and direct action against Urban Shield after it was moved to a remote suburb approximately thirty miles from Oakland, successfully disrupting its operations. Additionally, reflecting its internationalist politics, the coalition was able to push county legislators to ban countries with records of human rights abuse from participating in the training.

After building broad community opposition in cities across the Bay Area, in March of 2018 the coalition successfully moved the Alameda County Board of Supervisors to end Urban Shield. In 2019, the County reaffirmed its decision and Urban Shield was ultimately defunded. Through years of organizing resulting in our victory, the coalition struck a massive blow to police militarization in the Bay Area and beyond. We reframed the narrative from war on poverty, drugs, and terror to how it translates to war on community.

Just as Urban Shield represented a variety of crucial fights for our communities, the Stop Urban Shield campaign had to reflect the various movements that led these fights. Our coalition was made up of health workers, migrants, youth, and families who lost loved ones to police violence, and other communities impacted by war, SWAT raids, and policing. Our coalition had a clear demand—to end Urban Shield. We made it explicit that our campaign was an abolitionist campaign while also striking a balance to hold space for organizations with different orientations to abolitionist politics. Throughout our work, we revisited strategy several times, sometimes several times a year, we assessed losses and gains, and most importantly, built power in the process.

Our solution was to defund the program and redistribute the resources toward people-centered responses to disasters and emergencies that are rooted in community rather than law enforcement. Some of these responses would be what people have come to call "alternative" public safety responses, but some were also more community-based or public health–centered responses that existed and worked for years and then were defunded and abandoned, only to be replaced by responses totally controlled by law enforcement. The Stop Urban Shield campaign was a tangible representation of a defund policing campaign based on the divest/invest framework.

After we successfully defunded Urban Shield, we remained involved in the implementation process, including informing and shaping the process that dictated the future allocation of the funds.

REFLECTION

Stop Urban Shield offers a very clear and powerful success story when it comes to the struggles around defunding law enforcement. The campaign was effective in linking communities' struggles and mobilization against war and US imperialism to struggles against domestic policing. It also raised international consciousness among legislators, pushing them toward disengaging governments with records of human rights abuse. This campaign, built on years of abolitionist and internationalist work, identified and offered alternatives to policing and militarism, engaged contradictions within movements, moved bases in diverse communities and, through protracted struggle, redistributed resources, built power, and offered a much-needed victory.

Part 3

DIGITAL IDS: THE BODY AS A BORDER

19

Digital ID: A Primer

Sara Baker, The Engine Room[1]

O ver the past fifteen years, digital identity systems have exploded in their application and popularity with corporate and government actors. This technology expands or replaces paper-based identification by digitizing an individual's data and requiring them to authenticate their identity with the use of a phone, password, security token, or biometric data. While physical ID cards may still be used and linked to a range of digitized data about an individual, often digital IDs replace physical cards. Governments and institutions are increasingly relying on digital ID systems, especially in combination with biometric technology, for public service delivery, aid distribution, cash transfers, voting processes, national security, and more. Accordingly, these systems collect massive amounts of biographic, biometric, location, and relational data on individuals and communities.

Proponents claim that digital IDs will solve an endless list of problems: financial exclusion, lack of access to government services, inefficiencies in health care and welfare systems, underbanking, and lack of identification. The argument can seem compelling, but data collection is never neutral; data has become one of our greatest commodities. Digital IDs, for all their supposed promise, have repeatedly proved to increase states' power to surveil and further exclude marginalized populations—while generating massive profit for the companies that administer them.

Globally, one billion people lack formal identification, which limits their access to basic rights and services.[2] This is a real, systemic problem with devastating consequences, including denial of citizenship, property rights, freedom of movement, and access to resources. But international, state, and

131

private actors have promoted digital identification systems as a universalized intervention, ignoring fundamental risks and crucial differences in needs across countries, communities, and refugee camps. Digital IDs have been shown to not solve the issues that they claim to address; instead they exacerbate systemic problems for populations that are already heavily surveilled, controlled, monitored, and excluded.

This primer explains those dangers and breaks down the key arguments for and against digital IDs. It builds off The Engine Room's digital ID work, which includes reports on the use of biometric technology in humanitarian environments,[3] the lived experiences of people targeted by digital IDs,[4] and advocacy for people-centered systems,[5] as well as participation in initiatives ranging from the #WhyID global community of activists, researchers, and technologists[6] to UNHCR's Global Virtual Summit on Digital Identity for Refugees.[7] In this chapter, we seek to equip advocates and communities around the world with a greater understanding of the forces behind digital IDs, the risks, and a way forward.

Digital IDs: A Tool or a Barrier to Inclusion?

The convenience of a digital ID may seem appealing, but registration systems can often be inaccessible and exclude people by design. If you live outside an urban center, you may have to travel for hours to reach the closest registration office, carrying sensitive supporting documents like your birth certificate—if you have one. Setting up a system to issue digital IDs doesn't automatically fix underlying issues regarding access to documentation or inaccessible government bureaucracy. Imagine you can't access the necessary documents: you are stuck outside of this new ID system, and thus cut off from key social services.

Media and civil society reports show that accessibility is a consistent issue across digital ID systems, creating barriers for the elderly, people without internet access, rural communities, people with disabilities, LGBTQI+ people, and historically marginalized ethnic or racial groups. For example, in Nigeria, many registration sites are physically inaccessible for people with disabilities, and some people have reported giving up on trying to obtain an ID after finding there was no assistance available.[8] And when digital ID systems become required, barriers to access effectively deepen existing inequity and the exclusion of vulnerable or targeted groups of people.

In theory, digital IDs could expand access to rights and services, but without community collaboration and strong regulations, they frequently do the opposite for those with the least power. Governments and companies claim digital IDs are a way to connect historically marginalized communities to financial opportunities, public services, and elections—but if the design and rollout of the system excludes many in those very populations, then who exactly is the digital ID benefiting?

What's behind the ID

Imagine that you've found the money to fix your documents and get your digital ID. This could get you health care and rent assistance, which your family desperately needs, so you don't ask questions, even when the registration center staff takes your fingerprints and scans your face. But you feel uneasy: What data are they collecting? How are they using that information? Who has access? Is the government tracking every place you use your ID? Is it mandatory to connect your digital ID to your health records? Will having your ID on your phone amount to essentially handing over your unlocked phone to the police?[9]

Digital ID systems collect a frightening range of data, from basic personal information such as name, birthdate, and address, to more comprehensive biographic and relational data including education and occupational history, financial details, health conditions, and extended family contacts. Biometrics systems usually collect photographs, fingerprints, and iris scans, but may also record voice and walking stride patterns. By amassing all this data, digital IDs create representations of people, with alarming consequences. Each data point above refers to one aspect of a person, and the more data collected, the "clearer" the identity of that person becomes—or seems to become, as some data is subjective. Much of this data is sensitive, such as health conditions. And while you may be able to change your name or address, your biometric data is largely immutable.

The dangers of this massive data collection—which happens both at registration and throughout the use of your ID—are significant, especially because this data is typically shared among government agencies, companies contracted to administer ID systems, and potentially third parties.[10] Your data could be leaked or hacked, or the implementing government or institution can simply share your information with a range of other entities, without your knowledge or consent.[11]

By and large, governments and their private sector partners have not been transparent about how digital ID systems and processes work, where the data is stored, and who has access. For biometric data, these decisions could have irreversible consequences, especially in a pandemic and under growing authoritarianism.[12] When governments push digital IDs for the sake of national security, what they mean is increased surveillance, especially on those who are already most surveilled, such as people of color,[13] migrants,[14] and LGBTQI+ communities.[15] In Thailand, for example, focus group participants told The Engine Room that the government tracks the movements of Indigenous community leaders through digital IDs to monitor their participation in activism or other political activity.[16]

State surveillance is not the only concern. The private sector already extracts as much data from people as possible, and many of these same companies are governments' main partners in developing and maintaining digital ID systems. Companies and trade groups including JPMorgan Chase, Mastercard, and techUK actively court governments to convince them to build expansive digital ID systems—because data means money.

In 2018, Tunisian activists successfully lobbied legislators to add strong data protection amendments to a digital ID bill supported by a private contractor.[17] However, once the amendments were passed, the Ministry of the Interior withdrew the bill. Although activists were never able to uncover the name of the contractor in the public-private partnership, they were convinced the company pulled out of the contract because of the amendments, which would have prevented them from accessing troves of Tunisians' personal data. If there's no data to extract for profit, it seems there's no reason for the system.[18]

Who Holds the Power in IDs?

What would you do if your life depended on turning your biometric data over to authorities? If you had to trade data for food, shelter, or refuge? If the aid organization or host country you rely on shares your information with the groups at home that have threatened to detain or kill you? These are not hypotheticals. When biometric ID systems were introduced in Bangladeshi refugee camps in 2018, Rohingya communities feared the host government and the UNHCR would share their information with the very people who persecuted them in the first place, the Myanmar government.[19] This fear was realized when the UNHCR collected and shared the Rohingya data with Myanmar without their consent or knowledge.[20] Data collection and sharing, even by actors we consider "good," is far from neutral, and exacerbates existing threats or creates new dangers for people fleeing war, climate disasters, economic devastation, and other forms of violence.

In 2019, the World Food Programme (WFP) cut off food aid to Yemen for two months until the Houthi government agreed to implement WFP's biometric identity system for the over one million people who relied on this food aid to survive.[21] That same year WFP joined forces with data analytics company Palantir, known for its contracts with US intelligence and law enforcement agencies, including Immigration and Customs Enforcement, that enable mass surveillance, detention, and the deportation of immigrants.[22] In other words, an institution with a mission to feed refugees, migrants, and other displaced people uses that role to forcibly collect invasive biometric data, and the range of actors who have access to that data is unclear.

Data sharing between aid organizations and governments can create enormous risk. In humanitarian contexts, the issue of informed consent relating to the collection of sensitive data for digital IDs has become a crucial concern.[23] Refugees are fully reliant on host countries, multilateral institutions, and NGOs for their survival, a power imbalance that significantly undermines the integrity of informed consent processes. The Engine Room identified this problem repeatedly in our field research, where many refugees we interviewed did not feel able to assert their right to privacy or their right to know how their data is used.[24]

When such institutions hold biometric data on people who have already been targeted because of some fundamental aspect of their identity, that data is valuable to others. Forcibly displaced people have little choice but to trade their immutable identities for life-saving aid, even when they have been targeted, commodified, abused, or declared "dangerous" because of those very identities. We've gone from the era of Jim Crow to "the New

Jim Code," as biometric data collection ensures that oppressed people are counted, categorized, and contained.[25]

Consent also becomes meaningless outside of contexts of active conflict, as many institutions push societies toward a place where digital IDs become a requirement for accessing vital services, potentially violating the right to privacy and the many rights privacy enables. The use of digital IDs for "national security" and "public safety" can easily lead to violations of freedom of opinion and expression, freedom of assembly and association, and freedom of movement—and enable further state surveillance and violence.

Shifting ID Power Back to People

We must push back against the key drivers of digital ID systems: corporate interests, the profits of data extraction, and state investments in systems of control. The risks and the limitations of digital IDs clearly show they target—rather than serve—the people they are supposedly designed to support. This doesn't have to be the case. For digital IDs to be part of an effective solution to real societal problems, institutions must take a people-centered approach that addresses the diverse needs of the many communities to be served and upholds human and civil rights.

20

IDs and the Citizen:
Technologically Determined Identity in India

Usha Ramanathan

The idea of the citizen has been through many tellings in the history of independent India; and, each time, the circumstances and politics of the day have molded the meaning of citizenship. Alongside the changes in the meaning of citizenship, recent times have seen the strange story of biometrics unfold in ubiquitous and unforgiving ways. Untested when it was rolled out to the whole population in 2009, biometrics has not let failure be an impediment, leaving it to the individual to make the digital ID, embedded in biometrics, work successfully, or bear the consequences of its failing. A haze has settled over the relationship between citizenship and the biometric ID that has got denser as the years have slipped by. In the meantime, biometrics has wended its way into single-member households, persons above sixty or below fifteen years old, and those whose biometrics have "failed them" because they are bedridden or otherwise physically and visually challenged, and thus have had to appoint a "nominee" to lend their fingerprint—one person's fingerprint establishing another's identity.[1] This indeed is the story of the databasing of a whole population—which, in India, would mean over 1.3 billion people and counting.

Shrinking Citizenship

India became independent in 1947 and was immediately engulfed in a bloody partition that divided the country into India and Pakistan. It gave itself a Constitution in 1950, held the first elections in 1951–52, and passed the Citizenship Act in 1955, which recognized citizenship for all persons born in India. The "citizen" has been modified with each amendment made to the Citizenship Act. Two wars in 1965 and 1971, the latter culminating in the creation of Bangladesh, saw the movement of large numbers across the border into India, most of them seeking refuge from a vicious war. The border states, especially Assam, experienced a surge of people moving in and settling there. The growing numbers led to an agitation that expressed itself in the form of student protests,[2] which escalated into a political movement and culminated in a 1985 accord.[3] Reflecting the terms of the accord was an amendment to the citizenship law in 1986 acknowledging that the people of Assam are of "Indian origin." They were given deferred citizenship, with all rights recognized straightway except the right to vote, which was held back for ten years from the date their name was entered in the register.[4]

In 1987, the Citizenship Act was amended again, this time declaring that a person born in India would be a citizen only if, at the time of their birth, either of their parents was a citizen. This narrowed the claims to citizenship; but it was a 2003 amendment to this law that turned it upside down. If either parent of a person born in India was an "illegal migrant," the amendment said, there could be no stake in citizenship. By this time, political rhetoric had shifted away from the threat from across the border with Pakistan[5] to the "illegal" Bangladeshi migrant who, as it was understood, was taking away resources and jobs.[6] This amendment also stipulated that the government "may compulsorily register every citizen of India and issue a national identity card to him."[7]

The first comprehensive exercise to create a National Register of Citizens (NRC) was carried out in the state of Assam, spurred on by the Supreme Court.[8] It was a process that relied on documents and records, and notions of legacy and identity, which were elusive fragments—often fiction—and which saw 1.9 million people being declared stateless and illegal, to be sent into detention camps.[9]

One of India's largest technology corporations, Wipro, played a central role in the controversial NRC project in Assam. Initially, it advertised and celebrated its involvement in the NRC process on a page of its company website; then, when the process met with a barrage of criticism, it deleted the page. The page was later restored, but Wipro never explained why it had been deleted.[10]

Each of these changes to the citizenship law was of consequence to identity and belonging; but it was not till the law was amended, again, in 2019, that it became a matter of public dissent, debate, and protest. This amendment, enacted as the Citizenship (Amendment) Act, took away the tag of "illegal migrant" from "any person belonging to Hindu, Sikh, Buddhist, Jain, Parsi or Christian community from Afghanistan, Bangladesh or Pakistan who were also in the class of persons exempted from prosecution under immigration laws."[11] The significant omission was the Muslim, not so subtly implying that state repression in Muslim majority countries neighboring India is only of religious minorities, on the basis of their religious identities..

This was the unhidden politics of the right-wing party, the Bharatiya Janata Party (BJP), which had ridden to power on a Hindu majoritarian agenda in 2014, and returned to Parliament with a thumping majority in 2019. Soon after this electoral endorsement, the BJP government proceeded headlong into making, and enforcing, policy and laws that reconfigured both the people and the territory of India. So, for instance, on August 5, 2019, a few months after the BJP had returned to power, the special status recognized in the Constitution to the Muslim-majority state of Jammu and Kashmir was scrapped, and the state split into two "union territories," which would then fall under the control of the central government in New Delhi. The Citizenship Amendment Act was widely viewed as a declaration of who the BJP would accept as citizens, and who would stand excluded.

Countrywide protests met this amendment. Protesters were arrested, charged under an anti-terror law that sanctioned the holding of activists in prison for long periods.[12] Then COVID-19 struck, giving the state a ground to clear protest sites.[13] The disquiet hasn't ceased; it has merely been deferred.

These changing notions of citizenship were intricately linked with the unique ID project that made its entry in January 2009.

Toward a Knowable 360-Degree Citizen

In the fading years of the last century, India was engaged in an eyeball-to-eyeball confrontation with neighboring Pakistan, and the government of India set up a committee to report on the intelligence failures that had caught the country off guard. This is the committee that suggested that, to strengthen security, the government issue identity cards to people in border areas and along the coast.[14] TCS, another major Indian technology company, was tasked by the Ministry of Home Affairs to set out the contours of a citizen card project. TCS ingenuously gave it an acronym: NISHAN, meaning "mark." In 2002, TCS did a similar exercise for the state of Gujarat, drawing liberally on its earlier report.[15] This time, though, the purpose shifted—from security along the border to "simplify(ing) delivery of services."[16] The citizen card was designed to be mandatory and not optional, so as to allow only those registered access to various state services. Food distribution records, driver's licenses, banking and credit scores, health records, utility payments, criminal records, legal records were all to be linked to the citizen card.[17] This was an early description of the "360 degree" view of the citizen, built around a citizen card. In a few years, this morphed into the unique ID number (UID), but not before some twists and turns.

In 2006, Wipro put together a "strategic vision" for the unique identification of residents.[18] This time, the explanation proffered was the targeted delivery of welfare support to families living below the poverty line. The Committee of Secretaries that enlisted Wipro's aid saw determination of citizenship as "involved and complicated"[19] and decided that the UID[20] project—branded as Aadhaar—should start off as a "resident database" and then be extended to the National Population Register (NPR) once the nationwide census had been conducted in 2011.

The Unique Identification Authority of India (UIDAI) was established in January 2009 by executive notification—that is, it started without the backing of law.[21] The proposal for UIDAI included plans to generate and assign UIDs to residents, to identify "partner databases," and "to ensure collation of NPR with UID."[22]

In July 2009, Nandan Nilekani, a founder of the technology company Infosys, moved from the corporate world into government to take charge of the UID project.[23]

Untested Technology: Biometrics

Biometrics were introduced into the project at a time when no one knew if they could be successfully applied to 1.3 billion people and across time.[24]

A Biometrics Standards Committee set up by the UIDAI doubted that fingerprints would be able to achieve the accuracy needed for the project.[25] So, the UIDAI prevailed on the committee to add the human iris as an added biometric—untested, and its potential unknown.[26] The biometric database was never audited or, if it was, that information was not shared publicly. In the meantime, biometric failure is reported with striking regularity. In March 2012, a "fingerprint authentication" report of a study carried out by the UIDAI spoke to the uncertainties in the process.[27]

In 2015, the UIDAI website hosted a section titled "UBCC and Research." UBCC is an acronym for UIDAI Biometric Centre of Competence. "Nature and diversity of India's working population," it read, "adds another challenge to achieving uniqueness through biometric features."[28] Accordingly, its "mission" was "to innovate biometrics technology appropriate for Indian conditions." This was *five years* after biometric enrollment had begun. In 2017, the budget of the UIDAI revealed that no sums had been allocated to the UBCC, and a minister informed Parliament that the UBCC had never been set up.[29] And, on top of that, in 2017, when biometrics failed, a "nominee" could let their biometrics speak for the identity of another!

The Empowered Group of Ministers that "in principle" gave approval for setting up the UIDAI had directed that the NPR for the 2011 census be created through data collected on persons in the country, including their photographs and finger biometrics. The "NPR so created would be managed with the UID database."[30] These decisions were discarded by the UIDAI once it was set up. The Registrar General of India meekly became the UIDAI Registrar—that is, data gatherer.[31] The UIDAI, impatient to get everyone enrolled and create its own exclusive database, began to enroll people. This led to swift transitions in UIDAI's marketing messages for the program—from "Know Your Citizen," to "Know Your Resident" to "Know Your Customer" —revealing its all-too-plain profit motives.[32] Very soon into the project, the technology controllers had rolled out an ID that would serve the market, break down silos, and convert the digital footprints into data on which products, such as credit, could be built.[33]

There had to be a price, though. The state would seek its pound of flesh. It was claiming the personal information of its citizens as its property, mandating the linking of the UID number in ways, and places, that would let the state see without being seen. Mass surveillance was passed off as the "seamless delivery of (state) services."[34] The UID number was linked with police records, health services, fertilizer subsidies, bank accounts, driving licenses, mobile phones—and more. Soon, those controlling the technology were working from within the state—again—and pushing through the adoption of data stacks, such as the National Health Stack and the AgriStack, that would make people and their data accessible in many more fields.[35] This was a deliberate attempt to eliminate the right to privacy. It was the normalization of treating personal information as a "public good," and as a resource for private industry.[36]

A Case against Surveillance and for Privacy

The UID project was taken to court in 2012, and the verdict was delivered in September 2018.[37] The Supreme Court's majority did not strike down the project, or the law, but they did whittle down its scope. A significant dissent records the problems with the project including exclusion, erosion of the fundamental right to privacy, enhanced potential for surveillance through the breaking down of silos, failures of biometric technology, and the risk involved in companies with a relationship with the CIA and US Department of Homeland Security holding, managing, and using the biometric database.[38]

In the arguments before the court, the Attorney General asserted that privacy could not be a ground to challenge the project because privacy is not a right of the people.[39] That assertion, fortunately, was shot down in 2017.[40]

While the case was in the last stages of being heard in court, it acted as a restraint on the project. Since the judgment in the case, which was delivered in September 2018, the uses of the UID have exploded. There is still no law regarding data protection. An old colleague of Mr. Nilekani's from Infosys headed a committee on a "non-personal data framework," which seeks to free data, including personal information, from all restraint using the fig leaf of "anonymization."[41]

During this whole period there had been no audit of any part of the UID system—not until 2020, when the Comptroller and Auditor General (CAG), a constitutional office that audits how public moneys are spent, stepped up. The CAG found a flawed "de-duplication process" and a "database [that] continued to have faulty Aadhaars"; technology that was not updated; money wasted on enrolling children using biometrics when it was known that their biometrics could not properly identify them.[42] The CAG found a "huge volume of voluntary updates [on the UIDAI database] indicat[ing] that the quality of data captured to issue initial Aadhaar was not good enough to establish uniqueness of identity." UIDAI did not have a system to analyze the factors leading to authentication errors. It gave excuses for why it would not penalize deficient Biometric Service Providers despite the shortcomings in their services. Although it was mandatory that UID numbers and any connected data be stored on a separate "Aadhaar Data Vault" so the data would be secure, the UIDAI could not provide reasonable assurance that the entities involved adhered to the procedures. And so on it went.

In the meantime, more numbers are popping up everywhere: unique property identification numbers,[43] unique health IDs,[44] unique farmer's IDs.[45] These are set to join the over thirty pre-existing IDs on which the UIDAI based its own ID.[46]

The technological imagination that conjured up the UID project has little patience with people's rights. It refuses to confront the effect that this expansion of the power of the state has had on the people. It needs the state to extend its reach and seeks the coercive power of the state to get what it wants.

At the turn of the century, the internet, social media, and the mobile phone were exciting, and seemed to spell freedom. That has transmuted into anxiety and unfreedom through IDs, databases, the datafication of people, and the normalization of surveillance. Technology needs another imagination.

21

The Cost of Recognition by the State: ID Cards as Coercion—An Interview with Rodjé Malcolm and Matthew McNaughton

Matt Mahmoudi and Mizue Aizeki

Rodjé Malcolm is a human being consciously exploring ways of human "being." In the past he was executive director of Jamaicans for Justice—a human rights and social justice organization—where he provided leadership for varied programs to create a more just society. He often focuses on the ways we choose to "be" as an integral part of being human.

Matthew McNaughton is a digital development practitioner from Kingston, Jamaica. He currently holds the Edward S. Mason and the Ash Democracy Fellowships at the Harvard Kennedy School, where he is completing a master's in public administration. He cofounded the SlashRoots Foundation, a social impact organization utilizing digital practices to improve the design and delivery of public services and development programs in the Caribbean.

Mizue Aizeki: Could you tell us about SlashRoots and about the digital ID situation in Jamaica?

Matthew McNaughton: SlashRoots Foundation is a civic tech, nonprofit organization based in Kingston, Jamaica. We think about and focus on how to use digital technology to improve public service delivery, and on how digital technology can enable a more inclusive and equitable Caribbean society. SlashRoots often works in coalition with different organizations. For example, the National Identification System ("NIDS")[1] Focus Coalition was co-convened with Jamaicans for Justice (JFJ), a human rights and social justice organization that works at the intersection of legal response, research, policy, advocacy, education, and outreach to create a more just and equitable Jamaican society. The coalition comprised civil society organizations, individuals, think tanks, and other groups that came together to form a big tent of actors that contributed to an analysis of the discourse around the proposed national ID system.

Digital ID and identity were positioned as very much the foundational pieces of any kind of transition to a broader digital society. Yet, the first deep public discourse or public debate and legislative contests around the introduction of the ID system in Jamaica were not very constructive. It was fraught with a lot of misinformation, negative discussions, and lacked constructive deliberative engagement.

At that point, Rodjé and I had previously done some work together—convening around the data protection bill in Jamaica—and had built up trust and rapport. We sat down and identified overlaps between our two areas of interest in relation to digital rights. One was the second version of the proposed ID system, and we really wanted to engage in this process from a statutes perspective. We were interested in enabling a more constructive discourse and building towards a more citizen-centric and rights-respecting ID system.

Rodjé Malcolm: There have been two different versions of the digital ID system, and the thematic context that situates the engagement, whether in version one or two, is a fundamental question of recognition by the state. The implications of configuring the system of state recognition naturally raised questions of human rights, of data protection, and about the nature of our participation in society. The first broad context is how national IDs and digital ID systems can either create pathways or erect barriers for participation, and/or be a means of controlling how persons participate in society.

The second context is the question of digital IDs as a method of state recognition, and the associated tech platforms presenting mechanisms for undesirable forms of governance to manifest in ways that are unforeseen. We saw it relevant to enter this discussion seeing the examples across the world and the logical risks that would exist if there wasn't a rounded perspective in the formulation of the legal framework.

The third context, which is quite specific, is the nature of how Jamaica initially envisioned to configure its national digital ID system, which raised fundamental human rights concerns as it related to privacy, fundamental liberty, coercion, and access to services that—whether digital or not digital—required a human rights response.

In 2016, Jamaica established its modern national identification policy. It was not the first one, but the first that has been able to move forward. In 2017, the Jamaican government introduced legislation to establish a national identification registration system called NIDS. In that system, a mandatory provision was included for all biographic, biometric, and demographic information that you can conceive of, including your religion, race, occupation. There would be mandatory submission of national IDs for all public services, and a requirement that all public services must request national IDs. The legislation also included a range of other concerning things such as broad-based power for the prime minister to amend laws by order, if it made implementing a national ID system easier. For the first version of the ID system, there was no space for input—no public feedback, no citizen participation, and a largely accelerated legislative process.

Mahmoudi: What was the initial justification for the extensive data grab, whether biometric or biographical? How did the justification change?

Malcolm: Originally, the government wanted to obliterate the need for a census. They wanted to collect all biographic, biometric, and demographic information for national planning statistics, but the census is expensive—they won't say that now, but that's what they were saying originally. NIDS wasn't just mandatory for public services; it was a crime if you didn't enroll, punishable by $100,000, an extraordinarily coercive mechanism. What they also did, in a very early version that was later withdrawn, was create an affirmative obligation for you to update the system whenever there were any changes in any information, including a change in religion! That was crazy to me, but the rationale at the time was that this would provide ongoing information to the state about the population. This would ultimately put you in a perpetual census. Obviously, the dark side is that it is a subtle form of surveillance. And it is tangential to the purpose of identification, because it's exploiting the identification framework to do other types of social engineering for statistical purposes, broadly defined.

So national planning was one of their justifications. Data collection in Jamaica is fairly poor—this would be one way to do a lot in one system.

There was an attempt to jam a lot of different social, political, and governance interests into NIDS. This exacerbated and exposed a range of other risks and vulnerabilities, which eventually had to be abandoned—at least overtly abandoned—in the configuration of NIDS. It wasn't just taking fingerprints; they had the ability to mandate your retina scan, palm prints, footprints, vein patterns—they didn't always require it for everybody, but they maintained the *ability* to require it, just to give you a sense of the scope.

Another justification that was passively given was the ability to have fingerprints of the entire population in support of national security goals. The vanilla version was, "Oh, we can find missing people and identify bodies easily." Obviously, the less vanilla version, which is hidden in the shadows, is the ability to use someone's biometric and biographic details for any form of policing that was desired. You had to give your secondary addresses, even any aliases that you may have been called, mandatorily.

McNaughton: As Malcolm highlighted, in version one there were mandatory enrollment requirements. So, every Jamaican would be an affected party. In terms of who it might affect most, any individual who might have an aversion to participating in this broad scrape-up of information by the state was at risk. Not enrolling was a crime, and so the risk was quite broad. In terms of consultation, there was none initiated by the government in version one, and the only consultative process that took place was led by Malcolm and his organization, JFJ. The public's concerns about the bill became louder and louder, alongside a number of objections and a spreading of misinformation from multiple sources.

Malcolm: I just want to add two things. First, I would say there was no genuine consultation. The government would say that they consulted by presenting versions of the bill in a few closed meetings to people like the church groups and stakeholder groups, and this would have been before the bill was tabled. How I've referred to this is that there was no process for public participation in the legislative or consultative process because the consultation was purely with who the government chose to reach out to, which does not effectively align with the meaning of consultation. What it lacked was a participatory process, or an entry point into any type of consultation with the government.

Secondly, Matthew is 100 percent right when he says it affected all Jamaicans equally. Often, there's a framing of searching for some group by virtue of their identity or social status that's going to be excluded from services. In the Jamaican context, I haven't found that to be a relevant framing. There are certainly ways that it could differentially affect different groups, but it hasn't necessarily been affecting groups differentially based on the structure of the society. That's not to say that there is a differential impact based on how people interact with state recognition or interact with data collection. For example, the largest community that came out in version one that we worked with was the [people with] disabilities community, because the mechanism of enrollment was likely to differentially affect those with physical and intellectual disabilities. Therefore, we focused on the voices of those persons, and the government is actually most receptive to those groups, because it just didn't consider the potential unintended impact. I just want to nuance aspects of the framing that I often see in the global discourse that may not align us appropriately in framing the discussion about Jamaica.

Mahmoudi: Thank you for that nuance. It's incredibly important here that we take stock of the numerous impacts. Often in ID debates, there is the argument that certain groups need to be able to avoid the gaze of the state. In Denmark, where I was raised, it's people of color—because of discrimination, people go to the informal sector for work. So, there is a question around being able to avoid the state for survival. But you describe a system where people disadvantaged in their access to digital infrastructure would lose visibility by the state.

McNaughton: Yes, particularly when you get into version two, which was passed into law in December 2021, there are ways in which the proposed system will make certain markers that exist in our society either more visible—potentially facilitating the formalization of certain kinds of prejudice—or enable a kind of erasure, because the state does not recognize certain types of relations. But this is a different kind of exclusion from what you were talking about.

Concerns around the risk for systematic prejudicing do exist because of the information that is collected. When we talk about, for example, an address as one of the data points that will be collected and potentially be formalized, it lowers the friction of access to information about where someone lives. In version two, you are required to not only provide your primary address, but any other addresses that you frequent. In Jamaica, we have an issue where individual communities are prejudiced against, particularly within the frame of employment. Therefore, people are often cautious about being seen as from a particular community. Now NIDS obligates individuals, when they enroll in the system, to provide information about where they live, or risk receiving fines. The National Identification Registration Authority, charged with custody of the ID system, is required to formally verify this information before issuing the ID. But once that is complete, the address becomes linked to that individual and can subsequently be provided to other third parties through the NIDS system. As such, that data point against which bias exists within our society becomes more readily available and difficult to hide.

The other issue obviously relates to the issue of same-sex marriages, which Jamaica's constitution does not recognize. The NIDS also enables non-Jamaicans who are ordinarily residents to enroll. There are of course many other jurisdictions where people can engage and get married as a same-sex couple. As such, there is a conflict when you are both required to indicate your marital status and an ambiguity as to whether these individuals who are coming from jurisdictions where same-sex marriages are recognized are themselves being forced to indicate that they are, for example, single. So, there are other kinds of prejudices that emerge as a result of the design of the system.

Mahmoudi: Some of the questions that are incredibly potent are those challenging the dominant paradigm around how we talk about ID. I'm really interested in strategies that you have deployed to push back, and what the end goal really is for you?

Malcolm: Let's start with a question. What is life going to be like where the state uses the ID card—much like you saw with Aadhaar[2]—to coerce people into engaging into a relationship they don't want to have?

In version two, the scope of data collected is much narrower in response to the Supreme Court's decision on the privacy issue. And I want to emphasize the Supreme Court's relevance here, because the issues that the court ventilated, as raised by the claimants, were those that civil society raised during the legislative process. In version two, then, we get a voluntary system and much less data. There is no requirement for demographic information. There is a limited requirement; it's still extreme, but it's much less so, requiring only one biometric attribute—that being your fingerprint. The threshold of harm, between version one and two, is potentially reduced, but version two still presents a substantial risk of exclusion for those who are either privacy skeptics or by virtue of their various vulnerabilities—maybe they are from a certain community that is stigmatized; maybe they have reason to distrust the state. The major issue in Jamaica is really predatory policing and state abuse of poor people, and mostly poor Black people. There is therefore a real hesitation and skepticism in engaging with the state apparatus if you are likely to be "vulnerabilized'" by the state.

The question, therefore, that is presented is: "What's the cost of recognition by the state?" I want to be recognized by the state, which is a fundamental right that people should have if they're involved in the state. And the responsible configuration of a national ID system, digital or not, is to honor that fundamental relationship. Anything that obstructs that relationship has to be held to the highest scrutiny.

In version two, a major point for us was advocating for a reduction in the attributes that were mandatory for ready enrollment. And while enrollment was not mandatory, "the Authority" —the name of the body that is managing the ID system, short for "the National Identification Registration Authority"—has discretion over a broad collection of data points they can require an individual seeking to enroll to provide. In alignment with the principles of data minimization contained in our new Data Protection Act, we therefore advocated for the reduction in the attributes.

Shifting from the adoption to the operation question, what we have in our ID system are these auxiliary services attached to your enrollment that give rise to questions of human rights violations—questions of perfect privacy, surveillance, and even exclusion, based on status or identity. One simple one is "the Authority," which offers verification and authentication services. The bill leaves "verification services" undefined, but we understand them to be where you go to a third party to make a service transaction utilizing a verification service. It basically allows for the Authority to verify someone via a third party, should they want the Authority to verify them. I mean, this seems benign, but it is also really the bridge. It's a bridge technology and the bridge relationship between the person and the state that allows for the state to insert itself into private affairs by saying: "This person is verified; this person isn't verified." It doesn't have to happen, but that's the type of outcome that's possible.

The other is the Authentication Service, which is just basically using your card or your number to facilitate transactions of various kinds. This is the e-governance framework. These things create new things that we have to look at, and what the law requires in Jamaica is that data is generated at each point of verification or authentication, and that the Authority is legally required to maintain a record of every time a verification or authentication occurs. Although we asked several times for the data parameters to be specified and to be limited in law, what we were able to get was a regulatory instrument which will hopefully be coming in the first quarter of 2022. That's the next version of the work, which is mostly about the operations, not about the broad architecture.

But here's the risk: I use my card to go get a loan for a car. I want to upgrade my car, and I'm going to get a loan. I use my card to verify who I am. The financial institution runs a check on me. Because we're now going into e-governance and everybody wants to use their card, we are enabling the ability of the state to amass superrich data sets of where and how I am using my card—in other words, a rich data set on my pattern of life. This is a potential that never existed before. It exists principally because of how we have chosen to operationalize a digital ID system. Profiling, of course, creates algorithmic prejudice and various opportunities for exclusion. And there's so many more. But this was one really big operational component that's hidden behind the question of a just ID card or no ID card. It's really the "devil in the details" here.

Identification is the discursive center point: "We need to know who you are, it's a good thing for you to have an ID." But the system is designed to do way more than identify who you are. Rather than a simple process of, "Are you Rodjé or are you not Rodjé?" with the promise of making transactions easier, it creates an ongoing connection with the state at various service interactions, even if the state is irrelevant to that. What's presented to the potentially enrolled individual is: "Do I need to subscribe to this type of relationship, in order to be identified?" We will answer that question in the negative. But the configuration of the system requires that. So you create, again, a system where in order to be recognized, I must take on risks that are not inherent in my basic social contract with the state.

And that, I think, is a political question of this era when it comes to digital ID systems. I worry that this fundamental social contract question is not being contended with within the public narrative.

22

The UK's Production of Tech-Enabled Precarity: An Interview with Gracie Mae Bradley

Coline Schupfer

Gracie Mae Bradley was a founding member of the Against Borders for Children campaign, which in 2016 successfully stopped the collection of nationality and country-of-birth data through schools for immigration control purposes. From 2020 to 2021, she was interim director of the human rights organization Liberty. She is the author of Liberty's Care Don't Share *report on hostile environment data sharing and coauthor of the book* Against Borders: The Case for Abolition *(Verso, 2022).*

Coline Schupfer: Over a decade ago, the Conservative Party denounced the previous government's national identity project as a threat to civil liberties and pledged to scrap the proposed ID scheme to "reverse the rise of the surveillance state." What we see now, however, amidst a global health pandemic, are new plans of creating a digital ID. Can you describe the impacts of these new proposals?

Gracie Mae Bradley: Over the last couple of years the government has floated a lot of piecemeal proposals in the UK that include some element of identification, such as vaccine passports, voter ID, and a digital identity scheme, although they all claim to serve relatively different purposes. The proposed digital ID system—retailed to the press as something that carries numerous benefits, such as helping people register for the doctor or buy a pint at the pub—is still incredibly vague. But we know that the risk that comes with these piecemeal, overlapping proposals is that we end up with an ID system through the back door.

In theory, there is a very strong tradition against ID systems in the UK. When New Labour proposed a national ID scheme which would have entered everyone who applied for a British passport into a database, as well as the possibility of non-compulsory ID cards, a hard-fought battle by the NO2ID coalition and cross-party politicians meant that the coalition government scrapped all elements of the scheme (except for migrants, which is significant) in 2010. However, one of the key civil libertarian arguments mobilized in that battle was against the principle of "showing your papers" on demand in peacetime—this is often remembered as a fight against ID *cards*. What is forgotten and obscured goes beyond the problem with the principle of "papers, please." It's the problem of physical ID systems backed up by massive databases that all too often require biometric identifiers, centralizing state information on us, potentially allowing a much broader range of actors to a previously siloed data set, and mediating our access to essential goods and services.

I said that it was significant that New Labour's ID scheme was retained only for migrants. With the introduction of the hostile environment in the 2010s,[1] we've seen migrants' access to services used as a testing ground for exclusionary digital ID systems, initially through rudimentary data-sharing processes between government departments, and now what will effectively be a massive database for immigration enforcement purposes. The point I have long been making, however, is that such a system of entitlement checks will not be able to perform its desired exclusionary function unless it can check citizens and migrants. Landlord immigration checks, for example, affect me as a citizen, because I have to show ID, as do migrants. So as with so many threats to civil liberties, where we see measures justified on the grounds that they target a so-called unpopular group, we are seeing the implementation of an ID system that is affecting everyone.

Schupfer: How does this fit into the UK's broader digital strategies? And what are the risks here?

Bradley: There is an enormous risk—beyond the rights-infringing logic of the state in making migrants' access to essential goods and services increasingly conditional—that comes simply from poor data security and failure to uphold data protection rights. That might include personal information falling into the hands of a non-state actor, but it might also include data initially being collected consensually for one purpose, then being shared or used in nonconsensual, unrelated, or potentially harmful ways. We know that spies have used state surveillance architecture to find out more about their love interests. There was one very high-profile case of that happening with "test and trace" data too[2]—it subsequently emerged that the data wasn't even really being used for contact tracing. There is no guarantee that individuals with access to data sets like this will behave in an appropriate way, and given the government track record on data protection, there's a risk that people's private data will be leaked or stolen, leading to blackmail and fraud. The bigger the [data] stack, the bigger the honey pot.

Schupfer: Through the proposed system, individuals will be identifiable through a single identifier by the government and anyone else with access to the database. What rights are at stake here?

Bradley: A cornerstone of good digital security is not keeping all our eggs in one basket and using multiple identifiers. We use different credentials to access different services, so that if one is compromised, this doesn't affect everything. What a digital ID system risks doing is centralizing and attaching lots of different kinds of data, often collected for specific and limited purposes, to a single identifier, accessible by a range of actors. In some instances, this might happen in the case of an individual person that is of interest to the state, as was the case when the UK Home Office used the National Pupil Database—i.e., children's school records—for immigration enforcement purposes. But we should also look more broadly towards the growing use of profiling. As data sets get bigger, become interoperable, and include more and more intimate data, the possibility of attempting to infer things about people based on the perceived characteristics of others with similar profiles grows, and with it, the possibilities of stratifying and labeling people based on their profiles. Profiling can then be used to justify certain interventions you might make, what products you might sell to them, how risky they are to lend to, or how likely you think they are to violate their probation. State-backed ID systems and databases are in the current data ecology assets to be sold for enormous value to data brokers and entities that build profiling tools, and the state is also a market for those tools.

Schupfer: You have touched upon some of the risks, but there is also a lot of talk about how this new national ID system will increase GDP, prevent crimes such as fraud and human trafficking, and improve access to health care and other services, by making individuals easily identifiable. What's your prognosis on all these acclaimed benefits?

Bradley: A lot of the arguments presented are about convenience. When the government launched its digital identity proposal, there was a lot of fanfare about proof of age at pubs (of course!) and speeding up property checks for homebuyers. It was the same with vaccine passports: the government talked about pubs. It's about reducing friction and making it easier for people to purchase and consume, and for providers of goods and services to trust that the person they are dealing with is who they say they are. That is the business perspective. From the state's perspective, if you believe that certain people should be denied access to certain goods and services—for example, denying undocumented migrants access to the National Health Service—then a digital ID system makes it easier to ensure that access is denied and reserved only to those deemed deserving. This conditionality, of course, exerts control over the deserving and undeserving alike—in the case of the undeserving, it functions to exclude. In the case of the deserving, it produces subjects that need to retain that deserving status. Conditionality is never purely about access; it is also about control, and producing compliant subjects. These are technologies that on the current political terrain facilitate a logic of control.

Schupfer: You described digital ID as being about state control and movement control. What is the connection with the Home Office, and how is the government using digital ID data to implement the hostile environment?

Bradley: Mainstream discussions fail to consider who is likely to find it difficult to get ID. We know from research on the government's voter ID proposals that disabled people and low-paid workers are disproportionately likely to be excluded from voting by the proposals, for example.

More broadly, we need to talk about what identifying yourself in order to access what you need to live and flourish means in a society where rights are conditional on immigration status. Very often, borders are talked about as the edges of national territories. Yet contemporary bordering practices reach every aspect of daily life. The goal, as we have seen in the UK in the context of the hostile environment, is to deny "everything a person needs to live," as Theresa May herself described it. This means cutting off access to all essential goods and services and making it so difficult for people that they would rather leave than stay.

In order to do this, the Home Office has built a vast data-matching and -mining architecture that uses data from a whole host of other agencies, from the government's revenue and customs department, [known by the acronym] HMRC, to the Department of Education and the Department of Health, to landlords and employers, in order to check people's entitlements and exclude them from goods and services, and to get up-to-date contact information so that it can take enforcement action against them. All of the data-sharing agreements were concluded in secret, and the sharing happens without the consent or knowledge of the people whose data is being processed and, all too often, of those at the front line collecting it. In this context, you also have those with ID and those without, who could then be excluded from welfare schemes. So, you have teachers, doctors, and so on being made complicit in immigration enforcement without knowing, and you have important public policy objectives like children's education and the protection of public health being undermined, because people fear immigration enforcement if they interact with essential services.

Finally, it is worth mentioning that voluntary departures have not sky-rocketed with the onset of the hostile environment. These new technologies don't stop people from arriving or push them to leave. Instead, they dictate what kind of life people have when they stay in the UK. What we have seen is that there are more people living in fear of going to the police, and whose children are fearful of going to school. We see families without access to a safety net who do not come forward when they are unwell, who do not access homelessness services. People are being pushed further into the margins by cutting off regular avenues for support. And we are now seeing this logic of nonconsensual data sharing by public services applied to so-called "gang nominals" in the policing context; it has happened in the name of counterterror for a long time under the Prevent strategy, and we have also seen disabled-people who have protested having their benefits affected due to data sharing with the police.

Schupfer: You have underscored that these new technologies do not land in a neutral world, and that it is about differential access to rights. What is the impact on vulnerable populations?

Bradley: With a national digital ID system, what we would see is a singular identifier across a whole range of government services. Without firewalls, without people having been informed or having consented for their data to be used in a particular way, it will be much easier to mark them out for certain interventions. In the hostile environment data-sharing framework, what we see is an architecture of data sharing and matching that first sees the data collected by trusted essential services, then shared with the Home Office and used in immigration enforcement. In turn, the Home Office shares its list of people it believes are undocumented with other government departments and service providers, and then that person does not get access to banking or other essential services. It is quite rudimentary, but we can see that in effect this system—in conjunction with lack of controls, knowledge, transparency, or consent—essentially becomes a de facto immigration database, despite that not being the purpose for which health and education data is collected. When we ask ourselves what the risks are for vulnerable populations, we should consider that in the UK, in addition to the hostile environment for migrants, there are increasing trends towards pre-criminal intervention based on crude profiling and sharing, and using data to interfere with people's access to welfare.

Schupfer: Can you describe how digital ID works in conjunction with biometrics and facial recognition?

Bradley: Biometric surveillance magnifies the state's capacity to know where you are, what you are doing, and where you're going. Or make you worry that it can. Maybe you decide you don't want to go to that demonstration, or your sexuality is not known by your employer or your family so you decide not to see your partner, or maybe you're Muslim and you don't feel like you can continue to go to the same mosque without being profiled for different interventions. There is the issue of what the state knows about you, and what the state does with this information. For example, in one instance, the police shared data on attendees at a disability rights protest with the government. These people were then told that they do not need disability benefits since they are healthy enough to go and protest.

This all speaks to the macro effect of what it is like to live in a society where people are tracked and surveilled. "Nothing to hide, nothing to fear" is what we're often told. But who is and isn't suspect is not a fixed thing. You might think that you do not fall into one of these categories, but these categories shift. You are not seeking asylum now, but you might have to one day. This is not just about the state surveilling people. It's about the state interfering with your rights immediately. It's about figuring out as much as possible about people and treating people a particular way based on that assessment. It's about the state amassing enough data to build a profile and justify their treatment on that very basis.

Schupfer: Finally, to wrap up, I'd like to invite you to reflect on your biggest struggles as well as the biggest breakthroughs that you have experienced organizing against hostile government interventions. What have been some of your biggest takeaways?

Bradley: One of the most exciting collective endeavors that I've been part of was the Against Borders for Children campaign. In 2016, the government announced that the school census—data collection on pupils during each school term, with data sent to a central government department—would ask for nationality and country-of-birth data for the first time. In the context of a hostile environment, we, a scrappy collective of parents, teachers, activists, and artists, did not believe this data collection was in children's best interests. The announcement itself led to schools demanding to see children's passports, and only non-white pupils and children with "foreign"-sounding names being asked questions in front of their classmates. And we worried that the data would be used for purposes that had little to do with education, and everything to do with immigration control. To cut a very long story short, with virtually no funding but a lot of time, creativity, and a wide and deep coalition, we mobilized a boycott of the data collection. Over two hundred thousand children and parents actively refused to give nationality and country-of-birth data in solidarity with migrant children and families, and a soft boycott meant that no data was collected on a further two million pupils. During our campaign, which involved mobilizing unions, talks with the government, careful media work, guerrilla advertising on public transportation, and participatory art-making campaign actions to raise awareness of the right to opt out, it emerged that the government had intended for this data to be shared with the Home Office, and indeed, that a secret data-sharing agreement between the Home Office and the Department for Education existed. The government scrapped the data collection, but a system for sharing the addresses of undocumented families collected by schools continues, and we are still pressing the government to delete the nationality data that it did manage to get.

I suppose the key learning for me, at least, was to approach the issue from the ground of the world and the state as it is, not with some random view from nowhere but, as Mari Matsuda would tell us, from the perspective of oppressed people. Because we weren't institutionalized, we were nimble and we were bold. There were organizers of lots of different ages and life experience in our group, so we were able to share learnings and be pragmatic in avoiding past mistakes. We worked to uplift the voices of the migrant children who were targeted by these measures. And we didn't let this become reduced to a purely technical data rights issue, which is the kind of advocacy we often see from NGOs. It was about the right of every child to go to school and feel safe and inviting people to act together in upholding that. I learned a huge amount from that campaign and reflect on it still.

23

On Donkeys and Blockchains: A Conversation with Margie Cheesman

Matt Mahmoudi

Dr. Margie Cheesman is a Lecturer of Digital Economy in the Department of Digital Humanities at King's College London. Margie's ethnographic research engages with elite and marginalized stakeholders—from global migration governance institutions to asylum seekers and refugees. She has published key studies on experimental money and identity technologies, highlighting the justice concerns surrounding their adoption in humanitarian aid, welfare, and development projects.

Matt Mahmoudi: Let's talk about the digital elephant in the room first—blockchain. Or the idea that decentralization will solve our most pressing issues of the day. I make no secret of my general dismissal of it, not in small part as it's become a sort of a "catchall" solution to every problem that we could conceive of, related to trust.

Margie Cheesman: I think that the knee-jerk critical responses to blockchain are often well founded, because it has been the apotheosis of techno-solutionism. It's been, as you put it, a catchall solution to trust. Not just trust, but also the problematic centralization of computing and power that have come with the internet and the rise of Big Tech platforms in recent years.

It's also been seen as a solution to privacy invasions. Because blockchain is interconnected with cryptocurrency and with cryptographic techniques, it has been appealing as a method of performing anonymous transactions outside the clutches of states and banks.

But in my research, I found that the politics and implications of blockchain are incredibly complicated. It has so far revealed that, no, blockchain isn't a trust machine that removes the need for human intermediaries and institutions. No, it isn't always a force for a more equitable, decentralized politics. And no, it's probably not the global solution to privacy invasions, either.

At the same time, we need our knee-jerk critical responses to be backed up by detailed analysis. We're currently lacking ethnographic research on what actually happens when blockchains are implemented.

Mahmoudi: So, what is the value proposition of blockchain then? Where is decentralization seen to be helpful? We've obviously seen it hailed as the arbiter of equity, and at times framed as helping generate greater efficiencies in the distribution of resources in, e.g., refugee camps, where you did fieldwork such as in the Azraq and Za'atari camps of Jordan. Yet, time and time again, we see how spaces like camps are turned into test sites, labs funded by ambitious proposals that promise some sexy tech intervention but, in reality, cause tremendous harm. In Za'atari, we've seen some of the most notorious examples of ID experimentation—most egregiously, residents were subjected to iris scanners to pay for basic goods, as a means of countering alleged incidents of fraud. This, in turn, discourages newcomers from registering with, e.g., the UNHCR, in the first place, out of fear that the disproportionately invasive verification system is gathering biometric information that may end up in the hands of adversarial actors.

Cheesman: First of all, I really wanted to discuss with you a kind of thought experiment that I'm not sure has been done about the value proposition of decentralized infrastructure and its affinity with abolitionist thought. Potentially, decentralized infrastructures are—at their core—about a politics of redistributive justice. I've seen a number of activist blockchain projects which are about peer-to-peer exchange of money and resources—about meeting needs without the machinery of surveillance, capitalism, and financial institutions.

I mean, a lot of these decentralized projects use the rhetoric of privacy and surveillance resistance. And blockchain projects in general, like abolitionist projects, are all about seeking a kind of radical alternative to state-led governance and domination. So, whether it's communities of people, or communities of people and computers, I guess this is about looking at how decentralized *collectives* make community accountability and consensus mechanisms.

So . . . are there important and meaningful logics in this move towards decentralization? I think there are. And we've seen some interesting projects around cryptographically protected digital identities, such as the DE-CODE project in Barcelona, which people and collectives can use to own and manage their own data and how it flows between governments and the private sector.

However, as you alluded to before, these technologies are still—in practice—situated in structures of imperialism, securitization, capitalism, and techno-solutionism. The Za'atari situation, in other words, is hardly surprising—but it's not just in humanitarian contexts. We're seeing Meta's (formerly known as Facebook) blockchain-based global payment infrastructure "Diem" emerge. We've got the Indian government introducing a decentralized identity system to go along with Aadhaar. You know, this blockchain digital payment experiment I studied in my fieldwork in Jordan—it not only involves hundreds of thousands of Syrian refugees but is now also working on Rohingya refugees in Bangladesh.

Mahmoudi: And, we don't need to look very far in history to see calls for decentralization as, for example, a counter-narrative to the monopolization of communication infrastructure, in wake of Meta's global blackout. So basically, we're dealing with a solution that has logics that are potentially more emancipatory or at least more agentic, insofar that it affords a community some degree of autonomy that maybe other systems that are centralized don't.

But on the other hand, it's underpinned by racial capitalism, surveillance capitalism, heavy securitization as a result of post-9/11 measures, as you say. So where does that leave us, in terms of resisting modes of governance and modes of control that are centralized, knowing that decentralization offers one possible solution, but is inescapably bound up with logics and applications that still consolidate power among larger tech actors?

Cheesman: It's the rhetoric of decentralization in particular, and appeals to privacy, that are really powerful, but they're masking this underlying political economy. And these wider infrastructures that will not allow decentralized computing to be the solution.

And that leaves me feeling quite hopeless, because you know, it reveals that we need organizing; that we need actions that really dismantle the root issues. And that's one of the things that I was looking at in the Jordan research. The rhetoric really was around autonomy for refugees—in particular, empowerment of refugee women using blockchain-based digital wallets.

I examined how that rhetoric fitted in with refugee women's priorities and needs and how they saw, used, and experienced these new digital wallets. And I found that these new financial initiatives didn't only bolster existing infrastructures of securitization and control, but they are also, at their most crude, about controlling and monitoring ever further people's access to money, to spaces, and to resources—albeit using cryptography.

They also just didn't, in any way, address the actual concerns that people had living in those camps. In one of the conversations I had with someone who had a young family and a leg injury, she told me, "Look, I'd rather they provided us with donkeys than a digital wallet"—and this was because refugees in Azraq camp experience this incredible spatial oppression where there's no transport and infrastructure provided.

On top of that, there are labor regulations preventing more than one person per household from working at a time. So, these digital wallets were part of short-term initiatives that gave people paltry income for a matter of months, and then they were back without that digital wallet, and living in quite abject poverty in most cases.

These are incredibly carceral environments surrounded by military tanks. So, in all these ways, decentralized infrastructures can't do anything to dismantle or overcome root issues of domination and oppression of refugees, asylum seekers, people living in carceral conditions, and regimes of acute securitization and policing. We need to think about how we can address those structures. And, based on this evidence, blockchain isn't the answer.

Mahmoudi: In my reading, there's a tendency of treating folks who have citizenship status that is considered "lesser" than yours or mine, or whose immigration status is generally precarious, as a justification for investments in initiatives that can drive capital, and in particular venture capital (to fund tech projects) and political capital (to politically legitimize tech actors), towards tech companies and government authorities. The mere existence of refugees and undocumented immigrants—or Black and Brown people living in poverty—allows the state to say, "We're dealing with this urgent issue, by partnering with X tech initiative," while acquiring the means to accumulate ever-increasing amounts of invasive data; it allows the contracted tech initiative to say, "We're a serious actor with political backing, looking to disrupt poverty," which in turn drives larger tech giants and venture capitalists to invest in these nascent initiatives, allowing them to derive PR value from this act. The Microsofts, Metas, and Googles of the world swarm to proclaim that their next corporate social responsibility project is saving the lives of refugees and poor people. Yet, the same companies will turn around and contract with US Immigration and Customs Enforcement (ICE), the UK Home Office, or Frontex as guarantors of the hostile immigration environment.

This is why we cannot possibly talk about tech today, and in particular in the ID context, without also talking about racial capitalism; the economy that sustains these interventions is not fundamentally about demonstrating use by targeted communities—instead, it's about their mere existence as marginal subjects.

Cheesman: James Scott's framing of "legibility initiatives" that seek to render populations visible comes to mind. And, in particular, how this affects people with precarious forms of rights—migrant populations, especially.

I think an important issue here is the difference between formal identification and functional identification. A lot of these Big Tech initiatives and start-up projects are about using untested technologies in the so-called Global South, where they implement "functional" identity projects. And here "functional" refers to forms of identification that allow or grant people access to, usually, markets and sometimes basic services in refugee contexts. That might include, e.g., a UNHCR biometric ID that gives people political status as a refugee, and the functional ability to get bread or health care in a refugee camp.

This is very different from formal identification, such as citizenship, and the rights and protections that come with that. So, we're looking at a stratified system of belonging, of rights, and of justice. And these stratifications have shown, time and again, that they follow racialized, classist, and gendered lines.

What's clear about Big Tech, financial inclusion, and functional identity projects is that their motives aren't completely well-intentioned; they aren't simply about giving people access to the resources they need. They're about tracking people's transactional behaviors, sorting and classifying people on that basis, and using information to extract value and manage people's mobility.

Mahmoudi: What you're suggesting is also that we could imagine a stratified scenario in which there are citizens of nation-states, who can access and claim their rights through their social contract with their government, and then there are folks who, through, e.g., Meta's Diem currency, can access whatever menial Meta-approved services are available to them. This, to me, is what's at the core of a digitally reinforced global apartheid.

Cheesman: Yeah, I think we have to consider that as a possibility. And that's not to say that this potential vision isn't highly contested. Governments and regulators all over the world are increasingly critiquing and cracking down on decentralized cryptographic infrastructures that potentially circumvent formal financial institutions and formal identification.

A lot of decentralized projects are now also having to meet consumer rights regulations and so on. But we have to be concerned—we have to think forward and imagine all possible outcomes and scenarios.

And I think there are a number of really worrying possibilities here. Especially with regard to Meta's platform. Because under the banner of financial inclusion, Meta wants to expand markets and shine a light on people who aren't visible to Big Tech companies.

Mahmoudi: "Emerging markets" are, in other words, another way of referring to the possibility for new "real estate"; for new spaces and people to subject to the extractive forces of Big Tech, for the colonial capture of value. We are also, in tandem, learning about communities insisting on maintaining their invisibility from Big Tech companies, and often, by extension, the state. The line between the two is not always clear. In New York, many communities struggling against the aggressive deportation regime of ICE are anxious that some of the urban tech initiatives, owned by Big Tech companies, were relaying their digital information to immigration enforcement. Yet these urban tech initiatives provided free Wi-Fi, identification, affordable housing, etcetera. This is not a real choice; we're dealing with a trade-off between life and death either way.

Cheesman: Exactly, and I think that point is very important—that everyone has a right to invisibility and to be forgotten. But one of the ironies and paradoxes in the decentralized space, as I've suggested already, is that a lot of decentralized projects promote privacy and surveillance resistance.

There are cryptographic techniques like zero-knowledge proofs, which are ways of minimizing information shared with third parties, but in a way that still allows people to be authorized access to different kinds of services. But we're not seeing much evidence that those techniques are actually coming to fruition in a meaningful way that really transforms the lives of people whose mobility is controlled, who are surveilled, discriminated against, and policed.

Data minimization is another principle that a lot of critical academics, activists, and advocates are seeing as potentially enabling change, but even that is a struggle because of this hubris that institutions and companies have around data—that more data equals better aid, and also more money.

So, minimization is already quite a feat. Not collecting data . . . I mean, that would be great, wouldn't it?

As the aid industry has shown time and again, there's just reams and reams of information, a lot of which isn't used, a lot of which is duplicated. And part of the challenge in data infrastructure projects is cleaning all of that up. But that comes with some tricky implications as well, because once we have carefully ordered and synchronized data, then it's easier to enforce punitive measures and social sorting.

Mahmoudi: So, this is where we've landed, Margie: technologists can't just think about decentralized interventions in and of themselves. You have to think about these other structural dynamics that are playing out that also need to be tackled at the same time—securitization, the carceral state, racial capitalism. This is incredibly challenging in industries such as the humanitarian sector, where "neutral" technical fixes claim to "bypass" politics as technical fixes to complex forms of oppression. What else are we missing from the bigger picture?

Cheesman: I think that proponents of technological solutions to complex structural problems need to wake up to those political-economic structures, which is a really big task. But that's connected with the task of examining the needs and priorities of the actual people these projects are addressing—for example, if you're trying to include migrants, asylum seekers, and refugees in the financial system, or make invisible people visible.

Institutions and companies need to start thinking about whether that actually meshes with the needs and priorities of those people. And I don't think governments and Big Tech companies are doing that, because it doesn't fit their agendas.

Mahmoudi: That feels like a gargantuan ask for companies composed of technologists and engineers who probably didn't go into their spaces thinking they'd need to cultivate their inner activist, or obtain a sociology degree. They will undoubtedly be curious about the solution or world we imagine, sometimes from behind the ivory tower.

Cheesman: This is important. I came across that so much in my fieldwork as well. Academic work feels more slow-burning, and it blows loads of questions open. A lot of the time, the institutions you're working with don't want to hear that, and it is challenging to distill specific recommendations. I think we've got quite similar political positions on this one. We may work with them to record history and make the best possible difference, but it's difficult for our recommendations not to be "abolish technological experimentation," "just stop neoliberalism," and "end neocolonialism."

Mahmoudi: In other words, it's really difficult to speak of "recommendations" in abolitionist terms, because our recommendations fundamentally interrupt the status quo of the political economy around tech, how it derives value, how it reinforces borders. Because we can't recommend our way out of a system that needs to be fundamentally abandoned, rather than reformed.

24

CASE STUDY: How We Mobilized Civil Society to Fight Tunisia's Proposed Digital ID System

Al Bawsala and Access Now. Case study based on
conversations with Wafa Ben-Hassine

WHO WE ARE

Al Bawsala is an independent, Tunisian nongovernmental human rights organization. Access Now is a global organization that defends the digital rights of at-risk populations. On November 18, 2016, six associations led by Al Bawsala and Access Now called on the Tunisian government to reject the proposed biometric ID system.

KEY CONCEPTS

What is biometric ID?
Biometric technologies use physical and behavioral human characteristics, including body measurements, hand shape, and tone of voice, as a form of identification and access control. "Biometric identification" refers to the use of such technology and the practice of using biometrics to identify users/individuals.

What are concerns with chip technology?
Contactless chip technology is convenient, but it is not necessarily private. There are often concerns with regards to the weak surrounding privacy policy, the collection of large amounts of data, and the ability to track individuals through chip technology. Big Data collection, and ability to track individuals through chip technology. In our case, there were additional

concerns given the obscurity of the proposed project, the absence of free and informed user consent, and the lack of information about what data would be shared and collected, who would have access to it, and the intended (and unintended) uses of that data.

THE ISSUE

On August 5, 2016, Tunisia's Ministry of the Interior proposed a new draft law to the Assembly of the Representatives of the People, the legislative branch of government, to replace the existing identity card with a biometric identity document. The proposed biometric card would entail an electronic chip containing a person's identifying details—information already stored on the current national identity card—but would have cost the government $10.4 million at a time of severe economic difficulties. This new technology, it was said, would simplify administrative procedures, reduce risks of identity theft or document fraud, and provide greater security in the fight against terrorism. The proposed change was strongly criticized by civil society, particularly because in drafting the proposed law, the Ministry of the Interior had failed to consult the National Personal Data Protection Authority (known by the French acronym INPDP), which can issue an advisory opinion on any matter relating to personal data.[1]

The opacity surrounding the project raised particular concerns. The proposed system would collect personal information without disclosing where the data would be stored, how long it would be kept, or who would have access to it. There was no information about the company in charge of creating the biometric system, no provision for citizens to view or verify their personal data, and any person who attempted access illegally risked a five-year prison sentence.

Debates on the draft law were neglected, despite the high stakes and even though the proposed system directly violates the Tunisian constitution.[2] After the Council of Ministers' approval in August 2016, the bill was sent to the Committee on Rights and Freedoms and External Relations, and MPs were expected to examine the text and make necessary amendments. On July 7, 2017, the committee approved the draft text and forwarded the draft law for debate in a plenary session, scheduled for January 9, 2018.

ON CIVIL SOCIETY RESISTANCE

Several actors decided to use this time to define a strategy. Access Now and Al Bawsala began working on recommendations for the MPs on the Committee on Rights and Freedoms and External Relations. They studied each provision of the draft law and proposed necessary amendments. In early 2018, the committee, whose composition had changed in the interim, resumed discussions. This time, MPs appeared more sensitive to the risks posed by the draft law. Al Bawsala and Access Now representatives also maintained contact with different MPs on the committee, who kept them informed of scheduled meetings and the progress of the discussions, and with the president of the committee. This exchange allowed the activists to give their views on the biometric system and suggest recommendations directly.

On January 8, 2018, the "Consensus Commission," composed of influential members of the Assembly—a commission considered unconstitutional by legal scholars—met behind closed doors. The MPs considered the recommendations by civil society and discussed three proposed amendments. The first concerned the reading of the electronic chip, which should be read by contact and not remotely in order to protect chip data from being intercepted without the cardholder's knowledge or consent. A second amendment called for citizens to have access to their identity card's data, to allow them to understand what data is collected and kept and, where necessary, rectify any errors. The third amendment stipulated that the cardholder's photographs and fingerprints should be disposed of after the identity card has been issued.

Following those meetings, rumors began to circulate that the Ministry of the Interior was dissatisfied with the latest changes, which were more protective of personal data. The bill was scheduled for debate in plenary the following day. However, the morning of that discussion, it was announced that the Ministry of the Interior had withdrawn the draft law.

This marked a huge victory for civil society. Activists nonetheless remain cautious—the fact that the draft law had been withdrawn did not exclude the possibility of its reintroduction through other means or later forms, which could bypass parliamentary scrutiny.

Access Now and Al Bawsala were surprised that more civil society organizations did not voice concern with the digital identity card, especially when the country had just come out of a dictatorial regime that actively surveilled the communications of its people and profiled them. One question, however, still remains: Did the Ministry of the Interior already have a contract in place with a private company to establish, maintain, and furnish the required infrastructure to hold the personal data of millions of Tunisians?

REFLECTING ON THE PAST AND LOOKING FORWARD

According to Wafa Ben-Hassine, former global policy counsel at Access Now, if the team were to have done anything differently, it would have been submitting an official access to information request to the Ministry of the Interior. The request would have asked the ministry to clarify whether it was already engaged with a contracting company for the manufacturing of the chips, for instance. She shared some suggestions for others grappling with similar challenges:

- Organize with partner organizations even if their primary focus is not explicitly "digital." An issue like digital identity touches on many different aspects of a person's everyday life, from access to health care and welfare benefits to protecting the right to privacy.

- Reach out and "relativize" the issue with civil society as much as possible, so that a solid coalition can be built upon mutual interests.

- Build and maintain relationships with legislative actors and be familiar with their policy agendas. Digital technologies imbue every aspect of our lives, and important links can be established between digital rights advocacy objectives and an issue about which a legislator is already active, such as health care rights. This linkage goes a long way in working with legislative actors to challenge any proposed legislation that potentially infringes on people's rights.

25

CASE STUDY: Why We Must Fight for Alternatives to the UK's Digital-Only ID System

Maike Bohn, the3million

WHO WE ARE

the3million is the UK's largest EU citizens' rights group, formed after the 2016 EU referendum. We work to give a voice to EU citizens in the UK, to protect their rights, and to mobilize our communities. We do this by raising rights awareness, elevating grassroots voices, removing barriers to citizenship, and through specific actions and campaigns, such as #ProofEqualityNow and #DeniedMyBackup, that, among other things, call for a physical-document alternative for EU citizens required to provide proof of their immigration status. All our work is evidence-based, informed by lived experience reported to us, research, and collaborations with other organizations in the migration sector.

KEY CONCEPT

What is the UK'S EU settlement scheme?

The EU settlement scheme is an immigration status scheme put in place as part of the Brexit transition process that required citizens from the EU, Switzerland, Norway, Iceland, and Liechtenstein, along with their families, to apply for either settled or pre-settled status if they wanted to remain in the UK. The deadline for applications was June 30, 2021, and there are concerns that thousands of people living in the UK who missed the deadline have since lost their legal basis to remain in the UK. The latest quarterly

73

figures up to June 2022 showed that there were 267,350 late applications from people who should have applied before June 30, 2021, but did not. They did lose their lawful status—in principle, they should have regained lawful status once they put in an application and received a certificate of having done so, but those certificates are massively delayed, and employers, landlords, and other individuals often discriminate against people who don't have a determined legal status.

THE PROBLEM

In 2016, Britain narrowly voted to leave the EU. This decision meant that millions of EU citizens living in the UK had to apply for a new immigration status to continue living lawfully in the country. The logistics of this presented the UK with a huge challenge—unlike other European countries, it had never registered EU citizens before—and an opportunity, namely, to use this large cohort of people as guinea pigs for its planned move to a digital-only system for immigration status. Brexit opened the door to the digitization of millions of people's immigration status, part of an ongoing government-wide shift toward digitized immigration control by a government with a patchy track record when it comes to data management and data protection.

While the debate about the ethics and much-lauded "robustness" of digital status rages on, the UK experiment is played out amid the "hostile environment"—bureaucracy and legislation to make life so miserable for anyone without immigration status that they will "self-remove." For EU citizens living in the UK, this means that anyone not able to navigate the new, complex checking process via the Home Office website will face huge barriers to opportunity and healthy well-being. The status that EU citizens receive cannot truly be called digital—for example, in the form of some digital credential that belongs to them. Rather, they and the checking entity have to access government web portals each and every time a proof of rights is required, with each of these transactions logged and collected by the UK government. Since July 2021, EU citizens have been forced to depend on the digital-only system working twenty-four hours a day, every day, to prove their immigration status—when seeking a new job opportunity, finding a place to live, opening a bank account, getting treatment at a hospital, or returning home after a holiday abroad. To do this they also have had to be digitally literate, and have depended on access to an email account or telephone number connected to their status, broadband with no system outages, and others' willingness to engage with this system.

TACTICS AND SOLUTIONS

The UK government has ignored warnings from civil society organizations, including the3million, that this abrupt move to a digital-only immigration system is failing people and depriving them of autonomy over their status. In September 2020, when debating the new immigration bill, the UK Government refused to listen to the concerns of the3million and other NGOs who—campaigning under the hashtag #DeniedMyBackup—warned it of risks of discrimination if it didn't issue a physical document. The government chose to ignore all concerns and pushed ahead. The Immigration and Social Security Coordination Act 2020 passed without granting EU citizens a right to physical proof of their pre-settled or settled status, making them rely on a purely digital access portal instead.

The UK government is not only ignoring the fact that around 22 percent of people do not have the essential digital skills required for dealing with this process; it is also ignoring its own assessment that digital-only would cause serious issues for many and that a physical backup should be retained for now: "There is a clearly identified user need for the physical card at present, and without strong evidence that this need can be mitigated for vulnerable, low-digital skill users, it should be retained."[1] The3million has written repeatedly to the UK government, setting out legal and practical arguments as to why it is important that it give EU citizens the option of a physical proof of their status. This included a proposal for a cost-effective use of secure QR code technology. We are concerned that the government continues to place blind faith in its digital systems. System failures happen every day—the UK's COVID Test and Trace system, and technical glitches with the EU settled status scheme, to name but a few. In each case, those responsible had claimed that the system was robust and resilient.

The new digital system sits uneasily within a government department that lacks respect for individual rights and has shown an inability to learn from and assess feedback based on users' experience. To protect those who are most vulnerable, the3million filed a claim at the High Court on February 18, 2021, to challenge the policy on the basis that it discriminates against some of the most vulnerable members of our society, who are unable to access and prove their status using the online system. The case was ruled premature by the High Court, with the government stating that mitigating support processes would be put in place, in the form of a dedicated helpline. This helpline has proven to be highly problematic—overly complex and at times not accessible.

EU citizens in the UK are currently facing a perfect storm. They have to hand their personal data to the Home Office and its contractors to be able to stay in the UK, and at the same time, that same error-prone Home Office has been given unprecedented powers to restrict their data rights. They had their existing rights to live and work in the UK removed when Britain left the EU, they have to apply for and maintain a new immigration status, and, often for the first time, engage with the immigration control system in the UK. Their status can be refused or revoked in an instant as it is digital-only, and they have no control over how much of their data is shared between institutions via the Home Office.

LOOKING FORWARD

With tracking, targeting, and surveillance techniques becoming more sophisticated, we also need to develop better privacy protections for our data and to ensure that technological solutions do not become tools of exclusion through the back door. People need ownership of their status. In the largest survey to date of EU citizens' experience of the EU settlement scheme, the vast majority (89 percent) expressed unhappiness about the lack of physical proof of their status.[2]

We cannot allow these technological "solutions" to create even more divisions within our society by creating barriers to the right to work, the right to rent, and access to health care. EU citizens will have no choice but to have their every interaction with society logged into a database, and they will have no control over how much of their data is shared between institutions via the Home Office. In fact, they will struggle to access their data even if they request it. In a digitized immigration system, where decision-making is done through cross-checking of databases and algorithms, democratizing database management is arguably the most important issue of the twenty-first century.

Part 4

BORDERING EVERYDAY CITIES

26

Apartheid Tech: The Use and Expansion of Biometric Identification and Surveillance Technologies in the Occupied West Bank

Marwa Fatafta

> *Write down!*
> *I am an Arab*
> *My identity card number is 50,000*
> *I have eight children*
> *The ninth will come after a summer*
> *Will you be angry?*
>
> —Mahmoud Darwish, "ID Card"

On September 3, 2021, around 8 o'clock in the evening, eight Israeli soldiers entered the home of a Palestinian family in the occupied city of Hebron. They pulled thirteen small children out of bed and grouped them outside on the balcony, then an armed soldier came forward and—in a surreal move—he asked the trembling and half-asleep children to smile and "say cheese" before he snapped a photo of them with his smartphone.

In the disturbing video released by the Israeli human rights organization B'Tselem, one Palestinian mother is heard saying, "It's normal, it's normal," in an attempt to calm the terrified children.[1] While nothing is normal about this scene, the intrusion of Palestinian homes and privacy has become so habitual that Israeli soldiers were reported to compete in capturing the most photographs of Palestinian men, women, and children for prizes such as a night off from work duty.[2]

The photos, coercively captured, are fed into an extensive biometric surveillance database dubbed the "Facebook of Palestinians," which, in turn, powers a dystopian biometric surveillance project in the West Bank named "Blue Wolf."[3] The facial recognition system allows the Israeli army to identify Palestinians on a smartphone application by matching an individual's detected face to the database. Upon identification, the app flashes in traffic-light colors to alert soldiers if a Palestinian should be detained, arrested, or left alone.

This secretive system was uncovered by a *Washington Post* journalist, who also revealed the existence of a separate and much larger database called "Wolf Pack."[4] It contains the profiles of virtually every Palestinian in the West Bank, their photographs, family histories, education, and a security rating for each person.

Identification, as such, has been a vital instrument to aid and maintain Israel's settler colonialism and the surveillance and control of the Palestinian population living under military occupation. The deployment of a web of facial recognition cameras at military checkpoints, stretching across Palestinian cities in the West Bank and in East Jerusalem, has not only helped Israel expand this capability, but also automate the enforcement of an apartheid system in which territorial and temporal movement and access is thoroughly and fully controlled.

"Ruling by Records": A Short History of Identification and Colonialism

New technologies such as facial recognition systems are an extension of an old practice. Intelligence gathering and social sorting, through ID systems and population censuses, were an important cornerstone for colonial rule, or "ruling by records," as coined by Richard Saumarez Smith.[5] The British Mandate, for instance, introduced ID cards in Palestine during the Arab Revolt from 1936 to 1939 as "part of [the British] campaign to stave off Palestinian opposition to colonial rule and illegal Zionist immigration."[6]

Before the establishment of Israel, the Zionist movement inherited from the British Mandate of Palestine a treasury of records that mapped, in great detail, different aspects of Palestinian life including population registries, censuses, land registers, survey maps, tax lists, cadastral maps (those showing boundaries and ownership of land parcels), village statistics, and handbooks.[7]

Zionist researchers also collected their own data about Palestinians and their land from 1920 to 1948, of which the most famous and meticulous endeavor was "Operation Arab Village" conducted by the Shai, the intelligence service of the underground Zionist militia Haganah. It not only included data on Palestinian land, population, fauna and flora, weaponry, religion, businesses (such as cafés),[8] but also their wealth, family and marital affairs, and other everyday details. In two years, from 1945 to 1947, over six hundred Palestinian villages were surveyed and classified in a card-index system. This data-gathering and classification project, known as the "Village Files," was invaluable in the ethnic cleansing of Palestinian villages and towns in 1948, and marks the inception of surveillance and intelligence activity for military ends—the hallmark of Israel's surveillance-military regime.[9]

Israel is a surveillance state par excellence. It has established itself as a global leader in the sale and deployment of surveillance expertise and technologies, counting for the highest number of surveillance firms per capita in the world.[10] Its superiority stems not only from a tightly knit military-industrial complex but also from a history in which Israel, as a state, was born out of and into a surveillance regime.

In 1949, Israel introduced mandatory identification cards (hawiyya), which continue to be used today to control Palestinian land and movement, and, by extension, enforce a system of apartheid. The ID system is numerically coded and curated according to colors that denote the restrictions and limitations to which certain Palestinian communities are tied. "Blue" for Palestinian residents and citizens of Israel, and "green" for those living in the West Bank and Gaza. The color-coded tyranny of Israel's ID system makes for a highly elaborate and bureaucratic mechanism that creates and manages different realities for different populations.

It took decades for leading human rights organizations to acknowledge these different realities under Israel's rule as a system of apartheid, institutionalized racism, and systemized oppression.[11] Between the Mediterranean Sea and the Jordan River, Jewish Israelis are, according to a Human Rights Watch report, granted "a superior status under the law as compared to Palestinians living in the same territory when it comes to civil rights, access to land, and freedom to move, build, and confer residency rights to close relatives."

Facial Recognition: Automating Apartheid and Population Control

The objectives of Israel's surveillance, as a settler-colonial regime, revolve around the ability to control two key features of Palestinian life: land and people. As Helga Tawil-Souri explains in the case of surveillance of Palestinians in the city of Jerusalem:

> Territorial expansion cannot happen without surveillance: a regime needs to know how and which territory needs to be demarcated, fixed, protected, and enlarged; it needs to ascertain its safety in ruling that territory, thus requiring clear definitions of territories, borders, and populations. Land surveys and mapping, land laws and regulations, residency permits and citizenship, infrastructure building, among others, have been imperative for Israel's presence in and expansion around Jerusalem.[12]

Since Israel's annexation of the remainder of Palestine in 1967, constituting what is known today as the occupied territories, it has relied on low- and hi-tech surveillance technologies to control and subjugate over 4.5 million Palestinians, relying on a web of informants, biometric data collection, population registries, CCTV cameras, wiretapping, communications interception, watchtowers, military checkpoints, and now drones, spyware, predictive policing tools, and facial recognition cameras.

There are 705 permanent roadblocks installed by the Israeli occupation forces across the occupied West Bank whose purpose is to restrict and control Palestinian movement, 104 of which are permanent military checkpoints.[13] Tens of thousands of Palestinians have to cross these checkpoints on their way to work or school, or to get in and out of their towns and villages. Presenting an ID at checkpoints is mandatory, because it enables soldiers to verify whether a Palestinian has the necessary permission to move around, thus enforcing rules of segregation and apartheid.

In 2019, Israel upgraded twenty-seven military checkpoints with facial recognition technology to verify Palestinians' identities as they cross into Israel;[14] the technology was developed by Israeli company AnyVision, which describes itself as "world's leading developer of facial, body and object recognition platforms." According to a statement from the Israeli army, "the [new] inspection procedure at the crossings has become more efficient and significantly faster." Demonstrating the evolution of military checkpoints—from cement "flying" roadblocks, ad hoc checkpoints that are randomly installed then removed by the Israelis, to permanent infrastructures—during the years of the Second Intifada, the upgrade to biometric checkpoints not only further institutionalized these apartheid structures but made them "more efficient" and automated.

Jerusalem is another example. In 2000, the Israeli authorities introduced the project "Mabat 2000," composed of 320–400 CCTV cameras "capable of maneuvering 360 degrees to follow and track movements."[15] This network has been expanded over the years and upgraded to include facial-recognition and predictive-policing capabilities. According to the Palestinian digital rights organization 7amleh, over two hundred Palestinians on both sides of the Green Line—both within the occupied territories and Israel—have been preemptively arrested using data analysis technology. In 2017 and 2018, similar cameras were introduced in other Palestinian neighborhoods in East Jerusalem, including Sheikh Jarrah, Wadi el-Joz, and Silwan. Some of these cameras are pointing directly into people's homes.

In the occupied West Bank city of Hebron, which disturbingly embodies Israel's apartheid and segregation policies and has become a surveillance experimentation lab, the Israeli military installed face-scanning cameras to "help soldiers at checkpoints identify Palestinians even before they present their ID cards." A network of CCTV cameras, under the project banner of "Hebron Smart City," provides real-time monitoring of the city's population and, as one former soldier said, can sometimes see into private homes.[16]

In addition, the Israeli authorities have installed at the military checkpoint of Shuhada Street, in the heart of the Old City, a new remote controlled weapons system that uses image processing to identify and lock in on moving or static targets to fire stun grenades, tear gas, and sponge-tipped bullets at Palestinian protesters. The Israeli military spokesperson stated that the system is at its pilot stage and it will only fire sponge-tipped bullets.[17]

The Israeli company that has developed this technology, Smart Shooter, prides itself in the use of AI technologies and computer vision with the aim to revolutionize modern weaponry, and its vision is to sell its systems to all armies of the world.[18] In 2021, Smart Shooter developed a system for the

US Defense Department's Irregular Warfare Technical Support Directorate, which will be tested before implementation.[19]

The militarization of law enforcement surveillance operations have expanded in the aftermath of 9/11 and global counterterrorism wars. In this context, Israel has become a role model in exhibiting "homeland security" and "counterterrorism," as well as promoting itself as a successful example in these security approaches, not only through selling surveillance technologies, military-grade spyware, and high-tech weapons but also through holding seminars as well as exchange and training programs in Israel for law enforcement officers.

In the wake of the Black Lives Matter movement in the US, the debate on the militarization of US police and law enforcement scrutinized the nature of US-Israel military exchanges and training programs. Over the decades, a few thousand US law enforcement officers, including from Immigration and Customs Enforcement, Customs and Border Protection, the US Marshals Service, and city and state police departments and security agencies, have gone on military training trips to Israel in order to "study first hand Israel's tactics and strategies to combat terrorism."[20] These trips included visits to Israeli prisons, including the notorious Gilboa Prison, as well as the occupied Palestinian territories and the Golan Heights. Several media interviews with US officials who participated in those trips describe how they were "impressed" by Israel's invasive surveillance operations, including the use of predictive policing tools.[21] Some of the surveillance tactics have been copied in the US. For instance, an invasive Video Integration Center established by the Atlanta police department, whose police chief participated in a military training trip in 2008, was modeled after Israel police's surveillance system in the Old City of Jerusalem.[22] Similarly, the NYPD's notorious infiltration operation of Muslim American communities in the aftermath of 9/11 was based on the Israeli intelligence operations in the West Bank.[23]

As in the story of the Palestinian children forced to smile before an Israeli soldier for a coerced photo, there are harrowing testimonies on how surveillance has impacted Palestinians' public and private lives. Through a regime where no legal protection and safeguards exist for Palestinians, and where Israel rules by military orders and defies its responsibility to adhere to the International Covenant on Civil and Political Rights, intelligence on Palestinians and their private data, collected through coercive means by the

Israeli army, are offered to the private sector, enabling security firms to run, test, and enhance experimental prototypes for military ends.[24] The impact of biometric surveillance on Palestinian communities is particularly severe. When the conviction rate for Palestinians tried in Israeli military courts is 99.7 percent, it makes the consequences of a potential error in identification or authentication especially merciless.[25] Bias, discrimination, and the inability to course-correct for false detentions are not only feared risks associated with the use of these technologies; they are baked into a system whose very design aims to produce and sustain such results.

The Israeli military occupation and apartheid regime has created a dystopian surveillance lab in the occupied territories, where it continues to deploy, prototype, and enhance abusive and invasive biometric surveillance technologies that are tested and experimented directly on Palestinian individuals and communities, in violation of fundamental human rights and bodily security, agency, and dignity. Whereas the deployment and use of biometric surveillance technologies in public spaces is becoming increasingly scrutinized, and even banned in some cities, the Israeli surveillance tech industry and arms supply chains are flourishing under the premise of fighting terrorism and criminal activities.

27

The Encroachment of Smart Cities

Ben Green

I n October 2017, Eric Schmidt shared a vision that had animated Google's executives and founders for years:[1] "We started talking about all of these things that we could do if someone would just give us a city and put us in charge."[2] While the idea of putting a technology company in charge of a city might sound like a dangerous fantasy, it appeared as an exciting prospect to many technologists and policymakers.

Schmidt made this statement at a celebratory press conference in Toronto announcing that a version of this vision was coming true.[3] Toronto would be partnering with Google-affiliated company Sidewalk Labs to develop a portion of the Toronto waterfront. Canadian prime minister Justin Trudeau, another speaker at this press conference, shared Schmidt's zeal. He declared, "Sidewalk Labs will create [. . .] technologies that will help us build smarter, greener, more inclusive cities, which we hope to see scaled across Toronto's eastern waterfront and eventually in other parts of Canada and around the world."[4]

The partnership between Toronto and Sidewalk Labs represents just one notable instance of a recent trend in urban governance: "smart cities."[5] As proponents of smart cities describe, new digital technologies enable tremendous and revolutionary breakthroughs. Everyday objects will be embedded with sensors that monitor the world around them. Machine learning algorithms will use this data to predict events before they occur and optimize municipal services. Through apps, algorithms, and artificial intelligence, new technology will relieve congestion, restore democracy, prevent crime, and create free public services. Following this vision, governments and technology companies around the world have pursued smart cities as a novel approach to innovative and progressive urbanism.

Despite the optimistic rhetoric surrounding them, the promises of smart cities are illusory and come with significant dangers—particularly for people of color, immigrants, the poor, and other marginalized groups. Reconstructing urban life and municipal governance in pursuit of smart cities will lead to cities that are superficially "smart"—that is, full of technology—but under the surface are rife with injustice and inequity.

Smart cities reflect a new spin on neoliberal logics that have eviscerated cities for decades: prioritizing economic efficiency, placing the onus of citizenship on individuals, outsourcing public functions to private companies, and relying on law enforcement to address social disorder.[6] These dynamics are exacerbated by the austerity and resource scarcity that have plagued cities in particularly acute form since the 2007–2008 global financial crisis.

Thus, to the extent that the smart city revolutionizes urban life, it will be by transforming urban politics and power rather than by creating a technological utopia. Businesses stand to gain even greater control and political influence over urban life, while those on the margins face new forms of intrusive surveillance and policing.

There are, of course, real problems that cities face, and technology can play a role in alleviating some of them. But smart cities are not the answer. Smart city boosters suggest that new technologies will present objective, technical solutions to social issues. This facade of neutral answers obscures the social and political impacts of smart city technology. Furthermore, this approach stifles the consideration of alternative and more radical strategies for addressing social issues. By blocking off legitimate political debate in the name of technological progress, presumptions of neutrality bolster the status quo and obstruct more systemic reforms.

The intersections of surveillance, privatization, and policing are particularly salient forms of violence enacted through smart city initiatives.

Expanding Surveillance

Smart cities involve pervasive data collection, making it increasingly impossible to avoid being tracked. Sensors monitor the behavior of anyone with a Bluetooth- or Wi-Fi-connected device. And given the expansive reach of cameras and the use of facial recognition software, it is difficult to escape surveillance even by abandoning one's digital technology. The only way to avoid being tracked in a smart city is to stay out of the city altogether.

The smart city is a dream come true for companies eager to increase the scale and scope of data they collect about the public. Companies that place cameras and sensors on Wi-Fi kiosks, trash cans, and streetlights will gain previously unattainable insights into the behavior of individuals. And given the vast reach of hard-to-trace data brokers that gather and share data without the public's knowledge or consent, one company's data can end up in another's hands.[7] All of this data can be used to exclude people from credit, jobs, housing, and health care in ways that circumvent antidiscrimination laws.[8]

Private Control of Public Decision-Making and Resources

Many smart city initiatives rely on public-private partnerships and technology developed and controlled by tech companies. As a result, smart city projects shift control over municipal infrastructure and public resources from the public to for-profit technology companies.[9]

Major technology companies such as IBM and Cisco achieved these gains by "selling smartness," disseminating narratives about urban challenges and technological solutions to those challenges.[10] These companies see the potential for massive profits: one report estimated that the global smart cities market would be worth $237.6 billion by 2025.[11]

The partnership between Sidewalk Labs and Toronto presents a notable example of corporate ambitions to mine cities for profit. Sidewalk Labs aspired to even greater control of public resources than the already significant amount that Toronto had granted them. In February 2019, local journalists reported that Sidewalk Labs had expressed a desire to receive a portion of the property taxes and development fees associated with the project—estimated at $30 billion over thirty years—which would otherwise go to the City of Toronto.[12] Later that year, Sidewalk Labs shared its intentions to develop and manage a far larger plot of land than the twelve acres that Toronto had allotted it.[13]

The Links between Corporate Technology and Law Enforcement

The combination of expanded surveillance and public-private partnerships takes a particularly pernicious form in expanding the reach of law enforcement surveillance. Police can gain access to widespread surveillance by acquiring technology from companies, partnering with companies, and requesting access to data and video footage held by companies. Data collected through smart city efforts can also be fed into algorithmic systems to aid policing and immigration control.

Smart cities enable governments to enhance their surveillance capabilities in significant yet discreet ways. For instance, police in suburban Portland, Oregon, hoping to aid criminal investigations, have used Amazon's facial recognition software to identify more than one thousand people who have appeared in camera footage.[14] Often these expansions in surveillance arrive under the premise of more benign applications. In 2016, San Diego invested millions of dollars into "smart streetlights" developed by a General Electric subsidiary, hoping to study traffic and parking conditions. Although the data proved of little use in improving traffic, the video footage turned into a tool for police surveillance, including during Black Lives Matter protests in 2020.[15]

Partnerships between technology companies and law enforcement also play out over international lines. The multinational Chinese tech company Huawei created a $1.5 billion project to create smart cities in Africa.[16] In one project that was part of its "Safe City" program, Huawei installed 1,800 cameras, two hundred traffic surveillance systems, and a national police command center in Nairobi.[17] Some African governments have used Huawei's Safe City technology to spy on political opponents.[18]

By partnering with technology companies through behind-the-scenes partnerships and data-sharing arrangements, law enforcement can expand its surveillance without public knowledge or oversight. Documents obtained via public records requests showed that three hundred police departments in California have access, through Palantir, to data collected and stored by a Department of Homeland Security (DHS) data fusion center, without any requirement to disclose their access to this information.[19] In Los Angeles, automatic license plate readers recorded the location of more than 230 million vehicles in 2016 and 2017.[20] Through data-sharing agreements, this information can find its way into the hands of Immigration and

Customs Enforcement. Indeed, in 2020, several California municipalities broke their promises not to share any of their license plate reader data with ICE.[21] The secretive company Clearview licensed its facial recognition software to more than six hundred law enforcement agencies in 2019, including the FBI and DHS.[22] Similarly, police in New Orleans used predictive policing algorithms for several years without having gone through any public procurement process. Even members of the City Council were left in the dark.[23]

Fighting Back

Despite these trends and dangers, the harms of smart cities are not inevitable. Organized resistance can combat invasive and exploitative smart cities. Across the United States, communities have pushed for legislation that bans facial recognition and limits other forms of surveillance technology.[24] In Toronto, organizers challenged the Sidewalk Toronto initiative, building public resistance and prompting Sidewalk Labs to abandon the project.[25] Protests in Los Angeles helped push the Los Angeles Police Department to halt its use of predictive policing software.[26] These and other collective wins against smart cities provide the starting points for a playbook on resisting violent urban tech and creating room for alternative technological futures.

By exposing the injustices of smart cities, organizing and advocacy can subvert the path to political and economic capital for politicians and technology companies. Smart city proponents will surely adapt in response to these protests, however, prompting the need for a nimble resistance to smart city initiatives. COVID-19-induced recessions may herald a new era of municipal budget cuts, spurring a renewed demand for technological enhancements that stretch limited budgets. Resistance to large-scale projects such as Sidewalk Toronto may prompt governments and companies to move toward more understated business models such as providing software for investors, developers, and governments without the overt smart city branding.[27]

Ensuring a meaningful "right to the city"[28] in the coming decades requires shifting from a model of "smart cities" to "smart enough cities," rejecting visions of technologically optimized cities and attaining public control over technology.[29] Such power will not be handed over.

Efforts to resist smart cities must therefore neither start nor end with efforts to resist technology. Instead, rejecting smart cities requires rejecting the politics of carcerality, inequality, and austerity that produce smart cities. Remaking smart cities is a project of remaking cities themselves.

28

Control-X: Communication, Control, and Exclusion

Brian Jordan Jefferson

The silent and steadily expanding surveillance of communications networks across the United States has caught widespread attention in recent years. Many critics have pointed out that while access to information and communications systems is a prerequisite for participating in the global economy, it comes at the cost of privacy.[1] Common to these criticisms is a sense that inclusion into the official communications networks generates new avenues of social control that are less dependent on overt displays of authority and violence.

Alongside these debates, people are turning attention to the ways communications systems extend into the lives of people who are excluded from formal civic and economic life. For instance, a great deal of attention has been directed at how surveillance and communications networks once confined to the US-Mexico borderlands maintain, and in some cases intensify, the exclusion of Latin American immigrants from civil society.[2] And while the past two decades have witnessed a bipartisan coalition of lawmakers and security officials hailing the spread of cutting-edge technology as humane tools to monitor border crossers, activists, journalists, and scholars around the country have painted a much different picture.[3] Many have brought attention to the human consequences of the extraordinary surveillance apparatus built to detect and track immigrants. Here, emphasis is placed on how leading-edge technology *facilitates* inhumane treatment—including indefinite detention and deportation—instead of eliminating it from border and immigrant control.

Running parallel to these criticisms, a rising chorus has brought attention to the expanding surveillance capacities of the carceral state.[4] These discussions have revealed the degree to which the carceral state has been transformed through communications networks and the new modes of social exclusion generated as a consequence. Each branch of the criminal justice system has contributed to constantly unfolding networks of cellular towers, fiber-optic cables, fusion centers, and video cameras dedicated to monitoring and intercepting criminal suspects. Surveillance cameras watch over streets for specific faces and license plates; global positioning systems track the movement of convicts; predictive software processes police data to guide patrol units; and, more recently, police have added robotics into the repertoire.[5] These networks have helped codify War on Crime and War on Drug tactics and strategies in programming language, thus creating new justifications for old policies of social exclusion.

This chapter focuses on connections between these two instances of exclusionary control in border policing and the carceral state. Instead of focusing on the diverse, subjective experiences of surveilled individuals, the chapter explores the objective conditions that make their experiences possible in the first place. There are two reasons for this. First, concentrating on structural relations between border and carceral communication and control technologies highlights targets for abolition not apparent in everyday experience. The lion's share of exclusionary control technologies is located outside the realm of everyday experience, so understanding the *where, why,* and *how* of these infrastructures requires an approach capable of probing these realms. Second, the chapter aims to trace out common themes and objectives to help bolster immigrant rights and anti-criminalization alliances. By exploring overlapping themes and developments between border and carceral control, the goal is to highlight commonalities between immigrant rights and decriminalization efforts. The chapter does not document techniques of resistance as this book is subject to the surveillance of the very forces it seeks to undermine. Instead, it aims to cast light on the less apparent aspects of exclusionary communications and control systems for experienced organizers to review and develop appropriate counter-strategies.

The chapter begins by offering an abbreviated history of communications systems at the US-Mexico border and in the criminal justice system in the twentieth century. It discusses some of the more pronounced political projects to mobilize communications systems for purposes of excluding immigrants and convicted people socially, politically, and geographically. Then the chapter explores how these systems were integrated into everyday communications networks in the twenty-first century. Here, the chapter explores how such normalization has transformed the very structures of immigrant and carceral control. The third section describes the processes under scrutiny as "control-x," a term meant to emphasize the increasingly computer-operated function of cutting out or removing targeted people from society. The x also refers to the increasing ability of communications and control systems to swap out one group (undocumented immigrants) for another (crime suspects and convicted persons). The conclusion revisits how conceptualizing exclusionary control in terms of structural relations helps to develop broader and integrated concepts of communication, control, and social exclusion, and the political significance gained from doing so.

Crises and Exclusionary Control in the Twentieth Century

The development of exclusionary communication and control at borders and in the criminal justice system in the United States is no mere technical phenomenon. It is also a political one. During the early part of the twentieth century, the rise of organized labor across northern industrial cities provided impetus for various developments in law enforcement agencies. The early 1900s saw urban police incorporate telegraph networks to coordinate riot squads to manage rising labor agitations.[6] These networks built on the legacy of police boxes introduced decades prior, which were used primarily for police in the field to communicate with their stations. Some boxes also allowed civilians to communicate with the police. The early twentieth century also saw police in Detroit and San Francisco implement one-way radios in patrol vehicles.

At the US-Mexico border as well, state reactions to social crises have often served as a driving force behind technological development. The Great Depression offers an illustrative example of this. In the 1920s, the growing number of Mexicans fleeing the aftermath of revolution encountered anti-immigrant blowback upon entering the United States. Mexican agricultural workers found themselves demonized through propaganda such as the 1936 film *Reefer Madness* and laws such as the Marihuana Tax Act of 1937. The border itself evolved modestly during this time. The 1930s saw the beginnings of fence building along the southern border, reinforced with barbed wire, lampposts to make border crossers more visible at night, and crossing gates to scrutinize crossers.[7] Such developments continued throughout World War II. The uptick of Mexican farmworkers arriving in the US through the Bracero Program during this era catalyzed the further development of border communications systems including observation towers, radio-equipped gyrocopters, and radio transmitters.

A combination of political and technical factors in the 1960s galvanized the spread of communications and control across enforcement agencies. Once the Bracero Program ended in 1964, many white farmworkers in the Southwest complained that Mexican labor drove wages down.[8] Labor tensions were only exacerbated by the rising influence of the United Farm Workers, a union under Chicano/a and Filipino American leadership. The Immigration and Naturalization Service (INS) painted Mexican and Latin American immigrants as invasive aliens whose containment warranted collaboration with the Defense Department. Democrats representing groups such as the United Farm Workers and AFL-CIO joined with "law and order" Republicans in calls for a "hard-sealing" of the border.[9] These efforts were accompanied by pushes to end guest worker programs and ban the hiring of undocumented immigrants. All these tensions culminated with Nixon's proposal to establish a barrier across the entire southern border, the first proposal of its kind by a US president.

Increased border policing involved instituting a number of communications technologies. Government aircraft equipped with radar hovered over borderlands looking for crossers.[10] The decade saw surplus weapons and surveillance equipment from the Vietnam War flow into various domestic agencies. Urban police departments and the Border Patrol were among the leading recipients. Some of the gear made it to the southern border. In the early 1970s, the INS replicated an electronic fence developed by the Defense Department to divide North and South Vietnam along parts of the border. The fence was an intrusion detection system originally developed by the US Air Force to track communist guerrillas moving between Vietnamese borders.[11] Ground sensors, infrared sensors, radio towers, and many other communication technologies extended border infrastructure.

The process of border militarization occurred alongside national initiatives to modernize police departments throughout urban America. In the urban core, Lyndon Johnson's 1965 War on Crime fueled the spread of communications systems across the criminal justice apparatus. These systems were viewed as essential to modernizing the police. Johnson's Omnibus Crime Control and Safe Streets Act of 1968 provided the necessary funds to achieve this. In response to the rising reports of crimes associated with the civil rights, white feminist, and anti-Vietnam movements, the act created the Law Enforcement Assistance Administration (LEAA), which was tasked with modernizing urban police on a national scale. A few years later the Organized Crime Control Act increased the LEAA's budget from $75 million to $500 million to expand police agencies' equipment and technology.[12]

Nixon inherited the LEAA, which had up to then provided billions in technology and training to large police forces. It also spurred police departments' adoption of military-style communications systems. One of the LEAA's most lasting legacies was introducing the military's "command and control" philosophy into urban policing.[13] Command and control relied on widespread telecommunications networks that include radio towers and receivers, computer-aided dispatch systems, telephone lines, and patrol units dispatched according to spatial-statistical analysis. In this way, police departments played center stage in laying infrastructure for migration policing in urban settings. Meanwhile, the buildup continued along the US-Mexico boundary in the 1980s and 1990s. During these decades, the amounts of funding, staffing, and border infrastructure exploded alongside politically fueled anxieties of a country under siege primarily by Mexican migrant workers.[14] Flood lights were installed, fences were heightened, and helicopter patrols expanded to reinforce the border police's detection and capture system.[15] These processes of modernizing the communications systems and militarizing the everyday operations of border, immigration, and urban police set the foundation for even more radical changes in the wake of the attacks of September 11, 2001.

Communication, Control, and Exclusion in the Twenty-First Century

The many catalysts of exclusionary control technology—from transnational politics, to labor market mutations, to nativism, to racial demagoguery—continued to exert themselves as the century turned. What is more, these technologies enmeshed themselves into *everyday communications systems*, weaving exclusionary control into the fabric of day-to-day human-machine interactions. No catalyst was as influential in normalizing exclusionary control systems as the War on Terror. Politically, the war revitalized nativism across the political spectrum and geography of the country. It commanded bipartisan support to increase border policing and interior immigration policing via digital systems that integrate facial recognition, satellite monitoring, and thermal imaging.[16] Counterterrorism initiatives steered resources into urban security and public safety infrastructures, which altered the carceral state's landscape. In short, the political responses to the 9/11 attacks ushered in a new technical basis for communication, control, and social exclusion not only of terrorist suspects, but other groups already vilified in political discourse.

One key new institution to emerge from the war was fusion centers: surveillance headquarters that processed data from countless sources. These centers have merged counterterrorism, border policing, and law enforcement operations into a functional whole.[17] The Department of Homeland Security (DHS) created the National Fusion Center Association shortly after the 9/11 terrorist attacks, an eighty-member consortium of data centers that communicate information between the Coast Guard, departments of corrections, Customs and Border Protection, DHS, the Drug Enforcement Administration, highway patrols, the National Guard, local police departments, and private entities. Fusion centers brought together formerly dispersed networks of audio detection devices, drones, environmental sensors, CCTVs, ground sensors, and patrols. These centers flourished in an atmosphere where urban officials and residents clamored for cutting-edge systems to monitor foreigners. Three decades after the immigration and defense departments joined to build an electronic fence, the newly installed DHS announced plans for a "virtual fence"—a border made of automated tollway systems, checkpoints, control rooms, drones, facial recognition software, ID card systems, infrared cameras, license plate readers, military-grade surveillance cameras, motion sensors, and radar systems.[18] For border control agencies, the post-9/11 fence was meant to put information from all different branches of the state and many private businesses at their fingertips to assist them in identifying, intercepting, and deporting "unlawful" border crossers.

Although the virtual fence project collapsed, it marked a new era in immigration control, based largely on communication between various branches of the public and private sector. Customs and Border Protection (the parent agency of the US Border Patrol) built database systems to analyze mobile phone data from private data brokers, track the movements of immigrant visas, and flag license plates and student visitors.[19] Eventually Immigration and Customs Enforcement (ICE) gained access to the national license plate database, the world's largest of its kind, which contains 5 billion images and allows agents to track the daily activities of flagged plates and the vehicular movements of immigrants.[20] The sprawling database network developed by DHS has been indispensable to expanded efforts to deport immigrants and migrant workers. The ever-growing number of faces scanned and registered, license plates recorded and tracked, and profiles analyzed and flagged has been pivotal in ICE's dragnet-style raids in recent years.[21] These raids have led to mass detainments and deportations that have slashed through communities, disrupted households, and driven many non-citizens deeper into hiding. Border tech keeps migrants "in their place"—that is, in specific positions in international political, economic, and social systems—apart from the formal channels of civil society.

The transformations were not limited to border policing. Near the same time, carceral communications and control mutated via real-time crime centers (RTCCs) and mini–fusion centers operated by police departments.[22] RTTC bring together software-operated alert programs, CCTVs, automated dispatch systems, data analytics, and geographic information systems. Originally, they were meant to help commanders determine geographic distributions of patrol units and organize how patrols navigate the city.[23] Instead, however, they evolved into command centers for the police to monitor mobility and capture targeted subjects identified through human and machine communication. Like fusion centers, RTCCs take data from a sprawling network of cameras, detectors, and databases from multiple bureaucracies and produce targets for police. For instance, New York City's RTCC was mining data from over 5 million New York State criminal records, parole, and probation files; 20 million criminal complaints, emergency calls, and summonses; 31 million national crime records; and an astounding 33 billion public records just five years after launch.[24]

Similar to the technologies at the border, carceral technologies engendered new forms of exclusion based heavily on communication systems. Moreover, these systems achieved ever-tightening and widening grips on the everyday lives of targeted communities and individuals. Cities erected special architectures of CCTV surveillance around public housing, in public schools, and at street intersections. The deployment of such technologies also included the expansion of electronic ankle bracelets equipped with global positioning systems used to track parolees and probationers in real time.[25] These feed a constant stream of data to offices and patrol units in the streets. The net result is an entire network dedicated to monitoring criminalized people and places, thus ensuring their relative exclusion.

Conceptualizing the Control-X Function

The first, obvious feature of these histories is how both involve mobilizing computer-aided communications systems to remove unwanted groups from physical and social spaces. For unwanted border crossers, "control-x" involves both forms of control. At the border, the increasingly dense networks of radar-equipped planes, ground sensors, and human patrollers make entry an increasingly treacherous affair. These human-machine networks extend increasingly into the US interior, ensuring targeted immigrants are surveilled in order that they can be kept in marginal positions in ways that affect their mobility and sense of security. The interiorization of border communications systems has also proven fundamental for ICE in orchestrating mass deportations in cities across the United States.

For the carceral state, the extension of communications systems in and around criminalized areas similarly maintains social and spatial exclusion. At the level of the individual, electronic ankle bracelets communicating with parole offices and patrol officers constricts the mobilities of convicted persons. Moreover, electronic monitoring programs are increasingly also capable of surveilling consumption habits of monitored subjects, restricting agency within the context of consumer society.[26] At the community level,

CCTVs are installed in public housing complexes, thus reinforcing geographic differentiation along socioeconomic lines.

A second characteristic of exclusionary modes of control is the burgeoning political economy underwriting the spread of these policing technologies. Whereas the twentieth century witnessed primarily state-run campaigns to fortify borders and modernize urban law enforcement, the twenty-first is witnessing an increasingly proactive IT sector that is driving the process. These links between the IT sector, national government, regional governments, and local authorities constitute a structural mutation in communication, control, and social exclusion. For instance, in the 2010s, DHS opened its Silicon Valley office to seed money to start-ups to develop specified technologies. Around the same time, ICE awarded Palantir—whose other clients include policing agencies and the CIA—a $41 million contract to design a system that provides ICE agents with terabytes of information about a given individual: addresses, biometric traits, car insurance, criminal record, employment history, family relations, foreign exchange program enrollment, immigration history, phone records, utility bills, social media, and more.[27] The money continued to flow into the end of the decade. For instance, in 2017 ICE announced a $100 million contract for an automated system that discerns whether an individual immigrant is likely to be a productive member of society or a deviant. A subsidiary of the aerospace and defense corporation General Dynamics won the contract for the system, which analyzes foreign visitors' social media and publicly available information to produce the assessment. Amazon met with ICE in Silicon Valley in 2019 to pitch facial recognition software that used predictive analytics, tagging, and analysis software to identify people's faces along the US-Mexico border. By the end of the following year, ICE had so much data at its disposal it began to solicit tech companies to provide cloud services.[28]

Relations between the IT sector and the criminal justice system have also progressed significantly in the recent past. Following social uprisings over racial police violence, especially those in the wake of the protests in response to the police killing of Michael Brown in Ferguson, Missouri, in August 2014, the federal government responded with a national task force to explore technology-based solutions to police misconduct. The results of the task force saw the Department of Justice and the National Institute of Justice produce a report recommending a spate of technological fixes including new standards for biometrics, body-worn cameras, and CCTV surveillance networks to monitor police-community relations. The report also served as a basis for the Police Data Initiative, a national program wherein police worked with data scientists and tech corporations to bolster police accountability.

While we might enumerate the differences between immigrant and urban experiences with exclusionary communication and control systems, a technically focused consideration of these systems suggests they are converging, giving rise to an integrated apparatus capable of identifying group X (e.g., Latin American immigrants, low-income urban Black people) and swiftly executing exclusionary policies and practices. Moreover, this perspective encourages deeper scrutiny into the underlying political economy of exclusionary control. In specific, it provokes activists, researchers, and organizers to collectively piece together a wide sweeping and still emerging nexus of actors and motives in the vein of Angela Y. Davis's influential notion of the prison-industrial complex.[29] Focusing on the underlying structures of exclusionary control raises urgent questions: What other groups fall under its exclusionary gaze? What contemporary crises may fuel the further expansion of exclusionary systems? What are the most effective ways of forging intergroup alliances to reverse these trends?

Conclusion

The burgeoning modes of controlling excluded groups through communications systems merit new ways of thinking about governance, technology, and social equity. First, they require building on the abundance of research that focuses on how access to information communications technology is necessary for having access to official labor markets and public services. Specifically, our growing awareness of exclusionary modes of communication and control enjoin researchers to explore how these very same technologies also exclude various groups from these markets and services. Second, focusing on the rise and spread of exclusionary communication systems exposes the wide breadth of actors and institutions involved in the process. Civilians, enforcement agencies, IT companies, and telecommunications companies each play a role in weaving anti-immigrant and carceral operations into everyday communications systems. Moreover, such processes are not simply matters of policy but also material infrastructures that increasingly pervade the material environment.

These revelations are valuable to experienced activists and organizers, as they point to new areas of intervention. In the main, the expanding infrastructures of exclusionary control have been planned and installed outside the realm of public discussion and even perception. Academic researchers are uniquely equipped with tools to make these developments visible to the public so that they can devise appropriate strategies on local scales. More and more, activists and scholars discover the very same functions that border tech performs in other state technologies, not only in today's smart cities. Though far from identical, the similarities between these technologies offer an avenue for intersectional mobilization. Activists dedicated to establishing immigrant rights or abolishing carceral governance find common ground with respect to the proliferation of social control technology. An integrated theory of communication, control, and social exclusion can serve as an aid in charting out such common ground—hence the ongoing importance of historical and structural analysis.

29

Data Justice in Mexico: How Big Data Is Reshaping the Struggle for Rights and Political Freedoms

Arely Cruz-Santiago, Ernesto Schwartz-Marín, and Conor O'Reilly

Mexico has become a laboratory for new forms of both surveillance, and resistance. In a series of frontal challenges to human rights and political freedoms, state authorities have preyed on journalists, academics, human rights activists, and families of victims of enforced disappearances. Malware has become a means for the Mexican state to surveil its citizens in a systematic, highly invasive, and stealthy way. Mexican government expenditure on spyware has been one of the highest in the Americas.[1] Through spyware, misinformation campaigns, and selective uses of "dataveillance" and intelligence, alliances between government and organized criminal groups have emerged. But so have new forms of civil resistance and counter-forensics. This chapter provides a snapshot of the current Mexican scenario, its challenges and opportunities, to understand contemporary dilemmas born from the interaction between Big Data and the freedoms of speech, movement, and assembly.

Mexico is the country with the highest number of documented (ab)use cases of spyware technologies to track journalists, human rights defenders, and political opponents.[2] Digital infrastructures acquired and used by Mexican authorities include platforms for Big Data analysis such as "Echo" and spyware technologies that target mobile phone users. Echo is a global virtual signals intelligence system developed by Rayzone Group. The system allows for the collection of comprehensive, diverse, and detailed data on internet users on a massive scale within a country. The platform can analyze any device and operating system and does not require any pre-installation or physical equipment. It collects information on a particular point of interest (a target-centric approach), as well as from all internet users in a country (a data-centric approach).[3] Spyware technologies such as Pegasus (developed by the NSO Group) and Da Vinci (developed by Hacking Team) target mobile phones devices. In the case of Pegasus, once a phone is infected, a Pegasus operator can extract chats, photos, emails, and location data or activate microphones and cameras secretly without a user knowing. In August 2021, the Pegasus Project, a collaborative journalistic investigation into the NSO Group and its clients, revealed that Mexico was the first government to buy Pegasus, which it did in 2011, and is one of the world's heaviest known users of the spyware.[4]

The spyware was used to target journalists and their families, public health advocates who supported a tax on soda, and human rights defenders. For example, Jorge Carrasco, who led an investigation into the Panama Papers and Mexican corporations, had his mobile phone infiltrated in 2016. In the same year, news presenter Carmen Aristegui and her young son were attacked with spyware. Investigative journalists Javier Valdez, who reported stories on violence in the northern state of Sinaloa, and Regina Martinez, who uncovered corruption networks within the state of Veracruz, were killed in 2012 and 2015, respectively. Family members and colleagues close to them were later found to have the spyware in their phones. In a country already recognized as one of the deadliest for journalists, targeting through digital surveillance has exacerbated the intimidation, threats, and violence directed toward those exposing corruption and confronting organized crime in Mexico.[5]

The Mexican government insists that Pegasus has only been used to fight organized crime and for national security purposes. However, digital surveillance has extended to include peasant communities and victims of violence. In 2014, family members of and advocates for the forty-three Ayotzinapa Rural Teachers' College students had their mobile phones infiltrated.[6] NSO Group (Israel), Rayzone Group (Israel), and Hacking Team (Italy) are some of the twenty spyware companies that are known to have worked with Mexican local and federal authorities. From military-grade drones to remote computer systems, Mexico has become a laboratory for new forms of surveillance.

Along the US-Mexico border, a myriad of border surveillance tools and installations—including military drones, motion detectors, infrared sensors, and watchtowers—patrol Mexico's northern territories. Less acknowledged, however, is how US migration surveillance reaches further into Mexico. In 2018, it was revealed that the US Department of Homeland Security was seeking to extend its access to screening facilities in Mexican detention centers that record migrants' biometric data and send this information into US crime and immigration control databases.[7] Funded through the Mérida Initiative, a security partnership between the US and Mexico, this channel for more militarized support, predominantly justified in the context of the War on Drugs, is another important dimension of Mexico's complex surveillance architecture.

The latest iteration in this surveillance architecture is the recently approved change to the Federal Communications Law to create a national biometric database of mobile phone users, which requires all users to submit their personal information and biometric data to the Mexican State in order to access the cellular network.[8] Publicly framed as an attempt to safeguard the population and combat crime, the Mexican Congress passed the legislation in April 2021. The requirement applies to every mobile phone user in the country (currently 124 million mobile phone lines are in use). While details have not been provided regarding the type of biometric data that will be collected, it could entail fingerprints, iris scans, and facial and voice-recognition data. This program raises questions about privacy protection—especially after a previous attempt by state authorities to create a similar database containing personal information, whose data was leaked and sold for $30 in 2009 in various street markets in Mexico City.[9] The decision to create a biometric database for mobile phone users came with increasing fears that the government was recasting mobile phone surveillance spyware as a tool for tracking COVID-19 transmission rates.

Amid the COVID-19 pandemic, the Attorney General's Office (Fiscalía General de la República) acquired a geolocation system that provides real-time location of any mobile phone user and "Echo," a platform for Big Data analysis that collects data on internet users within the country. Massive surveillance of citizens goes against the principles of necessity and proportionality, and makes this type of technology easily available for other problematic and chilling uses.

The last two decades have seen a worrying trend in the expansion of Mexico's surveillance apparatus, progressing beyond orthodox "high policing"[10] and recognizable authoritarian state impulses toward a "multiveillant" society—one where highly fluid (in)security arrangements move beyond state-centric surveillance apparatuses into a hybrid network that brings together criminal organizations and government offices. For instance, in 2015, a WikiLeaks exposé showed that the systematic oil theft at PEMEX (Mexico's national oil company) was logistically organized and supervised via spyware. According to the leaked documents, the spyware was bought by elite members of the military working for PEMEX to safeguard national sovereignty.[11] Authorities estimate that PEMEX lost over $3 billion US dollars to the practice of fuel theft.[12]

Similarly, investigative journalists, human rights defenders, and activist citizens are developing their own technological capacities to confront the looming specter of control and intimidation, as well as forging collaborative networks to expose the surveillant state. Those targeted have in some instances deployed (trans)national practices of counter-surveillance. This includes, most notably, the investigation carried out in 2017 by Mexican civil society organization R3D, in collaboration with Citizen Lab, a research center at the University of Toronto, and the *New York Times*. Through a forensic analysis of the infected devices, the team discovered that at least twenty-five individuals had their mobile phones successfully hacked using Pegasus spyware.[13]

The complexity of the Mexican scenario compels us to analyze how citizen science and data journalism have stimulated new forms of transparency, accountability, and human security to counterbalance the surveillance tactics of governmental agencies and organized crime. However, proactive and reactive, citizen-led counter-surveillance techniques also pose important questions regarding trust: trust in government; trust in law enforcement; and trust in fellow citizens.

During an informal interview we conducted in 2018 with John Scott-Railton, a researcher from Citizen Lab in Toronto, he shared that most of the data security measures used by activists are artisanal and piecemeal rather than comprehensive and systematic.[14] He compared the existing approach to data security to the treatment of a chronic disease, where a perceived lack of immediate danger makes it hard for people to take action. Scott-Railton's remarks shed light into the asymmetries that shape our digital world. In the case of Pegasus spyware, a profit-making entity such as NSO Group will mostly have the upper hand in the surveillance arms race, making it hard—if not practically impossible—for ordinary citizens to take effective action on their own against digital intrusions.

The multiveillant society goes well beyond high-profile spyware cases and emerges in response to pervasive everyday insecurity—from crime and violence to economic exploitation and targeting by the state. The crucible of surveillance experimentation encompasses family members tracking loved ones when concerned about kidnap risk, or domestic workers sharing information with colleagues on abusive employers.[15] Surveillance is also deployed when employers monitor and test the trustworthiness of employees, or when private security specialists use GPS to track client journeys in dangerous regions. The multiple manifestations of quotidian surveillance activities—often for supportive oversight for loved ones, colleagues, peers, and clients rather than any nefarious targeting—are also constitutive of multiveillance.

In short, the multiveillant society encompasses counter-surveillance innovations fashioned by ordinary citizens. These innovations become digital sites of resistance characterized by the development of *sous*veillance—or "watching from below"[16]—and the forensic intelligence capacities of ordinary citizens and NGOs. These innovations emerge as a response to state inaction and impunity, but also as a strategy for citizens to keep each other in check in the face of a state that applies law in a very selective and arbitrary way. The possibility for social and legal justice through data remains an open question in Mexico and around the world. The counter-surveillance strategies to fight Pegasus spyware in Mexico are promising, but the growing militarization of the country and lack of accountability that has characterized security operations so far make it increasingly difficult for citizens around the world to fight large dataveillance operations. The concept of "multiveillance" allows us to grasp the complexity of surveillance operations and illuminate the sites of resistance emerging at the margins of a growing panopticon that seeks to shield those occupying positions of power from democratic oversight. Multiveillance points toward the need for collective solutions that go beyond the notion that the fight for digital justice is an arms race where tech-savvy activists and political dissidents clash against digital surveilling entities that have multimillionaire budgets, powerful connections, and clients on their side. To tackle the growing challenge of multiveillance, and seize the opportunities it presents, it is necessary to find concrete alternatives to surveillance capitalism[17] and state-led intelligence.

30

Corporate Tech and the Legible City

Ryan Gerety, Mariah Montgomery, Mizue Aizeki, and Nasma Ahmed

Public land deals negotiated under non-disclosure agreements. "Hourglass" economies with very high-wage jobs and very low-wage ones. Civilian-police surveillance networks.

Technology corporations are playing an outsized role in shaping cities—undermining urban democracy, consolidating wealth, and expanding authoritarian practices through their relationships to workers, local government, essential infrastructure, land, policing, and communications. While smart city and surveillance incursions are key elements of tech's approach to cities, the impact and ambition of these corporations are best understood more broadly, as a restructuring of governance and the economy. Corporate tech not only concentrates governance and economic power away from public control, but it actively reinforces and expands the parts of the state that marginalize the working class, immigrants, and Black and brown communities.

This essay is a collective exploration of those dynamics from our perspective as campaigners and activists who have come into direct conflict with technology corporations as we fight for more just cities—including confrontations with Amazon, Google, Uber, Mastercard, and public-private technology partnerships. In order to understand and strategize about those confrontations, we have convened and been part of conversations between advocates, organizers, and researchers confronting tech's growing role in changing employment, real estate development, policing, private surveillance, and more. These conversations brought together people working on different facets of tech and drew from diverse knowledge bases and approaches. Together, we began to conceptualize what we are up against: a sector that is transforming the political economy of the city.

In this essay, we draw from those conversations to share what emerged as important to understand about corporate tech's unique challenges to democracy, equality, and true safety and freedom.[1] We aim to contribute to an analysis of the political economy of cities that cuts across silos in academia, advocacy, and organizing, and prepares us to fight back, and fight forward, more effectively. We focus on the United States and Canada, where we have direct experience.

Background

Like corporations throughout history, tech firms operate in ways that reflect the economic and political incentives of the moment. The business models were developed as an optimized response to the neoliberal push to privatize and reduce government spending on public goods and services; the availability of low-cost labor due to outsourcing, union busting, and weakening labor protections; decreasing antitrust enforcement; increasing military, police, and migrant control budgets; and excess investment capital. Within this environment, tech corporations have paired economic concentration, labor exploitation, social control of marginalized populations, and a reduction of public goods with the capacity of technology to automate, optimize, scale, and control.

While corporate interests have long shaped and reshaped cities, since the 1980s that profit-making has taken the form of urban "revitalization," characterized by the influx of real estate investment and high-income white populations into cities, which drive longtime communities of color out of their homes.[2] To fuel this transformation, investment interests have compelled city governments to focus on competing with other municipalities to attract private capital to provide jobs and essential services.[3] In this sense, city leaders have been primed over decades to see the tech industry—as it has grown in wealth, scale, and centralization—as an all-encompassing solution to broad and complex urban challenges. And given the concentration of capital in major cities, technology corporations have been eager to play a dominant role.

We see these forces play out and transform our cities. And in particular, we have seen that tech corporations are able to take advantage of—and then reinforce—urban conditions of fiscal austerity, privatization, land speculation, displacement of communities of color, and inequality.[4] As a result, we see privatized broadband access, so-called smart cities projects, automation of government services, venture capital–funded solutions for transportation and logistics, carceral and policing technologies, public incentives for tech corporations, the transformation of urban housing to meet the needs of higher-income tech workers, and so on.

Meanwhile, tech billionaires are held up as leaders and visionaries, despite exacerbating inequality and turning our personal lives and preferences into massive profits.

Undermining Democracy

Across a myriad of cities and campaigns, we observe corporate tech using hard and soft power to shape cities and undermine democracy. We have found that a particular challenge is that the industry derives unique soft power from its claim on our collective imagination of the future. While we have seen this attempted capture of the future in every "smart city" project and "innovation" district, the Google Sidewalk Labs proposal is perhaps the best window into the bare audacity of private tech interests to make claims on our collective futures: "The moment is right for a vision of historic sweep. The world sits on the cusp of a revolution in urban life every bit as transformative as the arrival of the steam engine or electricity, powered by a new set of digital and design breakthroughs."[5]

This claim on our future is reinforced by the monumental size and financial success of a relatively small number of firms, and by our daily use of tech tools to do everything from finding a doctor, to getting groceries, to earning a living. Given this techno-optimistic narrative, even small tech firms can trade on representing the only viable path to "progress," and local officials, stripped of resources to provide an alternative, rarely stand in the way. Meanwhile, local news outlets that might investigate and challenge the promises of corporate tech have been hobbled by digital giants—Google and Facebook are capturing advertising dollars and people increasingly look for headlines aggregated by those firms instead of the organizations that actually report and write the content.[6] Meanwhile these same corporations control the digital spaces where culture and politics play out.

Of course, corporate tech's soft power is backed by momentous material power. Many have characterized the largest tech firms as more comparable to nation-states than to other corporations, and both organizers and public agencies express trepidation at taking on entities with such resources.[7] The market values of some tech firms far exceed the GDPs of many countries.[8] Even relatively young firms have access to tremendous amounts of investment capital. Additionally, tech companies often provide services and infrastructure that are necessary to city life, in competition with, or as a replacement for, public services. Whether tech firms are providing necessary services to the public directly or providing technology to government actors, democratic oversight and transparency are undermined—private firms control services through corporate terms of service and the code itself. Meanwhile governments readily embrace the neoliberal precept that the best way to govern is via public-private "partnerships."

Some of the inducements tech firms offer to influence local government are the same as those made by any major corporation: the promise of high-paid jobs, good press, and campaign contributions. Examples include Amazon's notorious second headquarters search and Google's strong-arm tactics in San Jose. However, tech also leverages its monopoly on digital infrastructure—its real and inflated advantage in technical know-how and data, and its direct, often strong relationships with potential voters (its users).

For example, during the California fight to ensure rights for app-based workers, organizers with relatively few resources have had to contend with Uber requiring voters (its customers and drivers) to view and click "confirm" or "OK" on messages that urged support for an anti-worker ballot initiative in order to use its app.[9] In effect, the company uses its digital infrastructure—direct connection to residents' phones—and its role in providing essential transportation to create and mobilize a new constituency to lobby for policies that benefit the company, while harming workers and the public. Most cities do not regularly communicate with residents directly via personal devices and often provide inadequate public transportation. Importantly, Uber was only able to compete with—and even erode—public infrastructure because of its seemingly endless access to private investment capital, which allowed it to undercut taxi rates, recruit drivers through large bonuses, operate in violation of local laws, and draw people away from public transit with artificially cheap prices.[10]

Taking advantage of the neoliberal orientation of cities, we have seen that the industry uses various carrots and sticks to exert control over local governance. For example, Google and Amazon have used non-disclosure agreements to secure the silence of elected officials when negotiating real estate development terms, to head off potential public opposition and sometimes secretly negotiate economic incentive terms.[11] Amazon led a successful effort to get the Seattle City Council to reverse a payroll tax in 2019, threatening to bankroll a repeal effort.[12] Tech firms also neutralize large swaths of civil society through philanthropy (and self-interested investments masquerading as philanthropy). In exchange, tech firms are able to secure good press, the cooperation of potential critics, and tax benefits.

We have also seen that during each and every crisis, corporate tech positions itself as the rescuer in the face of an inadequate welfare state—even when its largest firms avoid paying taxes that could enhance the state's ability to provide for public well-being. We see this with Amazon delivering essential goods during the pandemic, the incursion of tech giants into health care, and Uber and Lyft providing transportation to cover gaps in public infrastructure. At every turn, the tech industry inserts itself as an alternative to public goods, facilitating the provision of basic essential goods and services, while asserting a form of undemocratic leadership. We do not claim that this corporate assertion of supremacy over the possibility of public goods is new, but rather that tech has adopted and deepened this approach.

Taken all together, these factors create a power imbalance and a challenge to democratic city governance that is difficult to overstate.

Consolidating Wealth

As with the struggle against corporate tech's consolidation of political power in our cities, organizers and activists are grappling with tech's multifaceted consolidation of economic power. Technology corporations have consolidated enormous wealth in a variety of ways: gaining monopoly power, privatizing profits from public investment in research and development,[13] maximizing power over workers, leveraging excess investment capital,[14] and avoiding taxes.[15] In this section, we reflect on how corporate tech has contributed to wealth concentration, economic exploitation, underinvestment in public goods and services, and privatization—using both old-fashioned and novel techniques to gain economic power.

In our conversations, we heard communities describe contending with tech's economic power from distinct vantage points: either from the perspective of tech's economic consolidation and resulting gentrification in cities like the Bay Area, Seattle, and Toronto; or in conflicts over tech's model of economic extraction and exploitation in those cities and in other places around the world.

In tech-dominated cities like Seattle or San Francisco, the relatively few high-paying tech jobs mean that luxury services dominate, rents rise, and other residents are priced out or economically disadvantaged, exacerbating existing race, gender, and class hierarchies. While these places hold enough wealth to take care of everyone, the combination of highly compensated workers, tech corporations not paying their fair tax share, and government austerity measures means that society becomes highly exclusionary and unequal. Meanwhile, by concentrating wealth in a few cities, others fall behind and are sites where tech is merely extracting what it needs: labor, land, public contracts, customers, data, and so on.[16] Globally this translates into tech corporations in a few cities in wealthy countries extracting from the Global South and racialized communities across the globe—a process that has been referred to as "digital colonialism."[17]

In terms of tech's investment and extraction in cities, we find that these corporations seek out cities for at least three reasons: opportunities to monopolize dense markets with affluent segments, availability of a low-wage workforce, and sizable public infrastructure and services (ripe for privatization). By seizing upon market density to concentrate control and profit of local economies, a handful of monopoly platforms dominate our cities, from rental markets (Airbnb), to taxi services (Uber/Lyft), to retail (Amazon), logistics and delivery (Instacart/Postmates), and labor markets (Taskrabbit). In the case of Airbnb, this upends the housing market in high-tourism cities—leading to displacement and economic hardship.[18] And as previously noted, social media giants have siphoned investment from local media institutions. Across the board, these corporations use monopoly power and investment capital to outcompete individual local businesses and entrepreneurs.

Technology corporations are also consolidating wealth through the privatizing of urban infrastructure including broadband, transport, computing infrastructure, and tech solutions for city governance (such as lighting, garbage collection, and identity systems). Examples are the advertising-supported wireless kiosks in New York City from Google's Sidewalk Labs, or San Diego's "smart" light system, enhanced with surveillance technology developed by General Electric, Intel, and AT&T. Often this transfer of power and responsibility is invisible. It is in software, underground infrastructure, or in the "cloud." And as we have discussed, when tech corporations become an essential part of the city's functioning, they are able to wield increased power within the city.[19]

Crucial to tech's incursion into the city is its ability to cheaply take advantage of a concentrated workforce necessary for its seamless, low-cost services. Weakened labor protections and rising costs in cities open an opportunity to exploit the working class. Automated management and surveillance are a means to capitalize on that opportunity. App-based work is a canonical example, but it's also true of Amazon, now the second largest employer in the United States.

Amazon developed a system of automated management, surveillance, and discipline to maximize control over workers.[20] Drivers and warehouse workers are prodded and timed from one task to the next, while managers watch metrics rise and fall.[21] Over time, these technologies of control result in lower wages, higher injuries, and increased precarity.[22]

App-based work, an "innovation" sold as freedom and as solving underemployment, places large numbers of people in conditions of heightened risk, longer hours, fewer protections. In the simplest terms, it reinforces precarious underemployment as the standard operating model.[23] Rather than ensuring freedom, it ensures workers have little control over their work; risks are offloaded from the employer onto the worker.

As always, workers have resisted these new (but familiar) models of control, and recent worker organizing in Amazon warehouses in places like New York City; Bessemer, Alabama; the Inland Empire of Southern California; Chicago; and Minneapolis point in a hopeful direction.

Security, Legibility, and the Role of the City

When wealth is highly concentrated, the elite can drive cities to shrink beneficial public services and, instead, invest in the policing and control of the working class to serve business interests.[24] Investment in policing does not stop with law enforcement. City agencies that provide social benefits like housing, food, and medical assistance are also tasked with tracking and policing the residents receiving those services.[25]

Technology corporations that build tools to identify, categorize, and track position themselves as partners to integrate policing and control into every aspect of city governance.[26] License plate readers, facial recognition technology, and data integration services are just a few ways that tech offers cities a way to efficiently order, prioritize, and predict all aspects of urban life.

Bloated police budgets are attractive targets: Microsoft partnered with the New York Police Department to create the Domain Awareness System,[27] which it describes as one of the world's largest surveillance networks; Amazon has agreements with thousands of police departments to provide warrantless access to millions of "smart home" cameras.[28] There is also a growing market for smaller tech vendors.[29] Meanwhile, not only is there a revolving door between city chief technology officers and corporate tech,[30] but police are actively being recruited into tech corporations.[31]

While some technologies *could* improve city services for everyone, there are strong incentives for cities to enhance the experience of the wealthy with technology, while simultaneously excluding and surveilling others. Cities have even invested in technology to restrict access to public spaces, including sonic devices that dissuade teenagers from parks.[32]

Likewise, touchless transit cards may provide seamless access but also increase exclusion and surveillance. Not only does this tech exclude those without credit cards or smartphones, it can readily increase the power of local or immigration police to track and target people.[33]

When social services are digitized, the purported intent is to eliminate fraud, but in actuality, the impact is a reduction of caseworkers and beneficiaries and an increase in surveillance.[34] When Temporary Assistance for Needy Families (TANF) started to provide benefits through electronic cards, each transaction could be tracked and was used by the state to identify which stores people had visited. While digitalization and data integration could better serve residents, often expediency and austerity pressures dominate.

As tech giants reimagine the city for us, the city contorts to the divide between the wealthy and the working class: a frictionless urban interface for the wealthy (the smart city and other privatized digital services), and for the others, a system of control, criminalization, and extraction. Digital technology's propensity toward identifying, formalizing, and categorizing is a dangerous complement to a city designed on behalf of the wealthy, where inequality is managed through control and policing, rather than addressed through public goods and redistribution.

Conclusion

Tech's incursions into the cultural, political, and economic life of the city compound and reinforce each other. Economic inequality that prices working people out of their long-term communities erodes their social fabric, and in turn, their power to realize collective liberation, genuine democracy, and equality. Wide adoption of remote biometric surveillance technologies, such as police use of facial recognition software to track people in gentrifying neighborhoods, expands the authoritarian capacity of the state against all people. Workplace surveillance designed to extract maximum profit reinforces antidemocratic governance as a norm. To take on tech's harms in one part of urban life, we must understand those harms in the context of corporate tech's logic of political and economic control. With this more holistic view, we can do more than mitigate harm—we can create new alliances and strategies to make cities truly democratic and egalitarian.

31

Seeing the Watched: Mass Surveillance in Detroit

Tawana Petty

The racial and political implications of growing up in a predominantly Black city did not hit me psychologically until I became an adult and began to recognize how others around the world viewed us. Although I recall being told quite frequently as a child that I had to "grow up and get out of Detroit" to make something of myself, I hadn't internalized that it was because I was Black or that the city was full of Black people. I simply understood that there appeared to be a lack of opportunities for upward mobility in the city.

This lack of awareness led me to move to suburbs just outside Detroit, where the population was predominantly white. It wasn't until I moved to a middle-class suburban area that I began to realize that we weren't living in a post-racial America after all. I wasn't politicized as a child. I was taught to pursue a good job so that I could be self-determinant. And that if I worked hard enough, I could go anywhere and do anything I wanted—good advice on its face.

However, in my early twenties, I had a reality check about perceived success. My first week driving home to my suburban neighborhood, I was pulled over by police officers and asked, "Where are you headed?" I replied, "I'm headed home." I thought that would be a sufficient response, but one of the officers followed it up with, "Where is home?" To which I replied, "Home is here." I was not asked to exit my vehicle, nor was I asked to show my identification. However, what became clear to me was that I was under surveillance in that neighborhood. Maybe not in a digital sense, but definitely through the eyes of the law and, more than likely, my new neighbors.

This was something I was not accustomed to experiencing in my Black city. After the brief interrogation, I was "free" to go.

This experience was particularly daunting for me, because I did not grow up thinking critically about law enforcement. I have several officers in my family, and was always taught they were where you go for safety.

However, my personal experiences outside of those I knew growing up, or the ones related to me, gave me a more well-rounded view. One that allowed me to think about the profession systemically, beyond the individuals wearing the uniforms.

After a few short attempts at living just outside Detroit, I moved back home. It was a sort of sanctuary for me. Despite the dominant negative narratives that have plagued the city my entire life, I felt safer in Detroit than I did in the predominantly white communities I had ventured out to.

The pervasive story that the residents of Detroit were hopeless, helpless, non-contributory human beings who burned down their own city for no good reason during the 1967 "riots" made its way through the numerous conversations I found myself defending my city against. I was in my late twenties before I even realized that what happened in Detroit in 1967 was a rebellion and not a riot, like the race "riot" of 1943.

I was also in my late twenties before I learned the truth about the police brutality that plagued the city during the years of S.T.R.E.S.S. (Stop the Robberies, Enjoy Safe Streets). S.T.R.E.S.S. was a police unit founded in 1971 that terrorized Black residents in Detroit, particularly men.[1] The officers in the unit murdered no less than twenty-four men, twenty-two of them Black, in the short three years of its existence, and some officers were even proud of their record.[2]

When you grow up in a city frequently propagandized as the "murder capital of the world," it becomes easy to internalize that militarized policing and brutal carceral tactics are the lone roads to safety.[3] But, as I matured in my political understanding and anti-racism analysis, particularly around the ways that anti-Blackness shows up, I discovered that safety was being conflated with surveillance, and other forms of institutional violence were being leveraged through data systems, technological innovation, narrative, and policy.

When I was serving as a community researcher with Our Data Bodies (ODB), I learned that community members were feeling watched, but not seen. It appeared to be a running theme across all three cities we were engaged with.[4] Community members in Detroit, Michigan; Charlotte, North Carolina; and Los Angeles, California were describing systems that were extracting data from them, not for the benefit of increasing their quality of life but to ensure that punishments were carried out, or for purposes that benefited the institutions collecting and analyzing the data. Some of the community members also shared that they felt the mistakes they made in their lives were being integrated across systems and following them as they attempted to regain some footing in their lives. Formerly incarcerated community members described challenges in gaining meaningful employment and housing opportunities. Other community members described how poverty-induced water shutoffs were being leveraged to displace them from their homes, and that those shutoffs were trailing into other aspects of their lives, prohibiting their upward mobility.

It was during my research with ODB that Project Green Light's mass surveillance program began to ramp up in Detroit. The real-time crime surveillance program started with flashing green lights connected to surveillance cameras, monitored by law enforcement at eight or nine gas stations that stayed open late in 2016. In less than three years, it quickly morphed into over two thousand cameras connected to more than seven hundred businesses, including laundromats, educational facilities, public housing, recreation centers, and grocery stores. Law enforcement has the capability to monitor these cameras from fusion centers, on mobile devices, and from police precincts. The cameras are also leveraged to extract images for facial recognition technology.[5] Because of the racial bias inherent in facial recognition, Detroit had the first two *known* cases in the US of misidentification by law enforcement who leveraged the technology for arrests.[6] There have since been other cases, including the case of a fourteen-year-old girl who was misidentified while attempting to enter a Livonia, Michigan (a suburb of Detroit) skating rink, and then put out in the street alone at night.[7] Project Green Light, with its companion facial recognition, was also being leveraged by police against community members to issue $1,000 tickets during the pandemic, in a community that had a median household income before COVID-19 of under $35,000 per year. Since the pandemic, nearly 40 percent of the residents in Detroit have lost their jobs.[8]

Detroiters have made numerous attempts to rid ourselves of the Project Green Light mass surveillance program. We have organized town halls, protests, and petition drives, written op-eds and blogs, hosted panel discussions, taught workshops, published several articles in *Riverwise Magazine* (a Detroit community magazine), and collaborated with the ACLU of Michigan on a Community Input Over Government Surveillance ordinance, in an attempt to put strong regulations over the acquisition of police surveillance. Although the ordinance measure passed, it was unfortunately watered down during years of back and forth between Detroit City Council and local law enforcement, ultimately affording the Detroit Police Department the ability to leverage undefined "exigent" circumstances indefinitely, and behind closed-door sessions.[9]

Detroiters also created a campaign called "Green Chairs, Not Green Lights," in direct response to Project Green Light, where they encouraged community members to return to their front porches and see each other instead of watching each other—to think of the circumstances and resources that create safety in their communities outside of policing. They also created pod maps (also known as "circles of safety"), which challenged community members to think about the people in their circle that they would call on when in need. Youth repurposed pallets into green benches and gifted them to community members who attend the pod-mapping workshops. The Feedom Freedom Growers community garden hosted many of these conversations in collaboration with other community organizations.

Detroiters came together to create a Detroiters' Bill of Rights, which boasted a suite of rights including the right to affordable water, to affordable housing, to be free from surveillance and militarized policing, to access and mobility, to recreation, and many other civil liberties that would enhance the quality of life for hundreds of thousands of Detroiters.[10] These rights culminated in a proposed revision of the city's charter (constitution) that became known as "Proposal P," which was fought against by the governor, the mayor, law enforcement, and some community members who had internalized the misinformation campaign leveraged by the city and paid for by dark money.[11]

The fight for Proposal P went all the way to the Michigan Supreme Court during our pursuit to keep it on the ballot.[12] We won the right to protect our vote, but ultimately failed following a deluge of "Proposal P Is a Problem" campaign ads, billboards, text messages, mailers, radio and TV commercials, newspaper editorials, and door-to-door canvassing. Corporate money funded the campaign against Proposal P, and we were unable to raise enough money and reach enough community members with the truth.

Detroiters continue to be engaged in an active struggle against the surveillance gunshot detection program ShotSpotter. At the time of this writing, Detroit City Council is considering funding an additional $8.5 million toward the initiative.[13] American Rescue Plan funds that were initially allocated by the government to address COVID-19 are being redirected to the program by law enforcement, despite ShotSpotter's proven ineffectiveness at reducing, or even accurately detecting, gun violence.[14]

The struggle to be seen, to be treated as full human beings is a protracted one. It is an uphill battle in a world that has failed to internalize Dr. King's call for a radical revolution of values. As long as safety is conflated with surveillance and policing, our civil liberties remain at risk. True safety cannot be delivered by inflating police budgets or pouring exorbitant amounts of money into artificial intelligence. True safety can only be nurtured by a village that chooses to see each other. We can start to get there when more of us realize that mass surveillance is violence.

32

Necropolitics and Neoliberalism Are Driving Brazil's Surveillance Infrastructure

Rafael Evangelista

I write this on the day that Brazil, according to official data, approaches seven hundred thousand deaths from COVID-19. Although this tragedy affects everyone, it does not victimize all social classes and population groups equally. Under the logics of necropolitics[1] —that is, the politics of deciding who gets to live or die—the poorest, usually Black, have less access to good and secure jobs, which allow for remote work. They live in houses that make social distancing difficult in the event of a family member's illness, and have less time and resources to assist children in remote education activities. It is not by chance that there is intense social pressure for schools to reopen, even if teachers are at risk of contracting the virus, so that parents can meet the pressure of their bosses by dedicating themselves fully to their jobs.

Likewise, the poorest populations are the ones that have become most vulnerable to informational surveillance and monitoring technologies. They are the ones that most need government and social assistance, and the ones most dependent on the services of Big Tech platforms.

From 2019 to 2022, Brazil was commanded by Jair Bolsonaro, a politician whose fierce electoral base is made up of military and police forces, and who stood out for his public statements in favor of the torture and violence committed in Brazil's most recent dictatorial period (1964–85). From the time he won the elections, democratic sectors feared an authoritarian turn in the country. The president rehearsed attempts at institutional change, and he often signaled his support for the proliferation of everyday violence, perpetrated outside the law by his support base.

But the authoritarian dynamics in poorly consolidated democracies definitely do not follow a predictable roadmap. When the pandemic hit Brazil in early 2020, there was fear of an advance in social control technologies, such as contact tracing, and other measures that, justified by the need to care for the population, would imply greater informational control of individuals' activities. As expected, the country saw a push in the use of biometrics, remote education provided by Big Tech companies, and delivery services mediated by digital platforms.

However, the economic and political conjuncture brought other elements to the table. The result was an increase in the death rate that coincided with a decrease in health care for the population and the rampant adoption of invasive technologies for data collection and exchange. In this process, opportunistic private interests and a neoliberal logic of population reduction combined to form a lethal political concoction.

To understand the driving forces in the adoption of social control technologies in the context of the pandemic, it is important to observe the ideological pressure for budget cuts as much as any desire to control the population. It is a complex interplay between neoliberalism and necropolitics, an ideological pressure for economic austerity that uses technology to further privatization, coupled with a disregard for the lives of anyone who doesn't belong to the elite. Just as the signs of negligence show, as Beatriz Busaniche points out, a lack of commitment from Latin American countries to protect the data of their citizens, so too do they help to explain how surveillance technologies have been used in the region.[2] States' adoption of digital platforms and technologies has occurred in a way consistent with what Ruha Benjamin describes as a "lack of concern for how the past shapes the present."[3]

Three Paths of Action and Understanding

At the time of the global outbreak of the pandemic, I co-wrote an essay in which we posited that, globally and in the Brazilian context, there were three different paths for understanding the crisis.[4] In describing one of the paths, the "rupture," we pointed out that the worsening of the pandemic crisis would be the product of historical asymmetries and inequalities, and that the way to overcome the crisis involved dealing with these global social injustices.

Another of these paths denied the seriousness of the crisis, and made an attempt—already identified as a failure—to seek the old normality at any price, even if it cost lives. We call this understanding "exception," because it dealt with the pandemic as if it were a brief period of abnormality.

The third path was the "acceleration" of the adoption of information technologies, including surveillance, to stop the proliferation of the virus through mass isolation and the transposition of traditional work and teaching routines to the internet. This latter path would also lead to increased social control and inequality. Brazil, through Bolsonaro's policies, managed to combine the harms of "exception" and "acceleration" without any of the possible benefits of such paths.

Exception: "It Is Just a Little Flu"

Denying the seriousness of the virus from the beginning, with public statements that COVID-19 would be a "little flu," former president Bolsonaro boycotted attempts by Ministry of Health technicians to adopt comprehensive and integrated measures to combat the disease. Until the beginning of 2021, for example, the ministry's information channels still encouraged the consumption of ineffective drugs against COVID-19, such as hydroxychloroquine. Several patients arrived at Brazilian hospitals intoxicated with drugs such as the antibiotic azithromycin, as a result of the president's propaganda about an alleged "early treatment" for the disease. It was only beginning in April 2021, after pressure from the other powers of the Republic, that the Ministry of Health started to work on a unified and scientifically proven hospital treatment protocol to be distributed to health professionals in the country.

There has never been a consistent effort in Brazil to conduct mass testing in combination with contact tracing. When Google and Apple made the contact-tracing technology available, the Ministry of Health readily adopted it as part of its official software. The software was first made available as a source of information about the disease, and the contact tracing feature was later adopted. However, only patients with more advanced symptoms have been tested in hospitals, while the population has resorted to cheap—although, for the majority, still unaffordable—and unreliable tests performed in pharmacies. This means that there is no reliable data on who is infected and when they became infected, making the use of this type of application unfeasible. At least until the beginning of 2021, the application contained outdated or misleading information. For example, it disregarded the importance of aerosol transmission and focused on recommending hygiene and social distancing measures.

However, that did not mean that other measures of technological acceleration could not be adopted. They aligned with attempts to adapt to the so-called new normal, but they also stem from trends previously mentioned, the effects of which are exclusion and the production of more inequality.

Acceleration: Rampant Digitization

Bolsonaro did not plan to offer any type of financial aid to people economically affected by the pandemic. But Congress managed to put public pressure and approve a bill benefiting all workers without income, regardless of whether they had lost their jobs because of the crisis or for some other reason.[5]

Anyhow, the delivery of the aid involved an electronic registration process modeled after that of previous social enrollments, such as Bolsa Família (a social welfare program implemented during former president Lula's years). The recommendations for social isolation implied an attempt to digitize much of the social assistance work, even though more than a third of the country has poor access to the internet, and often exclusively through smartphones.

This pressure to remotely provide social assistance services led to an acceleration of biometric identification practices, without a robust public debate about their possible harms; the focus was, instead, solely on the promotion of their benefits, the cost efficiencies, and the supposed protections against fraud. Pensioners have been encouraged to offer biometric data for facial recognition through an app, in order to avoid going to a service agency. Brazil has a mostly Black population, but little discussion has taken place about the problems of this type of system in identifying populations of African origin. There are plans for making use of the biometric system mandatory in the future.

These developments also bolstered policies for the creation of a "citizen base register" a project that was instituted in late 2019. The decree for the register's creation specified specifies the objective of gathering both biographical and biometric data. Through this program, information previously dispersed in different databases of the federal government (driver's licenses, enrollment in social assistance programs, vehicle registration, income information, work registration, etc.) becomes interoperable. The so-called proof of life for pensioners, for example, uses biometric data borrowed from the electoral register. Civil society's criticisms of the project are concerned with the inadequacies in Brazilian law regarding the protection of personal data and the possible use of this information for authoritarian purposes. A governance committee was created for the project, but it only includes members of the federal government, with no participation from civil society or scientific societies.

As in other places in the world, the pandemic forced a reduction of social, professional, and educational meetings for Brazilians. In all these fields, there was a push toward remote activities. In schools and universities, however, this push added to an ongoing process of dismantling their own autonomous informational structures in favor of the adoption of technologies from large platforms, technologies linked to so-called surveillance capitalism.[6] Michael Kwet understands this kind of process as digital colonialism, in which Big Data technologies are used as tools for a system of global surveillance capitalism marked by the collusion between corporations and state agencies from the Global North.[7] He posits that digital colonialism and surveillance capitalism share a continuity with surveillance tactics used to police Black bodies.

Data collected by researchers from the Educação Vigiada project point to a growth of up to 19 percent in agreements Big Tech platforms made with universities and state departments of education in the first seven months of the pandemic.[8] Although it is not an astounding number, it indicates the intensification in the use of these systems. As they receive large investments from speculative capital and the financial market, Big Tech companies have been better able to cope with the sudden spike in demand caused by the rush to remote systems. Systems maintained autonomously by universities and public schools, which had already received little investment, are gradually being abandoned owing to alleged technical insufficiency and high costs. Because companies operating under conditions of surveillance capitalism derive economic value from the data they collect from users, they are able to offer these systems free of charge to educational entities.

Asymmetric Impacts

The presiding logic in adopting surveillance and monitoring technologies in Brazil, however, follows less a direct desire to control speech and political discourse—although that is also present—and more the neoliberal and necropolitical reasoning of minimizing state spending. In other words, deaths resulting from coronavirus and impoverishment ultimately relieve the state of providing assistance because they minimize the "burden" on government agencies. Officials from the Ministry of Economy saluted the pandemic's impact on the national pension system.[9] Brazilian Congress hearings showed that calculations made by the Ministry of Economy predicted the end of the pandemic by late 2020 and limited resources in the 2021 national budget to fight COVID-19.[10]

Both the adoption of Big Tech infrastructures in the education sector and the interoperability of governmental personal data function on the same principle—reducing spending and promising greater efficiency is more important than data protection, social justice, and civil rights.

Bolsonaro's adoption of surveillance technologies in Brazil should not be understood only as a result of the personal authoritarian inclinations of the former president of the Republic. It stems from a broader context of austerity, economic policies, and a historical indifference by the country's elite to the lives of the population. The election of a new president in 2022—Luiz Inácio Lula da Silva, who ruled the country from 2003 to 2010—signals the resumption of policies of care for the population and the growth of the domestic consumer market. The broad coalition that supports Lula, however, is complex, ranging from center-right to left. While this offers positive change, we must ensure that investment decisions to expand the social support system cannot use technology only as a means to reduce costs, at the risk of replicating neoliberal and necropolitical logics of control.

33

CASE STUDY: Why We Must Fight against COVID-19 Surveillance and Techno-Solutionism

J. Carlos Lara Gálvez, Derechos Digitales

WHO WE ARE

Derechos Digitales is a nonprofit organization whose main objective is the development, defense, and promotion of human rights in the digital environment. Our vision is to contribute toward a more just, inclusive, and egalitarian Latin American society.

BACKGROUND

The COVID-19 pandemic arrived in Chile in early March of 2020.[1] As with most countries in Latin America, the first measures to contain the spread were adopted with significant skepticism and distrust from the population, especially once they took the form of lockdowns and curfews and the imposition of walk-around permits that could only be obtained by those with internet connectivity and digital literacy.

But there was an additional factor feeding that distrust: namely, the arrival of the pandemic in the midst of a national political crisis. Starting in October 2019, a spike in the price of subway tickets in Santiago surfaced three decades of frustration and resentment against the country's political and economic system. Massive protests led to a political agreement to start a process for replacing the national constitution—one that came into force during the military dictatorship forty years ago[2] —in order to replace a structural limitation to social demands.[3]

Although the path toward a new constitution was paved, social unrest did not fade away. Large protests with instances of looting and violence—as well as alleged human rights abuses by the police, and the imprisonment of protesters—became a regular part of the landscape in larger cities. Polls showed record low approval ratings for the government and large support for ongoing protests. Violent police repression continued.

A PERFECT STORM

Months of deep distrust in the government were followed by a global health crisis. Just as new, large demonstrations were expected, the government decreed a state of emergency—the military returned to the streets, and new lockdowns and curfews were put in place.

But the government understood there was a need to resume normal life. A series of new initiatives utilizing digital technologies began. In March 2020, a website that had served as a hub for obtaining police services was repurposed to become the only platform where one could obtain permits to leave quarantine. The same month saw the launch of a smartphone application to obtain a password in order to access government services online. In April 2020, "CoronApp" was released to provide official information on the pandemic. Online platforms were used to apply for government financial aid.

At a time that called for some social distancing and isolation measures, technology-dependent tools to interact with the government would seem like an ideal solution,[4] but the wave of initiatives failed to account for key concerns held by civil society organizations such as Derechos Digitales. What was being done to address the significant digital gaps across socioeconomic status, age, and geography? How was the collected personal data being used, stored, and accessed?

A government that sowed distrust and relied on heavy policing was now asking the entire population to depend on its systems of data collection and processing in order to maintain access to services during a global health crisis. And without internet connectivity, those already at risk were also under threat of sanctions for violating health measures, or simply risked falling outside the reach of financial aid, with the exception of a few boxes filled with groceries reluctantly funded by the government.

OUR STRATEGY

In spite of all the modernity behind the digital platforms, the lack of a comprehensive health strategy behind each measure was criticized, and the compound effect of the government's ineffective measures resulted in one of the largest per capita rates of contagion in the world for most of 2020.[5] The lack of proper planning and testing for the digital platforms was apparent, and distrust in the government was quickly met with action from different people to highlight weaknesses in the programs.

The "virtual police station" website, which was the primary entity issuing permits to go outside during lockdowns and curfews, has repeatedly failed[6] and has been reported to disclose the unique identifiers of its users.[7] The application to remotely obtain a unique password in order to access government services was retired less than a day before going public, after its crude facial recognition system was easily circumvented with photo printouts.[8] The whole system behind those unique passwords was also subject to cyberattacks.[9]

Besides highlighting the government's serious lack of security awareness throughout the pandemic, civil society has been clamoring for more proper safeguards against a series of haphazard efforts to collect more information than necessary.[10] The government's choice to use a smartphone application was a salient example of pursuing techno-solutionism rather than taking a thoughtful approach to address societal needs.[11] An initial examination showed that the application's broad collection of data and narrow safeguards made it problematic, risky, and ultimately useless.[12] The lack of adequate personal data protection mechanisms is indeed a more salient risk when so much information can be collected by or disclosed to the police, especially when much of it relates to freedom of movement—and consequently the right to protest—in a country with a track record of police action directly targeting public assemblies and protests.[13]

After a wide effort to obtain detailed information through transparency requests yielded disappointing results, there are now ongoing efforts to obtain better information about the real use of personal data by the authorities.[14] We believe that without transparency, there can never be true accountability.

LOOKING FORWARD

Although more restrictions were put in place after the second coronavirus wave in 2021, the reliance on technological tools to "mitigate" pandemic conditions started fading out. The "CoronApp" smartphone app was quietly removed from Apple's App Store and Google Play. The national state of emergency elapsed in September 2021 and curfews came to an end. A mostly successful vaccination campaign and the positive impacts of health measures offer hints of a brighter future. But as hope is reborn, we're left to wonder: what was the point of collecting all this information?

34

CASE STUDY: How We Challenged the German Migration Office's Surveillance Technology

Lea Beckmann, formerly of GFF, Society for Civil Rights

WHO WE ARE

The Gesellschaft für Freiheitsrechte (GFF, Society for Civil Rights) is a Berlin-based human rights organization. We have successfully challenged the German Federal Office for Migration and Refugees (German acronym: BAMF) on its routine analysis of data from refugees' smartphones. The phone data evaluation is expensive, non-transparent, and generates hardly usable results—and it violates fundamental rights as well as data protection law. In our work, we use the law as our primary tool to fight for human rights, to make German and European law more just and humane.

KEY TERMS

What is GDPR, the EU's data protection law?

The General Data Protection Regulation (GDPR) is a directly binding EU law on data privacy and security that became mandatory in 2018. Among other things, the GDPR regulation addresses the transfer of data outside of European Economic Area/EU areas and imposes strict obligations on organizations that collect data or target people in the EU. Through the regulation, the EU has concretized its firm stance on data privacy and data protection, threatening high fines for any GDPR violations.

What is Germany's 2017 legislative package?

Since 2016, Germany has passed law after law tightening asylum legislation and cutting down on the legal protection of asylum seekers in Germany. These changes included, among many others, an obligation that asylum seekers reside for prolonged periods in preliminary reception centers,
sometimes in remote places—sanctions which allow for substantial cuts
to already low livelihood benefits for a variety of reasons, as well as unan-
nounced deportations, sometimes in the middle of the night. In 2017, a
legislative package was passed that specifically aimed at speeding up asylum procedures and deportations and, to this end, made it possible for the
BAMF to analyze mobile phone data of refugees who do not possess a passport. This includes an analysis of a person's browser histories, social media
activity, geodata, call lists, and contacts.

BACKGROUND

If asylum seekers cannot present a valid passport or, in lieu of that, a passport replacement, the BAMF routinely extracts and analyzes data from
phones, to corroborate their owner's stated identity and country of origin.
Among the data analyzed are country codes of contacts in the phone address book, incoming and outgoing calls and messages, and geodata from
photos and applications, as well as email addresses and usernames used in
applications such as Facebook, Booking.com, and dating apps. Additionally,
a special software supposedly detects the language an individual has used
in their messages, emails, and web browser history. The BAMF checks the
results for any evidence that the asylum seekers made untruthful statements
regarding their identity or country of origin.

Phone data analysis on refugees was introduced as a part of the greater
legislative package in 2017 that sought to speed up asylum procedures and
the enforcement of deportations. Proponents of the legal changes argued
for them on the basis of assumptions that not only lacked evidence but also
were influenced by the key narratives of a rising far-right and racist ideology. Notably, during this time, refugees were increasingly depicted either
as fraudulent migrants without legitimate asylum claims or as terrorists in
disguise, and thus, a threat to national security. IT assistance systems were
presented as a possible remedy to render the asylum process more efficient

and reliable, to regain control and to demonstrate power. The legislative package thus marked a striking shift in the German political debate from a predominantly (and outwardly) empathetic and welcoming attitude toward Syrian refugees that arrived in growing numbers in Europe in 2015, to an increasingly hostile, right-wing, and racist discourse.

WHAT'S AT STAKE?

Smartphones contain some of our most sensitive and personal data, whether that entails our bank account details, messages, or photos. By screening the mobile phones of tens of thousands of refugees without just cause, the BAMF is blatantly violating fundamental rights as well as data protection law—all of this without producing meaningful "results." It is difficult to ignore the depth of these transgressions, given that they are systematically invading the mobile phones of people who, in practice, have incredible difficulty accessing legal remedies.

The BAMF analyzes primarily the phone country codes and languages that asylum seekers have used and spoken. Therefore, the actual relevance of the data evaluations, which is only indicative of nationality at best (and tentatively so), remains small. Between 2018 and August 2022, the BAMF attempted to analyze a total of 57,888 phones. In most cases, the evaluations failed, or results were inconclusive. Even where the results were conclusive and thus "usable," the BAMF only consulted these in making asylum decisions in 20–48 percent of cases. Where the results were used, in the vast majority of cases, the analyzed data corroborated the information given by the asylum seeker. The numbers from the 2018 records are lacking, but with regard to the 2019, 2020, 2021, and 2022 records, only 2-4 percent of the used results indicated a contradiction between the phone data and the said identity or country of origin of the asylum seeker, summing up to as little as 271 individual cases.

False results lead to distrust toward applicants and increase the risk of their asylum applications being rejected. Regardless of the results and how they are being used, being required to turn over one's phone has a personal and psychological impact on refugees, particularly because they are left in the dark as to what was viewed or analyzed, or what results the phone analysis yielded. As one of our claimants described it, "It felt like I was handing my whole life over."

The phone data analysis reveals a double standard when it comes to privacy rights. Despite huge public awareness about data protection in Germany, generally, the phone data analysis scheme targeting refugees has sparked little attention. Instead, refugees are de facto used as guinea pigs for new surveillance technologies.

OUR STRATEGY

We analyzed data carrier evaluation reports, asylum files, internal BAMF regulations, as well as training documents for BAMF employees and the user manual for reading mobile data carriers, documents from the legislative process, and statements by legal scholars, refugee organizations, and associations, as well as other information that was made public through parliamentary inquiries. We compiled, translated, and published the results of this research in a comprehensive report, which formed the basis of the legal action that followed.[1]

The GFF, on behalf of three claimants that had their phones taken and analyzed, initiated lawsuits in May 2020. The objective of the lawsuits was to obtain a judgment by a High Court declaring the phone data searches unlawful or unconstitutional. Additionally, GFF launched a complaint with the Federal Data Protection Officer who oversees the Migration Office and ensures its compliance with data protection law.

The first challenge was to find claimants who were willing to legally challenge the rights infringement. Many refugees were hesitant to press charges against state authorities as they were afraid of compromising their relationship with the very authorities on which their future depended. For them, there was little to gain, personally, but much at stake. Additionally, there were other, more urgent challenges besides privacy rights infringement, which they had to confront on a daily basis.

LOOKING FORWARD

Finally, and after almost three years of legal battle, in February 2023, GFF celebrated a major legal victory: the Federal Administrative Court of

Germany in a landmark decision, found that the BAMF phone search on an Afghan woman was unlawful, because it searched her phone at registration, before translating and examining all available documents. It thus failed to assess milder means before reading out the phones, as required by the law. As the phone search in question constituted BAMF's standard practice regarding phone searches, the implications of the judgment are far-reaching. Since other available means (such as linguistic assessments and the evaluation of all available documents) usually clarify any remaining doubts about identity, and as the phone data extraction has very little conclusive value, the remaining scope of the application of the phone data evaluations seem negligible. GFF will closely follow up on the application of this landmark decision. Nonetheless, despite dropping numbers, BAMF continues to search phones. GFF still awaits the decision of the German Federal Data Protection Officer. While not being able to directly instruct the BAMF, the Federal Data Protection Officer can demand access to information and evaluate the compliance of phone data processing with current data protection law and, on the basis of those findings, declare violations. The Federal Data Protection Officer can thus help reveal more information and enable short-term changes.

Through translating and disseminating our research on ongoing government practices, we have also been able to generate some small, short-term impacts. Through this awareness-raising work, which has also attracted significant media coverage, there is more public knowledge about phone-searching practices in Germany than there is about such practices in most other countries. Our research report also sparked academic interest and has informed and enabled interdisciplinary research on the digitization of border governance in Germany and internationally. Within Germany, GFF's work has substantially shaped the discourse about phone data analysis and the ongoing critical debate about the lawfulness, necessity, and uses of phone data analysis on refugees.

35

CASE STUDY: Fighting San Diego's Smart Streetlights Super Surveillance System

Khalid Alexander and Lilly Irani, Transparent and Responsible Use of Surveillance Technology (TRUST) San Diego Coalition

WHO WE ARE

Khalid Alexander is a professor at City College and founder of Pillars of the Community, an organization that advocates for people targeted and negatively affected by law enforcement. Lilly Irani is an associate professor at UC San Diego and organizes with Tech Workers Coalition, an organization that builds worker and community power.

KEY CONCEPTS

What are smart streetlights?
Smart streetlights are public light fixtures that incorporate remote sensing technologies, such as cameras and other sensors. They use remotely controlled management systems to monitor the streets in real time.

What is CalGang?
CalGang is the largest California-wide gang database that, at its peak, held data on 150,000 people. Since state law AB 90 imposed transparency and oversight procedures in 2018, many cities have withdrawn from CalGang and created their own gang databases using tools such as the Palantir system. The data that is fed into the database, widely critiqued as overrepresenting Black and brown youth, is based on very loose criteria for inclusion. It has several consequences and often plays into decisions regarding deportation,

criminal investigation, the imposition of injunctions, and arrests. California's Street Terrorism Enforcement and Prevention Act (STEP Act) also allows judges to hand down harsher punishment ("gang enhancement" charges) for those classified as gang members.

THE ISSUE

In 2014, the San Diego police rounded up thirty-three Black men, many in the middle of the night while they slept, because of the neighborhood they grew up in, the way they dressed, and the music they listened to. What none of them could have known was that the district attorney had decided to test out an obscure, never-before-used provision of the California Penal Code (Section 182.5) and a little-known statewide database to charge them with fifty years of life in prison. The charges relied on a database called "CalGang," built by police officers who would label people as gang members based on clothing, location, loose associations, and hearsay. The charges also relied on "gang enhancement" charges made against people unlucky enough to be in the database. CalGang and gang enhancements had been used to target Black and Brown communities since 1988 with the passage of the California STEP Act, but this roundup felt different. It seemed that Penal Code 182.5 licensed prosecutors to charge *anyone* with gang crimes. Its unapologetic use in San Diego triggered a community response and demand for transparency in how surveillance is used by law enforcement. The destruction enabled by this law became apparent when even prosecutors of two of the men admitted that they didn't think the defendants had committed the underlying crimes, or even knew about them. But because they were "documented gang members," they were charged under 182.5 anyway.

Concerns about cases like these led Khalid Alexander to show up, five years later, to a forum on the installation of a new "smart streetlight" system in San Diego. The program had been sold publicly as an energy-saving program. But at the meeting San Diego police and a city bureaucrat revealed that 1,500 streetlights had already been installed, and information that it gathered was being routinely accessed by law enforcement. The presentation seemed clear: police and the city were embarking on a new super surveillance system with no oversight. "Don't worry . . . the system's ability to listen in on conversations is turned off," they said, adding that the cameras were directed at public property.

What should have been a large group of community members learning about a new invasive technology at a local library had a total of four people in attendance. Three of those people were representing the smart street-lights initiative: a city bureaucrat, a police captain, and an official from General Electric. The audience of one, Khalid Alexander, didn't understand the technology itself, but knew enough to be shocked. Police already watched and documented his neighborhood, criminalizing people through gang laws. Could they start doing this with technology from a distance?

Alexander began reaching out to other organizations, immigrant rights groups, and tech workers. The next community forum packed the house with people asking hard questions about the technology, its law enforcement uses, and the policies governing it. From that meeting sprung one of the most diverse coalitions in San Diego. We now have two ordinances geared toward overseeing the use of technologies by the City. While smart streetlights provoked a reckoning about surveillance infrastructures among organizers, a wide range of technologies—known and unknown—made up the surveillance dragnets of San Diego. The mayor ignored our call for a moratorium, so we turned to the City Council for champions. We drafted an ordinance that gave City Council the authority to approve or reject any surveillance technology acquisition, required city departments to create user policies and impact reports to gain Council approval, and required an annual renewal necessitating Council approval. Our ordinance created a Privacy Advisory Board to support City Council with recommendations on specific technology acquisition proposals. The board seats are reserved for representatives from communities especially impacted by surveillance and for information technology and civil liberties experts. No board member can have financial ties to companies selling surveillance technologies. We built on the American Civil Liberties Union's Community Control Over Police Surveillance model, but emphasized a slowed down and transparent process to allow communities to organize.

As of September 2022, the ordinance is law; however, our fight is not over. The coalition is now focused on the city's implementation of the ordinance, strengthening the text of the law, stopping harmful technologies, and supporting other movements fighting surveillance in our region. We see the overreach of surveillance technology as a continued threat that will require the community's continued vigilance and struggle.

ON CONNECTING THE DOTS, AND BUILDING STRONGER RESISTANCE

The ordinance campaign brought together the TRUST Coalition: over thirty community groups variously working toward immigrant rights, police reform and abolition, racial justice, worker power, housing advocacy, climate justice, and civil liberties and privacy. Academics and privacy professionals also spoke out as experts reinforcing community knowledge and testimony to city officials. This coalition came together because surveillance technologies connected a number of violent projects in San Diego: "Countering Violent Extremism" programs that surveilled, radicalized, and criminalized Muslim communities; real estate development that called for the policing of racial and class spatial boundaries; economic development projects that greenwash clean tech and high tech as climate justice; and, finally, smart city projects pushed by tech companies that tech workers did not want to build, instead wishing for alternatives to heavily military-oriented tech jobs. These connections came together in joint resistance through this coalition. They generated spontaneous connections at City Council budget meetings, with those calling to refund libraries, those calling to defund the police, and those calling to defund the streetlights taking up each other's messages during public comments.

Organizers in the coalition participated in a coalition steering committee, held community education forums, offered feedback on the ordinance proposal, and educated one another on the myriad and distinct ways in which surveillance affects different vulnerable communities. These activities offered opportunities for more experienced organizers to build capacity by engaging newer organizers, thus deepening the bench of organizers in San Diego. Organizers also mobilized community members at key moments during an election year to push the ordinance, first through key committees and finally through a full, unanimously supportive City Council vote.

The coalition sees the oversight ordinance as a tool for deepening organizing and connecting struggles of different communities whose fates are affected by capitalism, especially forms of capitalism that operate by creating hierarchies and casting some groups as less than human. While the ordinance is not focused on any one technology, our organizing work around smart streetlights allowed for political education and built the relationships it took to ultimately shut down the streetlights in 2020. The ordinance slows down the process of acquisition, both slowing the tech sector's profit accumulation and creating time for organizers to educate, deliberate, and act on the City's plans to expand surveillance. It also makes deliberations public through the Advisory Board process, creating opportunities for communities in solidarity to propose alternatives to surveillance that expand safety and stability for all. Industry will keep selling new surveillance technologies and politicians will keep seeking quick fixes for complex problems. No win is final. The work will require constant vigilance. Raising the alarm and drawing attention is not enough. Neither is a "win." Once the ordinance is in place, the deeper work of building people power against surveillance and criminalization begins.

AFTERWORD

Since writing this essay, assembly member-turned-mayor Todd Gloria moved from sharing the concerns of the TRUST coalition to vigorously supporting police pursuit of a sole-source contract with Ubicquia for a new citywide smart streetlights and automated license plate reader network. Despite the Privacy Advisory Board voting unanimously to reject the police proposal, the City Council has voted to ignore the advice of the board and allow the city to move forward with dubious policy safeguards. While the ordinance has been successful in slowing down the tech and forcing the city and tech companies to be transparent, our organizing has not persuaded the mayor and the police to refuse this surveillance dragnet. Every day provides us with more opportunities to learn and continue the struggle.

Part 5

LOOKING FORWARD

36

Abolish National Security

Arun Kundnani

While the COVID-19 pandemic raged in 2020, at least 15 million people participated in Black Lives Matter demonstrations across the US.[1] These multiracial protests represented a coming to terms with the country's history of racial violence. Among the predominantly young people protesting, there is a widespread awareness that war, prisons, and borders do not advance the well-being of the majority of people in the US, that turning the country into an "armed lifeboat" is no solution to climate crisis and zoonotic pandemics, and that wealth never "trickles down" to the majority under racial capitalism.

Within this movement, as with any, there is a diverse range of motivations and orientations. Of particular note is the abolitionist approach that has shaped a lot of recent Black-led mass struggle, influenced by Black feminist politics and queer organizing—and the radical notions of care these traditions embody.[2] Abolitionism is a mode of political thinking and practice that has emerged from twenty years of organizing against the prison-industrial complex by groups such as Critical Resistance.[3] Abolishing prisons and defunding the police are its most prominent aims but opposition to border violence and militarism has also been important. Abolitionism locates policing and incarceration within a broader set of structures that includes borders and military violence deployed abroad. Fifteen years ago, Angela Davis called for the expansion of anti-prisons organizing work to take on the global imprisonment networks of the "Global War on Terror."[4] Today, groups such as Dissenters are organizing against the entirety of the US's national security infrastructure from a Black abolitionist perspective.[5]

At the core of abolitionist politics is an attempt to reconceptualize the notion of security. The logic that dominates the criminal legal system, abolitionists argue, involves thinking of harm as a problem that can be solved through officially sanctioned punitive violence. This has two consequences. First, it means that the criminal legal system intensifies rather than reduces the circulation of violence, giving rise, in turn, to demands for more police and more prisons—a perpetual motion of criminalization. Second, it means that attention is diverted from examining the underlying social and economic causes of what we call "crime." Prisons instead serve to screen off the social problems that result from the "unmanageable political economy" of global capitalism.[6] But in doing so, those problems are worsened. The massive expansion in the number of prisons and the militarization of law enforcement are not responses to increased crime but an integral part of neoliberalism, which involves declaring large numbers of people as "surplus." Prisons are ways of hiding such people from view and forgetting about the social questions they raise; racism is essential to this process.

In such circumstances, abolitionists argue, calls to reform prisons and police forces to make them more humane are insufficient. So, too, are calls to differentiate more effectively between those who deserve to be incarcerated and those who do not. Such calls avoid a reflection on the root causes of the problems that prisons and police pretend to solve. Instead, abolitionism proposes the creation of an "array of social institutions that would begin to solve the social problems that set people on the track to prison, thereby helping to render the prison obsolete."[7] This broader sense of security would involve meeting educational, childcare, housing, and health care needs as well as decriminalizing drug use, sex work, and migration. By also creating a justice system based on reparation and reconciliation rather than retribution and vengeance, there would ultimately be no need for prisons.[8]

Of course, achieving that goal is not an immediate possibility. For now, the question is how to push for reforms to the criminal legal system that move in the direction of defunding and disbanding. The answer will depend upon local context and the balance of political forces. As well as building power through grassroots organizing, electoral initiatives will also play a role. The Movement for Black Lives coalition's Electoral Justice Project, for example, has proposed the BREATHE Act—legislation that would defund federal incarceration and law enforcement, abolish ICE and the Drug

Enforcement Administration (DEA), fund community-led, nonpunitive approaches to public safety, retroactively decriminalize drug use, invest in education, health care, housing, and environmental justice, and extend workers' rights.[9]

Abolitionism throws up as many questions as it answers. The work of imagining alternatives to the criminal legal system is ongoing. What is striking, however, is the generative possibilities of applying an abolitionist approach not only domestically within the US but also to its agencies of global security. In this, abolitionism draws upon the legacies of a Black internationalist politics in the US that found expression, for example, in the Student Nonviolent Coordinating Committee's organizing in the late 1960s against the Vietnam War and its work supporting national liberation in Puerto Rico and Palestine.[10] Like its criminal legal system, the US's global national security infrastructure spreads rather than reduces violence, in ways that are often organized through racism. And its military actions distract us from addressing the social and ecological problems the planet faces. Abolitionism implies that framing discussion of US military actions in terms of which kinds of "intervention" are legitimate and which are not is a limiting horizon that hides from view the structural drivers of endless war. Likewise, discussing who should be constrained by borders and who should not means avoiding reflection on the role that borders play in our social and economic systems and what the alternatives might be. An abolitionist framework entails understanding that genuine security does not result from the elimination of "threats" but from the presence of collective well-being. It advocates building institutions that foster the social and ecological relationships people need to live dignified lives, rather than reactively identifying groups of people who are seen as threatening. It holds that true security rests not on dominance but on solidarity, at both the personal and the international level. It is possible to address security problems like climate change and pandemic diseases only from an internationalist perspective. In the long term, it is illusory to achieve security for one group of people at another's expense.[11] In policy terms, an abolitionist approach would imply a progressive defunding and shrinking of the US's bloated military, intelligence, and border infrastructure, and the construction of alternative institutions that can provide collective security in the face of environmental and social dangers.

The US Racial Security Logic

The US currently spends over $1 trillion a year on a fantasy of national security. This amount, spread across military, intelligence, and border agencies, is over twice what it would have cost to provide both COVID-19 vaccines to everyone in the world and a global safety net to prevent anyone from falling into poverty because of the virus.[12] The Department of Defense budget alone accounts for more than half of all federal discretionary spending each year. The US military deploys 2 million men and women across at least eight hundred military bases in ninety countries and territories around the world. It conducted covert military operations in 154 countries in 2020.[13] It maintains an estimated arsenal of 3,800 nuclear warheads and plans to spend roughly $100 billion to purchase six hundred more nuclear missiles.[14] Beyond the military, the present-day US national security system includes agencies that were forged in the early Cold War, such as the CIA and the National Security Council, as well as more recent creations of the Wars on Drugs and Terror, such as the DEA and DHS. With frameworks like the Global War on Terror and War on Drugs, involving relationships of intelligence-sharing, training, arms exports, and financial assistance, the US is able to draw many other states into its security machinery, driving spirals of conflict across Latin America, the Middle East, South and Southeast Asia, and Africa. Hundreds of thousands have died in Mexico as a result of the US-encouraged militarized War on Drugs.[15] The US remains the world's largest arms exporter, with its share of arms exports rising to over a third of the global total over the last five years.[16] In the neoliberal era, the national security system has incorporated a web of think tanks and private security corporations involved in weapons manufacturing, military logistics, the provision of mercenaries and other armed personnel, cyber warfare, border fortification, and surveillance technology. These corporations in turn provide opportunities for Wall Street investors to profit from the taxpayer-funded national security system.

The scale of this infrastructure is almost completely accepted as the taken-for-granted background to US foreign policymaking. To question it is to place oneself outside of what is considered legitimate opinion in elite US politics. Threaded through this consensus is an ideological process which involves repeatedly identifying "bad actors"—whether embodied in nation-states or insurgent movements—and selecting methods of dominating them to produce a fantasy of security. The frameworks through which these "bad actors" are conceived have foundations in US racial and colonial history. Today, they have a global reach. From the frontier wars of the colonial period to the Global War on Terror, the construction of threats to security has involved what Michael Rogin calls the "fantasy of savage violence," the fear that racially subordinated groups might inflict their barbarism on the civilized.[17] Rebellions against racial and colonial domination are the indispensable emergencies around which US security policy and practice has usually been organized. Some of these emergencies are real, some exaggerated, and some entirely imagined. Their racial elements might be explicit or submerged. In any case, they provide opportunities for the mythic heroes of US expansion to exact racial revenge or rescue.[18] This involves what Franco Fornari describes as "the incredible paradox that the most important security function is not to defend ourselves from an external enemy, but *to find a real enemy.*"[19]

In a sense, the United States has never stopped fighting "savages" at its frontiers, even as the frontier expanded to the global battlefields of the Cold War, War on Terror, and War on Drugs.[20] The enemy in each case is characterized by an ascribed inherent failure to follow "civilized" rules of conflict. To conservatives, the enemy is of necessity alien to the values of Western civilization; to liberals, the enemy fails to uphold democracy and human rights. But these political differences conceal an implicit solidarity: with few exceptions, conservatives and liberals agree that national security means absolute domination over less civilized enemies. In this way, the US national security system proclaims its own innocence and virtue while it is, as Martin Luther King Jr. pointed out, "the greatest purveyor of violence in the world."[21]

But the weight of history does not fully explain the modalities of US national security policy and practice in the neoliberal era. Neoliberalism depends upon racially coded global divisions of labor that render vast swaths of the human population superfluous to capitalist production. Projects of racist policing, mass incarceration, border militarization, and counterterrorism are directed at managing this "surplus" humanity under neoliberalism. This, in turn, provides a material basis for recurring upsurges of nationalism and racism that flourish in the ruins of neoliberalism's dismantling of collective democratic action.[22]

This emphasis on security under neoliberalism has offered a new basis for the legitimacy of government itself. As former chair of the Federal Reserve Alan Greenspan said in 2007, "Thanks to globalization, policy decisions in the US have been largely replaced by global market forces. National security aside, it hardly makes any difference who will be the next president."[23] In other words, because economic policy is usually subsumed in global markets, neoliberal governments find it hard to derive consent from claiming to increase citizens' material well-being; instead, it is easier to legitimize themselves through claims of protecting citizens from myriad terrible dangers—namely, "national security." Racially marked populations, who have been dispossessed by neoliberalism, are then cast as new sources of danger, in the form of terrorists, migrants, or criminals.[24] Neoliberal political contest becomes a matter of parties competing over the identification of threats and the implementation of spectacles of violence in response. The result is a political culture bent out of shape: national security has an overbearing presence in policymaking circles but one that mainly sustains a fantasy of domination and avoids any coming to terms with its own structural failures.

Mourning for America

Such a situation is not unique to the US but is a tendency wherever neoliberalism dominates. However, the US context is distinguished by an ideological attachment to the fantasy of a never-ending 1990s, when, in the aftermath of the Cold War, US exceptionalism seemed to have made possible a stable, US-dominated world order, before China's twenty-first-century ascent to great power status. The delusion of returning to the US "primacy" of the 1990s has long since become obsolete as a viable means of providing national security. Yet in the Washington policymaking process, alternatives to such a strategy are simply not credible.[25] By not facing up to the irreversibility of its geopolitical decline and the environmental and social challenges it now confronts, the United States is putting off a collective mourning for the loss of an imagined America that was loved but no longer exists. This failure to grapple with the early end of the American century finds expression in liberal calls for a return to a "rules-based international system"—code for 1990s-style globalization—as much as in Trump's call to "make America great again." Refusing to come to terms with the collapse of a fantasy of US omnipotence produces a melancholic paralysis in the face of real dangers, even as the US national security infrastructure lashes out against the current list of targets: China, Russia, Venezuela, and Iran.[26]

Consequently, the gap between the official US narratives of national security and the actual security needs of ordinary people has become palpable. The US national security infrastructure has itself been a major contributor to the greatest danger facing the US population over the coming decades, the heating of the planet.[27] Indeed, rather than reduce its carbon emissions, the Pentagon presented the climate crisis as providing a new rationale for its existence, declaring the US military as a necessary source of order in a world of climate-driven mass migration and extremism.[28] The US national security system did not prevent over a million people in the US losing their lives to COVID-19, one of the world's highest per capita death tolls in the richest country in the world. Instead, it mobilized anti-Chinese sentiment in response to the pandemic to justify an escalation in spending to counter the rise of China.[29] Thus, even the catastrophes of climate crisis and zoonotic pandemics have been folded into the racialized logic of national security. The cycles of violence spun by the War on Drugs and the Global War on Terror have continued, despite those wars causing far greater loss of civilian life than drug traffickers or terrorists could ever have imagined.[30] The general pattern is that US policies exacerbate the insecurities they are ostensibly designed to minimize. They have utterly failed to deal with the actual dangers facing the US population.

Cracks in the System

But there are cracks in the dominant security logic that could be pried open. US public opinion is skeptical of the endless wars. Around two-thirds of Americans think the 2003 Iraq war was a mistake, and over half think the US should not have deployed military force in Afghanistan or Syria. Veterans are just as likely to oppose these wars as anyone else, irrespective of period of service, rank, or combat experience.[31] Not only is there opposition to US involvement in specific wars but there is also support for defunding the national security infrastructure as a whole: a majority in the US favors cutting the defense budget by 10 percent and reallocating those resources to disease control and other public services. Twice as many people support such a cut to the defense budget as oppose it.[32]

Yet despite its popularity, legislation introduced to achieve this defunding was easily defeated in Congress.[33] The body of opinion in favor of military defunding lacks the momentum and energy that comes from grassroots organizational power—the only force capable of overcoming the vested interests and ideological barriers that have stood in the way of coming to terms with US violence. Fifty years ago, when progressive movements in the US were last at a peak of organizational power, in the shadow of the Vietnam War, Congress did take steps to reduce the power of the national security infrastructure. The Ninety-Third Congress, from 1973 to 1975, was, according to Greg Grandin, perhaps the "most anti-imperial legislature in United States history."[34]

Seize the Time

What this all points to is the need for intensified organizing to build a political force capable of dismantling the US's global infrastructure of violence. We need to focus on everything from ending the global Wars on Terror and Drugs, to ending sanctions policies, to halting support for Israel and Saudi Arabia, to nuclear disarmament. We need to sustain peace and development through conflict resolution, debt relief, and reparations programs that empower local communities rather than make financial aid conditional on acceptance of US counterterrorism, counter-narcotics, or migration control initiatives. We need to draw on experiences of community-based security cultivated in locations where the state has failed to protect its citizens, such as among Indigenous peoples in the shadow of the War on Drugs in Latin America.

Finally, we will need to acknowledge and commemorate the injustices of the past, from settler colonialism to the War on Terror. We might begin by constructing a national landmark monument to recognize the lives lost to US military violence, from Wounded Knee to Waziristan.

Twice before in US history there has been a major opportunity to overcome racism, prioritize care over killing, and embrace the reciprocity that constitutes humanity—first, in the era of Reconstruction after the abolition of slavery, and then in the heyday of the Black freedom and anti-war movements of the late 1960s. As a third such opportunity begins to become a possibility in the United States—with climate and pandemic crises looming—we must once again seize the time to fulfill the promise of those earlier moments.

37

The First Step Is Finding Each Other

Timmy Châu

In August 2017, in response to escalated tensions on the Korean Peninsula inflamed by the Western media, President Trump made headlines, warning that any threats would be "met with fire, fury, and frankly power, the likes of which the world has never seen before."[1] It was in this context, with the US president threatening to massacre millions of everyday Korean people, that a constellation of organizers based throughout the so-called United States came together to assess and renew radical pathways to a world without US imperialism.[2]

Since I am the son of a survivor of the US-led war in Vietnam, my dinner table was a place where the traumas of war were both passed down and re-lived—stories recounting the sounds of B-52F bombers hovering overhead in the night or the smell of burnt foliage that lingered in the air of my mother's village after a napalm raid. I long struggled to connect these stories to my experience as a young community organizer in Chicago, politicized during the Ferguson uprising and working to challenge systems of policing and imprisonment within the US. Not long after college I started working with a collective of artists, activists, and organizers known as the Chicago Torture Justice Memorials, a radical consortium of movement builders fighting for reparations for the hundreds of Black and brown men and women tortured under former Chicago police commander Jon Burge. It was through this work I learned that many of the Chicago police officers responsible, including Jon Burge, were Vietnam War veterans, and the torture tactics they were using against poor Black and brown people across Chicago were developed and weaponized against Vietnamese people during their time as US soldiers in the war.

For me, learning about the brutal connections of violence linking the lives of Black and brown Chicagoans to the lives of Vietnamese people—the violence of US empire—was clarifying, and it pointed directly to why a broad-based anti-imperialist movement connecting local and international struggles within the heart of the US empire was needed. So, part of the charge of Dissenters, a youth-led anti-war organization initiated by myself and a group of my collaborators, was to strategize how we might fill that gap and lay the groundwork for a new generation of resistance positioned to challenge the violence of the US war machine. The struggles and experiences encompassed were diverse—some came out of the movement to abolish police and prisons, some from migrant and environmental justice efforts, and others fighting for a liberated Palestine. We all understood the US military as a critical intersection of oppression connecting our various zones of resistance. We also sought to rectify the liberal peace movement's failure to center the communities most impacted by US militarism by providing a space to offer support, training, and resources to the next generation of young rebels seeking to end war.

Throughout high school and college, I witnessed firsthand the way US military recruiters preyed on poor Black and brown communities. I struggled seeing many of my friends grapple with the choice to enlist in the military so they could pay for college and ensure a better future for themselves and their families. Their choice was not an uncommon one, and it is one of many reasons why we identified universities, including community colleges, as key sites of the US military-industrial complex—from its blood-soaked endowments to its military recruitment offices. Given our experiences organizing with young people, and that many of us were young people ourselves, we saw a specific role for a nationally networked organization with local chapters that would start by targeting militarism on college campuses, and in future phases would expand to regional and citywide demands. We understood campuses to be a strategic place to initiate youth anti-war organizing, because young campus organizers can leverage collective power over local institutions with direct ties to US militarism. Additionally, we sought to build a network of highly skilled young organizers that would toxify war in the collective consciousness and proactively respond to political crises sparked by US imperialism through strategic direct actions.

On January 2, 2020, we launched the organization at our inaugural Founders Training, bringing together twenty-five radical student organizers from around the country. Together we shared analysis, deepened skills, and forged new relationships, laying the groundwork for a growing constellation of anti-war resistance.

Our approach to leadership as organizers must be a collective one. From the radical art-makers and direct-action experts to the campaign researchers and movement healers, everyone has a role to play, and the roles are many. Since its launch, there are now Dissenters members plotting direct actions, training other young radicals, and implementing targeted campaigns at over twenty-five chapters across the United States.

War on All Fronts

US militarism encompasses the police, military, and ICE. Policing and the imprisonment of poor Black and brown folks within and outside US borders are a part of the same project of maintaining the US settler-colonial, white supremacist system. Beyond the direct exchange of tactics and munitions, these various arms of the state ultimately serve the same purpose—to preserve and protect the interests of the US political and corporate elite.

In addition to my work with Dissenters, I am co-Director of an organization called the Prison + Neighborhood Arts/Education Project (PNAP), which works to build inside/outside networks of mutual support and resistance between incarcerated and free-world activists, scholars, thinkers, and artists. At Stateville Correctional Center, a maximum-security men's prison in Joliet where we operate, many of the prison guards are former US military who, after receiving training and doing tours abroad, find work at the prison. There is a mural painted on the walls of the prison guard cafeteria depicting a guard dressed half in "Orange Crush" (the anti-riot prison guard outfit) and half in a US military uniform. For me, part of being an effective organizer starts with knowing with absolute clarity who are my allies and who are my oppressors. This mural, which I see every time I enter and exit the prison walls, is a reminder of who and what the prison stands for, illustrating the theoretical and material connection between the brutalizing labor of a prison guard in central Illinois and the armed military guard manning the gates of Guantanamo.

Containment has always been a modality of war—from the "strategic hamlets" of Vietnam to Japanese internment camps. Whether it's the War on Terror or War on Crime, the US state continually manufactures enemies to fill its prisons. The military- and prison-industrial complexes share the objectives of liquidating resistance and disappearing communities that are deemed as surplus. More than just a framework to be reapplied to the context of US war-making abroad, abolition pushes us to understand how the US military-industrial complex was made possible through African slavery and Indigenous genocide. It also allows us to understand how the US prison system and the war machine are two pillars of the regime of US empire.

Demilitarization and the Earth

The US military is the world's largest polluter. While this makes for a strong case that abolishing the military is our best shot at mitigating the catastrophic harms of climate change, it's not the full picture.

During the US colonial war in Vietnam, over 3.6 million hectares of forest and villages were doused in upward of 19.5 million gallons of toxic herbicide, with the aim of killing all vegetation to "expose the enemy." Roughly a decade earlier, American B-29s dropped over 866,914 gallons of napalm on the northern half of the Korean Peninsula, resulting in what would be described by some as a "wilderness of scorched earth."

In December 2021, a US Navy fuel storage facility started leaking gallons of toxic oil into the Red Hill aquifer, contaminating a critical source of drinking water for thousands of native Hawaiians. In response, Dissenters organizers mobilized as part of the Oʻahu Water Protectors coalition to demand accountability as well as the shutdown of the fuel tanks. Following months of sustained collective action, the Pentagon announced on March 7, 2022, that the Red Hill fuel tanks would be shut down and decommissioned.

These moments remind us that the Earth and its sacred, life-sustaining ecosystems are always casualties in a world at war, and how struggles to resist US imperialism are deeply connected with ongoing dispossession of Indigenous land and resource extraction. Actualizing a demilitarized future is a responsibility—one of many—we need to take on to repair our relationship to the earth.

Resisting the Endless War

The United States has been waging endless warfare and fueling a permanent war economy since its inception. Its tactics and targets have evolved over time, but its propensity for war is constant. An ever-increasing military budget means that its capacity for conventional warfare has only increased. That said, increasingly global flows of production and consumption have provided a strong incentive for the world's imperial powers, most notably the United States, to develop new strategies for securing their piece of the global economic pie. Tactics of warfare have been refined such that the total violence of war-making is strategically dispersed in a continuum of militarized micro-operations sold to the public through the framework of "security."

We are up against a decentralized, transnational architecture of war-making where dominant states increasingly rely on the facilitation of strategic arms deals and enlistment of private paramilitary contractors and non-state forces to secure political and economic interests. For example, since 2015, the US has sold roughly $10.7 billion worth of weapons to Saudi Arabia every year, directly fueling the horrific Saudi- and Emirati-led war in Yemen, in return for secure access to Saudi oil production and political support for the US imperial footprint in the Middle East.[3] It is an infrastructure tasked with violently policing the globally displaced and dispossessed to ensure the vitality of a global marketplace, forcibly maintained through continuous counterinsurgency operations and increasingly militarized borders. Technological advancements in communications and surveillance infrastructure have allowed imperial war machines to eradicate threats and quell resistance with precision. Adapting to the inherent instability of global capitalism has meant that hyper-militarized states have continually refined the art of crisis management, perfecting their ability to manufacture and exploit political and economic instability across the world in real time.

Within the US, public support for endless wars at home and abroad is maintained through a mass media controlled by political and corporate elites. Ideas and images posing any threat to the status quo are relentlessly policed. On top of the brutal repression faced in the streets, the liberal establishment weaponizes morality through the rhetoric of "nonviolence" to further defang resistance movements and circumscribe them to the realm of legality and electoral politics. Bipartisan support from politicians to increase funding for the police and the military, despite popular demands for defunding levied in 2020 by the largest protest movement in US history, reveals a political system more than willing to sacrifice lives on the altar of power and profit. We are taught from a young age that the US government is a democracy ruled by and for the people. The reality of our social conditions paints a vividly different picture—one where liberal democracy, rather than a source of freedom for the exploited masses, has simply refined the art of co-optation and improved its ability to ensure the masses are more freely exploited. The real progress, if any, to be found in liberal democratic regimes is in their ability to effectively redirect movements for social change into the calibrated bureaucracy of electoral politics, where transformative and radical demands for more life quickly become lukewarm reforms leaving the status quo untouched. Rather than acting as a mechanism for undoing war, the promise of democracy has been fundamental to making war possible.

As new weapons of war are added to the US lexicon of organized violence, old ones remain. The brutal histories of mass violence and exploitation at the hands of colonial empires stand as evidence that no weapon is off the table. Nothing is certain. What we know is that all empires fall. But this empire will not fall without a fight.

Starting Points

At first glance, the expansive network of institutions and industries waging war on our communities is overwhelming. Our oppressors are many and all around us.

On the flip side, it means we have plenty of targets on which to set our sights: a weapons manufacturing warehouse, a police fusion center, a campus military recruitment office, an ICE detention facility all become possible terrains to plan our next attack. If the instruments of war are leveraged at both a local and global scale, so too must our strategies of resistance.

In October 2021, Dissenters organizers around the country mobilized for a week of direct actions to launch our #DivestFromDeath campaign, to force local institutions to divest from US companies profiting from war including Boeing, Lockheed Martin, Northrop Grumman, General Dynamics, and Raytheon.[4] Together, these US war profiteers are central to a global death-making industry fueling violence within and beyond our borders. Year after year they provide billions of dollars of weapons manufacturing to arm authoritarian regimes in the Philippines and Israel, and to local police departments across the US. In 2021, Dissenters based in Chicago launched a protracted struggle called the #BoeingArmsGenocide campaign to force the City to sever its ties with Boeing—including calling for an end to the millions of dollars in tax subsidies it provided the company to keep its headquarters there since 2001. After six months of campaigning, including initiating inquiries by the Office of the Inspector General into Boeing's city contract, Dissenters successfully blocked what would have been another $2 million check to Boeing for its final tax reimbursement from the city—a historic victory. I've often struggled with the idea of international solidarity so often discussed by activists in leftist movements—what does it look like in practice? How do we build internationalism from below in real, material ways? The #DivestFromDeath and #BoeingArmsGenocide campaigns are our response to these challenges, as well as what it means for us at Dissenters to be in solidarity with our comrades abroad, allowing our networks to take direct action against a shared enemy engineering war across the globe.

In addition, Dissenters organizers at different campuses are also challenging the local manifestations of US militarism by fighting to get police and military recruiters off their campuses. Working alongside such formations as the #CareNotCops and the #CopsOffCampus coalitions, members are fighting to dismantle the police forces responsible for violence and harassment against predominantly Black and brown students as well as the gentrifying role those forces play against the surrounding communities they occupy.

We know the US military will not be dismantled overnight. As our mobilizations grow, we see these fights as strategic opportunities to begin chipping away at a global system in a localized context, as well as a way to connect our battle at home to the ones abroad. We also recognize local campaigns as a critical way for young rebels to flex our muscles of direct action and build networks of affinity along the way.

The scars of war run deep. Healing will take time. But every scar is also a reminder of the less-told strategies of survival that we also carry with us. Makeshift creativity and clandestinity are ours—our innovations, our kindling. We will use these strategies, born from the legacies of displacement, to set fire to the fiction of nationalism until every border is obsolete. Forced passageways can also become lines of communication—forging meaningful affinities, weaving together pockets of resistance, linking people around the globe into a fiery constellation of rebellious complicities.

We want to end Empire. Lucky for us, there are many ways to ignite the flames of resistance. The first step is finding each other.

38

The Red Deal: Indigenous Liberation and the Fight to Save the Planet

Nick Estes[1]

I n 2020, the Red Nation, a Native resistance organization I cofounded in 2014, released *The Red Deal: Indigenous Action to Save Our Earth*, "a movement-oriented document for climate justice and grassroots reform and revolution." The Red Nation is dedicated to the liberation of Native peoples from capitalism and colonialism. Our work is focused on Indigenous treaty rights, land restoration, sovereignty, self-determination, decolonization, and liberation.

The Red Deal centers anti-capitalism *and* decolonization in social justice struggles and in the fight against climate change as well. The necessity of this approach is grounded in both the history and future of this land, and it entails the radical transformation of all social relations between humans and the earth.

Prison abolition and an end to border imperialism are key aspects of the Red Deal. In the United States today about 70 million people—nearly one-third of adults—have some kind of criminal conviction that prevents them from holding certain kinds of jobs. If we add this number of people to the approximately 8 million undocumented migrants, the sum is about half the US workforce, two-thirds of whom are not white. *Half* of the workforce faces employment discrimination because of mass criminalization and incarceration.

The terror inflicted on Black, Indigenous, Latino, migrant, and poor communities by border enforcement agencies and the police drives down wages and disciplines poor people by keeping them in a state of perpetual uncertainty and precariousness. As intensifying climate breakdown and imperialist interventions continue to fuel migration, especially from Central America, the policies of exclusion and control—as manifest through border walls, detention camps, and increased border policing—continue to feed capital with cheap, throwaway lives. For this reason, we need to thoroughly challenge national citizenship—as something that grants "legal" privileges to life for some and denies it others. What right does a colonizing settler nation have to say who does and doesn't belong? By fighting for equitable access to employment and social care for all, we can break down imperial borders, rather than reproduce them.

History has not ended. The fight over the past, present, and future is unfolding right now. There are alternative visions to maintaining the hegemony of the United States and its position as a "world power." We need a revolution of values that re-centers our relationships to one another and to the earth over profits.

Excerpt from the Red Deal

The Red Deal: Indigenous Action to Save Our Earth identifies five priority areas for divestment.[2] Given the great harm to the planet and humans they embody, divesting from them, the Red Nation writes, "will decrease violence on a mass scale. Divestment will also increase the quality of life and genuine safety of millions across the world who suffer at the hands of U.S. wars; wars against terrorism; wars against poverty; and wars against Indians."

The priority areas are Defund Police, La Migra, and Child Protective Services; End Bordertown Violence (a "bordertown" refers to a settlement sitting outside a Native reservation); Abolish Incarceration (prisons, juvenile detention facilities, jails, border security); End U.S. Occupation Everywhere; and Area 5: Abolish Imperial Borders.

In light of the theme of this book, we excerpt "Abolish Imperial Borders" below.

Area 5: Abolish Imperial Borders

Why is this important?

Western European countries have long held that the exercise of dominance over territory requires the definition and protection of borders. This pattern of dominance over territory and the militant defense of borders crossed the Atlantic Ocean with the arrival of the British, Spanish, French, and Portuguese colonialism. When the United States came into existence after a revolution of the bourgeoisie broke away the British crown, it embraced the European idea of controlling territory through border supremacy. This was codified in the Monroe Doctrine of 1823 that allowed the fledgling United States to exert its influence in the so-called "New World" without disturbance from "Old World" (European) colonial powers.

Since that time, borders have been used to control and restrict the movement of people (but only certain people) but free up and allow the movement of capital. The United States recognizes no borders other than its own when it seizes land through violent military force or topples governments of other nations who refuse to bend to the will of its corporations. This is the definition of imperialism, and borders play a key role.

Referring to the U.S.–México border, the U.S. media has proclaimed that we are in the midst of a "border crisis." This narrative, largely promoted by the U.S. National Security apparatus, paints the border as a threat to national security and to U.S. sovereignty. While this narrative has long justified U.S. imperialism as a means to "secure" the nation, it has been on steroids since September 11, 2001, and the creation of an entirely new arm of the U.S. government: the Department of Homeland Security.

This merging of borders with nationalism, capitalism, and imperialism requires us to develop a comprehensive analysis of how borders restrict, control, and govern the movement of Indigenous and other racialized people. The U.S. military force and capital have no borders; only people of limited means are bound by these borders. And what of our other-than-human relatives like animals? Their migration routes and free movement to fertile lands are denied by the border. The infamous livestock reduction program that was implemented by the U.S. government in the 1930s in the Navajo Nation is an example of this. Citing a lack of space for grazing, colonial administrators set out to reduce the number of sheep to "fit" the size of the Navajo reservation. But the borders of the Navajo Nation did not exist before the nineteenth century.

And they certainly weren't enforced as such through programs like livestock reduction prior to that period, which was a time when the United States aggressively sought to consolidate its territory and quell any competing claims to land held by Indigenous nations. Had imperial enclosures not been placed around the Navajo Nation, sheep could graze anywhere and Navajo families could follow in traditional seasonal movement patterns. Yet today, Indigenous people and our other-than-human kin are caged in our own lands.

These forms of border imperialism demonstrate how important it is to recognize the regulatory control that borders represent. This control happens through the surveillance of bodies, management of exclusion, and administration of punishment. Borders function as structures of segregation and weapons of empire. The abolition of border imperialism is critical to the idea that the free movement of people is an intrinsic human right, as stated in the United Nations Universal Declaration of Human Rights. Given the mass migration of humans and other-than-humans from the Global South to the Global North, which itself is caused by U.S. imperialist-colonialist practices and capitalist-driven climate change, we must open and abolish all borders to assist in the free movement of all life. Let us not forget: no one is illegal on stolen land except those who have stolen it.

What needs our urgent attention?

- Pan-African migration northwards into Europe
- Migration of plants and wildlife to natural feeding and breeding grounds
- Tribal reservations that are bisected by the U.S.-México Border

What can you do about it?

- Fight for sanctuary resolutions at the Tribal level
- Organize events that connect Indigenous peoples from the Global South (Bolivia, Brazil, Guatemala, etc.) with Indigenous movements in North America, Asia, and the Middle East

- Indigenous nations should play a role in the international community, specifically in the areas of international relations with other Indigenous nations and communities across the world (excluding nations that are complacent with the U.S. imperialist project)

39

Trying Harder to Build a World Where Life Is Precious: An Interview with Ruth Wilson Gilmore

Mizue Aizeki

Ruth Wilson Gilmore is professor of earth and environmental sciences and director of the Center for Place, Culture, and Politics at the City University of New York Graduate Center. Cofounder of many grassroots organizations including the California Prison Moratorium Project, Critical Resistance, and the Central California Environmental Justice Network, Gilmore is the author of the prize-winning Golden Gulag: Prisons, Surplus, Crisis, and Opposition in Globalizing California *(UC Press).*

Mizue Aizeki: Over the past thirty years, in the US we have experienced the explosive growth of a massive apparatus of migrant control. Can you help us understand the political and economic context in which deporting immigrants with criminal convictions became a heavy focus of the US social control regime?

Ruth Wilson Gilmore: That's really a great question, and I think that the answer to that question has many different dimensions. And the good thing is, if there are many dimensions, it means there are lots of ways to fight. Every dimension is an opportunity for a campaign, or an organization, or a struggle—and for a win.

The move to using the magic wand of criminalization to justify an extremely brutal and enormous roundup, incarceration, and deportation regime has origins long before 9/11. While 9/11 consolidated certain principles that were written into the Patriot Act, before that, in 1996, there was the Antiterrorism and Effective Death Penalty Act (AEDPA). And before that, in the waning days of the Carter administration [1977–81], resources were made available to localities to detain people who were moving from or fleeing their home countries, particularly Cuba and Haiti, for whatever reasons—economic, political, sexual freedom, gender identity freedom. As a result, other localities started to see opportunities. By the early 1980s, as Marlene Ramos shows, there were several municipalities in New Jersey that decided they would expand their jails in order to make space available to what was then the US Immigration and Naturalization Service (INS), and figure out how to make their jail space, management policies, and personnel practices conform to the demands of the federal government.

After 9/11, the dramatic reduction (outsourcing) of federal employees in security areas reversed, and federal security jobs started to rise again. Well, not surprisingly, if there is an expansion in a particular employment sector, especially in the public sector, that means some unions will be there to help those workers organize—as it should be. Unions in the United States are at one of the lowest levels of worker participation in history since the Wagner Act was passed during the Great Depression. In practical political terms, what should the response be? Organize.

Post-9/11, with the expansion of ICE personnel and Border Patrol, union organizers rolled in and started organizing, especially ICE and CBP. And then the question was put to the union organizers and the membership, many of whom come from households whose members include people who might well be vulnerable to deportation and incarceration and so forth: "Where is the line bright enough to distinguish 'deserving' from 'underserving' immigrants, even if it's also agreed that everybody should have proper documentation to be in the United States?" And what was their default position? "Go after the criminals." It was part of the union organizing strategy to get people to want to be in the union *and* to get the union approved by the Department of Homeland Security. The union said, "Give us a union, and we will do the job to pursue, detain, deport."

It's really kind of astonishing. Here are unions, municipalities, the spread of federal money, and state and local lockups with surplus space looking for someone who will rent it from them. All of these things are part of the constantly churning prison-industrial complex. Then there is yet another aspect to this problem, and it's a critical one for how to understand the context of struggle in the United States. Central to all this is what I call the "anti-state state."[1] By that I mean a state apparatus in all its dimensions in which important actors (elected, appointed, rank-and-file) rail against the very state (or, better said, particular aspects of the state) in which they work, or hope to work.

The anti-state state presents to itself and the world a dilemma. Which is to say, if an elected or appointed official takes a job in order to make the thing that makes the job possible disappear, then on what basis does that individual, or party, or other formation persist in the job rather than just lock the office door, go home and never come back again? And the answer is to find some default activities to support that appear, in a political context, self-legitimating. Police, for example, and firefighting are two; one would think public education and public health and hospitals would be, but they are not. And then there's the military, and to some degree, material infrastructure. I say "to some degree" because infrastructure neglect has been the story of the past fifty years in the United States. What happened in Texas in February 2021 is a perfect example of it. The idea that a power grid can fail in a state that produces oil and liquid natural gas and has plenty of open windy spaces to produce turbine power is astonishing. It's astonishing. But this is the anti-state state.

Aizeki: And the magic wand of criminalization requires the construction of enemies, right?

Gilmore: As I said, what is the default? The default tends to be characterized by the following way of thinking: We, all of us, can only secure our freedom in the context of having a perpetual enemy who must always be fought and can never be vanquished. Who is the enemy? Well, the enemy is variable, but right now in the United States one of the many enemies is any person who is not documented. Additional enemy status is conferred on not only those who are not documented in terms of permanent legal presence in the United States, but also, in numbers more dramatically, those who *are* documented in terms of what their encounters with law enforcement in the United States have been. When we put that together, we have a huge group of people. There are those who are not documented to work, which is about half the total number of not documented persons in the USA (around 5 million). And then there are those who are documented not to work—because of a disqualifying arrest or conviction, which creates significant barriers to securing jobs—which is about 65 million people. These numbers add up to at least half the entire US labor force, regardless of what their birth certificates say, who are all vulnerable to becoming or remaining precarious and to being persistent targets of, or abandoned by, the activities of the anti-state state. I raise this number to inspire organizers across many kinds of struggles and formations to think about the potential solidarities rather than disintegrations that might arise in the context of building campaigns.

One central contradiction that will never go away, that must be encountered and fixed, encountered and fixed, arises from the following: On the one hand, many of us who are abolitionist hold as a minimal given that no human is illegal, and where life is precious, life is precious. But, on the other hand, the view that settler colonialism, neocolonialism, and war have caused the actual or effective theft of the ability of people to make livings and make lives suggests a need to erect boundaries within which people can flourish (for example, establishing a commons and ruling what participating in it should never entail). The question emerges: How and under what circumstances can we imagine abolition geographies conducive to abundance, but which cannot be dominated again by the forces of unfreedom? And if the geographies can't be dominated again by forces of unfreedom, then there's got to be some kind of barrier or border or impediment to those forces. We get into this loop of enemy, counter-enemy, enemy, counter-enemy. And I haven't yet figured out how to overcome that loop, but I think about it all the time. All the time, as I try to think and think again how, in abolition terms, freedom is a place.

Aizeki: You have done a whole lot to help us understand carceral state logics and the prison-industrial complex. Under the current mass deportation framework, it is widely accepted among Democrats and Republicans that immigrants with criminal convictions are a legitimate and necessary target of the homeland security state. What are your thoughts on how we respond to that?

Gilmore: Well, this of course is what the unionization campaign I described earlier made into a legitimizing platform to secure the right to collective bargaining. The terrible few. The numbers are small and the fearmongering is persistent and frequently irresistible. I've often pointed out that at the original Critical Resistance conference in 1998, we talked about suffering harm, losing loved ones to murder and other forms of violence. Although hack polemicists from the left and right accuse abolitionists of moaning about innocents unfairly seized, abolition actually demands meticulous understanding of the bureaucratic, fiscal, and ideological conditions that channel people who suffer organized abandonment to the forces of organized violence. In that, the struggle to end (rather than better punish) interpersonal harm has caught the organizational imagination of people around the world.

There are all sorts of intermediate situations, including situations of harm and violence, in which things done differently can well produce a different outcome. This is the moment where I say INCITE! Women of Color Against Violence (which over time because INCITE! Women, Gender Non-Conforming, and Trans people of Color Against Violence) came into being because they saw that carceral feminism was not saving anybody. For them, women subjected to violence were not being saved by the fact that police were more involved in responding to violence against women, because that involvement was always after the violence, not before. And that, combined with the fact that police responding to violence often also enact more violence, and often the women who called for help would themselves wind up locked up, made those who started INCITE! say, "This is no way to end violence against women. What should be done instead? What do women who are vulnerable to violent interactions with household or intimate partners need?" What they figured out was, number one, they've got to be able to live somewhere where they are safe—and it's never a lockup. Two, they've got to not be dependent on the person perpetrating the violence for food and shelter or for income. And three, they've got to be—if they have dependents on their own—able to be confident that they can take care of them. These are very basic matters. Very, very basic. Which is a long way from saying that once a woman has been beaten, calling the police and punishing the beater is what justice is. Instead, it's saying, ending violence against women is what justice is, and then asking, "How?" Many people have been working a really long time trying to figure this stuff out. The Creative Interventions StoryTelling Organizing Project (STOP) that Mimi Kim and comrades built up is another resource for those who want to pursue different paths. In other words, these methods don't just arise from the heads of people in cozy desks in academia, but on the streets and in the organizations and by trial and error. And believe me, there are many errors. But the errors so far indicate what trying again might look like, because practice makes different.

Aizeki: How would you encourage us to think about the relationship of the state and corporations in the prison-industrial complex and the migrant policing regime?

Gilmore: If 100 percent of the private lockups—shorthand for a prison, jail, or detention center—closed tomorrow, whether they are holding migrants or the other kind of locked-up person, how many people would be freed? Zero. That is because the privates—which are significantly more successful in lobbying DHS for contracts than they've ever been in getting contracts for state and county jails—are only parasites at the end of the day. Nothing happens because they are there; they are there because the thing happens. They are the shiniest, most visible parasites on the bodies of the beast. But it's the beast, not the parasite that matters.

That is to say, rather than imagining that a group of corporations come to some state agencies and say, "Let us lock people up," or "Let us exploit people who are locked up," there is actually a whole world that unfolds before our eyes into which capitalists—builders, contractors, vendors—keeping their eyes on the movement of the social wage prize, insert their influence, ordinarily characterized as cost-saving promises (a theme that would require an entire additional interview to debunk).

Here are key elements: There are uniformed and civilian personnel whose salaries depend on locking people up and on holding people against their will for part or all of their lives. That is the biggest expenditure for the entire system, including migrant detention—wages and salaries.

Another expenditure is utility companies—these companies sell light and power and sometimes water to all of these lockups. Utility companies constitute the second biggest expenditure for the system. And then there are construction companies that build them and maintain them. Investment bankers make huge amounts of money selling debt to state and municipal authorities that use the money to expand the facilities to lock people up. Finally, the towns, whether they are big or small, where prisons and detention centers are located, seek facilities because they imagine they are going to have some kind of positive economic effect in the form of job multipliers (jobs whose presence happens because money spent by the facility or its employees creates local economic activity), or tax revenue.

Towns sometimes try to get rid of the facilities because they don't bring the kind of effect that people had imagined because elites had promoted it. There are many reasons for this failure, and a key explanatory factor is because the people who make the money from the facility don't spend it in those towns or live in them *because* there are prisons in them. They go somewhere else to spend their money, not surprisingly. There are exceptions, which ordinarily carry additional explanatory factors—such as the local economy is somewhat less singularly dependent on the prison (tourism, power plants, other public service employments such as forestry, land management, and so on).

So, there are all these parasites on the beast. There are those that are near the beast and are becoming part of the beast, like those that make electronic monitor ankle monitors, "ankle shackles" really, as James Kilgore insists we call them. Various people, whether they work for a public agency, a for-profit contracting firm, or a not-for-profit, are players in electronic monitoring. They are contracted to play supervisory roles in either monitoring undocumented people who get to "stay home," or monitoring people who have been arrested or convicted of things who get to "stay home." They are all parasites on the beast. But they are not the beast. And since it's come up, there are increasing numbers of nonprofit service providers, some helmed by formerly incarcerated people, that keeps the system aggrandizing.

It's a problem I referred to earlier: the US at all levels with few exceptions has tended toward, governmentally speaking, becoming the territorial expression of the anti-state state. To repeat, people run for elected office or try to keep elected office by promising people whose opinions count—which is to say voters—that if elected, they will make the government disappear. They will get government out of everyday life, they say. They promise to reduce taxes and make regulations go away. At the heart of the matter is the fact that the anti-state state aggrandizes itself through fulfilling obligations that people across quite a broad political spectrum accept as necessary. That's how the beast functions. And that's where the work of books like this and the organizing of the sort that this book lifts up matters—to denaturalize that acceptance and open consciousness to the possibility of life otherwise. It's stunning that the current regime appears natural, necessary, and inevitable, whereas it's a relatively recent politically produced phenomenon.

Aizeki: In the United States, the "good immigrant" versus "bad immigrant" frame has continued to limit our political possibilities. Since Obama, the federal government has repeatedly issued guidelines for what categories of immigrants ICE regards as priorities for arrest and deportation. Under Biden, ICE has broadly prioritized those which the government determines are a threat to "national security or, public safety"—for example, people with certain criminal convictions or anyone arrested for crossing the border after November 1, 2020. The immigrant rights movement often pushes back by weighing in on which immigrants should be the "real" priority, and, more recently, has pushed for more latitude to argue who is not a "threat"—rather than challenging the idea of prioritization overall. Given the ongoing challenges in the political landscape, how do we build political space for those deemed to be the "bad immigrants?"

Gilmore: You're exactly, right. Jesus fucking Christ—you can put that in the interview, "Jesus fucking Christ." I really want to know where these "capitulate first and then fight later" proposals originate—the logic of capitulation. Because what you just described vis-à-vis people without documentation in the United States is similar to proposals that people put forward to try to get only certain people exempted from having to post bail if they are arrested—narrowing pretrial presumption of innocence when, as far as I recall from the Constitution, the presumption is supposed to be universal. Further, many people in the anti-prison, anti-detention center are always paranoid about ALEC [the right-wing American Legislative Exchange Council], which has indeed written lots of this boilerplate legislation for various and sundry anti-state state activities. True enough. But this other boilerplate is equally bad. It comes from powerful think tanks and advisors, and it's organized around what people think they can win now rather than what the world should be. This is the moment a reader will say, "But Gilmore! Surely better to have relief for some than for none!" Of course! Some of the most resolutely abolitionist activities consist in getting prisoners compassionate release—one by one by one. The point is not the numbers; the point is the kind of specific capitulations written into much legislation that puts a

Krypton lock on the gate after the few have left rather than leaving open the possibility for more and more to be emancipated. That's the problem.

So let me repeat in slightly different words: I never object to any human getting out of jail. I never think, "Oh now, they should have been left there because there's some other person who should get out before them." That is not the point. The point is, while these carefully worded proposals to capitulate before the first debate happens might get a handful of people out, that handful of people also remains vulnerable to being charged and sent back in.

Some will say, "We can get these people released and this is good." But can they ensure that people will stay released? On the one hand, making it harder for everyone else to get out is already heinous, and, on the other hand, there's not anything that keeps the released free.

There is virtually no action involved in these kinds of proposals that tries in any meaningful way to rehearse a different outcome, to explore the possibility of thinking of the world differently and of having a different outcome. And the default is constantly, constantly, constantly—after forty years of nonstop, relentless, mind-numbing criminalization—that people take as the given that the problem is crime. People just take that as a given.

And I know things are getting really hectic in the United States because so many people are completely broke. I keep reading that gun crimes are up, carjackings are up. All these events are happening because everybody was cut loose because of the pandemic, and people are broke and are figuring out how to get unbroke, so they hold up someone, they do a home invasion, they steal cars. This reinforces the view that the problem is crime, and if we can only get on the far side of that problem, we can identify the deserving and innocent people—and these people are inevitably characterized as those who are seeking the American Dream, they are here to work. Then the question is, who does the difficult dirty and dangerous jobs in the United States? Whether it's delivering for Amazon, cleaning up office buildings, or being frontline health care workers, who aren't the highly paid doctors, or anything like that. Who are they? And we see a continuum of people, including modestly educated people who are the exact same kind of folks who are vulnerable to criminalization. Their vulnerability deepens for many reasons, including that they have been forbidden from having status as "employees" because they are gig workers or other casual workers, and because of the inadequacy of the minimum wage they're working two and three jobs, which means also they are doing things when they are tired and hungry. Their vulnerability also makes it more likely that they will come into the crosshairs of the police. I am talking about people who are vulnerable to be criminalized. People who wait. People who are tired.

Which then makes me say the following: it is not that capitalism made this happen in a playbook blueprint, but rather that capitalism requires inequality and racism helps to enshrines that inequality. I use racism broadly, to indicate group-differentiated vulnerability to premature death.

Aizeki: How can organizing against the prison-industrial complex (PIC) bring people with a range of interests to see the world differently?

Gilmore: The boosters who promote lockups can sometimes be persuaded to change their minds, and sometimes they get booted out of office by other kinds of political actors. Some anti-lockup campaigns have focused on persuading localities either to oppose having a prison, jail, or detention center or to agree to close one. Which then raises the question about what kinds of resources might go to towns that decide to turn away from prisons and look toward other kinds of economic development. It also raises questions about socialism—in terms of how we work to ensure the well-being of people in both urban and rural areas.

We had a struggle in Delano, California, during the 1990s and early 2000s. It was a really long campaign initiated by the California Prison Moratorium Project, and shortly thereafter joined by Critical Resistance, to stop the State of California from building a new prison. Among the many people who we organized with over the years of that campaign were members of the California State Employees Association (CSEA). This huge union local represented all kinds of people including many who worked in prisons—but not guards. And the best way I can summarize why they would come to the table and talk to us is, from their point of view, a teacher is a teacher—the local represented teachers—a locksmith is a locksmith, a secretary is a secretary, a mechanic is a mechanic—they can do what they do under all kinds of circumstances. The only people who absolutely need prisoners are guards. The CSEA could envision a different use of the social wage—of public spending on health, education, housing, and social welfare. And in fact, most of their members who were public-sector employees were engaging with the social wage, as state spending provided their wages or salaries in the free world. At the time of this campaign in the early 2000s, the union realized, "We might lose a few jobs in the lockup, but what we will gain in the free world is worth it." It wasn't as if some moralistic pathos were central to the union's position; they were thinking about members, jobs, publics, futures.

Aizeki: One of the things in the 2021 Biden immigration bill to "address the root causes of immigration" from El Salvador, Guatemala, and Honduras reminded me a bit of the "Weed and Seed" program brought to Los Angeles following the 1992 uprisings, which tied social programs with law enforcement. The proposal is to increase funding to these countries "conditioned on their ability to reduce the endemic corruption, violence, and poverty" that causes people to migrate, without any acknowledgment of the role the United States has played in driving migration by way of, among other things, militarism, imperialism, and neoliberalism. This is another example of how criminalization and "solutions" to address crime that reinforce the power of the PIC have so deeply saturated the migration control system. Does that make sense?

Gilmore: It does make sense, and you inspire me to talk about things that are not solutions, that people need to think about.

The United States and a good deal of the rich world, including the very vibrant economies of what used to be the crown of what many called the Third World (like India and even China), face a common problem. The problem that these political economies face has everything to do with the disjuncture between the kinds of well-being that are possible given the amount of income, and therefore by extension wealth, that people produce, and what the actual conditions of people in or related to these places might be. To go from that very abstract statement to something more specific in the US case, we know that the US middle class—in capitalist terms the great accomplishment of the post–World War II period—has been shrinking, shrinking, shrinking. The way that that shrinking class fraction has maintained its standard of living has been through the use of debt. Debt continues to fuel the economy. The participation of US private sector workers in union-protected jobs has, as I mentioned earlier, been at an all-time low point, and it was actually the union-protected jobs more than anything else that produced the conditions of possibility for that shrinking middle class to exist. It wasn't all professional people. It was wage workers, people with good pay and good benefits that enabled them to buy houses and cars and all sorts of stuff—what we called Fordism. That pattern, while specific to the United States, gives us a little bit of insight into the struggles and possibilities elsewhere as well.

In places that are dominated by or heavily reliant on extractive regimes—which includes many, but not all, countries in Latin America, for example—people have experienced huge disruptions. This is because the level of demand for the raw commodities extracted from the ground or from agriculture—whether those commodities are lithium, oil, copper, cotton, and so on and so forth, or things to be turned into biofuels—has gone down. Or if overall demand hasn't gone down, the price of the commodities has dropped because more and more places have altered their agricultural and extractive activities to produce the commodities that they assume will continue to be in high demand by growing economies, whether it's the United States, China, or the EU. All of this stuff is happening. And as a result of those kinds of struggles, plus the struggles of various regimes that allow or disallow that kind of industrial policy, all of this then produces the objective conditions which are pushing people out of where they are at, whether their income is high, middle, or low, and pulling people to places like the United States. Even with the squeezing or the reduction of the middle class, the US still has the kind of economy in which there is so much activity that it's possible to imagine making a living and making a life. In response, people in the United States and people in the EU and elsewhere say, "We can solve the migrant problem by having the home or the sending country restrict the people trying to leave or by paying an intermediate country to encamp them"—which is what the EU is doing with Turkey—to hold everybody and keep them from coming into the EU.[2]

This tells us that these are regimes that various nation-state governments, as well as the supranational EU, have put into place to throw up as much friction as possible to impede the movement of people across territories. And for our would-be colleagues in the United States who somehow think there is an easy solution that will keep people somewhere else, it requires that abolitionists show anyone who is listening to them what the actual ground of social struggle looks like—without falling into another trap, which is related to the magic of criminalization. And that is the trap that many people get into, including so-called abolitionists who declare the reason people leave El Salvador and come to the United States is because there is so much crime in El Salvador. So, that implies refugees are innocent people fleeing crime, and thus the logic continually refreshes and reinforces the notion that crime is the problem, so any solution must be a solution to crime. There is no context, no social life, no struggle over social reproduction that presents problems. If we understand social reproduction as the problem, then the solution has to be about improving social life, wherever. Lots of people don't want to pick up sticks and travel from wherever to the United States. Some do, of course. It ought to be possible for people to do either thing—stay or leave—but not as a matter of charity or pity.

Aizeki: In an interview you did with Antipode, I was struck by the community group that you work with in Amadora (Portugal). I am hoping you could share a story to help us think about how organizing requires consciousness-building as well as complexity.[3] Going back to something you said earlier, once you know how complex a problem is, you identify all these interventions.

Gilmore: I'll tell you a story. I first met my comrades in Amadora through a mutual friend, Sónia Vaz Borges—she is Portuguese, parents from Cabo Verde—who some years earlier started reading groups, as well as community organizing projects connected to basic things. She moved away, and her comrades started inviting me to do workshops at a long-standing community center. These comrades have an organization called Platforma Ghetto—the words mean what they sound like, "Ghetto Platform." A few of them are musicians who perform; they have all kinds of day jobs, many of them teachers who work with kids. Long before I met them they started putting together occasional universities which I call "pop-up universities." Each university would last for three days. The organizers would give it a name like University Marcus Garvey or University Malcolm X, and they would have presentations and workshops, often arranged around somebody passing through Lisbon from Brazil, or someone might be passing through from Guinea Bissau, as well as local militants with expertise in various areas. That's how I first got involved. I think my first workshop was on Pan-Africanism and communism. So, I go, several of us present talks, and then there's this intense debate among the entire packed room. The audience was mainly but not exclusively Afro-descended people, many first-generation children of immigrants, or themselves passing through, going to school in Lisbon from Angola, Mozambique, Cabo Verde, Brazil.

The pop-up universities always host huge deep debates about the questions and problems raised by the presentation. Very, very intense. And as I went back to do various workshops over time, I got familiar with the various dominant positions. And there was a Black consciousness (as in Steve Biko Black consciousness) faction, and a Marxism (as in Amílcar Cabral Marxism) faction. They were the poles, and the group would have it out. But—and this is the big point—they had it out not to win the point, but to continue developing their consciousness. In the context of those gatherings, I learned and learned again in a way what I've kind of been brought up to know. But what I had learned got a little bit dissipated through some life experiences, especially that kind of categorical imperative in the United States where more and more people—certainly not everybody, but more and more people—assert that an identity and experience is all you need for analysis.

In the community gatherings people constantly figure out new things to bring sharper work to bear on collective organizing. In 2015 Flávio Almada and other core activists asked me and Craig [Gilmore] to offer a presentation about policing and Black Lives Matter. We talked about what was happening in the USA to the best of our understanding, and discussed what we understood as strengths and vulnerabilities. And then the debate started. It was profound. One of the participants—who had offered simultaneous translation because we presented in English—said, "Fine, we always get to the end of our debate, but we don't often say, 'Maybe we need a new campaign.' And I think with police we should do something. What are we going to do?" A debate followed, and finally another comrade proposed, "Why don't we start modestly, just by talking to people in the neighborhood. People trust us, people know us. Why don't we start talking to people about not calling the police? Let's start really modestly." People thought that sounded like a good idea.

About ten days later, the police invaded the neighborhood. They just showed up. Some child threw a rock, and the cops took the kid off with them. The kid was gone and nobody knew where. Some comrades made their way to nearest station to find out if the kid was there. The police beat them up in the station and held them for days. Totally racially abused them, tortured them. Finally, they were released; we have photo documentation, they were a mess. Our comrades brought charges against the police for torture, racial abuse, etcetera, and the trial went on for some time. Amazingly, the judges heard out our comrades and the police were convicted. The police appealed and their conviction was upheld. The organizing continues and a serious abolition agenda is melding with a radical class and immigrant agenda that had developed over a long time of organizing and studying—both and.

This tells me many things about the community. One, people are willing to do things. Two, danger is here like anywhere. And, three, people understand there are many different weapons we can use to fight. It's not that the courts solved anything, but going to court was one way to publicize the police violence and make visceral in the halls of government what it is that people in largely immigrant communities have been experiencing with the police and get that read into the record. And because Portugal is a small country, and the television stations covered the trial and interviewed people every day after the hearings, it got attention. They didn't televise the trial but said, "Here is the update." This has helped to lift the contemporary anti-racist movement. Which means of course there are various perceptions about what the movement's motion should be tending toward: symbolic inclusion or radical restructuring.

And the end of the story is, there is always another start. Which is what excites me the most. And I know it's true also in the United States. People have and can use all sorts of different weapons, plus the courage of their convictions in terms of what they actually want. The faction I run with is the one that refuses to carve out the "relatively innocent" and abandon everyone else. Organized abandonment is what gets us into crisis, and organized violence will not stop, magically, at some barrier of innocence in a system organized to partition, differentiate, and exclude.

Thinking our way into the abolition future is thinking our way to realizing protection from calamity and opportunities for well-being. Nothing is guaranteed, but this sort of complex activity makes it more likely that the voluptuous possibility of life can be realized.

Editors and Contributors

Editors

MIZUE AIZEKI is Executive Director and founder of the Surveillance Resistance Lab. For nearly twenty years, Mizue has focused on ending the injustices—including criminalization, imprisonment, and exile—at the intersections of the criminal and migration control systems. Previously, Mizue was a Senior Advisor at the Immigrant Defense Project (IDP) and the founder and Director of the Surveillance, Tech and Immigration Project. At IDP, Mizue developed the advocacy program and led multiple campaigns to end the entanglement of local law enforcement and federal immigration policing, including the fights to end Secure Communities in New York State and the New York City detainer campaigns. She also led the ICE Out of Courts Campaign in New York and IDP's ICE raids and community defense programs. Mizue's photographic work appears in, among other publications, *Dying to Live: A Story of U.S. Immigration in an Age of Global Apartheid* (City Lights Books, 2008) and *Policing the Planet: Why the Policing Crisis Led to Black Lives Matter* (Verso, 2016).

MATT MAHMOUDI is a lecturer, researcher, and organizer. He's been leading the "Ban the Scan" campaign, Amnesty International's research and advocacy efforts on banning facial recognition technologies and exposing their uses against racialized communities, from New York City to the occupied Palestinian territories. He was the inaugural Jo Cox PhD scholar at the University of Cambridge, studying digital urban infrastructures as new frontiers for racial capitalism, where he remains an Affiliated Lecturer in Sociology. He helped to initiate and organize with the No Tech for Tyrants (NT4T) collective to hold the UK government to account on its Silicon Valley entanglements. His work appears in *The Sociological Review, International Political Sociology*, and *Digital Witness* (Oxford University Press, 2020). His forthcoming book is *Migrants in the Digital Periphery: New Urban Frontiers of Control* (University of California Press, 2023).

COLINE SCHUPFER is a human rights lawyer and consultant in intersectional justice at the Open Society Foundations. For the past ten years, she has engaged in advocacy, action research, and policy work, and has helped build structural legal aid projects in several countries across Europe and Asia. She previously worked and consulted for the Open Society Justice Initiative and the International Institute for Environment and Development, where she developed community-based public interest litigation and legal empowerment initiatives. Coline is a member of the Global Strategic Litigation Council for Refugee Rights' working group on legal status and lawful stay, and an advisor to the Girls Human Rights Hub. She has written for the *Border Criminologies* blog, *Opinio Juris*, and the *Asia-Pacific Journal on Human Rights and the Law.*

Contributors

NASMA AHMED is a technologist and facilitator based in the Dish with One Spoon Territory. Nasma is currently the director of the Digital Justice Lab, an initiative building toward a more just and equitable digital future.

KHALID ALEXANDER is a professor at City College and founder of Pillars of the Community, an organization that advocates for people targeted and negatively impacted by law enforcement.

SARA BAKER is a feminist activist, writer, and trainer. She has done digital rights research, advocacy, and organizing with The Engine Room and the Association for Progressive Communications.

LEA BECKMANN is a Berlin-based human rights lawyer. She formerly worked at Gesellschaft für Freiheitsrechte (GFF, Society for Civil Rights), an NGO focusing on strategic litigation. She was responsible for GFF's anti-discrimination work and coordinated strategic lawsuits regarding, among other issues, queer and trans rights, privacy rights of asylum seekers, and racial policing.

WAFA BEN-HASSINE is a human rights lawyer and principal on the Responsible Technology team at Omidyar Network. Previously, she was the Middle East and North Africa policy manager and global policy counsel for Access Now. In 2011, Wafa served as Tunisia's first-ever legislative aide in the Constituent Assembly.

RUHA BENJAMIN is professor of African American studies at Princeton University, founding director of the Ida B. Wells Just Data Lab, and author of the award-winning books *Race After Technology: Abolitionist Tools for the New Jim Code* (2019) and *Viral Justice: How We Grow the World We Want* (2022), among other publications.

MAIKE BOHN is cofounder of the3million and managing director of Oxford in Berlin. Her work focuses on breaking down digital, scientific and political walls and has helped to protect EU citizens' rights in the UK post-Brexit.

TIMMY CHÂU is a Vietnamese organizer and abolitionist based in the city of Chicago. He is a founding member of Dissenters and currently supports the organization on the Advisory Team. Timmy is on the Leadership Committee of the Prison + Neighborhood Arts / Education Project (PNAP), where he works to build inside/ outside networks of mutual support and advocacy between incarcerated and free-world activists, scholars, thinkers, and artists .

ARELY CRUZ-SANTIAGO is a human geographer and Science and Technology scholar based at the University of Exeter. Her research focuses on the politics of forensic knowledge production and grassroots forensic DNA databases. Her current Leverhulme Trust project, "Forensic Citizens: Science and Expertise in Latin America," analyzes citizen forensic practices to find disappeared persons in the region. From 2018 to 2021, Arely was a co-investigator in the project Data Justice, funded by the Economic & Social Research Council (ESRC).

IDA DANEWID is lecturer in gender and global political economy at the University of Sussex and a visiting research fellow at the Sarah Parker Remond Centre at University College London. Her research focuses on racial capitalism, anti-colonial political thought, and interconnected histories of raced, sexed, carceral, and ecological violence. Ida is the coeditor of *The Black Mediterranean: Bodies, Borders and Citizenship.*

NICK ESTES is a member of the Lower Brule Sioux Tribe, a writer, and co-host of the *Red Nation Podcast.* He is an assistant professor of American Indian studies at the University of Minnesota and the author of *Our History Is the Future: Standing Rock versus the Dakota Pipeline, and the Long Tradition of Indigenous Resistance* (2019).

RAFAEL EVANGELISTA is a social scientist with a PhD in social anthropology. He is a professor at State University of Campinas (Unicamp), member of the Latin American Network of Surveillance, Technology and Society Studies (Lavits), and author of the book *Beyond Machines of Loving Grace: Hacker Culture, Cybernetics and Democracy* (2018).

MARWA FATAFTA is a Palestinian researcher and writer who has written extensively on technology, human rights, and internet freedoms in Palestine and the wider Middle East and North Africa region. She leads the work of Access Now on digital rights in the MENA region as the MENA Policy Manager. She is also a policy analyst at the Palestinian think tank Al-Shabaka: The Palestinian Policy Network.

MARGIE CHEESMAN is a Lecturer in Digital Economy in the Department of Digital Humanities at King's College London. Margie's ethnographic research engages with elite and marginalized stakeholders—from global migration governance institutions to asylum seekers and refugees. She has published key studies on experimental money and identity technologies (like digital currencies, blockchains, and biometrics), highlighting the justice concerns surrounding their adoption in humanitarian aid, welfare, and development projects. Margie also works with the

Minderoo Centre for Technology and Democracy (Cambridge) and the journal *Big Data & Society.*

RYAN GERETY is the Director of the Athena Coalition and a Senior Advisor at United for Respect. Ryan has spent the last fifteen years working with activists and organizers to understand and respond to the technological acceleration of structural inequality. She was previously at the Ford Foundation and the Open Technology Institute at New America. Ryan studied computer science and political economy at the University of New Mexico.

BEN GREEN is a postdoctoral scholar in the Michigan Society of Fellows and an assistant professor in the Gerald R. Ford School of Public Policy. He is the author of *The Smart Enough City: Putting Technology in Its Place to Reclaim Our Urban Future* (2019). Ben is also an affiliate at the Berkman Klein Center for Internet & Society at Harvard.

JEFF HALPER is an Israeli anthropologist, the head of the Israeli Committee Against House Demolitions in Jerusalem, and a founding member of the One Democratic State Campaign. He is the author of *An Israeli in Palestine* (2008); *War against the People: Israel, the Palestinians and Global Pacification* (2015); and *Decolonizing Israel, Liberating Palestine: Zionism, Settler Colonialism, and the Case for One Democratic State* (2021).

NISHA KAPOOR is associate professor of sociology at the University of Warwick in the UK. She is author of *Deport, Deprive, Extradite: 21st Century State Extremism* (2018) and coedited *The State of Race* (2013).

LILLY IRANI is an associate professor at UC San Diego and organizes with Tech Workers Coalition, an organization that builds worker power in the tech industry.

BRIAN JORDAN JEFFERSON is associate professor of geography and geographic information science at the University of Illinois Urbana-Champaign. He is author of *Digitize and Punish: Racial Criminalization in the Digital Age.*

LARA KISWANI is the executive director of the Arab Resource & Organizing Center (AROC), serving poor and working-class Arabs and Muslims across the San Francisco Bay Area, and organizing to overturn racism, forced migration, and militarism. She is also a faculty member in the College of Ethnic Studies at San Francisco State University. Lara has been active in movements against racism and war, for Palestinian self-determination, and international solidarity for the last twenty years.

ARUN KUNDNANI is the author of *What is Antiracism? And Why It Means Anticapitalism* (2023), *The Muslims Are Coming! Islamophobia, Extremism, and the Domestic War on Terror* (2014) and *The End of Tolerance: Racism in 21st Century*

Britain (2007). He was an editor of the journal *Race & Class* and a scholar-in-residence at the Schomburg Center for Research in Black Culture, New York Public Library.

J. CARLOS LARA GÁLVEZ is co-executive director at Derechos Digitales, a Latin American organization working at the intersection of human rights and digital technologies. He has experience as an analyst, instructor, and researcher on issues related to data privacy, surveillance, freedom of expression, and access to knowledge in the digital environment.

JENNA M. LOYD is an associate professor in the Department of Geography at the University of Wisconsin-Madison. She is the author of *Health Rights Are Civil Rights: Peace and Justice Activism in Los Angeles, 1963–1978* (2014), coeditor of *Beyond Walls and Cages: Prisons, Borders, and Global Crisis* (2012), and coauthor, with Alison Mountz, of *Boats, Borders, and Bases: Race, the Cold War, and the Rise of Migration Detention the United States* (2018).

TODD MILLER is an author and journalist who lives in Tucson, Arizona. His books include *Build Bridges, Not Walls: A Journey to a World without Borders* (2021); *Empire of Borders: The Expansion of the US Border around the World* (2019); *Storming the Wall: Climate Change, Migration, and Homeland Security* (2017); and *Border Patrol Nation: Dispatches from the Front Lines of Homeland Security* (2014). He writes a weekly column for *The Border Chronicle*.

PETRA MOLNAR is a lawyer and anthropologist researching the impact of technology on people crossing borders. She is the associate director of the Refugee Law Lab at York University.

MARIAH MONTGOMERY is an organizer working with local coalitions to harness our collective resources to challenge corporate power and build the common good. In recent years, she has focused predominantly on the impact of Big Tech firms on political and economic democracy and justice in cities. She is currently the national campaigns director at PowerSwitch Action.

JOSEPH NEVINS is a professor of geography at Vassar College in Poughkeepsie, New York. With Suren Moodliar and Eleni Macrakis, he is a coauthor of *A People's Guide to Greater Boston* (2020). His other books include *Dying to Live: A Story of U.S. Immigration in an Age of Global Apartheid* (2008) and *Operation Gatekeeper and Beyond: The War on "Illegals" and the Remaking of the U.S.-Mexico Boundary* (2010).

CONOR O'REILLY is a professor in transnational crime and security at the University of Leeds. His research projects focus on global challenges and insecurities. As principal investigator of the Newton Fund Project M.A.K.E., he led work to tackle kidnapping in Mexico and coproduced counter-kidnapping tools for ordinary Mexican citizens (an app, a graphic novel, and a telenovela web-series). From

2018 to 2021, he was a co-investigator in the project Data Justice, funded by the Economic & Social Research Council (ESRC).

CHAI PATEL joined the Joint Council for the Welfare of Immigrants in 2015. Prior to that he was in the Human Rights department at the law firm Leigh Day, working on abuse and human rights claims, and on the death penalty team at Reprieve, focusing on international strategic litigation, casework, and investigation.

TAWANA PETTY is a mother, organizer, poet, and author. Her work focuses on racial justice, equity, privacy, and consent. She is a Just Tech Fellow with the Social Science Research Council and Executive Director of Petty Propolis, a Black women–led artist incubator. Tawana was honored with a Certificate of Special Congressional Recognition in 2018, was named one of 100 Brilliant Women in AI Ethics in 2021, and in 2023 was honored with an AI Policy Leader in Civil Society Award.

USHA RAMANATHAN is currently exploring the philosophy of law. She works on the jurisprudence of law, poverty, and rights. Ramanathan conducts research, writes, and speaks on a wide range of issues, including the nature of law, industrial disasters, mass displacement, eminent domain, manual scavenging, civil liberties (including the death penalty), beggary, criminal law, custodial institutions, the environment, and the judicial process. For over a decade, she has been tracking and engaging with the Indian identity project and has written and debated extensively on issues related to technology and the human conditions of freedom and liberty. She was awarded Access Now's Human Rights Heroes Award in 2019.

ERNESTO SCHWARTZ-MARÍN is a scholar working in the fields of biomedicine, forensics, and citizen science at the Sociology, Philosophy and Anthropology Department of Exeter University. Schwartz-Marín's work explores the development of participatory models to intervene in humanitarian crises via grassroots databases and citizen-led science. He was the Principal Investigator of the Economic & Social Research Council-funded project, Data Justice (2018-2021).

PAROMITA SHAH is the executive director of Just Futures Law. For over twenty years, Paromita has specialized in strategies to combat immigration detention, enforcement, and criminalization, and previously served as the associate director of the National Immigration Project of the National Lawyers Guild.

SILKY SHAH is the executive director of Detention Watch Network, a national coalition building power to abolish immigration detention in the US. She has worked as an organizer on issues related to immigration detention, the prison-industrial complex, and racial and migrant justice for twenty years.

MIRIAM TICKTIN is Professor of Anthropology at the CUNY Graduate Center and publishes widely on topics such as immigration, humanitarianism, and racial and gendered inequalities. Most notably, she is the author of *Casualties of Care:*

Immigration and the Politics of Humanitarianism in France. Her book, *Against Innocence*, is forthcoming in 2024.

HARSHA WALIA is a Panjabi Sikh writer and organizer based in Vancouver, unceded Coast Salish territories. Through such collectives and coalitions as No One Is Illegal, Defenders of the Land, and Anti-Capitalist Convergence, she has been an unpaid, grassroots organizer in migrant justice, anticapitalist, feminist, and anticolonial movements for the past two decades. Her day gig is in an antiviolence service provider organization supporting survivors of gender-based violence. Harsha is the award-winning author of *Border and Rule: Global Migration, Capitalism, and the Rise of Racist Nationalism* (2021) and *Undoing Border Imperialism* (2013). She is a coauthor of *Never Home: Legislating Discrimination in Canadian Immigration*, as well as *Red Women Rising: Indigenous Women Survivors in Vancouver's Downtown Eastside.*

Acknowledgments

We started this project in 2019. On the drawing board was a collection of incisive voices who fight against and speak saliently and urgently about technology resistance as border resistance. The thought of dialoguing across so many of them in one single anthology was but a pipe dream. Yet, a pandemic and a few political crises later, we have assembled a hopefully instructive volume made possible by the generous contributions of activists, scholars, and communities from the transatlantic context and beyond.

To the contributors, a heartfelt thanks for sharing their most precious and incisive work, thoughts, and ideas, and for working collaboratively with us as we juggled the few dozen essays that make up this volume. We are grateful for the wisdom and radical vocabulary of possibility passed down through the work featured in the book. A massive thanks, in particular, to Anthony Arnove and Naomi Murakawa at Haymarket for their patience, encouragement, and guidance and support, Ashley Smith for his editorial guidance, Brian Baughan for the incredible copyediting, and Jameka Williams for getting us to the finish line. Much appreciation to Anuj Shrestha for the incredible artwork that graces the cover.

It is in that vein that we wish to thank, for early conversations about this book, those who generously offered their time, energy, and support: Ujju Aggarwal, Laura Bingham, Matthew Burnett, Jordan Camp, Ben Hayes, Christina Heatherton, Craig Gilmore, Rachel Herzing, Jazmín Delgado, Monica Greco, Laura Liu, Jenna Loyd, Patrisia Macías-Rojas, Todd Miller, Cynthia Oka, Greg Ruggiero, and Linta Varghese. Many thanks to Joseph Nevins for his invaluable editorial support and guidance, and Camelia Manring for support with transcription and footnotes.

For shared work, contributions, and generative dialogue on these issues, we deeply appreciate the groundwork laid by *Who's Behind ICE: The Tech and Data Companies Fueling Deportation,* and Mijente's #NoTechforICE campaign. In that spirit, we send a huge thanks and much solidarity to Jacinta Gonzalez (Mijente), Paromita Shah, and Julie Mao (Just Futures Law), and Aaron Lackowski (Empower).

To friends and travel companions who inspired or in any way helped us form and rethink our ideas, as well as those who helped us fight this fight in recent years, we thank: Giulia Torino, Lorena Gazzotti, Surer Mohamed, Alina Utrata, Mallika Balakrishnan, and the No Tech For Tyrants collective, Soniya Munshi, Rashida Richardson, Donald Anthonyson, Subhash Kateel, Aarti Shahani, Maria Muentes, Carlos Garcia, Mia-Lia Kiernan, Nancy Nguyen, Carl Lipscombe, Janis Rosheuvel, Fatoumata Gassama, Samuel Anthony, Jean Montrevil, Khalil Cumberbatch, Abraham Paulos, Sarath Suong, Isaac Ontiveros, Thomas Mariadason, Laura Whitehorn, Jose Saldana, Melissa Tanis, Geoff Boyce, Suren Moodliar, Javier Valdes, Angad Bhalla, Peter Markowitz, Marisol Arriaga, Hannah Shapiro, Pooja Gehi, Lynly Egyes, Andrea Ritchie, Mariame Kaba, Sarah Gillman, Sameera Hafiz, Angie Junck, McKenzie Funk, Sarah Lamdan, Ian Head, Ghita Schwarz, Konstantin von Krusenstiern, Jennifer Guglielmo, David Hernández, John O'Malley, Ted Robertson, Kevin Rudiger, Roxane Auer, Mayra Peters-Quintero, Cynthia Conti-Cook, Rini Chakraborty, maisha quint, Deyanira Del Rio, Betsy Plum, Natalia Aristizabal, Carlos Menchaca, Zach Ahmed, Daniel Schwartz, and Jonathan Stribling-Uss. For your foundational work and unwavering commitment to fighting for the rights of immigrants with criminal convictions, we thank Manny Vargas, Nancy Morawetz, Alina Das, Jessica Rofé, Ravi Ragbir & Amy Gottlieb and the Defense Committee, and other colleagues at the Immigrant Defense Project over the years. Apologies and much appreciation to anyone we may have not named who has been part of this journey. We know there are many more of you, and we are deeply grateful for all your support and contributions.

The editors would also like to personally thank individuals who have supported them, whether now or in the past.

Coline thanks: Helen and Dave, and my siblings Kara, Cosette, and Mayk, for your love and untiring support, despite the distance that separates us across three different continents. For the constant encouragement, love, and for always being a source of inspiration and motivation— a thank you to Olivia Long, Loureen Sayej, Tania Karas, Sultana Tafadar, Solomon

ACKNOWLEDGMENTS 291

Sacco, Sumaiya Islam, Sara Hossain, Zaza Namoradze, Ayoub Ayoub, Hashem Abushama, Rachel Sherrington, Gabriella McGinley-Boyce, Tiffany Shakespeare, Agan Juanda, Mercedes Melon, Laura Lázaro Cabrera, Maryam H'madoun, Heena Khaled, Nathan Murphy, Anna Wright, Charlie Roper, Martín (Chun) Gebhardt, Jo Kroese, Adam Riley, Kane Maskell, Elliot King, and Tempe McMinn—thank you for your friendship and mentorship, and for your commitment to always creating spaces for conversations that matter. To Francisco Riccheri, por aportar tanta luz y tantas risas a nuestra humilde vida. To Matthew Burnett, not only for introducing me to both Mizue and Matt, but also for your intellectual guidance and encouragement, for your incredible legal empowerment work, and for being a role model to aspire to. And to Mizue and Matt, for I will always cherish these months with you, everything I learned, thank you for the solidarity, as well as for your persistence, perceptiveness, and dedication to the field.

Matt thanks: Matin, Mohsen, and Mitra, my eternal love and thanks for your unwavering support and emotional investment. For the love, fierce friendships, regular sanity check-ins, companionship, peer review, and world-building of Amy Costelloe, Luke Naylor-Perrott and Natalia Hussein, Damini Satija, Theo Weiss, Ali Neilson, Lucie Vovk, Inès Aït Mokhtar, Rebecca Vaa, Alia Al Ghussain, Sophie Dyer, Max Kashevsky and Naomi Marshall, Niyousha Bastani, Corinne Cath-Speth, Tellef Raabe, Anna Eitrem, Aurelie Skrobik, Danielle Cameron, Emma Murphy, Elise Williams, Ailsa McKeon, Marlena Wisniak, Sam Dubberley, Waed Abbas, Charlotte Phillips, Rebekah Larsen, and Isabel Guenette-Thornton. To you all: Thank you. To mentors who helped sketch the contours of the machinery we're fighting, and who have helped me along the way in vocalizing the necessary politics to fight it: Graham Denyer-Willis, Ella McPherson, Sharath Srinivasan, Mustafa Ali, Ali Meghji, Angèle Christin ––I can't thank you enough. To the Anthro Co-Write collective, facilitated by Laurie Denyer-Willis: thanks for your digital hospitality, for providing creative space to think, write, and edit, during challenging circumstances. To Mizue and Coline, a lifetime of gratitude for your companionship, solidarity, and relentless work towards fostering radical political imagination and a more just future.

Mizue thanks: Argelia, Hernan, Diana, Natalie, and Alexis for building family with us where we all found ourselves. Hiroko and Shin for your perseverance in creating a different future and for making our home wherever we were, Shizuko for always being there when needed, and to Takane, Sawato, Carol, and Lynn for your support despite the distance. To all my colleagues at IDP who joined forces to fight what others deemed futile and, in the process, built a politics of possibility, I share much appreciation and fond memories (and to Genia Blaser, Michelle Parris, Jane Shim, Marie Mark, and Alli Finn, thanks for your partnership in building key projects and new possibilities). To Colin Absalom and Jose Molina and their loved ones, thank you for the shared struggle and for showing the possibilities for a better, kinder world. To those of you who have helped me for decades (before DHS even existed!) to organize spaces and opportunities, and to think through politics, projects, pathways, regardless of how infrequent our communication or our geographical distance, much gratitude and love—Alex Caputo-Pearl, Connie Razza, Craig Gilmore, Fred Seavey, Hany Khalil, Katherine Beckett, Layla Welborn, Mark Salzer, Max Elbaum, Mike Murashige, Rachel Herzing, Ruth Wilson Gilmore, and Yuki Kidokoro. Much appreciation to Jack Weidner, Saya, and Ujju for your feedback on my essay, and to Sophia Giddens for your support and guidance for a new pathway forward. To the inaugural crew of the Surveillance Resistance Lab, many thanks for building this project together. Deep gratitude to Joseph Nevins for years of struggle and solidarity as we've journeyed together, and to Amina and Sayako, for always shining the light and providing the hope for all we are fighting for. Coline and Matt, it's been quite a ride—much appreciation for the rigorous, energizing, and caring collaboration and solidarity across borders, and for the laughter amongst the learning.

Notes

Foreword: Borders & Bits: From Obvious to Insidious Violence

1   Tim Craig, Sean Sullivan, and Silvia Foster-Frau, "Charges of Racism Swirl as Haitian Americans, Allies Unite to Protest Migrants' Treatment," *Washington Post*, September 21, 2021.

2   Of course, this is only one of many long-standing efforts by the US government to stymie Haitian mobility. See Jenna M. Loyd and Alison Mountz, *Boats, Borders, and Bases* (Oakland: University of California Press, 2018); Todd Miller, "U.S. To Haitians: Stay Home and Bear the Burden," NACLA, March 8, 2010; Todd Miller, *Border Patrol Nation: Dispatches from the Front Lines of Homeland Security* (San Francisco: City Lights, 2014).

3   Grateful American, "Biden 1994: 'If Haiti Just Quietly Sunk into the Caribbean . . . It Wouldn't Matter," September 23, 2021, YouTube video, 0:37, https://www.youtube.com/watch?v=Wwf4FyA0B0M.

4   Human Rights Watch, "US: Treatment of Haitian Migrants Discriminatory," September 21, 2021.

5   Human Rights Watch, "US: Treatment of Haitian Migrants Discriminatory."

6   Reece Jones, *Violent Borders: Refugees and the Right to Move* (London: Verso, 2016); see also Heba Gowayed, *Refuge: How the State Shapes Human Potential* (Princeton, NJ: Princeton University Press, 2022).

7   The Trump administration's Title 42 policy, which Biden extended, justifies the expulsion of migrants as a means to prevent the spread of COVID-19. Rebecca Morin, "CDC Extends Trump-Era Policy That Allows Migrants to Be Expelled over COVID Concerns," *USA Today*, August 3, 2021.

8   Eve Hayes de Kalaf, "How Some Countries Are Using Digital ID to Exclude Vulnerable People around the World," *The Conversation*, August 3, 2021; see also Eve Hayes de Kalaf, *Legal Identity, Race and Belonging in the Dominican Republic: From Citizen to Foreigner* (London: Anthem Press, 2021).

9   See Bridget Wooding and Richard Moseley-Williams, *Needed but Unwanted: Haitian Immigrants and Their Descendants in the Dominican Republic* (London: Catholic Institute for International Relations, 2004); Edward Paulino, *Dividing Hispaniola: The Dominican Republic's Border Campaign against Haiti, 1930–1961* (Pittsburgh, PA: University of Pittsburgh Press, 2016).

10 E. Tendayi Achiume, "Report of the Special Rapporteur on Contemporary Forms of Racism, Racial Discrimination, Xenophobia and Related Intolerance," U.N.S.G. A/HRC/48/76, September 22, 2021 (this is an complementary report to the prior report issued on November 10, 2020).

11 See Elaine M. Howle, *The CalGang Criminal Intelligence System: As the Result of Its*

Weak Oversight Structure, It Contains Questionable Information That May Violate Individuals' Privacy Rights (Report 2015-130), California State Auditor, Sacramento, CA, 2016.

12   See Emily Galvin-Almanza, "California Gang Laws Are Normalized Racism," *The Appeal*, October 4, 2019.

13   Aubrey Clayton, "How Eugenics Shaped Statistics: Exposing the Damned Lies of Three Science Pioneers," *Nautilus*, October 27, 2020.

14   Mizue Aizeki et al., *Smart Borders or a Humane World?* Immigrant Defense Project's Surveillance, Tech & Immigration Policing Project, and the Transnational Institute, October 2021.

15   Petra Molnar, "Robots And Refugees: The Human Rights Impacts Of Artificial Intelligence And Automated Decision-Making In Migration," in *Research Handbook on International Migration and Digital Technology*, ed. Marie McAuliffe (Cheltenham, UK: Edward Elgar Ltd., 2021), 134–51. See also Petra Molnar, "Technology on the Margins: AI and Global Migration Management from a Human Rights Perspective," *Cambridge International Law Journal* 8, no. 2 (2019): 305–30.

1. The Border Is Surveillance: Abolish the Border

1   Harriet Grant and John Domokos, "Dublin Regulation Leaves Asylum Seekers with Their Fingers Burnt," *The Guardian*, October 7, 2011.

2   Mathilde Schmitt, "The Dublin Regulation, a Nightmare for Asylum Seekers," *Sensus*, October 19, 2019.

3   Chloé Berthélémy, "Eurodac Database Repurposed to Surveil Migrants," *EDRi*, March 10, 2021.

4   Kaamil Ahmed and Lorenzo Tondo, "Fortress Europe: The Millions Spent on Military-Grade Tech to Deter Refugees," *The Guardian*, December 6, 2021.

5   Johana Bhuiyan, "Vast Immigration Surveillance Program in Dire Need of Reform, Biden Administration Warned," *The Guardian*, February 23, 2022.

6   Lucie Audibert and Monish Bhatia, "From GPS Tagging to Facial Recognition Watches: Expanding the Surveillance of Migrants in the UK," Institute of Race Relations, October 26, 2022.

7   J. Khadijah Abdurahman, "A Body of Work That Cannot Be Ignored," *Logic*, December 25, 2021.

8   Mijente, Just Futures Law, and No Border Wall Coalition, *The Deadly Digital Border Wall*, 2021, https://notechforice.com/wp-content/uploads/2021/10/Deadly.Digital.Border.Wall_.pdf.

9   Tamir Israel, "Facial Recognition at a Crossroads: Transformation at Our Borders and Beyond," Samuelson-Glushko Canadian Internet Policy & Public Interest Clinic (CIPPIC), September 30, 2020.

10   E. Tendayi Achiume, "Report of the Special Rapporteur on Contemporary Forms of Racism, Racial Discrimination, Xenophobia and Related Intolerance," U.N.S.G. A/75/590, November 10, 2020.

11   Human Rights Watch, "UN Shared Rohingya Data without Informed Consent," June 15, 2021.

12   Simone Browne, *Dark Matters: On the Surveillance of Blackness* (Durham, NC: Duke University Press: 2015).

13   Puck Lo, *From Data Criminalization to Prison Abolition*, Community Justice Exchange, https://abolishdatacrim.org/en/report/surveillance-capitalism-surveillance-carceralism#paragraph-81.

14   Toni Morrison, "Home," in *The House That Race Built* (New York: Pantheon Books, 1997).

15   Peter Nyers, *Irregular Citizenship, Immigration, and Deportation* (London: Routledge: 2018).

2. Multiplying State Violence in the Name of Homeland Security

1   Immigrant Defense Project, "Life Beyond Borders: Oral Histories," 2021, https://lifebeyondborders.org/stories/jose.

2   Neil Smith, "Giuliani Time: The Revanchist 1990s," Social Text 16, 4 (Winter 1998); Stuart Hall et al., *Policing the Crisis: Mugging, the State and Law & Order*, 2nd ed. (Basingstoke, UK: Palgrave Macmillan, 2013).

3   "The 9/11 Commission Report: Final Report of the National Commission on Terrorist Attacks Upon the United States," as cited in Todd Miller, *Empire of Borders: The Expansion of the US Border around the World* (London: Verso, 2019).

4   Muzaffar Chishti and Jessica Bolter, "Two Decades after 9/11, National Security Focus Still Dominates US Immigration Systems," *Migration Policy Institute,* September 22, 2021.

5   See Daniel Kanstroom, *Deportation Nation: Outsiders in American History* (Cambridge, MA: Harvard University Press, 2007); Moon-Ho Jung, *Menace to Empire: Anticolonial Solidarities and the Transpacific Origins of the US Security State* (Oakland: Univeristy of California Press, 2022).

6   See Rachel Ida Buff, *Against the Deportation Terror: Organizing for Immigrant Rights in the Twentieth Century* (Philadelphia: Temple University Press: 2018); Kanstroom, *Deportation Nation.*

7   See Kunal Parker, *Making Foreigners: Immigration and Citizenship Law in America, 1600–2000* (New Histories of American Law) (Cambridge: Cambridge University Press, 2015).

8   Ruth Wilson Gilmore and Craig Gilmore, "Restating the Obvious," in *Indefensible Space: The Architecture of the National Insecurity State*, ed. Michael Sorkin (New York: Routledge, 2008): 141–62.

9   Hall et al., *Policing the Crisis.*

10   Jordan Camp, *Incarcerating the Crisis: Freedom Struggles and the Rise of the Neoliberal State* (Oakland: University of California Press, 2016).

11   Joseph Nevins, *Operation Gatekeeper and Beyond: The War on "Illegals" and the Remaking of the U.S.-Mexico Boundary* (New York: Routledge, 2010); Peter Andreas, *Border Games: Policing the US-Mexico Divide* (Ithaca, NY: Cornell University Press, 2000). See Arun Kundnani's chapter in this volume.

12   Harsha Walia, *Border and Rule: Global Migration, Capitalism, and the Rise of Racist Nationalism* (Chicago: Haymarket Books, 2021).

13   Dawn Paley, *Drug War Capitalism* (Oakland: AK Press, 2014).

14   Arun Kundnani, *The Muslims Are Coming! Islamophobia, Extremism, and the Domestic War on Terror* (London: Verso, 2014).

15   Naomi Murakawa, *The First Civil Right: How Liberals Built Prison America* (New York: Oxford University Press, 2014).

16   *Nevins, Operation Gatekeeper and Beyond.*

17   See Patrisia Macías-Rojas, *From Deportation to Prison: The Politics of Immigration Enforcement in Post–Civil Rights America* (New York: NYU Press, 2016).

18   See Kanstroom, *Deportation Nation.*

19   This included the creation of a new category of immigration-specific offenses—

"aggravated felonies"—to severely limit, and in most cases eliminate, the rights of immigrants with particular convictions.

20 A. Naomi Paik, *Bans, Walls, Raids, Sanctuary: Understanding U.S. Immigration for the Twenty-First Century* (Oakland: University of California Press, 2020).

21 Peter H. Schuck and John Williams, "Removing Criminal Aliens: The Pitfalls and Promises of Federalism," Yale Law School Faculty Scholarship Series Paper 1659 (1999): 371.

22 Roberto Lovato, "Building the Homeland Security State," NACLA, October 31, 2008.

23 Deepa Fernandes, *Targeted: Homeland Security and the Business of Immigration* (New York, NY: Seven Stories Press: 2007).

24 "About DHS," https://www.dhs.gov/about-dhs.

25 On racial surveillance and hypervisibility, see Simone Browne, *Dark Matters: On the Surveillance of Blackness* (Durham, NC: Duke University Press: 2015). On the Pentagon's practice gathering biometrics to achieve military dominance, see Annie Jacobsen, *First Platoon: A Story of Modern War in the Age of Identity Dominance* (New York: Dutton, 2021).

26 Ana Muñiz, "Bordering Circuitry: Crossjurisdictional Immigration Surveillance," *UCLA Law Review* 66 (2019): 1636–80.

27 Todd Miller, *More Than a Wall: Corporate Profiteering and the Militarization of US-Mexico Borders*, Transnational Institute, September 16, 2019; William I. Robinson, *The Global Police State* (London: Pluto Press, 2020).

28 Anna Pegler-Gordon, *In Sight of America: Photography and the Development of U.S. Migration Policy* (Berkeley: University of California Press, 2009).

29 Kundnani, *The Muslims Are Coming!*, 64.

30 DHS, "Endgame: Office of Detention and Removal Strategic Plan, 2003–2012," August 2003, chap. 1, pp. 1–5.

31 DHS, "Endgame," chap. 4, p. 1.

32 Margaret Mendelson, Shayna Strom, and Michael Wishnie, *Collateral Damage: An Examination of ICE's Fugitive Operations Program*, Migration Policy Institute, February 2009.

33 "Fact Sheet: ICE Fugitive Operations," https://www.ice.gov/doclib/news/library/factsheets/pdf/fugops.pdf.

34 American Immigration Council, "The Cost of Immigration Enforcement and Border Security," January 20, 2021.

35 DHS, "U.S. ICE Budget Overview: Fiscal Year 2022 Congressional Justification," November 12, 2021.

36 Zolan Kanno-Youngs and Charlie Savage, "Trump Official's Last Day Deal with ICE Union Ties Biden's Hands," *New York Times*, February 1, 20121; Dara Lind, "How the Border Patrol Union Became Trump's Closest Shutdown Allies," *Vox*, January 3, 2019 See the Ruth Wilson Gilmore interview in this volume.

37 Naomi Murakawa, *The First Civil Right: How Liberals Built Prison America*, 16

38 Nicholas Kulish, Caitlin Dickerson, and Ron Nixon, "Immigration Agents Discover New Freedom to Deport under Trump," *New York Times*, February 25, 2017.

39 American Immigration Council, "The Criminal Alien Program (CAP)," August 1, 2013.

40 Mizue Aizeki, "Mass Deportation under the Homeland Security State: Anti-violence Advocates Join the Fight against Criminalization of Immigrants," *Scholar & Feminist Online* 15. no. 3 (2019).

41   DHS, "Yearbook of Immigration Statistics: Table 39.".

42   ICE, "ICE Arrests More than 3,100 Convicted Criminal Aliens and Immigration Fugitives Nationwide," April 2, 2012.

43   "Operation Cross Check: 3,100 Arrests," April 12, 2012, YouTube video, 2:09, https://www.youtube.com/watch?v=RrI7c_-UdC0.

44   "Remarks by the President in Address to the Nation on Immigration," The White House, November 20, 2014; for liberal law-and-order ideologies, see Murakawa, *The First Civil Right*.

45   See *Policing the Planet: Why the Policing Crisis Led to Black Lives Matter*, ed. Jordan T. Camp and Christina Heatherton (London: Verso, 2016), 3.

46   DHS Yearbook of Immigration Statistics 2020, https://www.dhs.gov/immigration-statistics/yearbook/2020

47   Spencer Woodman, "Palantir Provides the Engine for Donald Trump's Deportation Machine," *The Intercept*, March 2, 2017; for data commodification markets, see Robinson, *Global Police State*; on the research institutions, see Ben Hayes, "The Surveillance-Industrial Complex," in *Routledge Handbook of Surveillance Studies* (Abingdon, UK: Routledge, 2012): 167–75.

48   Didier Bigo, "Globalized (In)security: The Field and the Ban-Opticon," in *Terror, Insecurity and Liberty: Illiberal Practices of Liberal Regimes after 9/11*, ed. Didier Bigo and Anastassia Tsoukala (London: Routledge, 2008).

49   See Todd Miller, *Border Patrol Nation: Dispatches from the Front Lines of Homeland Security* (San Francisco: City Lights, 2014).

50   Immigrant Defense Project and Center for Constitutional Rights, "Defend against ICE Raids and Community Arrests," July 2019

51   Immigrant Defense Project, "ICE Policing through the Pandemic," December 17, 2020; "Blueprint for Terror: How ICE Planned Its Largest Immigration Raid in History," https://mijente.net/icepapers

52   Ed Pilkington, "'These Are His People': Inside the Elite Border Patrol Unit Trump Sent to Portland," *The Guardian*, November 11, 2021.

53   Yessenia Funes and Dhruv Mehrotra, "CBP Drones Conducted Flyovers near Homes of Indigenous Pipeline Activists, Flight Records Show," *Gizmodo*, September 18, 2020.

54   "The 287(g) Program: An Overview," American Immigration Council, July 8, 2021.

55   Kris W. Kobach, "The Quintessential Force Multiplier: The Inherent Authority of Police to Make Immigration Arrests," *Albany Law Review* 69, no. 1 (2006): 181.

56   "Law Enforcement Support Center Fact Sheet," ICE.

57   Muñiz, "Bordering Circuitry."

58   Stop LAPD Spying Coalition, https://stoplapdspying.org/policing-strategies-and-tactics. See Hamid Khan's chapter and the Stop Urban Shield case study in this volume.

59   Brendan McQuade, *Pacifying the Homeland: Intelligence Fusion and Mass Supervision* (Oakland: University of California Press, 2017)

60   "Targeting Operation Division Overview," ICE, https://www.ice.gov/doclib/about/offices/ero/pdf/todCenterOverviews.pdf.

61   Max Rivlin-Nadler, "How ICE Uses Social Media to Surveil and Arrest Immigrants," *The Intercept*, December 22, 2019.

62   Mizue Aizeki, Laura Bingham, and Santiago Narváez, "The Everywhere Border: Digital Migration Control Infrastructure in the Americas," *Transnational Institute, State of Power: Digital Futures*, February 14, 2023, https://www.tni.org/en/article/

the-everywhere-border

63 "International Operations," ICE, https://www.ice.gov/about-ice/homeland-security-investigations/international-operations; see Joseph Nevins and Todd Miller's chapter in this volume.

64 Aizeki et al., *Smart Borders or a Humane World?*

65 "DHS Agreements with Honduras, Guatemala and El Salvador," DHS, October 3, 2019.

66 Ana Muñiz, *Borderland Circuitry: Immigration Surveillance in the United States and Beyond* (Oakland: University of California Press, 2022).

67 Privacy Impact Assessment Update for the Enforcement Integrated Database (EID) Criminal History Information Sharing (CHIS) Program, DHS/ICE/PIA-015(h), January 15, 2016.

68 Paley, *Drug War Capitalism.*

69 Global Detention Project, *Immigration Detention in Mexico: Between the United States and Central America*, February 2021, https://www.globaldetentionproject.org/immigration-detention-in-mexico-between-the-united-states-and-central-america.

70 Antonio Flores, Luis Noe-Bustamante, and Mark Hugo Lopez, "Migrant Apprehensions and Deportations Increase in Mexico, but Remain Below Recent Highs," Pew Research Center, June 12, 2019, https://www.pewresearch.org/fact-tank/2019/06/12/migrant-apprehensions-and-deportations-increase-in-mexico-but-remain-below-recent-highs/.

71 Miller, *Empire of Borders*, 37.

72 Mizue Aizeki and Paromita Shah, *HART Attack: How DHS's Massive Biometrics Database Will Supercharge Surveillance and Threaten Rights*, IDP Surveillance, Tech & Immigration Policing Project, Just Futures Law, and Mijente, May 2022, https://surveillanceresistancelab.org/resources/hart-attack-how-dhss-massive-biometrics-database-will-supercharge-surveillance-and-threaten-rights/.

73 Nina Toft Djanegara and Privacy International, *Biometrics for Counter-Terrorism: Case Study of the US Military in Iraq and Afghanistan*, May 2021.

74 DHS, Privacy Impact Assessment for the United Nations High Commissioner for Refugees (UNHCR) Information Data Share, DHS/USCIS/PIA-081, August 13, 2019.

75 "Written Testimony for a Hearing Titled 'Securing the Border: Fencing, Infrastructure, and Technology Force Multipliers,'" DHS, May 13, 2015.

76 Will Parrish, "The U.S. Border Patrol and an Israeli Military Contractor Are Putting a Native American Reservation under 'Persistent Surveillance,'" *The Intercept*, August 25, 2019; Mijente, Just Futures Law, and No Border Wall Coalition, *The Deadly Digital Border Wall*, https://notechforice.com/wp-content/uploads/2021/10/Deadly.Digital.Border.Wall.pdf.

77 "Robot Dogs Take Another Step Towards Deployment at the Border," DHS, Science and Technology Directorate, February 1, 2022.

78 "Research & Development," Department of Homeland Security, updated June 13, 2023, https://www.dhs.gov/science-and-technology/research; Miller, "More Than a Wall."

79 Nandita Sharma, *Home Economics: Nationalism and the Making of "Migrant Workers" in Canada* (Toronto: University of Toronto Press, 2006): 51.

80 Miller, *Border Patrol Nation*; Morley Musick, "Meet the Boy Scouts of the Border Patrol," *The Nation*, January 21, 2020.

81 "Immigrant Rights Groups Demand the Truth about ICE's Citizen

Academy," Beyond Legal Aid, May 18, 2021, https://www.beyondlegalaid.org/
updates/2021/5/18/ice-academy-foia.

82 Miller, *Border Patrol Nation*.

83 Aizeki et al., *Smart Borders or a Humane World?*

84 Emily Widra and Tiana Herring, "States of Incarceration: The Global Context 2021,"
Prison Policy Project, September 2021.

85 "U.S. Defense Spending Compared to Other Countries," Peter. G. Peterson
Foundation, July 9, 2021.

86 Aizeki et al., *Smart Borders or a Humane World?*

87 Hayes, "Surveillance-Industrial Complex."

88 See Reece Jones, *Violent Borders: Refugees and the Right to Move* (London: Verso,
2016).

89 Susan Bibler Coutin, "Exiled by Law: Deportation and the Inviability of Life,"
Governing Immigration Through Crime, ed. Julie A. Dowling and Jonathan Xavier
Inda (Stanford, CA: Stanford University Press, 2013): 233–47.

90 Achille Mbembe, "Necropolitics," trans. Libby Meintjes, *Public Culture* 15, no. 1
(2003): 11–40.

3. Empire's Walls, Global Apartheid's Infrastructure

1 Associated Press (El Cinchado), "U.S. Agents Aid in Guatemalan Crackdown on
Hundreds of Migrants Headed North," *The Guardian*, January 16, 2020.

2 US Senate Democratic Staff, "DHS Run Amok? A Reckless Overseas Operation,
Violations, and Lies," October 13, 2020, pp. 2–4. Emphasis added.

3 See, for example, Maya Averbuch, "US Border Agents Went Rogue and Illegally
Detained Hundreds of Migrants in Guatemala," *Vice*, October 14, 2020.

4 Tim Cresswell, *On the Move: Mobility in the Modern Western World* (New York:
Routledge, 2006), 2.

5 See Joseph Nevins, "The Speed of Life and Death: Migrant Fatalities, Territorial
Boundaries, and Energy Consumption," *Mobilities* 13, no. 1 (2018): 29–44.

6 Michael Hirsh, "We Weren't Ready for a World without Walls," *Foreign Policy*,
November 7, 2019.

7 See Matthew B. Sparke, "A Neoliberal Nexus: Economy, Security and the Biopolitics
of Citizenship on the Border," *Political Geography* 25, no. 2 (2006): 151–80.

8 See Joseph Nevins, *Operation Gatekeeper and Beyond: The War on "Illegals" and the
Remaking of the U.S.-Mexico Boundary* (New York: Routledge, 2010).

9 Ainhoa Ruiz Benedicto, Mark Akkerman, and Pere Brunet, *A Walled World:
Towards a Global Apartheid*, Centre Delàs d'Estudis per la Pau (Barcelona),
November 2020.

10 Border fencing goes back to at least the late 1930s, See C. J. Alvarez, *Border Land,
Border Water: A History of Construction on the US-Mexico Divide* (Austin: University
of Texas Press, 2019).

11 Joseph Nevins and Timothy Dunn, "Barricading the Border," *NACLA Report on the
Americas* 41, no. 6 (2008): 21–25.

12 See Timothy Dunn, *Blockading the Border and Human Rights: The El Paso Operation
That Remade Immigration Enforcement* (Austin: University of Texas Press, 2010);
Nevins, *Operation Gatekeeper and Beyond*.

13 Sparke, "A Neoliberal Nexus."

14 Peter Andreas, "Redrawing the Line: Borders and Security in the Twenty-First
Century," *International Security* 28, no. 2 (Fall 2003): 96.

15   Lucy Rodgers and Dominic Bailey, "Trump Wall: How Much Has He Actually Built?" *BBC News*, October 31, 2021.

16   Melissa Correa, "VERIFY: How Much of President Trump's 450-Mile Border Wall Is Actually a New Barrier?" KHOU*11, January 13, 2012.

17   Alvarez, *Border Land, Border Water.*

18   Iván Chaar-López, "Sensing Intruders: Race and the Automation of Border Control," *American Quarterly* 71, no. 2 (2019): 495–518.

19   Mizue Aizeki et al., *Smart Borders or a Humane World?* Immigrant Defense Project's Surveillance, Tech & Immigration Policing Project, and the Transnational Institute, October 2021.

20   Lucas Chancel et al., *World Inequality Report 2022*, World Inequality Lab, wir2022. wid.world.

21   William I. Robinson, *The Global Police State* (London: Pluto Press, 2020), 41.

22   See Christine Leuenberger, "Crumbling Walls and Mass Migration in the Twenty-First Century," in *Open Borders: In Defense of Free Movement*, ed. Reece Jones (Athens: University of Georgia Press, 2019), 177–90; and Elisabeth Vallet, "Border Walls and the Illusion of Deterrence," also in *Open Borders*, 156–68.

23   Ron E. Hassner and Jason Wittenberg, "Barriers to Entry: Who Builds Fortified Boundaries and Why?" *International Security* 40, no. 1 (2015): 157–90.

24   See Rory Carroll, "Botswana Erects 300-Mile Electrified Fence to Keep Cattle (and Zimbabweans) Out," *The Guardian*, September 9, 2003; Marcela García, "The Other Country Building a Border Wall," *Boston Globe*, September 30, 2022; Reece Jones, *Violent Borders: Refugees and the Right to Move* (New York: Verso, 2017); Todd Miller, *Border Patrol Nation: Dispatches from the Front Lines of Homeland Security* (San Francisco: City Lights, 2014).

25   See John Washington and José Olivares, "Internal CBP Documents Detail 'Transnational Effort to Shut Down Asylum," *The Intercept*, March 22, 2022; and Will Weissert and Zeke Miller, "Mexico Agrees to Invest $1.5b in 'Smart' Border Technology," Associated Press, July 12, 2022. See also Levi Vonk with Axel Kirschner, *Border Hacker: A Tale of Treachery, Trafficking, and Two Friends on the Run* (New York: Bold Type Books, 2022).

26   See Miller, *Border Patrol Nation.*

27   "International Operations," ICE, https://www.ice.gov/about-ice/homeland-security-investigations/international-operations.

28   See "CBP Attachés" at https://www.cbp.gov/border-security/international-initiatives/cbp-attaches (last updated May 22, 2022).

29   Todd Miller, *Empire of Borders: The Expansion of the US Border around the World* (London: Verso Books, 2019), 25–27.

30   Quoted in Laura Carlsen, "Armoring NAFTA: The Battleground for Mexico's Future," *NACLA Report on the Americas* 41, no. 5 (2008): 17-22.

31   See Miller, *Border Patrol Nation*; and Aizeki et al., *Smart Borders or a Humane World?*

32   Brooke Jarvis, "The Scramble to Pluck 24 Billion Cherries in Eight Weeks," *New York Times Magazine*, August 12, 2020.

33   Miriam Jordan, "Farmworkers, Mostly Undocumented, Become 'Essential' During Pandemic," *New York Times*, April 2, 2020.

34   See, for example, Avram S. Bornstein, "Border Enforcement in Daily Life: Palestinian Day Laborers and Entrepreneurs Crossing the Green Line," *Human Organization* 60, no. 3 (2001): 298–307.

35   Meron Rapoport, "The Line Separating Israel and Palestine Has Been Erased. What Comes Next?" *+972 Magazine*, August 10, 2022.

36   See Joseph Nevins, *Dying to Live: A Story of US Immigration in an Age of Global Apartheid* (San Francisco: City Lights Books, 2008); Joseph Nevins, "Policing Mobility, Maintaining Global Apartheid—from South Africa to the United States," in *Beyond Walls and Cages: Prisons, Borders, and Global Crisis*, ed. Jenna M. Loyd, Matt Mitchelson, and Andrew Burridge (Athens: University of Georgia Press, 2012), 19–26.

37   See Joseph Nevins, "The Right to the World," *Antipode* 49, no. 5 (2017): 1349–67.

38   See Todd Miller, *Storming the Wall: Climate Change, Migration, and Homeland Security* (San Francisco: City Lights Books, 2017); and Todd Miller, Nick Buxton, and Mark Akkerman, *Global Climate Wall: How the World's Wealthiest Nations Prioritise Borders over Climate Action*, Transnational Institute, October 2021.

39   Harsha Walia, *Undoing Border Imperialism* (Chico, CA: AK Press, 2014). See Nick Estes's chapter in this volume.

40   Such struggles are, of course, present in myriad ways. See, for example, Madjiguène Cissé, "The Sans-Papiers: A Woman Draws the First Lessons," in *We Are Everywhere: The Irresistible Rise of Global Anticapitalism*, ed. Notes from Nowhere (London: Verso, 2003), 38–45; and Amelia Frank-Vitale and Margarita Núñez Chaim, "'Lady Frijoles': las caravanas centroamericanas y el poder de la hipervisibilidad de la migración indocumentada," *EntreDiversidades. Revista de ciencias sociales y humanidades* 7, no. 1 (2020): 37–61.

41   See Zoltan Grossman, "The Kindness of Strangers: Today's Refugees in Hungary and My Family during WWII," *Common Dreams*, September 21, 2015; Natasha King, *No Borders: The Politics of Immigration Control and Resistance* (London: Zed Books, 2016); and Eleanor Beardsley, "At Risk of Arrest, Villagers Aid Migrants Crossing French-Italian Border," NPR, February 10, 2017.

4. Fortress Europe's Proliferating Borders

1   Much of this chapter is drawn from a case study I authored that was included in Mizue Aizeki et al., *Smart Borders or a Humane World?* Immigrant Defense Project's Surveillance, Tech & Immigration Policing Project, and the Transnational Institute, October 2021. An especially big thank-you to Joseph Nevins for his help in rewriting and editing this chapter.

2   Harry Taylor, "Greece Extends Border Wall to Deter Afghans Trying to Reach Europe," *The Guardian*, August 21, 2021.

3   Matthew Chance et al., "Violence Erupts on Poland-Belarus Border as Polish Guards Fire Water Cannon on Migrants Throwing Rocks," CNN, November 16, 2021.

4   Jamie Grierson, "Channel Drownings: What Happened and Who Is to Blame?" *The Guardian*, November 25, 2021.

5   See Giuseppe Campesi, *Policing Mobility Regimes: Frontex and the Production of the European Borderscape* (London: Routledge, 2021).

6   The latest incarnation of the "sans-papiers" movement in France (the movement by/ for undocumented immigrants), which initially called itself "Les Gilets Noirs" ("The Black Vests," playing on the Yellow Vest movement) but has now largely morphed into the "La Chapelle Debout Collective," has pointed to France's repeated role in regime change in African countries from Libya to Burkina Faso, its investments in strategic raw materials, and the fact that fourteen African nations are still obliged by a colonial pact to put 85 percent of their foreign reserve into a French bank. See

Mawuna Remarque Koutonin, "14 African Countries Forced by France to Pay Colonial Tax for the Benefits of Slavery and Colonization," Pan African Visions, January 14, 2014.

7   See Matthew Carr, *Fortress Europe: Dispatches from a Gated Continent* (New York: The New Press, 2016).

8   Ainhoa Ruiz Benedicto and Pere Brunet, *Building Walls: Fear and Securitization in the European Union*, Transnational Institute, November 2021.

9   See Aizeki et al., *Smart Borders or a Humane World?*

10 "The EU Is Being Asked to Pay for Border Fences to Keep Migrants Out," *The Economist*, October 30, 2021.

11 Regarding Ceuta and Melilla, see Marcello di Cintio, *Walls: Travels along the Barricades* (New York: Soft Skull Press, 2013).

12 Euan Ward and Aida Alamai, "More Than 20 Migrants Die in Effort to Enter Spanish Enclave in Africa" *New York Times*, June 25, 2022

13 See Ainhoa Ruiz Benedicto, Mark Akkerman, and Pere Brunet, *A Walled World: Towards a Global Apartheid*, Centre Delàs d'Estudis per la Pau (Barcelona), November 2020; Sam Edwards, "The High-Tech 'Makeover' of Europe's Deadly Border with Africa," *Rest of World*, May 26, 2021.

14 "IDEMIA and Sopra Steria Chosen by EU-LISA to Build the New Shared Biometric Matching System (sBMS) for Border Protection of the Schengen Area," IDEMIA, June 4, 2020. See the "Border Wars" series from the Transnational Institute.

15 Nick Waters, Emmanuel Freudenthal, and Logan Williams, "Frontex at Fault: European Border Force Complicit in 'Illegal' Pushbacks," *Bellngcat*, October 23, 2020; Statewatch, "Frontex: Agency's Initial Response to Alleged Involvement in Pushbacks," February 24, 2021; Helena Smith, "Greece Accused of 'Biggest Pushback in Years' of Stricken Refugee Ship," *The Guardian*, November 5, 2021.

16 Mark Akkerman, *Expanding the Fortress: The Policies, the Profiteers, and People Shaped by EU's Border Externalization Programme*, Transnational Institute, May 2018.

17 Charles Heller, Lorenzo Pezzani, and Maurice Stierl, "Disobedient Sensing and Border Struggles at the Maritime Frontier of Europe" *Spheres: Journal for Digital Cultures* 4 (2017): 1–15.

18 Human Rights Watch, *Abused and Expelled: Ill-Treatment of Sub-Saharan Migrants in Morocco*, February 2014.

19 See, for example, International Rescue Committee, "Libya: Record Numbers Intercepted at Sea and Detained; IRC Calls for Their Immediate Release," press release, September 2, 2021.

20 Ian Urbina, "The Secretive Prisons That Keep Migrants Out of Europe," *New Yorker*, December 6, 2021.

21 This comes from a series of conversations with one of the activists working on site.

22 Helena Smith, "Greek Riot Police Fire Teargas at Refugees Campaigning to Leave Lesbos," *The Guardian*, September 12, 2020.

23 Jannis Papadimitriou, "Lesbos after Moria Fire: 'People Are Still Living in Tents by the Sea,'" DW, September 8, 2021.

24 Aurelien Breeden, "Outcry in France after Police Clear Migrant Camp," *New York Times*, December 23, 2020.

25 See Fallon and Molnar's chapter in this volume.

26 Rob Picheta, "Passengers to Face AI Lie Detector Tests at EU Airports," CNN, November 2, 2018.

27   Zach Campbell, Caitlin Chandler, and Chris Jones, "Sci-fi Surveillance: Europe's
      Secretive Push into Biometric Technology," *The Guardian*, December 10, 2020.

28   Picheta, "Passengers to Face AI Lie Detector Tests at EU Airports."

29   Julie Kleinman, *Adventure Capital: Migration and the Making of an African Hub in
      Paris* (Berkeley: University of California Press, 2019).

30   Katja Lindskov Jacobsen, "Experimentation in Humanitarian Locations: UNHCR
      and Biometric Registration of Afghan Refugees," *Security Dialogue* 46, no. 2
      (2015): 144–64; see also Petra Molnar, "Technology on the Margins: AI and
      Global Migration Management from a Human Rights Perspective." *Cambridge
      International Law Journal* 8, no. 2 (2019): 305–30.

31   See Reece Jones, *Violent Borders: Refugees and the Right to Move* (New York: Verso,
      2017).

32   See Alarm Phone, a hotline for people in distress on the sea, https://alarmphone.
      org/en/; Forensic Oceanography, a project to help trace the lethal effects of border
      regimes, https://forensic-architecture.org/category/forensic-oceanography; and
      Mosaik Support Center, part of Lesvos Solidarity, which has created sustainable
      support structures for refugees and locals, https://lesvossolidarity.org/en/what-we-do/
      mosaik-support-center.

33   Ty McCormick, "Highway Through Hell," *Foreign Policy*, October 4, 2017.

34   See Nina Perkowski, "Frontex and the Convergence of Humanitarianism, Human
      Rights and Security," *Security Dialogue* 49, no. 6 (2018): 457–75; and Miriam
      Ticktin, "Thinking Beyond Humanitarian Borders," in "Borders and the Politics
      of Mourning," ed. Alexandra Delano and Benjamin Nienass, special issue, *Social
      Research: An International Quarterly* 83, no. 2 (Fall 2016): 255–71.

35   See Miriam Ticktin, *Casualties of Care: Immigration and the Politics of
      Humanitarianism in France* (Berkeley: University of California Press, 2011).

36   Étienne Balibar, *We the People of Europe: Reflections on Transnational Citizenship*
      (Princeton, NJ: Princeton University Press, 2004).

5. Frontex and Fortress Europe's Technological Experiments

1   "New Pact on Migration and Asylum," European Commission, September 23, 2020.

2   Katy Fallon, "EU Announces Funding for Five New Refugee Camps on Greek
      Islands," *The Guardian*, March 29, 2021.

3   Petra Molnar (@P_Molnar), "Press Conference, Lesvos," Twitter, March 29, 2021,
      https://twitter.com/_PMolnar/status/1376492846707056648?s=20.

4   "New Pact on Migration and Asylum."

5   Mark Akkerman, *Financing Border Wars: The Border Industry, Its Financiers and
      Human Rights* (Amsterdam: Transnational Institute and Stop Wapenhandel, March
      2021).

6   "Artificial Intelligence–Based Capabilities for European Border and Coast Guard,"
      Frontex, March 26, 2021.

7   Statewatch, "Frontex: More Power, No Responsibility? Mega-agency Lacks Real
      Accountability Structure," April 19, 2022.

8   Matthias Monroy, "Border Surveillance: Frontex Installs Cameras in the
      Stratosphere," Security Architectures in the EU, October 4, 2022.

9   Petra Molnar, "Surveillance Sovereignty: Migration Management Technologies and
      the Politics of Privatization," in *Migration, Security, and Resistance: Global and Local
      Perspectives*, ed. Graham Hudson and Idil Atak (Oxford: Routledge, 2022).

10   Statewatch, "Funds for Fortress Europe: Spending by Frontex and EU-LISA,"

January 28, 2022.

11 "Situational Awareness and Monitoring Division," Frontex, frontex.europa.eu.

12 Statewatch, "Data Protection, Immigration Enforcement and Fundamental Rights: What the EU's Regulations on Interoperability Mean for People with Irregular Status," November 16, 2019.

13 EDRi, "Intensified Surveillance at EU Borders: EURODAC Reform Needs a Radical Policy Shift," September 8, 2021.

14 Petra Molnar, *Technological Testing Grounds: Migration Management Experiments and Reflections from the Ground Up*, EDRi and the Refugee Law Lab, November 2020.

15 Petra Molnar, "Inside New Refugee Camp Like a 'Prison': Greece and Other Countries Prioritize Surveillance over Human Rights," *The Conversation*, September 27, 2021.

16 Chantal Da Silva, "EU Alarmed by Greece's Use of Sound Cannons at Border to Deter Asylum Seekers," Euronews, June 4, 2021.

17 EURACTIV.com with AFP, "Greece Defends Use of Anti-migrant Sound Cannons," June 9, 2021.

18 Ryan Gallagher and Ludovica Jona, "We tested Europe's New Lie Detector For Travelers And Immediately Triggered A False Response," *The Intercept*, July 26, 2019.

19 Molnar, *Technological Testing Grounds*.

20 Alastair Jamieson, Kirsten Ripper, and Alasdair Sandford, "Greece Is 'Europe's Shield' in the Migrant Crisis, Says EU Chief von der Leyen on Visit to Turkey Border," Euronews, March 3, 2020.

21 "Europe Must Act," No More Camps: Monthly Update, February 2021.

22 Molnar, "Inside New Refugee Camp Like a 'Prison.'"

23 Hannah Davis, "At Poland's Borders, Ukrainians Are Welcomed While Refugees from Elsewhere Face a Growing Crackdown," *The New Humanitarian*, May 26, 2022.

24 "Poland Seeks to Bolster Border with New Tech amid Migrant Influx," Reuters, October 4, 2021.

25 Patrick Breyer, "EU-Funded Technology Violates Fundamental Rights," *About: Intel*, April 22, 2021.

26 Ruha Benjamin, *Race After Technology: Abolitionist Tools for the New Jim Code* (Medford, MA: Polity Press, 2019).

27 Katy Fallon, "How the Greek Island Lesbos Became a Stage for Europe's Far Right," Al Jazeera, May 6, 2020.

28 Katy Fallon, "'It's an Atrocity against Humankind': Greek Pushback Blamed for Double Drowning," *The Guardian*, February 17, 2022.

29 EURACTIV.com with AFP, "EU Border Agency Frontex 'Covered Up' Greek Pushbacks: Reports," July 29, 2022, https://www.euractiv.com/section/justice-home-affairs/news/eu-border-agency-frontex-covered-up-greek-pushbacks-reports/; Giorgos Christides and Steffen Lüdke, "Frontex Involved in Illegal Pushbacks of Hundreds of Refugees," *Spiegel International*, April 28, 2022, https://www.spiegel.de/international/europe/frontex-involved-in-illegal-pushbacks-of-hundreds-of-refugees-a-9fe90845-efb1-4d91-a231-48efcafa53a0.

30 Akkerman, "Financing Border Wars."

31 Molnar, *Technological Testing Grounds*.

32 Statewatch, "A Clear and Present Danger: Missing Safeguards on Migration and Asylum in the EU's AI Act," May 12, 2022.

33   Maeve Higgins, "How the $68 Billion Border Surveillance Industrial Complex Affects Us All," *VICE World News*, June 11, 2021.

34   Petra Molnar, "Technology at the Margins: The Human Rights Impacts of AI in Migration Management," *Cambridge Journal of International Law* 8, no. 2 (2019): 305–30.

35   EDRi, "Regulating Migration Tech: How the EU's AI Act Can Better Protect People on the Move," May 9, 2022.

36   "Abolish Frontex," https://abolishfrontex.org/.

37   European Council on Refugees and Exiles, "Frontex: One Investigation Closes as Another Begins and the Agency's Role in Return and Ability to Purchase Firearms under Scrutiny," March 5, 2021.

38   Petra Molnar and Sarah Chander, "OPINION: The AI Act: EU's Chance to Regulate Harmful Border Technologies," Thomson Reuters Foundation News, May 17, 2022.

6. Abolish Migration Deterrence

1   Joseph Nevins, *Dying to Live: A Story of US Immigration in an Age of Global Apartheid* (San Francisco: City Lights Books, 2008); Harsha Walia, *Undoing Border Imperialism* (Chico, CA: AK Press, 2014).

2   Samuel Moyn, *The Last Utopia: Human Rights in History* (Cambridge, MA: Harvard University Press, 2012).

3   Until then, people whom the US resettled were granted parole on an ad hoc basis by the Department of Justice.

4   Jenna M. Loyd and Alison Mountz, *Boats, Borders, and Bases: Race, the Cold War, and the Rise of Migration Detention in the United States* (Oakland: University of California Press, 2018).

5   Greg Grandin and Gilbert M. Joseph, eds., *Insurgent and Counterinsurgent Violence during Latin America's Cold War* (Durham, NC: Duke University Press, 2010); Karina Oliva Alvarado, Alicia Ivonne Estrada, and Ester E. Hernández, eds., *US Central Americans: Reconstructing Memories, Struggles, and Communities of Resistance* (Tucson: University of Arizona Press, 2017); Aviva Chomsky, *Central America's Forgotten History: Revolution, Violence, and the Roots of Migration* (Boston: Beacon Press, 2021).

6   Nevins, *Dying to Live*; Timothy J. Dunn, "The Militarization of the US-Mexico Border in the Twenty-First Century," in *Handbook on Human Security, Borders, and Migration*, ed. Natalia Ribas-Mateos and Timothy J. Dunn (Cheltenham, UK: Edward Elgar, 2021).

7   Jason De León, *The Land of Open Graves: Living and Dying on the Migrant Trail* (Oakland: University of California Press, 2015).

8   Jeremy Slack and Daniel E. Martínez, "The Geography of Migrant Death: Violence on the US-Mexico Border," in *Handbook on Critical Geographies of Migration*, ed. Katharyne Mitchell, Reece Jones, and Jennifer L. Fluri (Cheltenham, UK: Edward Elgar, 2019).

9   Guy S. Goodwin-Gill, "The Right to Seek Asylum: Interception at Sea and the Principle of Non-refoulement," *International Journal of Refugee Law* 23, no. 3 (2011): 443.

10   Alison Mountz, *The Death of Asylum: Hidden Geographies of the Enforcement Archipelago* (Minneapolis: University of Minnesota Press, 2020).

11   Thomas Gammeltoft-Hansen and James C. Hathaway, "Non-refoulement in a World

of Cooperative Deterrence," *Columbia Journal of Transnational Law* 53 (2014): 235.

12   Reece Jones, *Violent Borders: Refugees and the Right to Move* (New York: Verso, 2017); Gerda Heck and Sabine Hess, "Tracing the Effects of the EU-Turkey Deal," *Movements: Journal for Critical Migration and Border Regime Studies* 3, no. 2 (2017); Todd Miller, *Empire of Borders: The Expansion of the US Border around the World* (London: Verso Books, 2019).

13   Bentham also advocated for the principle of proportionality. Travis C. Pratt and Jillian J. Turanovic, "Celerity and Deterrence," in *Deterrence, Choice, and Crime: Contemporary Perspectives*, ed. Daniel S. Nagin, Francis T. Cullen, and Cheryl Lero Jonson (New York: Routledge, 2018).

14   Michael Tonry, "An Honest Politician's Guide to Deterrence: Certainty, Severity, Celerity, and Parsimony," in Nagin, Cullen, and Jonson, *Deterrence, Choice, and Crime*, 367.

15   Notable exceptions include Sharon Pickering and Leanne Weber, "New Deterrence Scripts in Australia's Rejuvenated Offshore Detention Regime for Asylum Seekers," *Law & Social Inquiry* 39, no. 4 (2014): 1006–26; and Mary Bosworth, "Immigration Detention, Punishment and the Transformation of Justice," *Social & Legal Studies* 28, no. 1 (2019): 81–99.

16   Gammeltoft-Hansen and Hathaway, "Non-refoulement."

17   Stacy Pollard, "Perspective: Why Deterrence Is Not the Answer to Reducing Asylum-Seeking Migrant Flows," *Homeland Security Today*, January 18, 2019; Jonathan Kent, Kelsey Norman, and Kate Tennis, "Building Walls and Deporting People to 'Safe' Countries Is Not Deterrence, It's Defense," *Just Security*, February 12, 2020.

18   Thomas Gammeltoft-Hansen and Nikolas Feith Tan, "Beyond the Deterrence Paradigm in Global Refugee Policy," *Suffolk Transnational Law Review* 39 (2016): 637.

19   Bhupinder S. Chimni, "The Geopolitics of Refugee Studies: A View from the South," *Journal of Refugee Studies* 11, no. 4 (1998): 350–74.

20   Nagin, Cullen, and Jonson, *Deterrence, Choice, and Crime*.

21   Emily Ryo, "Detention as Deterrence," *Stanford Law Review Online* 71 (March 2019): 244.

22   Cited in Adam Cox and Ryan Goodman, "Detention of Migrant Families as 'Deterrence': Ethical Flaws and Empirical Doubts," *Just Security*, June 22, 2018.

23   Wendy A. Vogt, *Lives in Transit: Violence and Intimacy on the Migrant Journey* (Oakland: University of California Press, 2018), 30.

24   Cox and Goodman, "Detention of Migrant Families."

25   The writing on this topic is vast. See Ruth Wilson Gilmore, *Golden Gulag: Prisons, Surplus, Crisis, and Opposition in Globalizing California* (Oakland: University of California Press, 2007); for additional resources, see URL.

26   For resources, see URL.

27   Caitlin Dickerson, "'We Need to Take Away Children': The Secret History of the U.S. Government's Family-Separation Policy," *The Atlantic*, September 2022, 36–76.

28   This is another expansive literature. See Bridget Anderson, Nandita Sharma, and Cynthia Wright, "Why No Borders?" *Refuge: Canada's Journal on Refugees* 26, no. 2 (2009): 5–18; for additional resources, see URL.

29   Ruth Wilson Gilmore, *Change Everything: Racial Capitalism and the Case for Abolition*, ed. Naomi Murakawa (Chicago: Haymarket Books, forthcoming).

30   A. Naomi Paik, *Bans, Walls, Raids, Sanctuary: Understanding US Immigration for the*

Twenty-First Century (Oakland: University of California Press, 2020), 113, 117.

31   Joseph Nevins, "Migration as Reparations," NACLA, May 24, 2016.

32   See "New Way Forward for Immigrant Justice," Immigrant Justice Network, 2021.

33   Suketu Mehta, "Why Should Immigrants 'Respect Our Borders'? The West Never Respected Theirs," *New York Times*, June 7, 2019.

34   Harsha Walia, *Border and Rule: Global Migration, Capitalism, and the Rise of Racist Nationalism* (Chicago: Haymarket Books, 2021), 213.

7. Cruel Fictions in the Black Mediterranean

1   Eric Allison, "Home Office Issues 'End of Life Plan' to Hunger-Striking Asylum Seeker," *The Guardian*, November 16, 2013.

2   "Enforcement of Immigration Legislation Statistics," Eurostat, accessed July 30, 2021, https://ec.europa.eu/eurostat/statistics-explained/index.php?title=Enforcement_ of_immigration_legislation_statistics; Mark Akkerman, *Outsourcing Oppression: How Europe Externalises Migrant Detention beyond Its Shores*, Transnational Institute and Stop Wapenhandel, 2021.

3   Cited in: David Morley, Julian Henriques, and Vana Goblot. *Stuart Hall: Conversations, Projects and Legacies*. (London: Goldsmiths Press, 2017), p.197.

4   See, indicatively, Sabine Broeck and P. Khalil Saucier, "A Dialogue: On European Borders, Black Movement, and the History of Social Death," *Black Studies Papers* 2, no. 1 (2016); Ida Danewid, "White Innocence in the Black Mediterranean: Hospitality and the Erasure of History," *Third World Quarterly* 38, no. 7 (July 2017): 1674–89, https://doi.org/10.1080/01436597.2017.1331123; Camilla Hawthorne, *Contesting Race and Citizenship: Youth Politics in the Black Mediterranean* (Ithaca, NY: Cornell University Press, 2022); The Black Mediterranean Collective, ed., *The Black Mediterranean: Bodies, Borders and Citizenship*, Mediterranean Perspectives (Cham, Switzerland: Palgrave Macmillan, 2021); P. Khalil Saucier and Tryon P. Woods, "Ex Aqua: The Mediterranean Basin, Africans on the Move, and the Politics of Policing," *Theoria* 61, no. 141 (December 2014): 55–75, https://doi.org/10.3167/ th.2014.6114104; Christina Sharpe, *In the Wake: On Blackness and Being* (Durham, NC: Duke University Press Books, 2016); S. A. Smythe, "The Black Mediterranean and the Politics of Imagination," *Middle East Report*, no. 286 (Spring 2018): 3–9. For a related argument, see Nicholas De Genova, "The 'Migrant Crisis' as Racial Crisis: Do Black Lives Matter in Europe?" *Ethnic and Racial Studies* 41, no. 10 (August 2017): 1–18, https://doi.org/10.1080/01419870.2017.1361543.\\uc0\\u8221{} {\\i{}Ethnic and Racial Studies} 41, no. 10 (August 21, 2017

5   In his classical text from 1993, Gilroy theorizes the Black Atlantic as a space of enslavement, exploitation, and racial terror that has been central to the making of the modern world. For him, the Black Atlantic also gave rise to a transnational counterculture of resistance that has the power "to conjure up and enact new modes of friendship, happiness, and solidarity." Paul Gilroy, *The Black Atlantic: Modernity and Double Consciousness* (London: Verso, 1993), 38.

6   The Black Mediterranean Collective, *The Black Mediterranean*, 11.

7   Sharpe, *In the Wake*, 21.

8   Cristina Lombardi-Diop, preface to *The Black Mediterranean*, 4.

9   On the racial and colonial history of mobility controls, see Simone Browne, *Dark Matters: On the Surveillance of Blackness* (Durham, NC: Duke University Press, 2015); Nadine El-Enany, *(B)Ordering Britain: Law, Race and Empire* (Manchester, UK: Manchester University Press, 2020); Encarnación Gutiérrez Rodríguez, "The

Coloniality of Migration and the 'Refugee Crisis': On the Asylum-Migration Nexus, the Transatlantic White European Settler Colonialism-Migration and Racial Capitalism," *Refuge* 34, no. 1 (2018); Radhika Mongia, *Indian Migration and Empire: A Colonial Genealogy of the Modern State* (Durham, NC: Duke University Press, 2018); Nandita Sharma, *Home Rule: National Sovereignty and the Separation of Natives and Migrants* (Durham, NC: Duke University Press, 2020).2015 See also Sabrina Axster et al., "Collective Discussion: Colonial Lives of the Carceral Archipelago: Rethinking the Neoliberal Security State," *International Political Sociology*, forthcoming.

10   Mongia, *Indian Migration and Empire*, 43.

11   On the migrant crisis as a racial crisis, see Genova, "The 'Migrant Crisis' as Racial Crisis.""plainCitation":"Genova, "The 'Migrant Crisis' as Racial Crisis.""","noteIndex":13},"citationItems":[{"id":2622,"uris":["http://zotero.org/users/local/8pGGmI9c/items/XKAMJUTK"],"itemData":{"id":2622,"type":"article-journal","abstract":"We are currently witnessing a remarkable conjuncture between the escalation, acceleration, and diversification of migrant and refugee mobilities, on the one hand, and the mutually constitutive crises of "European" borders and "European" identity, on the other, replete with reanimated reactionary populist nationalisms and racialized nativisms, the routinization of antiterrorist securitization, and pervasive and entrenched "Islamophobia" (or more precisely, anti-Muslim racism

12   Smythe, "The Black Mediterranean and the Politics of Imagination," 5.

13   Ida Danewid, "'These Walls Must Fall': The Black Mediterranean and the Politics of Abolition," in The Black Mediterranean Collective, *The Black Mediterranean*, 145–66.

14   W. E. B. Du Bois, *Black Reconstruction in America 1860–1880* (New York: Simon and Schuster, 1999), 199. See also Angela Y. Davis, *Abolition Democracy: Beyond Empire, Prisons, and Torture* (New York: Seven Stories Press, 2005).

15   No Border Kitchen Lesvos, "Forced Stop of Hunger Strike," April 11, 2020, https://noborderkitchenlesvos.noblogs.org/post/2020/04/11/forced-stop-of-hunger-strike/.

16   On border abolition, see Gracie Mae Bradley and Luke de Noronha, *Against Borders: The Case for Abolition* (London: Verso Books, 2022); Bridget Anderson, Nandita Sharma, and Cynthia Wright, "Editorial: Why No Borders?" *Refuge* 26, no. 2 (2009); Harsha Walia, *Border and Rule: Global Migration, Capitalism, and the Rise of Racist Nationalism* (Chicago: Haymarket Books, 2021).

17   Saidiya Hartman, *Lose Your Mother: A Journey Along the Atlantic Slave Route* (New York: Serpent's Tail, 2021), 234.

8. CASE STUDY: How We Fight Against (Tech-Facilitated) Persecution of Uyghurs in China and Abroad

1   Adrian Shahbaz, *The Rise of Digital Authoritarianism*, Freedom House, 2018; Human Rights Watch and Stanford Law School Mills Legal Clinic, *"Break Their Lineage, Break Their Roots": Chinese Government Crimes against Humanity Targeting Uyghurs and Other Turkic Muslims,"* April 2021.

2   This is further exemplified by the crackdown on the Hong Kong democracy movement, which Chinese authorities have also labelled "terrorist." See Uyghur Human Rights Project, "Persecution of Uyghurs in the Era of the 'War on Terror,'" press release, October 16, 2007.

3   Human Rights Watch, *"Break Their Lineage."*

4   Human Rights Watch, *"Break Their Lineage."*
5   Dake Kang and Yanan Wang, "China's Uighurs Told to Share Beds, Meals with Party Members," Associated Press, November 30, 2018.

9. CASE STUDY: Why We Took the UK to Court for Its Discriminatory Visa Streaming Algorithm

1   "Home Office Drops 'Racist' Algorithm from Visa Decisions," *BBC*, August 4, 2020.
2   The "Go Home" vans, also known as "Immigration Enforcement Vans," were a controversial Home Office campaign that was launched in 2013 and discontinued in 2014. The campaign involved vans driving around some areas of the UK with billboards on them instructing migrants to "Go Home" or face arrest.

10. Building the #NoTechforICE Campaign

1   A fingerprint sharing program where information collected by police at booking is automatically shared with DHS. See Aizeki chapter in this volume.
2   See #NoTechforICE campaign website, https://notechforice.com.
3   Immigrant Defense Project, Mijente, and the National Immigration Project of the National Lawyers Guild, *Who's Behind ICE? The Tech and Data Companies Fueling Deportations*, October 2018, hereinafter Mijente et al., *Who's Behind ICE?*
4   Aria Bendix, "Amazon Has Canceled Its New York City HQ2 Plans. Here's Why Many New Yorkers Opposed the Project," *Insider*, February 14, 2019.
5   Chris Mills Rodrigo, "Majority of Independent Shareholders Vote to Review Thomson Reuters' ICE Contracts," *The Hill*, August 9, 2021.

11. Big Tech, Borders, and Biosecurity: Securitization in Britain after COVID-19

1   Jim Waterson, "Boris Johnson Urges UK Top Tech Firms to Join Coronavirus Fight," *The Guardian*, March 13, 2020.
2   Juliette Garside and Rupert Neate, "UK Government 'Using Pandemic to Transfer NHS Duties to Private Sector,'" *The Guardian*, May 4, 2020; Oscar Williams, "Secret Data and the Future of Public Health: Why the NHS Has Turned to Palantir," *New Statesman*, May 21, 2020; Corporate Watch, *The UK Border Regime: A Critical Guide*, 2018.
3   Arun Kundnani, *The Muslims Are Coming! Islamophobia, Extremism, and the Domestic War on Terror* (London: Verso, 2014).
4   Kundnani, *The Muslims Are Coming!*
5   Tarek Younis and Sushrut Jadhav, "Islamophobia in the National Health Service: An Ethnography of Institutional Racism in PREVENT's Counter-radicalization Policy," *Sociology of Health and Illness* 42 no. 3 (2020): 610–26.
6   Maya Goodfellow, *Hostile Environment: How Immigrants Became Scapegoats* (London: Verso, 2019).
7   Spencer Woodman, "Palantir Provides the Engine for Donald Trump's Deportation Machine," *The Intercept*, March 2, 2017; Erica Consterdine, "Hostile Environment: The UK Government's Draconian Immigration Policy Explained," *The Conversation*, April 26, 2018.
8   Corporate Watch, *The UK Border Regime.*
9   Nafeez Ahmed, "How the CIA Made Google: Inside the Secret Network behind Mass Surveillance, Endless War, and Skynet," *INSURGE Intelligence*, January 22,

2015.

10   Privacy International, "All Roads Lead to Palantir," October 2020.

11   Ashlee Vance and Brad Stone, "Palantir, the War on Terror's Secret Weapon," *Bloomberg*, November 22, 2011.

12   Naomi Klein, "How Big Tech Plans to Profit from the Pandemic," *The Guardian*, May 13, 2020.

13   Sam Biddle, "How Peter Thiel's Palantir Helped the NSA Spy on the Whole World," *The Intercept*, February 22, 2017.

14   Rohail Saleem, "Palantir Secures Another Multi-Million Pound Defense Contract from the British Government," *wccftech*, December 5, 2019.

15   Martin Williams, "'Spy Tech' Firm Palantir Made £22m Profit after NHS Data Deal," openDemocracy, August 23, 2021.

16   Mijente et al., *Who's Behind ICE?*

17   "Guidance for Public Health Officers: Potentially Infectious Persons," Department of Health and Social Care, 2020.

13. Global Palestine: Exporting Israel's Regime of Population Control

1   Neve Gordon, *Working Paper III: The Political Economy of Israel's Homeland Security/ Surveillance Industry*, Surveillance Study Centre at Queen's University, Kingston, Canada, 2009.

2   See Yotam Feldman, *The Lab* (film), 2013, http://vimeo.com/65082874; for other resources, see URL.

3   Halper, *War against the People: Israel, the Palestinians and Global Pacification* (London: Pluto Press, 2015), 168–90, 249–74.

4   Jeff Halper, *Decolonizing Israel, Liberating Palestine: Zionism, Settler Colonialism, and the Case for One Democratic State* (London: Pluto Press, 2021), 47–49, 84–85.

5   Another significant "front" of Israeli migrant and population control concerns the presence of some forty thousand African asylum seekers (which Israel calls "infiltrators" or "job seekers" in order to avoid its obligations under international law). See Human Rights Watch, *"Make Their Lives Miserable": Israel's Coercion of Eritrean and Sudanese Asylum Seekers to Leave Israel*, September 2014.

6   Halper, *War against the People*, 67–85.

7   Jeff Halper, "Israelizing the American Police, Palestinianizing the American People," *The Link* 53, no. 5 (2020). My phrasing of the Israeli position follows the remarks of Israel Katz, the Israeli minister of intelligence, to the Belgian government after the ISIS terrorist attacks there in 2016.

8   Halper, "Israelizing the American Police"; Mark Neocleous, "The Universal Adversary Will Attack: Pigs, Pirates, Zombies, Satan and the Class War," *Critical Studies on Terrorism* 8 no. 1 (2015), 15–32; Mark Neocleous, *The Universal Adversary: Security, Capital and "The Enemies of All Mankind"* (Abingdon, UK: Routledge, 2016).

9   "Netanyahu Says Palestinians Can Have a 'State Minus,'" *Times of Israel*, January 20, 2017.

10   For a full presentation on the Matrix of Control, see Jeff Halper, *An Israeli in Palestine* (London: Pluto, 2011), 150–74; Halper, *Decolonizing Israel, Liberating Palestine*, 93–100.

11   Harsha Walia, *Border and Rule: Global Migration, Capitalism, and the Rise of Racist Nationalism* (Chicago: Haymarket Books, 2021).

12   Oren Yiftachel, *Ethnocracy: Land and Identity Politics in Israel/Palestine*

(Philadelphia: University of Pennsylvania Press, 2006).

13 See Noura Erakat, *Justice for Some: Law and the Question of Palestine* (Stanford, CA: Stanford University Press, 2019).

14 Ilan Pappé, *The Ethnic Cleansing of Palestine* (Oxford: Oneworld, 2006). Kindle edition.

15 Erakat, *Justice for Some*, 55–57.

16 Stephen Graham, *Cities Under Siege: The New Military Urbanism* (London: Verso, 2010), 253.

17 Halper, *War against the People*, 266.

18 SIBAT, *Israel Homeland Defense Sales Directory, 2012–13* (Tel Aviv: Israeli Ministry of Defense, 2013).

19 Israeli Export and International Cooperation Institute, *Israel: Homeland Security Industry*, 2013.

20 Halper, *War against the People*, 266–74.

21 Gordon, *Working Paper III*, 33–35.

22 Gordon, *e*, 10.

23 Hanan Sher, "Facets of the Israeli Economy—The Defense Industry," Israel Ministry of Foreign Affairs, June 1, 2002.

24 Gordon, *Working Paper III*, 12.

25 Halper, *War against the People*, 267–69.

26 iHLS, *It Is Better to Be Smart than Safe – The Growing Buzz Surrounding Safe Cities*, 2013.

27 Jimmy Johnson, "A Palestine-Mexico Border?" NACLA, June 29, 2012.

28 Elbit Systems, "Elbit Systems' Hermes 450 Unmanned Air Vehicle to Support U.S. Homeland Security on Arizona's Southern Border," press release, June 30, 2004.

29 "Mexico Adds More Israeli Surveillance Platforms," *Defense Industry Daily*, February 18, 2009.

30 Johnson, "A Palestine-Mexico Border?"

31 From AIPAC, as cited in Halper, *War against the People*, 250.

32 Amnesty International, "With Whom Are Many US Police Departments Training? With A Chronic Human Rights Violator—Israel," August 25, 2016, https://www.amnestyusa.org/with-whom-are-many-u-s-police-departments-training-with-a-chronic-human-rights-violator-israel/.

33 Israeli Export and International Cooperation Institute, *Israel*.

34 This has not gone without protest. In 2014, forty-three reservists sent a letter to Prime Minister Netanyahu and the military declaring, "We are unable, morally, to serve in such a system which harms the rights of millions of people." Gili Cohen, "Reservists from Elite IDF Intel Unit Refuse to Serve over Palestinian 'Persecution,'" *Haaretz*, September 12, 2014.

35 Hei Hu Quan, "Spies in the Ointment: The Israeli Espionage of Global Communications," *Conspiracy Central Blog*, July 26, 2007.

14. Chicago's Gang Database Targeting People of Color

1 Case No. 17-Cv-3258, United States District Court for the Northern District of Illinois Eastern Division, 2017.

2 Griselda Flores, "Massive Chicago Gang Database Under Fire: Database Is Racially Skewed, Data Shows; and Violates Spirit of Sanctuary City, Advocates Say," *Social Justice News Nexus*, December 3, 2017.

3 Erase The Database, *Tracked and Targeted: Early Findings on Chicago's Gang*

Database, February 2018.

4   GoodKids MadCITY, "Pass the Peace Book Ordinance Now!" MoveOn, 2021.
5   Carlos Ballesteros, "Southwest Side Construction Worker Quickly Deported to Mexico While Awaiting DACA Decision," *Injustice Watch*, July 3, 2020.
6   Irene Romulo, "Deported Immigrants Are Best Served by Organizer Networks, Not a 'Benevolent Administration,'" *Prism*, January 20, 2022.

15. Building Community Power in Unequal Cities

1   *The 9/11 Commission Report: Final Report of the National Commission on Terrorist Attacks Upon the United States* (New York: W.W. Norton, 2004).
2   Stop LAPD Spying Coalition and Free Radicals, "The Algorithmic Ecology: An Abolitionist Tool for Organizing Against Algorithms," March 2, 2020.
3   Stop LAPD Spying Coalition, *Before the Bullet Hits the Body–Dismantling Predictive Policing in Los Angeles*, May 2018.

16. CASE STUDY: Why We Are Suing Clearview AI in California State Court

1   James Clayton and Ben Derico, "Clearview AI used nearly 1m times by US police, it tells the BBC," *BBC News*, March 27, 2023
2   Charlie Osborne, "Controversial Facial Recognition Tech Firm Clearview AI Inks Deal with ICE," ZDNET, August 17, 2020, https://www.zdnet.com/article/controversial-facial-recognition-tech-firm-clearview-ai-inks-deal-with-ice/.
3   "Renderos et al v. Clearview et al (Facial Recognition Surveillance)," Just Futures Law, https://www.justfutureslaw.org/legal-filings/clearview.
4   Office of the Privacy Commissioner of Canada, "Clearview AI's Unlawful Practices Represented Mass Surveillance of Canadians, Commissioners Say," press release, March 2, 2021.
5   Privacy Determination, Office of the Australian Information Commissioner, November 3, 2021.
6   Vincent Manancourt, "Controversial US Facial Recognition Technology Likely Illegal, EU Body Says," *Politico*, June 10, 2020.
7   "Italy Fines US Facial Recognition Firm Clearview AI," *Agence France-Presse*, March 9, 2022.
8   Natasha Lomas, "Sweden's Data Watchdog Slaps Police for Unlawful Use of Clearview AI," *TechCrunch*, February 12, 2021;
9   "Clearview AI Wins Boost in Challenge of UK Data Privacy Fine," *Bloomberg Law*, October 28, 2023, https://news.bloomberglaw.com/ip-law/clearview-ai-wins-boost-in-challenge-of-uk-data-privacy-fine.

18. CASE STUDY: Stop Urban Shield: How We Fought DHS's Militarized Police Trainings

1   Stop Urban Shield, http://stopurbanshield.org/about-the-campaign/participating-organizations/.

19. Digital ID: A Primer

1   Many thanks to Alli Finn for their support in editing this chapter.
2   World Bank, "Principles on Identification for Sustainable Development: Toward the Digital Age," 2018.
3   The Engine Room and Oxfam, *Biometrics in the Humanitarian Sector*, May 2018.

4   Sara Baker and Zara Rahman, *Understanding the Lived Effects of Digital ID: A Multi-Country Study*, The Engine Room, January 2020.

5   Quito Tsui and Teresa Perosa, "Digital IDs Rooted in Justice," The Engine Room, October 2022.

6   6 See #WhyID, https://www.accessnow.org/whyid/.

7   The summit's conclusions and recommendations can be found at https://www.unhcr.org/idecosystem/wp-content/uploads/sites/69/2019/12/Conclusions_and_Recommendations.pdf.

8   Sara Baker, "Digital ID in Zimbabwe: A Case Study," The Engine Room, 2020.

9   Jay Stanley, *Identity Crisis: What Digital Driver's Licenses Could Mean for Privacy, Equity, and Freedom*, ACLU, May 2021.

10 See Karan Saini, "Aadhaar Remains an Unending Security Nightmare for a Billion Indians," *The Wire*, May 11, 2018; PTI, "Plea Alleges Unauthorized Access of Aadhaar and Banking Data by GPay," *Financial Express*, September 15, 2021.

11 Mastercard, for instance, has been involved in several digital ID initiatives, including its new partnership with a digital health platform for patients to verify identity on their mobile phones. Heather Landi, "Mastercard Makes Healthcare Move with Digital ID Solution Patients Can Use on Their Smartphones," *Fierce Healthcare*, April 2, 2021.

12 Adrian Shahbaz and Allie Funk, *False Panacea: Abusive Surveillance in the Name of Public Health*, Freedom House, 2020.

13 Privacy International, "Ethnic Minorities at Greater Risk of Oversurveillance after Protests," June 15, 2020.

14 Mijente et al., *Who's Behind ICE?*

15 Jane Lytvynenko, "Data Collection and State Surveillance Put LGBTQ People at Risk Online and Off," *BuzzFeed*, July 14, 2020.

16 Madeleine Maxwell and Sara Baker, "Digital ID in Thailand: A Case Study," The Engine Room, 2020.

17 See the Tunisia case study in this volume.

18 Emna Sayadi, "Biometric ID vs. Privacy: Tunisians Win on Privacy! But It's Not Over Yet," *Access Now*, January 11, 2018.

19 Madeleine Maxwell, Zara Rahman, and Sara Baker, "Digital ID in Bangladeshi Refugee Camps," The Engine Room, 2019.

20 Human Rights Watch, "UN Shared Rohingya Data without Informed Consent: Bangladesh Provided Myanmar Information That Refugee Agency Collected," June 15, 2021.

21 Aaron Martin and Linnet Taylor, "Biometric Ultimata—What the Yemen Conflict Can Tell Us about the Politics of Digital ID Systems," Global Data Justice, June 21, 2019.

22 Nathaniel Raymond, Laura W. McDonald, and Rahul Chandran, "Opinion: The WFP and Palantir Controversy Should Be a Wake-up Call for Humanitarian Community," *Devex*, February 14, 2019.

23 Ben Hayes and Massimo Marelli, "Facilitating Innovation, Ensuring Protection: The ICRC Biometrics Policy," *Humanitarian Law & Policy*, October 18, 2019.

24 Zara Rahman and Sara Baker, "Digital ID in Ethiopian Refugee Camps: A Case Study," The Engine Room, 2020.

25 Ruha Benjamin, *Race After Technology: Abolitionist Tools for the New Jim Code* (Medford, MA: Polity Press, 2019).

OK:

20. IDs and the Citizen: Technologically Determined Identity in India

1   Government of Tripura, Food Civil Supplies and Consumer Affairs Department, "Notification," 2019.

2   The student protest began in 1979, and was waged in opposition to immigrants—a source of anxiety that had been exacerbated by the numbers of people moving across the border from Bangladesh (erstwhile East Pakistan) in the period leading up to, and during, the Liberation War that ended on December 16, 1971. The protests were also about the lack of economic development of the state.

3   Memorandum of Settlement between the Government of India and the Assam Movement, *Accord between AASU, AAGSP and the Central Government on the Foreign National Issue (Assam Accord)*, New Delhi, 1985, https://peacemaker.un.org/sites/peacemaker.un.org/files/IN_850815_Assam%20Accord.pdf.

4   *Citizenship (Amendment) Act 1986* (India), section 6A.

5   "The Kargil Review Committee Report," 1999, http://www.claudearpi.net/wp-content/uploads/2019/08/Kargil-Report.pdf. On July 29, 1999, three days after the Kargil War ended, the Indian government set up the Kargil Review Committee in order to "examine the sequence of events and make recommendations for the future." The report included a suggestion about IDs for persons living along the border: "Likewise, steps should be taken to issue ID cards to border villagers in certain vulnerable areas on a priority basis, pending the extended issuance of identity cards to other or all parts of the state. Such a policy would also be relevant in the North-East, Sikkim and part of West Bengal."

6   "Illegal Immigrants Have To Be Deported: Advani," *Times of India*, February 16, 2003, https://timesofindia.indiatimes.com/india/illegal-immigrants-have-to-be-deported-advani/articleshow/37657208.cms; Law Commission of India, *1I Report on the Foreigners (Amendment) Bill*, 2000, https://www.google.com/url?q=https://lawcommissionofindia.nic.in/reports/175thReport pdf&sa=D&source=docs&ust=1642588444064610&usg=AOvVaw1DzfxTeSzsh6d4m2Py2ZbR. The Law Commission's report, too, was rooted in this anxiety about the "illegal migrant" who was crowding the country and taking away resources and jobs.

7   *Citizenship (Amendment) Act 1986* (India), section 14A.

8   *Assam Sanmilita Mahasangha & Ors. Versus Union of India & Ors.*, Supreme Court of India, 2014. https://main.sci.gov.in/judgment/judis/42194.pdf.

9   "Assam NRC: What Next for 1.9 Million 'Stateless' Indians?" *BBC*, August 31, 2019, https://www.bbc.com/news/world-asia-india-49520593.

10 Priya Pathak, "NRC Protests: Wipro Celebrates Company's Role in NRC Project in Assam, First Deletes Page Then Restores It," *India Today*, December 23, 2019, https://www.indiatoday.in/technology/news/story/wipro-celebrates-its-role-in-nrc-project-in-assam-first-deletes-page-then-restores-it-1630865-2019-12-23.

11 *Citizenship (Amendment) Act 1986* (India), section 2(1)(b).

12 Express Web Desk, "In Pictures: How 2020 Was Bookended by Anti-CAA and Farmers' Protests," *Indian Express*, 2020, https://indianexpress.com/article/india/2020-protests-caa-jnu-jamia-shahee-bagh-7118839/; "UN Experts Urge India to Release Protest Leaders," United Nations Human Rights Office of the High Commissioner, June 26, 2020, https://www.ohchr.org/EN/NewsEvents/Pages/DisplayNews.aspx?NewsID=26002&LangID=E.

13 "After a 101-Day Sit-In, Shaheen Bagh Protest Cleared Due to Coronavirus Lockdown," *The Wire*, March 24, 2020, https://thewire.in/rights/shaheen-bagh-cleared-coronavirus-lockdown.

14   "Kargil Review Committee Report," 1999.
15   Gujarat Informatics Limited, "Citizen Card: Pre-Feasibility Study,"
     Tata Consultancy Services, July 2002, https://www.gidb.org/pdf/
     citizenCardPrefeasibilitystudyfinalreport.pdf.
16   Gujarat Informatics Limited, "Citizen Card."
17   Gujarat Informatics Limited, "Citizen Card."
18   S. IK. Das, *Making the Poor Free? India's Unique Identification Number* (New Delhi:
     Oxford University Press, 2015).
19   DNA Web Team, "National Population Register: Know about NPR and Its
     Importance," DNA India December 24, 2019, https://www.dnaindia.com/india/
     report-national-population-register-know-all-about-npr-and-its-importance-2806669.
20   I use the term "UID" and not "Aadhaar," which is the brand name given to the
     number. The Unique Identification Authority of India (UIDAI) says it decided on
     the name after a nationwide competition, but its similarity to the Aadhar Trust, co-
     set up by Nandan Nilekani, the tech magnate who was the chair of the UIDAI from
     2009 to 2014, to fund an earlier venture in taking on a government function, is a
     coincidence difficult to ignore.
21   A bill was introduced in Parliament in December 2010, after enrollment in the
     UIDAI database had been underway for over two months. This was rejected by a
     Standing Committee of Parliament in December 2011. A law was finally enacted
     in March 2016, at a moment when it looked like the Supreme Court might hear
     and decide on the case challenging the database project. One of the main grounds
     of the challenge was that the UIDAI database had proceeded without the backing
     of legislation, rendering the whole project vulnerable to the charge of being illegal
     and unconstitutional; the hurried passage of the law in 2016 served to get past this
     challenge.
22   Before its establishment as a statutory authority, UIDAI was functioning as an
     attached office of what was then the Planning Commission (now NITI Aayog).
     See Government of India Planning Commission, "Gazette Notification No.-A-
     43011/02/2009-Admn.I," *Gazette of India*, January 28, 2019, https://uidai.gov.in/
     images/notification_28_jan_2009.pdf.
23   "Nilekani Takes Charge, Says First Set of IDs in 12–18 Months," *Times of India*,
     July 24, 2009, https://timesofindia.indiatimes.com/india/Nilekani-takes-charge-
     says-first-set-of-IDs-in-12-18-months/articleshow/4812763.cms?referral=PM.
24   A UIDAI document, dated January–February 2010 read: "There is a lack of sound
     study that documents the accuracy achievable on Indian demographics (i.e., larger
     percentage of rural population) and in Indian environmental conditions (i.e.,
     extremely hot and humid climates and facilities without air-conditioning). In fact,
     we would not find any credible study assessing the achievable accuracy in any of
     the developing countries." See Unique Identification Authority Of India (UIDAI),
     "Notice Inviting Applications For Hiring Of Biometrics Consultant," A-11016/07/10-
     UIDAI, 2010, p. 4, https://docplayer.net/18863674-Notice-inviting-applications-for-
     hiring-of-biomet-rics-consultant-a-11016-07-10-uidai.html.
25   Unique Identification Authority Of India (UIDAI), "Biometrics Design Standards
     For UID Applications," December 2009, http://www.corporatelawreporter.com/wp-
     content/uploads/2013/05/Biometrics-Design-Standards-For-UID-Applications.pdf.
26   Unique Identification Authority Of India (UIDAI), "Role of Biometric Technology
     in Aadhaar Authentication," March 2012, https://www.yumpu.com/en/document/
     view/10178448/uidai-role-of-biometric-technology-in-aadhaar-authentication, pp. 3,

11, 44.

27   Illustratively, the report read: "The fingers are labelled Green, Yellow, or Red—depending on their suitability for single finger authentication. In addition, some residents could be determined to be not suitable for reliable fingerprint authentication." See UIDAI, "Role of Biometric Technology in Aadhaar Authentication," p. 20.

28   Usha Ramanathan, "The Law Needs to Catch Up with Aadhaar, but Not in the Way Jaitley Is Promising," *The Wire*, March 3, 2016, https://thewire.in/rights/the-law-needs-to-catch-up-with-aadhaar-but-not-in-the-way-jaitley-is-promising.

29   Unique Identification Authority of India (UIDAI), "Annual Report 2017–18," 2018, https://uidai.gov.in/images/Annual-Report-ENG-2017-18-Final-18072019.pdf. On page 66, for example, UIDAI admitted that no sum was allocated or used for UBCC.

30   *Justice (Retd) KS Puttaswamy v. Union of India judgment*, 2018, https://main.sci.gov.in/supremecourt/2012/35071/35071_2012_Judgement_26-Sep-2018.pdf. In this case, an affidavit was filed on behalf of the Planning Commission of India, within which the UIDAI had been sited, in response to the challenge to the UID project.

31   Government of India, "MemorandIf UnderIding Between the UIDAI and I Registrar GenerIf India for the Implementation of the UID Project," 2011, https://uidai.gov.in/images/mou/partners/uidai_and_rgi_mou_16_march_2011.pdf.

32   Government of India, Ministry of Law and Justice, "The Aadhaar (Targeted Delivery of Financial and Other Subsidies, Benefits and Services) Act 2016," Sections 3(1), 9, https://uidai.gov.in/images/targeted_delivery_of_financial_and_other_subsidies_benefits_and_services_13072016.pdf.

33   Usha Ramanathan, "The Function Creep That Is Aadhaar," *The Wire*, April 25, 2017. https://thewire.in/government/aadhaar-function-creep-uid; Nandan Nilekani, foreword to "Credit Suisse: Indian Financials Sector," Credit Suisse, June 29, 2016, https://research-doc.credit-suisse.com/docView?language=ENG&format=PDF&document_id=1062747711&source_ id=emcsplus&serialid= HHGAYGkeu%2F8DPBafQyAl7ZsraQAIh%2BJEOzQ81xi1Xb8%3D&cspId=null.

34   Ramanathan, "The Function Creep That Is Aadhaar."

35   National Digital Health Blueprint, "Notice: Placing the Report on National Digital Health Blueprint (NDHB) in Public Domain for Comments/Views Regarding," July 15, 2019, https://www.nhp.gov.in/NHPfiles/National_Digital_Health_Blueprint_Report_comments_invited.pdf; Shagun Kapil, "AgriStack: The New Digital Push in Agriculture Raises Serious Concerns," *Down to Earth*, June 23, 2021, https://www.downtoearth.org.in/news/agriculture/agristack-the-new-digital-push-in-agriculture-raises-serious-concerns-77613.

36   Government of India, Ministry of Budget, India Budget, "Data of the People, by the People, for the People," 2018–19, https://www.indiabudget.gov.in/budget2019-20/economicsurvey/doc/vol1chapter/echap04_vol1.pdf.

37   *Justice (Retd) KS Puttaswamy v. Union of India Judgment*, 2018.

38   *Justice (Retd) KS Puttaswamy v. Union of India Judgment*, 2018.

39   *Justice (Retd) KS Puttaswamy v. Union of India Order* (2015), https://main.sci.gov.in/judgment/judis/42841.pdf.

40   *Justice (Retd) KS Puttaswamy v. Union of India Judgment*, 2017. It was in the challenge to the UID project that the government took the stand that people do not have the right to privacy, which is why the title of the case is the same in both case decisions.

41 Kris Gopalakrishnan, *Report by the Committee of Experts on Non-Personal Data Governance Framework*, Ministry of Electronics and Information Technology, 2020, https://static.mygov.in/rest/s3fs-public/mygov_159453381955063671.pdf.

42 Report of the Comptroller and Auditor General of India on the Functioning of Unique Identification Authority of India, 2021, https://cag.gov.in/uploads/download_audit_report/2021/24%20of%202021_UIDAI-0624d8136a02d72.65885742.pdf.

43 "Centre to Launch Unique ID Number for All Plots of Land by 2022: Report," *The Wire*, March 29, 2021, https://thewire.in/government/centre-to-launch-unique-id-number-for-all-plots-of-land-by-2022-report.

44 National Health Authority, "National Digital Health Mission: Strategy Overview," 2020, https://ndhm.gov.in/assets/uploads/NDHM_Strategy_Overview.pdf.

45 Ajay Kumar Shukla, "Centre's Digital Database for Farmers under Agristack Programme on Off-Track Mode," *Economic Times Government*, June 25, 2021, https://government.economictimes.indiatimes.com/news/governance/centres-digital-database-for-farmers-under-agristack-programme-on-off-track-mode/83831338.

46 Government of India, "Aadhaar: List of Acceptable Supporting Documents for Verification," November 2, 2020, https://uidai.gov.in/images/commdoc/valid_documents_list.pdf.

21. The Cost of Recognition by the State: ID Cards as Coercion

1 NIDS is the abbreviation for the National Identification System developed by the Jamaican government.

2 See Usha Ramanathan's chapter in this volume.

22. The UK's Production of Tech-Enabled Precarity

1 See Nisha Kapoor's chapter in this volume.

2 In 2020, the British government implemented a National Health Service "track and trace" system to monitor and control the spread of the COVID-19 pandemic. See, e.g., Sarah Bosley, "What Is the Test, Track and Trace System in England?" *BBC*, May 26, 2020; Robert Booth, "What Has Gone Wrong with England's Covid Test-and-Trace System?" *The Guardian*, October 13, 2020.

24. CASE STUDY: How We Mobilized Civil Society
to Fight Tunisia's Proposed Digital ID System

1 Tunisia's Organic Act No. 2004-63 of 27 July 2004 on the Protection of Personal Data.

2 Tunisian Constitution, Article 24.

25. CASE STUDY: Why We Must Fight for Alternatives to the UK's Digital-Only ID System

1 "Prove Your Right to Work – Beta: The Report from the Beta Assessment for Home Office's Prove Your Right to Work Service on 2 March 2018," United Kingdom Central Digital and Data Office, July 24, 2018.

2 "Experiences and Impact of the EU Settlement Scheme," the 3million and Northumbria University Newcastle, February 28, 2019.

26. Apartheid Tech: The Use and Expansion of Biometric Identification and Surveillance Technologies in the Occupied West Bank

1   B'Tselem, "Central Hebron: Soldiers Enter Residential Building and Conduct Lineup for School-Age Children," November 17, 2021.

2   Elizabeth Dwoskin, "Israel Escalates Surveillance of Palestinians with Facial Recognition Program in West Bank," *Washington Post*, November 8, 2021.

3   Dwoskin, "Surveillance of Palestinians."

4   Dwoskin, "Surveillance of Palestinians."

5   Richard Saumarez Smith, "Rule-by-Records and Rule-by-Reports: Complementary Aspects of the British Imperial Rule of Law," *Contributions to Indian Sociology* 19, no.1 (January 1985): 153–76.

6   Elia Zureik, "Colonialism, Surveillance, and Population Control: Israel/Palestine," in *Surveillance and Control in Israel/Palestine: Population, Territory, and Power*, ed. Elia Zureik, David Lyon, and Yasmeen Abu-Laban (London and New York: Routledge, 2011), 3–40.

7   Michael R. Fischbach, "British and Zionist Data Gathering on Palestinian Arab Landownership and Population during the Mandate," in *Surveillance and Control in Israel/Palestine*, 297–312.

8   Elisha Baskin, "Documents Reveal: This Is How the Defense Spied on Arab Cafes in Haifa," National Library of Israel, May 11, 2017.

9   Fischbach, "British and Zionist Data Gathering."

10 "The Global Surveillance Industry," Privacy International, July 2016.

11 Human Rights Watch, *A Threshold Crossed: Israeli Authorities and the Crimes of Apartheid and Persecution*, April 2021.

12 Helga Tawil-Souri, "Surveillance Sublime: The Security State in Jerusalem," *Jerusalem Quarterly*, no. 68 (Winter 2016).

13 United Nations Office for the Coordination of Humanitarian Affairs, "Over 700 Road Obstacles Control Palestinian Movement within the West Bank," October 8, 2018.

14 Daniel Estrin, "Face Recognition Lets Palestinians Cross Israeli Checkpoints Fast, but Raises Concerns," NPR, August 22, 2019.

15 7amleh, "Facial Recognition Technology & Palestinian Digital Rights.".

16 Dwoskin, "Surveillance of Palestinians."

17 Hagar Shezaf, "Israeli Army Installs Remote-Control Crowd Dispersal System at Hebron Flashpoint," *Haaretz*, Sep 24, 2022.

18 "Israel's 'Smart Shooter' Revolutionizes World of Military," i24NEWS English, July 5, 2020.

19 Meredith Roaten, "Israeli Firm Delivers Advanced Targeting System," *National Defense*, September 6, 2021.

20 Jewish Voice for Peace, *Deadly Exchange: The Dangerous Consequences of US-Israel Law Enforcement Exchanges*, September 2018.

21 Alex Kane and Sam Levin, "Internal ADL Memo Recommended Ending Police Delegations to Israel Amid Backlash," *Jewish Currents*, March 17, 2022.

22 Jewish Voice for Peace, *Deadly Exchange*.

23 Matthew Petti, "Do Small Town Cops Need Training in Israeli Counterterror Techniques?" *Reason*, June 20, 2022.

24 Sophia Goodfriend, "'We Violated People's Privacy for a Living': How Israel's Cyber Army Went Corporate," *+972 Magazine*, November 23, 2021.

25 Noam Sheizaf, "Conviction Rate for Palestinians in Israel's Military Courts:

99.74%," *+972 Magazine*, November 29, 2011.

27. The Encroachment of Smart Cities

1   From 2015 to 2017, Eric Schmidt was the executive chairman of Alphabet, the parent company of Google and Sidewalk Labs. Schmidt had been Google CEO from 2001 to 2011 and Google executive chairman from 2011 to 2015.

2   Emily Badger, "Google's Founders Wanted to Shape a City. Toronto Is Their Chance," *New York Times*, October 18, 2017.

3   Sidewalk Labs, "Announcing Sidewalk Toronto: Press Conference Live Stream," October 17, 2017, YouTube video, 54:15, https://www.youtube.com/watch?v=A_yg_BsJy_o.

4   David McGuffin, "Plans To Develop High-Tech 'Smart City' In Toronto Met With Resistance," NPR, February 16, 2020.

5   Ben Green, *The Smart Enough City: Putting Technology in Its Place to Reclaim Our Urban Future* (Cambridge, MA: MIT Press, 2019).

6   Giuseppe Grossi and Daniela Pianezzi, "Smart Cities: Utopia or Neoliberal Ideology?" *Cities* 69 (2017): 79–85.

7   Federal Trade Commission, "Data Brokers: A Call for Transparency and Accountability," Federal Trade Commission, May 1, 2014.

8   John Podesta et al., "Big Data: Seizing Opportunities, Preserving Values," Executive Office of the President, May 2014.

9   Green, *The Smart Enough City*.

10 Jathan Sadowski and Roy Bendor, "Selling Smartness: Corporate Narratives and the Smart City as a Sociotechnical Imaginary," *Science, Technology, & Human Values* 44, no. 3 (2019): 540–63.

11 Grand View Research, "Smart Cities Market Worth $676.01 Billion By 2028," press release, February 15, 2022.

12 Lauren Feiner, "Alphabet's Sidewalk Labs Wants a Cut of Toronto Taxes to Build a Smart City There," *CNBC*, February 15, 2019.

13 Stephen Diamond, "Open Letter from Waterfront Toronto Board Chair, Stephen Diamond regarding Quayside," *Waterfront Toronto*, June 24, 2019.

14 Drew Harwell, "Oregon Became a Testing Ground for Amazon's Facial-Recognition Policing. But What if Rekognition Gets It Wrong?" *Washington Post*, May 1, 2019.

15 Jesse Marx, "Smart Streetlights Are Now Exclusively a Tool for Police," *Voice of San Diego*, July 20, 2020.

16 Jean Marie Takouleu, "AFRICA: Huawei Sets up a $1.5 Billion Fund to Boost African Smart Cities," *Afrik21*, June 6, 2019.

17 Bulelani Jili, "Surveillance Technology a Concern for Many in Africa," *New Africa Daily*, December 29, 2020.

18 Joe Parkinson, Nicholas Bariyo, and Josh Chin, "Huawei Technicians Helped African Governments Spy on Political Opponents," *Wall Street Journal*, August 15, 2019.

19 Caroline Haskins, "300 Californian Cities Secretly Have Access to Palantir," *Vice*, July 12, 2019.

20 April Glaser, "Sanctuary Cities Are Handing ICE a Map," *Slate*, March 13, 2018.

21 Suhauna Hussain and Johana Bhuiyan, "Police in Pasadena, Long Beach Pledged Not to Send License Plate Data to ICE. They Shared It Anyway," *Los Angeles Times*, December 21, 2020.

22 Kashmir Hill, "The Secretive Company That Might End Privacy as We Know It,"

New York Times, updated November 2, 2021.

23   Ali Winston, "Palantir Has Secretly Been Using New Orleans to Test Its Predictive Policing Technology," *The Verge*, Feburary 27, 2018.

24   Jay Peters, "Portland Passes Strongest Facial Recognition Ban in the US," *The Verge*, September 9, 2020.

25   Bianca Wylie, "In Toronto, Google's Attempt to Privatize Government Fails—for Now," *Boston Review*, May 13, 2020.

26   Thomas Macaulay, "LAPD Ditches Predictive Policing Program Accused of Racial Bias," The Next Web, April 22, 2020.

27   Okalo Ikhena, "Announcing Delve: Discovering Radically Better Urban Designs," Sidewalk Labs.

28   David Harvey, "The Right to the City," *New Left Review*, September 2008.

29   Green, *The Smart Enough City*.

28. Control-X: Communication, Control, and Exclusion

1   See Zygmunt Bauman, *Globalization: The Human Consequences* (New York: Polity Press, 1998); for more resources, see URL.

2   See Jonathan Xavier Inda, *Targeting Immigrants: Government, Technology, and Ethics* (Malden, MA: Blackwell Publishing, 2006); for more resources, see URL.

3   McKenzie Funk, "How ICE Picks Its Targets in the Surveillance Age," *New York Times*, October 2. 2019; Mizue Aizeki et al., *Smart Borders or a Humane World?* Immigrant Defense Project's Surveillance, Tech & Immigration Policing Project, and the Transnational Institute, October 2021.

4   Simone Browne, "Digital Epidermalization: Race, Identity and Biometrics," *Critical Sociology* 36, no. 1 (2010): 131–50; Brian Jordan Jefferson, "Computerizing Carceral Space: Coded Geographies of Criminalization and Capture in New York City," *Environment and Planning A: Economy and Space* 50, no. 5 (2018): 969–88; Elizabeth E. Joh, "The New Surveillance Discretion: Automated Suspicion, Big Data, and Policing," *Harvard Law and Policy Review* 10 (2016): 15.

5   Elizabeth E. Joh, "Policing Police Robots," *UCLA L. Rev. Discourse* 64 (2016): 516.

6   Anthony Townsend, *Smart Cities: Big Data, Civic Hackers, and the Quest for a New Utopia* (New York: W. W. Norton, 2013).

7   C. J. Alvarez, *Border Land, Border Water: A History of Construction on the US-Mexico Divide* (Austin: University of Texas Press, 2019); Sandro Mezzadra and Brett Neilson, *Border as Method, or, the Multiplication of Labor* (Durham, NC: Duke University Press, 2013).

8   Inda, *Targeting Immigrants*.

9   Greg Grandin, *The End of the Myth: From the Frontier to the Border Wall in the Mind of America* (New York: Metropolitan Books, 2019).

10   Chaar-López, "Sensing Intruders."

11   Timothy J. Dunn, *The Militarization of the U.S.-Mexico Border, 1978–1992: Low-Intensity Conflict Doctrine Comes Home* (Austin: Center for Mexican American Studies, 1996); Paul Edwards, *The Closed World: Computers and the Politics and Discourse in Cold War America* (Cambridge, MA: MIT Press, 1996).

12   Brian Jefferson, *Digitize and Punish: Racial Criminalization in the Digital Age* (Minneapolis: University of Minnesota Press, 2020).

13   Alex Vitale, "Command and Control and the Miami Model at the Republican National Convention: New Forms of Policing Protests," *Mobilization* 12, no. 4 (2007): 403–15.

14 See Nevins and Miller's chapter in this volume.

15 Joseph Nevins and Timothy Dunn, "Barricading the Border," *NACLA Report on the Americas* 41, no. 6 (2008): 21–25.

16 Jennifer Correa and James Thomas, "From the Border to the Core: A Thickening Military-Police Assemblage," *Critical Sociology* 45, nos. 7–8 (2019): 1133–47.

17 Stephen Graham, *Cities Under Siege: The New Military Urbanism* (London: Verso, 2010).

18 Ginger Thompson, "Work Under Way on 'Virtual Fence,'" *New York Times*, May 8, 2009.

19 Nathan Busch, "Public-Private Partnership in Homeland Security: Opportunities and Challenges," *Homeland Security Affairs* 8, no.11 (2012): 1–24.

20 Funk, *How ICE Picks Its Targets*.

21 Funk, *How ICE Picks Its Targets*.

22 Art Murray and Nola Joyce, "The Future of Law Enforcement," *KM World*, March 31, 2017.

23 New York Police Department, *Best Practice: Real Time Crime Center: Centralized Crime Data System*, New York City Global Partners Innovation Exchange (New York: NYPD, 2010).

24 Jefferson, "Computerizing Carceral Space."

25 James Kilgore, "Progress or More of the Same? Electronic Monitoring and Parole in the Age of Mass Incarceration," *Critical Criminology* 21 (2013): 123–29.

26 Jefferson, "Computerizing Carceral Space."

27 Funk, *How ICE Picks Its Targets*.

28 Funk, *How ICE Picks Its Targets*.

29 Angela Y. Davis, *Are Prisons Obsolete?* (New York: Seven Stories Press, 2003).

29. Data Justice in Mexico: How Big Data Is Reshaping the Struggle for Rights and Political Freedoms

1   "Gobierno Espía: Vigilancia Sistemática a Periodistas y Defensores de Derechos Humanos en México," R3D, June 2017.

2   "El Estado de la Vigilancia Fuera de Control," R3D, November 2016.

3   Rayzone Group, "ECHO Global Virtual SIGINT System," July 2020; Thomas Brewster, "Israeli Surveillance Companies Are Siphoning Masses of Location Data from Smartphone Apps," *Forbes*, December 11, 2020.

4   Forbidden Stories and Amnesty International had access to a leaked database of more than fifty thousand phone numbers selected as targets by clients of the NSO Group since 2016. Around fifteen thousand of the phone numbers were from Mexico. Organized Crime and Corruption Reporting Project (OCCRP), "Mexico," A World of Surveillance, 2022.

5   "Mexico," Reporters Without Borders, accessed February 15, 2022.

6   OCCRP, "Mexico."

7   Joshua Partlow and Nick Miroff, "U.S. Gathers Data on Migrants Deep in Mexico, A Sensitive Program Trump's Rhetoric Could Put at Risk," *Washington Post*, April 6, 2018.

8   Diario Oficial De La Federación, "DECRETO por el que se reforman y adicionan diversas disposiciones de la Ley Federal de Telecomunicaciones y Radiodifusión," April 14, 2021.

9   Pepe Flores, "A la Venta los Datos de Celulares del RENAUT en México,"

Hipertextual, June 4, 2010.

10   Conor O'Reilly, "The Pluralization of High Policing: Convergence and Divergence at the Public–Private Interface," *British Journal of Criminology* 55, no. 4 (2015): 688–710.

11   Valeria Durán, Raúl Olmos, and Daniel Lizárraga, "El General Espía," *Contra la Corrupción*, 2019.

12   Alberto Nájar, "'Huachicoleo' en México: las Consecuencias Económicas del Desabasto por el Combate al Robo de Combustible," *BBC News Mundo México*, January 11, 2019.

13   Azam Ahmed and Nicole Perlroth, "Using Texts as Lures, Government Spyware Targets Mexican Journalists and Their Families," *New York Times*, June 19, 2017.

14   John Scott-Railton, in discussion with the authors, October 31, 2018.

15   Data Justice, https://www.datajustice.mx/.

16   Simone Browne, *Dark Matters: On the Surveillance of Blackness* (Durham, NC: Duke University Press, 2015). See also Jascha Hoffman, "Sousveillance," *New York Times Magazine*, December 10, 2006.

17   Shoshana Zuboff, *The Age of Surveillance Capitalism: The Fight for a Human Future at the New Frontier of Power* (New York: PublicAffairs, 2019).

30. Corporate Tech and the Legible City

1   We use the term "corporate tech" to include corporations whose primary means of power and profit is collecting and managing information.

2   David Harvey, "The Right to the City," *New Left Review*, September 2008.

3   David Harvey, "From Managerialism to Entrepreneurialism," *Geografiska Annaler: Series B, Human Geography* 71, no. 1 (1989): 3–17.

4   Giuseppe Grossi and Daniela Pianezzi, "Smart Cities: Utopia or Neoliberal Ideology?" *Cities* 69 (2017): 79–85.

5   See Sidewalk Labs proposal: https://storage.googleapis.com/sidewalk-labs-com-assets/ Sidewalk_Labs_Vision_Sections_of_RFP_Submission_7ad06759b5/Sidewalk_Labs_ Vision_Sections_of_RFP_Submission_7ad06759b5.pdf

6   Barbara Schecter, "Big Tech's Gain Has Been Publishers' Pain, Industry Group's Report Finds," *Financial Post*, October 22, 2020.

7   Reijer Hendrikse, "Neoliberalism Is Over—Welcome to the Era of Neo-Illiberalism," openDemocracy, May 7, 2020; Paul Apostolicas, "Silicon States: How Tech Titans Are Acquiring State-Like Powers," *Harvard International Review* 40, no. 4 (2019): 18–21; Alexis Wichowski, "The U.S. Can't Regulate Big Tech Companies When They Act Like Nations," *Washington Post*, October 29, 2020.

8   Omri Wallach, "The World's Tech Giants, Compared to the Size of Economies," *Visual Capitalist*, July 7, 2021.

9   Andrew Hawkins, "Uber and Lyft Had an Edge in the Prop 22 Fight: Their Apps," *The Verge*, November 4, 2020.

10   Joy Burkholder et al., *Uber State Interference: How Transportation Network Companies Buy, Bully, and Bamboozle Their Way to Deregulation*, National Employment Law Project, January 2018; Len Sherman, "Can Uber Ever be Profitable?" *Forbes*, June 2, 2019.

11   Elizabeth Dwoskin, "Google Reaped Millions in Tax Breaks as It Secretly Expanded Its Real Estate Footprint Across the U.S.," *Washington Post*, February 15, 2019; Martin Austermuhle, "Amazon Insists on Silence from Twenty HQ2 Finalists," WAMU, January 30, 2018.

12   Alana Semuels, "How Amazon Helped Kill a Seattle Tax on Businesses," *The Atlantic*, June 13, 2018.

13   Mariana Mazzucato, "The Entrepreneurial State," *Soundings* 49, no. 49 (2011): 131–42.

14   Rodrigo Fernandez et al., "Engineering Digital Monopolies: The Financialisation of Big Tech," *SOMO*, December 2020.

15   Michael Kwet, "Digital Colonialism: The Evolution of US Empire," *TNI Longreads*, March 4, 2021.

16   Maryann Feldman, Frederick Guy, and Simona Iammarino, "Regional Income Disparities, Monopoly and Finance," *Cambridge Journal of Regions, Economy and Society* 14, no. 1 (2021): 25–49.

17   Kwet, "Digital Colonialism."

18   Dayne Lee, "How Airbnb Short-Term Rentals Exacerbate Los Angeles's Affordable Housing Crisis: Analysis and Policy Recommendations," *Harvard Law & Policy Review* 10 (2016): 229.

19   Keith Breckenridge, "The Global Ambitions of the Biometric Anti-Bank: Net1, Lockin and the Technologies of African Financialisation," *International Review of Applied Economics* 33, no. 1 (2019).

20   Remarks by Courtenay Brown, United for Respect Leader, "Testimony before the Senate Finance Subcommittee on Fiscal Responsibility and Economic Growth," Public Hearing on: Promoting Competition and Economic Growth in the Technology Sector, US Senate, December 7, 2021.

21   Jay Greene, "Amazon's Employee Surveillance Fuels Unionization Efforts: 'It's Not Prison, It's Work,'" *Washington Post*, December 2, 2021.

22   Brishen Rogers, "The Law and Political Economy of Workplace Technological Change," *Harvard Civil Rights–Civil Liberties Law Review* 55 (2020): 531.

23   Ian Carlos Campbell, "Gig Work Is Precarious No Matter the Country," *The Verge*, September 24, 2021.

24   Jamie Peck, "Austerity Urbanism: American Cities under Extreme Economy," *City* 16, no. 6 (2012): 626–55.

25   Virginia Eubanks, *Automating Inequality: How High-Tech Tools Profile, Police, and Punish the Poor* (New York, St. Martin's, 2017).

26   For example, "Justice and Public Safety," Amazon Web Services (AWS).

27   "Technology," New York City Police Department, https://www1.nyc.gov/site/nypd/about/about-nypd/equipment-tech/technology.page.

28   Lauren Bridges, "Amazon's Ring Is the Largest Civilian Surveillance Network the US Has Ever Seen," *The Guardian*, May 18, 2021.

29   Kristina Libby, "Silicon Valley Has Quietly Been Selling Ineffective Tech 'Solutions' to Police Departments," *Salon*, August 16, 2020; Adam Satariano, "Pitch to the Police," *New York Times*, February 7, 2020.

30   For example, "Mayor de Blasio Appoints John Paul Farmer as Chief Technology Officer," City of New York, press release, April 23, 2019.

31   Steven Morgan, "Are Ex–Police Officers the Next Recruits to Help Fill the 1.5 Million Cybersecurity Jobs by 2019?" *Forbes*, April 13, 2016.

32   Michaela Winberg, "30 Philly Parks Contain Sonic Devices That Target Teenagers with Terrible Sounds," Billy Penn, June 18, 2019.

33   "Oyster, Octopus and Metro Cards: What Happens to Our Data?" Privacy International, October 26, 2012; Mizue Aizeki and Rashida Richardson, eds., *Smart-City Digital ID Projects: Reinforcing Inequality and Increasing Surveillance*

through Corporate "Solutions," Immigrant Defense Project, December 2021.

34   Eubanks, *Automating Inequality.*

31. Seeing the Watched: Mass Surveillance in Detroit

1   Matthew D. Lassiter and the Policing and Social Justice HistoryLab, *Detroit Under Fire: Police Violence, Crime Politics, and the Struggle for Racial Justice in the Civil Rights Era*, University of Michigan Carceral State Project, 2021, https://policing.umhistorylabs.lsa.umich.edu/s/detroitunderfire/page/rememberingstressvictims.

2   Stateside Staff, "Documentary Looks Back at Violent History of Detroit Police's S.T.R.E.S.S. Units," Michigan Radio, August 22, 2018.

3   "FBI Stats Show Detroit Remains Nation's Murder Capital," *Associated Press*, May 11, 1987.

4   Virginia Eubanks et al., *From Power to Paranoia: Our Data Bodies Project 2016 Report*, Our Data Bodies (O.D.B.) Project, May 2017.

5   Elisha Anderson, "Controversial Detroit Facial Recognition Got Him Arrested for a Crime He Didn't Commit," *Detroit Free Press*, July 11, 2020.

6   Randy Wimbley and David Komer, "Black Teen Kicked Out of Skating Rink after Facial Recognition Camera Misidentified Her," Fox 2 Detroit, July 16, 2021.

7   "Civil Liberty Advocates Caution Use of Project Greenlight during Pandemic Response," *WXYZ Detroit*, May 11, 2020.

8   Lauren Slagter, "More than 4 in 10 Detroiters Have Lost Jobs during Pandemic," *Michigan News University of Michigan*, May 26, 2020.

9   Bryce Huffman, "Detroiters Get Oversight of Surveillance Technology, but Is It Enough?" *Bridge Detroit*, May 26, 2021.

10   Nushrat Rahman, "Bill of Rights for Detroiters Could be First Change to City Charter in 8 Years," *Detroit Free Press*, July 29, 2020.

11   Vincent Duffy, "Duggan and Adams Win Mayoral Primary, Proposal P Fails in Detroit," Michigan Radio, August 4, 2021

12   Hunter Wasser, "Michigan Supreme Court Ruled 4–3 Thursday to Keep Detroit Proposal P Charter Revision on Aug. 3 Ballot," *Ballotpedia News*, July 30, 2021.

13   Sarah Rahal, "Detroit City Council Set to Revisit $8.5M Expansion of ShotSpotter," *Detroit News*, September 12, 2022.

14   "U-M Policy Brief Raises Concerns about Acoustic Gunshot Detection Systems Used by Police Departments," Gerald R. Ford School of Public Policy, September 1, 2022, https://fordschool.umich.edu/news/2022/u-m-policy-brief-raises-concerns-about-acoustic-gunshot-detection-systems-used-police.

32. Necropolitics and Neoliberalism Are Driving Brazil's Surveillance Infrastructure

1   Achille Mbembe, "Necropolitics," trans. Libby Meintjes, *Public Culture* 15, no. 1 (2003): 11–40

2   Beatriz Busaniche, "Negligencia, La Inminente Amenaza a Nuestra Privacidad," *Global Data Justice*, December 17, 2020.

3   Ruha Benjamin, *Race After Technology: Abolitionist Tools for the New Jim Code* (Medford, MA: Polity Press, 2019).

4   Rafael Evangelista and Rodrigo Firmino, "Brazil. Modes of Pandemic Existence: Territory, Inequality, and Technology," *Data Justice and COVID-19: Global Perspectives* (2020): 100–107.

5   Mani Tebet Marins et al., "Auxílio Emergencial Em Tempos de Pandemia,"

Sociedade e Estado 36 (2021): 669–92.

6   Shoshanna Zuboff, *The Age of Surveillance Capitalism: The Fight for a Human Future at the New Frontier of Power* (New York: PublicAffairs, 2019); Rafael Evangelista, "Review of Zuboff's *The Age of Surveillance Capitalism*," *Surveillance & Society* 17, no. 1/2 (2019): 246–51.

7   Michael Kwet, "Digital Colonialism: US Empire and the New Imperialism in the Global South," *Race & Class* 60, no. 4 (2019): 3–26.

8   Leonardo Ribeiro da Cruz and Jamila Rodrigues Venturini, "Neoliberalismo e Erise: O Avanço Silencioso do Capitalismo de Vigilância Na Educação Brasileira Durante a Pandemia da Covid-19," *Revista Brasileira de Informática na Educação* 28 (2020): 1060–85.

9   Julia Lindner and Mateus Vargas, "Morte de Idosos Por COVID-19 Melhora Contas da Previdência, Teria Dito Chefe da Susep," *Terra*, May 28, 2020.

10 Lorenna Rodrigues and Fabrício de Castro, "Achávamos Que a Pandemia Estava Acabando Não Por Má-fé, Foi Um Engano, Diz Guedes," *Terra*, June 1, 2021.

33. CASE STUDY: Why We Must Fight against COVID-19 Surveillance and Techno-Solutionism

1   "Ministerio De Salud Confirma Primer Caso De Coronavirus En Chile," Ministerio De Salud, Gobierno De Chile, March 3, 2020.

2   Jorge Contesse, "A Constitution Borne Out of Actual Bullets: A Reply to Sergio Verdugo," *Verfassungsblog*, November 10, 2019.

3   Jorge Contesse, "Chile's Constitutional Awakening: In Chile, Protests against Metro Fare Price Hikes Led to An Unprecedented Constitutional Process," OpenGlobalRights, April 13, 2020.

4   "Individuals Using the Internet (% Of Population)—Chile," World Bank.

5   Valentina Fuentes and Philip Sanders, "Once A Covid Role Model, Chile Now Among the World's Worst," *Bloomberg*, June 16, 2020.

6   Paulo Quinteros, "El Portal De La Comisaría Virtual Está Completamente Inoperante," *La Tercera*, April 2, 2020.

7   Leonardo Casas, "Detectan Divulgación Masiva De RUT Contenidos En Base De Datos De Comisaría Virtual," *Biobiochile.Cl*, December 4, 2020.

8   Felipe Delgado, "Registro Civil Anunció Que Bajó La App Para Obtener Clave Única: Hubo Denuncia Sobre Su Seguridad," *Biobiochile.Cl*, March 29, 2020.

9   Alejandra Jara and Victor Rivera, "Hackeo A Gobierno Digital Obliga a Iniciar Proceso De Actualización De La Clave Única," *La Tercera*, October 15, 2020.

10 J. Carlos Lara, "Arrestos Más, Arrestos Menos," Derechos Digitales, October 26, 2020.

11 Evgeny Morozov, *To Save Everything, Click Here: The Folly of Technological Solutionism* (New York: PublicAffairs, 2013).

12 "Coronapp: La Inutilidad Del Atajo Tecnológico Desplegado Por El Gobierno Y Sus Riesgos," Derechos Digitales, April 16, 2020.

13 Amnesty International, *Eyes on Chile: Police Violence and Command Responsibility during the Period of Social Unrest*, , October 2020.

14 Michelle Bordachar, "Faltas en materia de transparencia y protección de datos personales en el despliegue de tecnologías de vigilancia para combatir el Covid-19," *CEJIL*, December 15, 2021.

34. CASE STUDY: How We Challenged the German Migration Office's Surveillance Technology

1   Anna Biselli and Lea Beckmann, *Invading Refugees' Phones: Digital Forms of Migration Control in Germany and Europe*, Gesellschaft für Freiheitsrechte, 2019.

36. Abolish National Security

1   Larry Buchanan, Quoctrung Bui, and Jugal K. Patel, "Black Lives Matter May Be the Largest Movement in US History," *New York Times*, July 3, 2020.

2   Barbara Ransby, *Making All Black Lives Matter: Reimagining Freedom in the 21st Century* (Oakland: University of California Press, 2018).

3   Amna A. Akbar, "How Defund and Disband Became the Demands," *New York Review of Books*, June 15, 2020.

4   Angela Y. Davis, *Abolition Democracy: Beyond Empire, Prisons, and Torture* (New York: Seven Stories Press, 2005), 111.

5   "Our Vision," Dissenters, https://wearedissenters.org/our-vision/. See Timmy Châu's chapter in this volume.

6   Davis, *Abolition Democracy*, 113.

7   Davis, *Abolition Democracy*, 92.

8   Angela Y. Davis, *Are Prisons Obsolete?* (New York: Seven Stories Press, 2003), 15–21, 91, 107–11.

9   "The Breathe Act Bill Summary," Movement for Black Lives' Electoral Justice Project, July 1, 2020.

10 James Forman, *The Making of Black Revolutionaries* (Seattle: University of Washington Press, 1997).

11 Abolitionist arguments align with notions of human security. See David Gee, "Rethinking Security: A Discussion Paper," Ammerdown Group, May 2016.

12 William Hartung, "The Trillion-Dollar National Security Budget," *TomDispatch*, July 25, 2017; Esmé Berkhout et al., *The Inequality Virus: Bringing Together a World Torn Apart by Coronavirus through a Fair, Just and Sustainable Economy*, Oxfam International, January 2021, p. 17.

13 Nick Turse, "Will the Biden Administration Shine Light on Shadowy Special Ops Programs?" *The Intercept*, March 20, 2021.

14 Hans M. Kristensen and Matt Korda, "United States Nuclear Forces, 2020," *Bulletin of the Atomic Scientists* 76, no. 1 (January 2020): 46–60; Elisabeth Eaves, "Why Is America Getting a New $100 Billion Nuclear Weapon?" *Bulletin of the Atomic Scientists*, February 8, 2021.

15 Molly Molloy, "Homicide in Mexico 2007–March 2018: Continuing Epidemic of Militarized Hyper-Violence," *Small Wars Journal*, April 27, 2018.

16 Pieter D. Wezeman, Alexandra Kuimova, and Siemon T. Wezeman, "Trends in International Arms Transfers, 2020," Stockholm International Peace Research Institute (SIPRI), March 2021, p. 2.

17 Michael Rogin, "'Make My Day!': Spectacle as Amnesia in Imperial Politics," *Representations* 29 (Winter 1990): 99–123.

18 Susan Faludi, *The Terror Dream: Myth and Misogyny in an Insecure America* (New York: Picador, 2008).

19 Franco Fornari, *The Psychoanalysis of War* (Bloomington: Indiana University Press, 1975), xvii.

20 Davis, *Abolition Democracy*, 121.

21 Martin Luther King Jr., "Beyond Vietnam," April 4, 1967.

22 Arun Kundnani, "The Racial Constitution of Neoliberalism," *Race & Class* 63, no. 1 (2021): 51–69; Wendy Brown, *In the Ruins of Neoliberalism: The Rise of Antidemocratic Politics in the West* (New York: Columbia University Press, 2019).

23 Quoted in Adam Tooze, *Crashed: How a Decade of Financial Crises Changed the World* (New York: Viking, 2018), 574.

24 Ruth Wilson Gilmore, *Golden Gulag: Prisons, Surplus, Crisis, and Opposition in Globalizing California* (Oakland: University of California Press, 2007).

25 Patrick Porter, "Why America's Grand Strategy Has Not Changed: Power, Habit, and the US Foreign Policy Establishment," *International Security* 42, no. 4 (2018): 9–46.

26 Paul Gilroy, *After Empire: Melancholia or Convivial Culture?* (Abingdon, UK: Routledge, 2004).

27 Neta C. Crawford, *Pentagon Fuel Use, Climate Change, and the Costs of War – Updated and Revised*, Watson Institute for International and Public Affairs, Brown University, 2019, p. 1.

28 US Department of Defense, "Climate Change Adaptation Roadmap," Department of Defense, 2014, pp. i, 2, 4; Nick Buxton and Ben Hayes, *The Secure and the Dispossessed: How the Military and Corporations Are Shaping a Climate-Changed World* (London and Amsterdam: Pluto Press and Transnational Institute, 2015).

29 Tom Bowman, "Pentagon Pushes for Bigger Effort to Deter China's Growing Military Might," *NPR*, March 16, 2021.

30 "Global Terrorism Index 2015: Measuring the Impact of Terrorism," Institute for Economics and Peace, 2015, p. 14. This report draws on definitions and data from the Global Terrorism Database maintained by the National Consortium for the Study of Terrorism and Responses to Terrorism at the University of Maryland. Its definition of terrorism excludes most forms of state political violence and therefore omits the vast majority of violent incidents in the Global War on Terror.

31 Ruth Igielnik and Kim Parker, "Majorities of US Veterans, Public Say the Wars in Iraq and Afghanistan Were Not Worth Fighting," Pew Research Center, July 10, 2019.

32 Mark Pocan, "The American People Agree: Cut the Pentagon's Budget," Data for Progress, July 20, 2020.

33 Stephen Semler, "Cut the Military Budget and Give us $2,000 Checks with the Money," *Jacobin*, February 23, 2021.

34 Greg Grandin, *Empire's Workshop: Latin America, the United States, and the Rise of the New Imperialism* (New York: Metropolitan Books, 2006), 62–63.

37. The First Step Is Finding Each Other

1 Associated Press, "Trump: NKorea Will Be Met with 'Fire and Fury,'" August 8, 2017, YouTube video, 0:38, https://www.youtube.com/watch?v=8p1JIgTuKQk.

2 I use "so-called" to acknowledge a nation-state's settler colonial dimension and resist normalization of its claim to the land.

3 Bruce Riedel, "It's Time to Stop US Arms Sales to Saudi Arabia," *Brookings*, February 4, 2021.

4 "Divest from Death," https://wearedissenters.org/divest-from-death/.

38. The Red Deal: Indigenous Liberation and the Fight to Save the Planet

1 This piece is drawn from my longer article, "A Red Deal," *Jacobin*, August 6, 2019.
2 The Red Nation, "The Red Deal: Indigenous Action to Save Our Earth. Part One: End the Occupation," April 2020, p. 10.

39. Trying Harder to Build a World Where Life Is Precious

1 Ruth Wilson Gilmore, *Golden Gulag: Prisons, Surplus, Crisis, and Opposition in Globalizing California* (Berkeley: University of California Press, 2007).
2 "EU-Turkey Statement & Action Plan," European Parliament, https://www.europarl.europa.eu/legislative-train/theme-towards-a-new-policy-on-migration/file-eu-turkey-statement-action-plan.
3 "Geographies of Racial Capitalism with Ruth Wilson Gilmore—an Antipode Foundation film," June 1, 2020, YouTube video, 16:18, https://www.youtube.com/watch?v=2CS627aKrJI.

Index

7amleh, 183
9/11 Commission, 18, 109
2020 New Pact on Migration and Asylum.
    See New Migration Pact

Aadhaar. *See* unique ID number (UID),
    India
Abdurahman, J. Khadijah, 13
Abolish Frontex, 51
abolition: Black Mediterranean and,
    60–61; conditions that create violence
    and, xii, 271, 278–279; conscious-
    ness-building and, 279–280; creation
    as, xiii, 246; criminalization and,
    275–276, 278–279; decriminalization
    as, 246–247; freedom and, 270; gen-
    erative possibilities of, 247, 281; global
    refugee regime system and, 278–279;
    migrant justice as, 60; security and,
    246–247; unions and, 276–278; US
    history of, 245
abolition of: border- and surveillance-in-
    dustrial complex, 7; borders, 15,
    264–266; Frontex, 51; gang databas-
    es, 104–107; global apartheid, 6–7;
    immigration detention, 120–123;
    migration deterrence, 57; military-in-
    dustrial complex, 245–247, 257–258;
    prison-industrial complex, 245–247;
    racial capitalism, 7; US national secu-
    rity apparatus, 27–29, 252–253
Access Now, 169, 171–172
Achiume, E. Tendayi, xi
Against Borders for Children campaign,
    159–160
Ahmed, Fahd, 85–91
Al Bawsala, 169, 171–172
Alexander, Khalid, 238, 239–240
Amazon, 75–76, 213, 215, 216

American-Israeli Public Affairs Committee
    (AIPAC), 98
Andreas, Peter, 33
anti-state state, 269, 273
apartheid, European. *See* European
    apartheid
apartheid, global. *See* global apartheid

Balibar, Étienne, 45
BAMF. *See* Federal Office for Migration
    and Refugees (BAMF)
Beccaria, Cesare, 54
Ben-Hassine, Wafa, 172
Bentham, Jeremy, 54
Biden, Joe, ix
Big Data: data analytics as, 75; data bro-
    kers as, 75; data criminalization and,
    14; dataveillance as, 84, 203; digital
    colonialism and, 227; Mexican use of,
    203–206; US Immigration and Cus-
    toms Enforcement and, 25
Big Tech. *See* corporate tech
biometrics: Brazil's COVID-19 pandemic
    response and, 226; consent, lack of,
    135–136, 169–170; ICE's use of, 12,
    76; definition of, 117, 169; Indian
    citizenship and, 140–142; Israeli
    apartheid and, 180, 183, 185; Jamai-
    can National Identification System
    and, 146–147; New Jim Code and,
    135–136; policing and, 158–159
bitachon, 99
Black Atlantic, The (Gilroy), 59
Black Lives Matter demonstrations, US,
    245
Black Mediterranean, 59–60
Black Mediterranean Collective, 59
Black Youth Project 100 (BYP100),
    102–103

About Haymarket Books

Haymarket Books is a radical, independent, nonprofit book publisher based in Chicago. Our mission is to publish books that contribute to struggles for social and economic justice. We strive to make our books a vibrant and organic part of social movements and the education and development of a critical, engaged, and internationalist Left.

We take inspiration and courage from our namesakes, the Haymarket Martyrs, who gave their lives fighting for a better world. Their 1886 struggle for the eight-hour day—which gave us May Day, the international workers' holiday—reminds workers around the world that ordinary people can organize and struggle for their own liberation. These struggles—against oppression, exploitation, environmental devastation, and war—continue today across the globe.

Since our founding in 2001, Haymarket has published more than nine hundred titles. Radically independent, we seek to drive a wedge into the risk-averse world of corporate book publishing. Our authors include Angela Y. Davis, Arundhati Roy, Keeanga-Yamahtta Taylor, Eve Ewing, Aja Monet, Mariame Kaba, Naomi Klein, Rebecca Solnit, Olúfẹ́mi O. Táíwò, Mohammed El-Kurd, José Olivarez, Noam Chomsky, Winona LaDuke, Robyn Maynard, Leanne Betasamosake Simpson, Howard Zinn, Mike Davis, Marc Lamont Hill, Dave Zirin, Astra Taylor, and Amy Goodman, among many other leading writers of our time. We are also the trade publishers of the acclaimed Historical Materialism Book Series.

Haymarket also manages a vibrant community organizing and event space in Chicago, Haymarket House, the popular Haymarket Books Live event series and podcast, and the annual Socialism Conference.